The Other Government

Mark J. Green

THE OTHER GOVERNMENT

The Unseen Power of
Washington Lawyers

Grossman Publishers

A Division of The Viking Press
New York   1975

First published in 1975 by Grossman Publishers
625 Madison Avenue, New York, N.Y. 10022

Published simultaneously in Canada by
The Macmillan Company of Canada Limited

Printed in U.S.A.

Library of Congress Cataloging in Publication Data

Green, Mark J.
  The other government.
  Includes index.
  1. Lawyers—District of Columbia. 2. Practice of
law—District of Columbia. I. Title.
KF298.G65   340′.09753   74–32345
ISBN 0–670–52934–6

Acknowledgments

Begun in the summer of 1969, this book has emerged from a five-year gestation. Its midwives have been Ralph Nader, who understood the need for a comprehensive look at Washington lawyers because he understood their influence, and Dan Okrent, whose editorial guidance was invariably telling and good-natured.

Washington lawyers themselves proved reluctant subjects. Uneager to criticize publicly fellow brothers-at-the-bar and discouraged from doing so by an unnecessarily restrictive Canons of Ethics, most lawyers interviewed refused to allow use of their names. This shyness produced a larger number of confidential attributions than was ideal, a limitation apparently unavoidable in a study of lawyers.

Still, three hundred interviews with both lawyers and nonlawyers alike did take place from June 1969 to September 1974 to form the cornerstone of this book. Since so much of what Washington lawyers do is undocumented and hidden, only personal knowledge and the oral tradition could provide the information necessary to stitch together their patterns of behavior. Among those interviewed were ninety lawyers who are or have been partners or associates of Covington and Burling. In addition, Lloyd Cutler and John Pickering of Wilmer, Cutler & Pickering were seen twice for a total of six hours. Mr. Cutler agreed to the first interview only after the American Bar Association ruled, in response to his inquiry, that his co-operation with me would not be considered unethical "advertising and soliciting" under the Canons of Ethics.

I am alone responsible for the content of *The Other Government,* but there have been numerous individuals indispensable to the book's ultimate delivery, and I wish to thank Craig Kubey, Jeffrey Peters, Judith Friedlaender, Willem Van den Brock, Joel Seligman, Susan Grafeld, Pauline Postotnik, Michael Haroz, Andra Hotchkiss, Linda Blitz, Toby Edelman, Karen Schneider, Ellen Posner, Caroline Lalire,

244618

vii

and many others whose names cannot be disclosed but who should be acknowledged.

Finally, I have been fortunate to have worked with and drawn inspiration from two people who, in the great tradition of Louis Brandeis and Reginald Heber Smith, provide a model of the people's lawyer serving the public interest—Ralph Nader and Ramsey Clark.

Mark Green
October 2, 1974
Washington, D.C.

To my parents

Contents

The Other Government

WHO

Are Washington Lawyers Just Lawyers?

Earthshakers, Lawmakers, Message-Takers: A Tour

A lawyer is a person skilled in circumvention of the law.
—Ambrose Bierce

The problem is not that you can buy a congressman for $10,000, but can buy a Washington lawyer for $100,000.
—Former FCC Commissioner Nicholas Johnson

As the Washington, D.C., Tourline bus creeps along Rock Creek Parkway, the guide diligently points out the Lincoln and Jefferson memorials, the Washington Monument, and John Kennedy's grave at Arlington National Cemetery. Some of the bright blue-and-white buses carry awed tourists not merely to symbols of power but also to the places of power themselves—Congress, the Supreme Court, the White House. But a bus with a guide knowledgeable in the reality rather than the formality of Washington could have taken its visitors by the other government—those thirty-five large law firms, of more than twenty attorneys each, which practice powerlaw.

Lawyers in general have long exercised obvious public influence—which is why Tocqueville, himself a lawyer, called them "our highest class" a century and a half ago. The trusts, the railroad reorganizations, the regulatory agencies, as well as the legal fiction that corporations are people—these are largely the inventions of Wall Street and Washington lawyers. A. A. Berle thought that law firms "have contributed little of thought, less of philosophy and nothing at all of responsibility or idealism. What they have contributed, however, is the creation of a legal framework for the new economic system, built largely around the modern corporation."* Author Ferdinand

---

* Reference notes begin on page 291.

Lundberg rendered a harsher judgment. "Most of the deeds and misdeeds of the robber barons," he said, "were in actuality the mere projections of lawyers' schemes. . . . They are the brains of American Capitalism." Even Robert Swaine, prototype of the Wall Street lawyer, had some second thoughts about the lawyer's role in the economy. In 1949, fearing the growing danger of "Big Business, Big Labor and Big Government," he issued a challenge to his colleagues: "It behooves all of us who render 'specialized service to business and finance' to seek such solutions of the legal problems of our clients as . . . will avoid the abuses of economic power to which our profession too often contributed in past decades."

This injunction is particularly relevant for Washington lawyers. Senators and Presidents come and go, even the chairmen of Exxon and IBM shift, but Covington & Burling; Wilmer, Cutler & Pickering; Arnold & Porter; Hogan & Hartson; and Clifford, Warnke, Glass, McIlwain & Finney remain—a continuous source of expertise and pressure in Washington. Though far less prominent than public officials, Washington lawyers have burrowed themselves into the federal establishment. They influence a whole range of policy matters that deal with the way we live—the drugs and food we consume, the cars we drive, the taxes we pay, the air we breathe, the things we view and read. Though they represent only specific clients, their pressure on public policy can intimately touch 210 million nonclients as well.

Thus, what the social Philadelphia lawyer was two generations ago and the financial Wall Street lawyer one generation ago, Washington lawyers are today—as the locus of public power shifts from pedigree, to money, to politics. They are to all lawyers and citizens what the heart is to the body: by dint of central location and essential function, both are the reigning organs of their respective body politic. In short, Washington lawyers are among the most powerful people in the country today.

Unlike other lawyers, capital attorneys will often draft bills, not wills; lunch with a cabinet secretary rather than perorate before a judge; consider a court terra infirma yet feel confident in a Senate markup session; represent not aggrieved individuals but billion-dollar corporations that make dents even on a trillion-dollar economy; view "politics" not with opprobrium but as an occupation. This is a function, again, of location. In Detroit they talk of cars and in Akron, tires. In Washington, they talk about government. Lawyers, like everyone else there, accommodate to that reality.

Clients with federal problems, consequently, seek out federal lawyers. They may need counseling on how to avoid potential conflict with the government (if firms A and B merge, will the Justice Department bring an antitrust case?) or how to resolve an actual conflict (as when the Securities and Exchange Commission [SEC] sues a slew of corporate managers for insider trading) or how to persuade the government to confer a benefit on their deserving company (a statutory tax exemption, a Pentagon procurement contract, a loan from the Export-Import bank).

These assignments involve Congress, the courts, the White House, and the administrative agencies. The latter bodies have come to equal in influence the three formal branches of government. They have evolved in four rough stages: 1887–1890 saw the creation of the Interstate Commerce Commission (ICC) and the passage of the Sherman Antitrust Act; from 1913 to 1916 a progressive Woodrow Wilson set up the Federal Reserve System, the Federal Trade Commission (FTC), the U.S. Tariff Commission, and the U.S. Shipping Board; during the New Deal many of the regulatory agencies—the SEC, the Federal Communications Commission (FCC), the Civil Aeronautics Board (CAB)—were created to treat a wounded economy; and the 1970s have witnessed the overnight creations of agencies (the Cost of Living Council, the Federal Energy Administration) with vast powers.

These organizations have substantial authority to help or hurt the nation's 1.5 million corporations. They can dispense great wealth via licenses, subsidies, contracts, and approved rate schedules, or can limit great wealth by tax, antitrust, and regulatory standards. The big six regulatory commissions (the FCC, the SEC, the CAB, the ICC, the Federal Power Commission [FPC], the Federal Maritime Commission [FMC]) have direct authority over some $120 billion of commerce. The Pentagon contracts out $40 billion in weapons contracts annually. The banking industry can do little without approval from the Federal Reserve Board, the comptroller of the currency, or the Federal Deposit Insurance Corporation. The Internal Revenue Service and the Environmental Protection Agency have the ability to make any manufacturing firm in the country miserable.

Unsurprisingly, corporations, through their Washington counsel, try to turn these enterprises to their advantage. They appreciate the value of Attorney General Richard Olney's oft-quoted opinion to a railroad executive in 1892: "The older such a commission [the ICC] gets to be, the more inclined it will be found to take the business and railroad view of things. . . . The better course is not to destroy the Commission but to utilize it."

Despite their obvious public importance, it is fine with Washington law firms that they are not tourist attractions. They are their most successful, in fact, precisely when they are their least visible. Then, Washington lawyers are, at least ostensibly, keeping their clients and themselves out of trouble. When client and counsel become a focus of media attention—witness ITT's self-inflicted anguish in 1972—something is often terribly wrong. With some notable exceptions such as Clark Clifford, prominent Washington counsel appear in newspapers far less frequently than Ethiopian diplomats or local high-school athletes. "They [law firms] thought of their organizations in much the same manner as clergymen think of the church—as an institution that should not be studied," wrote legal sociologist Edwin Smigel. H. Thomas Austern, senior partner at Covington & Burling, was more blunt. "Our public work is in court or agency records," he said; "the rest of our practice is no one's business but ours, and we won't talk about it."

Such reluctance is predictable. By temperament, training, and the strictures of the *Code of Professional Responsibility*, attorneys are discreet. Perhaps, too, a historic unpopularity makes lawyers sweaty under the public spotlight. From a thirteenth-century description of Saint Ives ("He was a lawyer, yet not a rascal, and the people were astonished") to Benjamin Franklin ("God works wonders now and then: Behold! A lawyer and an honest man") to Groucho Marx

("How do you get along at the office?" he once asked a lawyer. "Do you trust each other? Or does each have a separate safe for his money?")—it is clear that lawyers, like Listerine and Presidents, are perhaps respected, but not necessarily loved. In a 1973 Harris poll of those institutions in which Americans had confidence, law firms won only 24 per cent approval, ranking behind doctors, garbage collectors, organized religion, the Congress, local government, and the police.

Of course, Watergate did little to enhance this image of Washington lawyers. "My first reaction was . . . how in God's name could so many lawyers get involved in something like this," John Dean told the Senate Select Committee before millions of television viewers. By mid-1974 the American Bar Association had referred the names of 115 lawyers to state bar groups for possible disciplinary action because of their Watergate involvement. One wonders, for example, just what Hogan & Hartson partner William Bittman had in mind as he ferried large chunks of cash between phone booths and his office.

Unpopular, perhaps, but not unsuccessful. Washington lawyers, in Olney's words, have helped "utilize" the commissions so extensively that law firms have become a growth industry. In the past ten years alone Arent, Fox, Kinter, Plotkin & Kahn has grown from 19 lawyers in 1963 to 112 in 1974; Hogan & Hartson from 47 to 81; and Arnold & Porter, despite the shock waves from the fall of its former name partner, Abe Fortas, from 30 to 85. In fact, growth appears inevitable because of the happy lot of lawyers: they prosper when times are good, as mergers and stock offerings increase, *and* when times are bad, as bankruptcies rise and government regulation must be kept at bay. "The phone's been ringing off the wall," reported one pleased lawyer in late 1973 whose clients were urgently making energy inquiries.

In all there are 18,000 members of the District of Columbia bar. Approximately 4000 work for the government;* another 3500 prac-

---

* Approximately one-half of the Representatives and two-thirds of the Senators are lawyers. This dominance of government by lawyers is not peculiar to the 1970s or to Washington. Of fifty-six signers of the Declaration of Independence, thirty-three were lawyers. Twenty-five of our thirty-eight Presidents have been lawyers. It was estimated in 1963 that 40 per cent of all American diplomats were then lawyers. In 1973 twenty-three of our fifty governors had a legal background. So do the presidents of Harvard, Yale, Michigan, Indiana, Iowa, Ohio State, Chicago, and Rut-

tice outside the D.C. metropolitan area. The remaining 11,500 private attorneys—up 300 per cent from just 3700 two decades ago—range from those who practice in elegant uptown law firms to those criminal lawyers of "Fifth Street," who are said to "keep most of their files in their hip pocket." Whereas there is one lawyer for every six hundred people in the United States, in our nation's capital there is a lawyer for every fifty-two people. In fact, if you pass nine white males in downtown Washington, the odds are one will be a lawyer.

Their income and fees can be lush. As ex-Senator George Smathers gushed to a reporter in 1969: "I'm going to be a Clark Clifford. That's the life for me! I've found the pastures outside are a lot greener than I had reasoned. A fellow with my background can make more money in thirty days out here than he can in fifteen years as a Senator."

Of a nationwide gross legal product of $9 billion, members of the private Washington bar earn approximately $307 million. It is not hard to understand why this figure is so high. "There are so many zeros on the ends of the problems clients have," one lawyer told *Washington Post* reporter John MacKenzie; "when they're dealing in a $50 million business, what do they care about the fee?"—a fee that is tax deductible as well. These rewards apparently surprised practicing New York City lawyer Richard Nixon:

> He was struck by how easy it was, after all, for him to make [money]. One story he told friends concerned a big corporation which came to him for advice about a plan to establish a division in France. They wanted his advice on the likelihood of political stability in France. Nixon, after some thought, told them simply that France would be stable while De Gaulle was alive, and he was much impressed to find that the clients were happy to part with twenty-five thousand dollars for this insight. . . . It does not appear to have crossed Nixon's mind that there was anything curious about an economic system in which great corporations had become so superfatted that they could disburse small fortunes to acquire information available to the most casual newspaper reader.

---

gers. Lawyers now head 12.4 per cent of 774 leading corporations, including du Pont, Sears Roebuck, Pfizer, Coca-Cola, American Smelting and Refining Company, Ashland Oil, National Steel, Textron, and Singer.

Down in Washington, D.C., El Paso Natural Gas gave $449,703 to Sharon, Pierson, Semmes, Crolius & Finley in 1971 alone to lobby for a bill to overturn three Supreme Court decisions in order to let it acquire the Pacific Northwest Pipeline Corporation; in its seventeen-year struggle for the pipeline, El Paso spent at least $15 million. In 1973 Braniff Airways paid Arnold & Porter $524,206, Continental Airlines paid Hydeman & Mason $408,715, and American Airlines paid Prather, Levenberg, Seeger, Doolittle, Farmer & Ewing $211,026 and Wilmer, Cutler & Pickering another $82,768 to keep it out of trouble. Al Prather is pleased with these rewards, but he does at least understand the problem: "Only an extremely wealthy individual [or institution] can really afford a first-rate lawyer for any extended problem. It is worse than medicine, as any person who even gets a divorce will soon tell you."

These large fees are generated by senior partners making $150 plus an hour and twenty-five-year-old associates generating $30 an hour. From this, senior partners can earn over $200,000 annually, and the average D.C. partner earned $60,000 in 1967, highest in the nation. Law graduates start at $18,000 annually (in 1910 they received $600, in the late 1920s $2400, and as recently as 1967 only $10,000). This opening salary of $18,000 is more than twice the income of the average American wage-earner, compares favorably with the average of *all* lawyers' salaries in Oklahoma ($18,000) and Georgia ($15,000), and is often more than the salary of the young lawyers' fathers.

Earthshakers and lawmakers? Yes, Washington lawyers can be that. But they are not merely that. To conform stereotype to reality, some demythification of Washington superlawyers is necessary.

They do not invariably save or scuttle great corporations with a Big Phone Call. As often as they give orders to an agency official they take orders from their corporate clientele. They can be message-takers and spear-carriers for interests to whom lawyers are merely a further instrument for obtaining market power. "I have had many lawyers tell me what I cannot do," J. P. Morgan reportedly said of his lawyer; "Mr. [Elihu] Root is the only lawyer who tells me how to do what I want to do." Thus, Washington counsel can be mere actors in a play scripted by corporations and reviewed by public officials. As actors they can leave them laughing or weeping, but they are still actors.

In addition, not every legal task involves issues of state at the highest levels. Often Washington lawyering can be a grim, gritty, tortuous way to earn a living, as its practitioners pore over galleys of briefs for typographical errors or search out the byzantine Federal Register for that crucial clause on which the interests of their client hinge. This is the ho-hum banality that is law everywhere. Many Washington lawyers are wonderful brief writers, Toscaninis of analysis and research, but they are uncomfortable with a client or senator or judge. Peter Hutt, general counsel at the Food and Drug Administration (FDA) and a former Washington corporate lawyer, emphasizes that "numerous administrative lawyers never go near the administrative agency with which they are concerned." Others may know cold a seemingly obscure area of law, such as the "dumping" of foreign goods in the United States (which have a cheaper price here than abroad)—a knowledge which earns impressive fees but few listeners at cocktail parties. A significant percentage of the partners at the large Washington law firms achieved their rank by perspiration, not inspiration, by technical thoroughness more than political contacts. Washington law reflects the Triumph of the Grinds at least as much as the Triumph of the Influence-Peddlers.

That they may be actors or grinds does not diminish the importance of Washington lawyers, who still remain essential links in the chain of governmental power. But neither does it mean that they perform their work with the ideological glee that an Andrew Carnegie did. For Washington practice can lead to serious conflicts between personal views and professional chores. Compare, by way of explanation, Washington and Wall Street law firms. The latter are often Republican and old money; they largely handle financial affairs, as the proximity of permanent corporate clients and their law firms convert lawyers into housekeepers of corporate business. The great New York firms trace back to the mid- and late 1800s. They thus have a strong sense of history and tradition, leading to conformity and stratification.

A dark suit is still expected, and at Cravath, Swaine & Moore there continue to be separate bathrooms for associates and partners.

On the other hand, most Washington law firms developed at the time of the New Deal or later. Less old, they are less traditional; some of the leading firms have sprung up only in the past decade, something unheard of on Wall Street. Like Washington itself (Democratic administrations have ruled twenty-eight of the past forty-two years), Washington law firms are decidedly more Democratic than Republican. And they deal more with public policy than with purely financial matters. As a result, they attract more liberal lawyers, those with a professed interest in social issues and government service, those less interested in the workings of the stock market than in the workings of the government.

But it is precisely this evolution that has led to the essential dilemma of Washington practice: liberal lawyers toiling for illiberal clients on great policy issues.

Whatever the progressive rhetoric of this legal estate, critics argue, it advocates positions that make the wealthy more so, consumers weaker, and corporations less accountable. One solution is to be a corporate lawyer by day for America, Incorporated, but a public-interest lawyer at night and on weekends for the American Civil Liberties Union (ACLU). Still the conflict remains. For some the political excitement of Washington practice becames a liability. "Hell, I won't work in a Washington firm," remarked one recent law graduate, who opted for Manhattan. "At least in New York I won't worry about my conscience."

In interviews many Washington lawyers denied any problems of conscience or ethics by repeatedly invoking the phrase "Everyone's entitled to a lawyer." But like "A man's home is his castle" or "Guns don't kill, people kill," this verity has some truth and much exaggeration. The issue is not so much *whether* a certain client deserves representation but *how* he is to be represented. When two companies have a contract dispute in Denver, the rest of the community or country barely notices. But an industry-wide practice before a federal agency can, as noted, affect millions of citizens—a situation which should make Washington lawyers especially sensitive to client practices. In addition, it is not at all unusual in Washington to participate in one-sided proceedings lacking an adversary, as in the agencies or in Congress. This can put the ethical lawyer in a quandary, since he is an officer of the court in addition to being an attorney for a client. "Where the adversary process does not operate," argues the eminent Professor Paul Freund of Harvard Law School, "the lawyer has a wider scope and obligation to see around a problem unconstrained by what may be too parochial concerns of his clients, and to advise accordingly." Louis Brandeis saw this problem also and stressed that responsible lawyers should represent not merely clients but the situation.

Washington lawyers should therefore maintain their professional independence from clients who may want fig leaves for illegal behavior or allies in unethical behavior. What do you do if your corporation client insists on a course of action which is nasty, brutish, and illegal? There are three alternatives. You persuade yourself that the activity is not nasty, brutish, or illegal; or you persuade yourself that it is not your function to judge but to carry out the orders of others; or you say no. SEC commissioner A. A. Sommer, Jr., in the context of securities matters, predicted that "the attorney will have to function in a manner more akin to that of the auditor than to that of the advocate. This means several things. It means he will have to exercise a measure of independence that is perhaps uncomfortable if he is also the close counselor of management in other activities, often including business decisions. . . . It means he will have to do the same thing the auditor does when confronted with an intransigent client—resign."

When they are not resigning (which is, of course, a rare event), exactly how do Washington lawyers do what they do? What is the basis of their accomplishments? Certain skills of Washington law firms are of such vintage and proven success that they can be roughly reduced to the Ten Commandments of Washington Law:

I. *Reputation*—In a city where so much is decided so informally, where a salutation as common as hello is, "Who are you with?", where the impression of power *is* power, reputation can be a critical asset, keeping judges attentive and agencies respectful. The late Hugh Cox of Covington & Burling began an argument in a bank usury case by saying deferentially, "I don't mean to burden this court," at which point Judge Oliver Gasch interrupted to note that "it's never a burden to listen to you speak," thereby sinking the hearts of Cox's legal adversaries. When the billboard interests objected to the Commerce Department's attempt to promulgate nationwide size, spacing, and lighting standards in 1966, they retained Cox's colleague Howard Westwood, a tenacious and brilliant lawyer. This prompted a department official to write in an intraoffice memorandum, "If the Outdoor Advertisers are smart enough to get Howard Westwood, we ought to be smart enough to know we have a real fight on our hands."

A grand reputation can be won in various ways. It can be a function of former government service (Thurman Arnold is still remembered as a ferocious trustbuster despite his two decades of corporate practice), the fame of Presidential counseling (Clark Clifford first served Harry Truman), political contacts (former senator George Smathers has—as all former senators have—Senate floor privileges), the ability to have outlived your peers (as Paul Porter has), a stable of blue-chip clients (as Lloyd Cutler has collected),* accumulated expertise (after years of communications advocacy, Ernest Jennes is like the FCC's eighth commissioner), or even a little self-promotion (Lee Loevinger enjoys telling audiences that whenever he enters an antitrust case the government capitulates, which titillates clients even though it happens not to be true).

II. *Intelligence*—The most enduring basis for a prominent reputation is, quite simply, brains. A lawyer's won-and-lost record reflects it, his fees show it, and a lawyer's reputation can turn on it. Hugh Cox's rank rested in no small part on his sheer analytic brilliance (in 1935 he received the highest grades ever given an American Rhodes

---

* San Francisco lawyer James Lorenz has articulated the myriad and reinforcing benefits of important clients: "Having clients with power, they can resolve things short of going to court. Because many of their clients have enough money to employ them on a continuing basis and to provide them with a good deal of work, they can establish continuing relationships with the people who are involved in making decisions in the society. Since they handle big involved cases, they are more likely to be handling 'interesting' cases, and more able to recruit bright young lawyers."

Scholar). Or imagine a former articles' editor at the *Columbia Law Review*—who clerked for a Supreme Court justice, then joined a large Washington law firm, and now dictates his briefs, keeps three secretaries busy, and can outthink, outargue, and outlast any government attorney. Although part truth and part hyperbole, this self-image is maintained by a fair percentage of Washington lawyers.

Reputation and intelligence are, of course, valuable assets for any professional. But beyond these personal traits, the brick and mortar of Washington law firms are specific techniques to build reputation into power. In summary form, these *modi operandi* follow.

III. *Reconnaissance*—In a place where information can be power, Washington lawyers often act as legal radar. On a continuing basis they scan their assigned territories for potential hostile activity and report back to their clients.

IV. *Interlocking Interests*—If a lawyer sits on the board of his corporate client or has worked for an agency he now appears before, the conventional Washington wisdom assumes he may have a bit more insight into what's wrong and how to fix it.

V. *Preferential Access*—If a District of Columbia lawyer cannot get to see the influentials, all his talent and effort may be so much confetti in the wind. Access without brilliance may be preferred to brilliance without access.

VI. *Lobbying*—Access gets you through the door; lobbying is what you say when you sit down. It is a primary *raison d'être* of capital counsel, who practice in Washington precisely because they try to tilt federal policy to their clients' interests.

VII. *Law-writing*—Even better than lobbying sympathetic legislators for a law is writing it for them. As computer programmers realize —who controls the input, controls the output.

VIII. *Inundation*—In representing giant corporations with vast resources, there is a temptation toward argumentation by inundation; the more briefs and motions the better. Whatever their comparable quality, a heavyweight can always beat a flyweight.

IX. *Delay*—Those who enjoyed *Bleak House* would appreciate the often exquisite dilatory tactics of Washington lawyers; for those seeking to avoid regulation, no decision is often a favorable decision.

X. *Corruption*—As with tax evasion and marital infidelity, we know that lawyers do illegal things—but we do not know how often. High stakes, desperate wealthy clients, and compromisable officials can combust into corruption, involving unethical lawyers as well.

Subsequent chapters will elaborate more fully all of these techniques and trace their actual applications. For some combination of them threads through all of what Washington lawlords do, especially the most prestigious and paradigmatic, such as Covington & Burling and Lloyd Cutler.

It is on these two that this book focuses. The law firm and the lawyer: the old, huge, and diversified institution and the crafty, resourceful individual. Because Covington & Burling has for years been the city's leading law firm, lawyers there are important not so much for their personal skills, which may be substantial, but precisely because they are at Covington & Burling. There is an institutional dynamic at the large firms such as C&B. The firm name supersedes and absorbs those of any of its lawyers (Covington has been dead for thirty-two years, Burling for eight), who come to appreciate the continuity of a collective that will long survive them. Lloyd Cutler, on the other hand, although creating a firm in his image, is interesting less for his firm than for his own personal struggle to the top of the greasy pole. Cutler has parlayed reputation and technique into prominence within the last decade, like some expansion team challenging a sport's dynasty. And having broken into the city's Legal Establishment, he has come to personify it. Covington and Cutler, then, in their ways, today exemplify the art of lawcraft as it is practiced in the City of Results.

The Covington Culture:
"Only a Bunch of Lawyers"

Why may not that be the skull of a lawyer? Where be his quiddities now, his quillets, his cases, his tenures, and his tricks?
—Hamlet, *Act V, Scene 1*

Not all my efforts were devoted to representing the forces of reaction in opposition to the children of light.
—*Dean Acheson of Covington & Burling*

Two blocks due north of the White House, occupying the top five floors of the Motion Picture Association Building at 888 Sixteenth Street, Covington & Burling has a panoramic view of the Washington world—which seems only fitting for the firm repeatedly characterized as the Everest of the city's bar. With 150 lawyers as of 1974, it is one of Washington's oldest law firms, its largest, and its most influential as well. "They run their own show, pick their own tactics. They're a major institution," said Timothy J. May, a Covington alumnus, with more than a little trace of awe. "I would love to be a senior partner at C and B, sitting on top of the pyramid." Do C&B lawyers consider themselves the best law firm in the city? ex-associate Gerald Norton was asked. "Not in the city," he answered, "in the *country.*"

Just as it is difficult to imagine that eon before the earth gurgled up Mount Everest, it is hard to comprehend a period when Covington & Burling was not number one.

A visitor enters Covington & Burling's seventh-floor lobby to see ornate gold lettering heralding the firm name on dark walnut paneling. To the left of the elevator is the library, a source of great firm pride. Its twenty thousand volumes rival some law school libraries, and, according to the Covington & Burling intraoffice manual, "The Library . . . is nationally renowned for its collection of federal legislative histories." To the right is a spacious reception area, which was the subject of a 1969 firm memorandum: "As the reception rooms and the waiting room are to accommodate our clients and visitors, all office personnel will understand the necessity of maintaining their informal dignity and, hence, of not using them for socializing, congregating, etc."

There is the steady hum of many typewriters; voices are muted. Purposeful-looking young men stride quickly about, while polite, largely middle-aged secretaries steer around the unfamiliar. There are few black faces. For those waiting, copies of *U.S. News and World Report* and the *Wall Street Journal* are neatly lined up on a visitors' coffee table. The furniture is tasteful and obviously expensive, though not opulent. On the floors there are rugs on rugs and, on the walls, prints of early-American hunting scenes. Off long corridors are small, spare rooms for associates, but large corner offices—with massive shelf space, comfortable divans, and wonderful views out of windows that never open—are reserved for the most senior partners. The ambience seems one of dignity, stability, tradition—something like a cross between a de luxe European hotel and an exclusive men's club.

But above all, there is a sense of history. In its fifty-five-year life the firm masthead has bannered some of the great names of the national bar—Judge J. Harry Covington, Edward Burling, Dean Acheson, John Lord O'Brian—yet today few other than Washington legal cognoscenti could name any of its members. There is no firm autocrat such as a Paul Cravath, a John W. Davis, or a John McCloy of the old Wall Street law firms; no Clifford, Corcoran, or Cutler dominates it. Instead, all work under the names of two dead men and under a ruling five-man management committee run by tax lawyer John Sapienza, who has the dynamism of a high-school librarian, the mind of a Swiss watchmaker, and a flair for understatement. "I don't know why we receive so much attention," he has said. "After all, we're only a bunch of lawyers trying to conduct a practice."

What they practice is the essence of Washington law. Whether it requires agency advocacy, congressional lobbying, courtroom litigation, or corporate counseling, Covington & Burling has the numbers, depth, and experience to staff almost any conceivable case in the nation's capital. The firm's forte is working those executive and regulatory agencies which determine who gets what. Still, although not known as a leading political firm—of the sort Clark Clifford created and Charles Colson hoped to create—C&B is hardly a novice of the legislative process. For an organization whose founder was a congressman (Covington) and which added former Senator John Sherman Cooper in 1973 (recently named to be the first U.S. ambassador to East Germany), this should not come as a surprise. A former firm lawyer recalled that as an associate he had accepted the law firm's conventional wisdom that it did "100 per cent pure legal work." But when he went to work in John Kennedy's White House, he discovered differently: "I found out they had clients which I hadn't realized had legislative interests."*

New client files at Covington & Burling increase at the rate of some two hundred a year. They come because of the firm's general reputation for quality technical work or because the wisdom is that a firm as experienced as C&B in Washington must know where the trap doors to power are. Thus, Covington & Burling represents seven of the top fifteen defense contractors, including McDonnell Douglas, North American Rockwell, Litton, and General Electric; at any given time it is doing Washington legal work for some 20 per cent of

---

* Within the past eight years, C&B, among its other efforts, has done the following on Capitol Hill: opposed bills to strengthen the Federal Trade Commission and consumer class actions on behalf of the National Canners Association; worked on behalf of the Trans-Alaska Pipeline for the State of Alaska; represented the National Association of Credit Management in its fight against the Fair Credit Reporting Act; euchred through the Congress an antitrust exemption permitting the merger of the National Football League with the American Football League; lobbied for the Newspaper Preservation Act on behalf of several newspapers and for an accelerated depreciation allowance on behalf of several international corporate clients; represented the Association of Maximum Service Telecasters in its opposition to legislation limiting the height of certain radio and TV towers; opposed franchise agreement bills for the Electronic Industries Association; and did general tax lobbying for a clutch of financial firms such as the Connecticut Mutual Life Insurance Company and the National Association of Mortgage Insurance Companies. Between 1970 and 1972, aside from general lobbying work, firm members testified on legislative matters alone a total of fifty-four times (twenty-seven times as merely interested individuals and twenty-seven times for specific clients).

Fortune's top 200 firms, including, among others, Exxon, International Business Machines (IBM), Gulf Oil, International Telephone and Telegraph (ITT), du Pont, Bethlehem Steel, Procter and Gamble, American Cyanamid, Campbell Soup, Kennecott Copper, American Smelting and Refining. It also takes on trade associations, such as the National Canners Association, the National Machine Tool Builders Association, and the Electronic Industries Association, as well as important individuals, such as Edward Ball, the industrialist who shut down his Florida East Coast Railway for eight years rather than tolerate his employees' unionization efforts. The firm's major areas of expertise include antitrust, communications, food-and-drug, railroad, and tax work; at one time within the past decade, for example, it had 150 active tax clients with some 320 separate tax problems. C&B also undertakes *pro bono publico* work on behalf of victimized groups, usually in the poverty-law area; it has a regular program whereby it sends two associates to work full time at the Neighborhood Legal Services Program.

Agency practice or *pro bono* work can be challenging, but it is Covington's international practice—which accounts for an estimated 10 per cent of the firm's resources—that is truly alluring to many of its attorneys. Shuttling between foreign capitals, meeting with world leaders on transnational problems, debating unprecedented issues before foreign tribunals, dining in elegance—international lawyers enjoy their world of secrecy, glamour, and large stakes. This specialty quite predictably attracts young law graduates who speak a foreign language and have seriously studied international law. If it were not for the Canons of Ethics and the law firm's sense of dignity, "Join Covington & Burling and See the World" posters might go up at law-school placement offices everywhere.

But as in domestic law, there is beer amid all the cognac. Not every case involving international issues sees a Cyrus Vance negotiating an end to war or a John McCloy single-handedly representing the Western oil firms against the oil-exporting nations. On the one hand, Dean Acheson, Howard Westwood, William Dobrovir, and William Allen spent parts of four years representing Venezuela in its effort (eventually successful) to extradite its former dictator, Marcos Pérez

Jiménez, from Florida to stand trial in Venezuela. On the other hand, when C&B lawyers investigated in 1967 "whether the District of Columbia might be held liable for a portion of the cost of repair to a nine-inch brick fence and retaining wall between the Ghanian Embassy and property belonging to the Canadian Embassy," they did not exactly feel like international moguls.*

In sum, it is not difficult to trace the firm's pattern of domestic- and foreign-client representation. As made clear by its congressional work and client list, the largest law firm in Washington represents the management of the nation's largest corporations on cases of great public importance for great fees. For Judge J. Harry Covington, if alive today, it would be a dream come true.

It was late 1918. The First World War had been won, and a triumphant Woodrow Wilson was moving inexorably ahead to personal defeat and illness. General Motors was ten years old, Babe Ruth was an obscure pitcher, and J. Harry Covington smelled opportunity in Washington. True, the number of Washington law firms had increased from only four in 1880 (two specializing in patent law and two in collections) to sixty-five in 1915, including some with regulatory expertise in the ICC and food and drug law. But the federal income tax and the Federal Trade Commission, relatively new creations, were beginning to generate legal business; then there was also the expected flow of international war claims.

At forty-nine, Covington was looking for a third career. He had been a successful politician, serving as a United States congressman from Maryland for three terms (1909–1914). During his congressional tenure, he chaired the House Interstate Commerce Subcommittee which created the bill that established the Federal Trade Commission. He was one of a group of influential progressive Democrats who in 1912 helped maneuver the Democratic nomination to

---

* Covington & Burling earned $1.5 million in the 1950s and $1.8 million in the 1960s representing foreign clients. Among the leading clients in this twenty-year period were Pakistan ($992,828), Denmark ($570,336), and Colombia ($129,045). Other nations represented included Greece, Venezuela, South Africa, Portugal, Peru, Canada, Finland, Holland, Iran, Lebanon, Ecuador, Israel, Cambodia, Korea, and Guinea.

Woodrow Wilson. Wilson did not forget his friends, appointing Congressman Covington chief justice of the Supreme Court of the District of Columbia (now the United States District Court). While on the bench Judge Covington taught at Georgetown Law Center and made an extensive survey of labor conditions in the West for President Wilson, helping shape the government's war labor policy.

If anyone was situated to see and seize opportunity in Washington, it was Judge Covington. He had the contacts of a politician, the respect accorded a chief judge, and an obvious amount of personal charm. Well known and well liked, he was a friendly, gregarious raconteur, wore a pince-nez with a black ribbon to add a dash of dignity, and had a deep interest in old American prints. And in 1918 he wanted to be a Washington lawyer.

So did Edward Burling, a man of a decidedly different bent. Tall, angular, almost awkward, he was a reserved Iowan whereas Covington was very much the outgoing and patrician Eastern Shore Marylander; he was intellectual where Covington was political, a Republican Bull Mooser rather than a Progressive Democrat. During the war Burling served as chief counsel for the U.S. Shipping Board. In 1917 he started the Chicago law firm of Bentley & Burling but was persuaded by Judge Covington to combine their complementary talents in a Washington legal practice. "Burling was the genius and Covington the wheeler-dealer," reflected one firm graduate, "an unbeatable combination."

Covington & Burling opened for business on January 1, 1919, and six months later it moved into the old Union Trust Building, where it would remain for fifty years. By 1921 business had flourished enough for the firm to expand. Joining as a name partner was one George Rublee, the man who had introduced Covington to Burling, and who had been at Harvard Law School (class of 1895) and on the U.S. Shipping Board with Burling. Rublee seemed to combine equal measures of dilettantism and activism. He had spent years on a European social whirl bankrolled by a business success, yet had worked with Brandeis on his Senate investigation of Secretary of Interior Richard Ballinger, as well as with Woodrow Wilson on the League of Nations. He was a large man, six feet two and lumbering, yet he possessed the style and contacts of international high society. "To the young firm," recalls one C&B senior partner, "Mr. Rublee lent class." .

Paul Shorb and Newell Ellison also joined the firm that year; they were both farm boys and George Washington law graduates and became, respectively, the firm's leading tax expert and the firm manager three decades later. A final addition in 1921 was a lawyer who had just concluded a two year clerkship with Justice Louis Brandeis, the twenty-eight-year-old Dean Acheson.

During the 1920s, the firm grew steadily in size and billings. Its cases were partly local but largely national and governmental, with Rublee handling some international work. Some 60 per cent of the fees earned between 1923 and 1932 derived from the firm's burgeoning tax practice, then under Shorb's leadership. Judge Covington spent much of his time generating business, while "Ned" Burling managed firm affairs; only rarely did either venture near a courtroom.

It was with the New Deal in the 1930s that the firm began its rise to the top of legal Washington. Helping billings, of course, was an energetic President and his regulatory designs. "I disagreed with the New Deal strongly," Burling once said, "but it was a great benefit to lawyers because so many businessmen all over the country began squealing about what was happening to them and had to hire lawyers. And so when you ask me about bureaucracy, I say, 'Oh, I'm for it.' How would I eat otherwise?" Many lawyers came to understand this pleasant truth, but the Covington firm above all others was in a position to exploit it. The firm was relatively large, diverse, with name talent and an expertise in politics and regulation—Messrs. Covington and Rublee, for example, being more responsible than anyone for the creation of the Federal Trade Commission. Following in this tradition, a young H. Thomas Austern in 1933 "was making the NRA's [National Recovery Administration] Blue Eagle dance to his tune," said firm member Howard Westwood, while Westwood himself helped shepherd the bill creating the Civil Aeronautics Board through Congress. As an activist administration began to regulate business, C&B began to get more business.

On January 1, 1934, the firm became Covington, Burling, Rublee, Acheson & Shorb. (Acheson left for a year to become undersecretary of the treasury but returned after he resigned owing to a dispute with President Roosevelt over the gold standard.) The firm existed with this name for the next fifteen years. During this period it grew from twelve lawyers to fifty-six, so that by 1949 it was more than twice as large as the city's second largest law firm. The work was hard ("Of course we worked nights, Saturdays and Sundays," Westwood remembers with relish) and profitable: the firm thrived, not only during the New Deal but also postwar, as billings rose 80 per cent between 1945 and 1948.

This prosperity existed despite internal firm upheavals. In February 1942, after only a few days' illness, Judge Covington died, leaving his relatives a $249,000 estate and the firm his name. Acheson had gone to the State Department the previous year and would not permanently return until 1953. And Rublee retired in 1944, somewhat embittered by his great failures. He had lost his earlier struggle to get the United States to join the League of Nations; and as director of the Intergovernmental Committee on Refugees in the late 1930s, he negotiated to save German Jews, only to see his near achievement slip out of reach by the outbreak of World War II.

The firm readjusted to these losses, and to wartime. It began to hire some female lawyers at the associate level and started systematically to recruit law students; a summer program for second-year law students was developed as an adjunct to recruiting. At the partner level, the firm took on two lawyers who came to be regarded as the firm's most brilliant members: John Lord O'Brian in 1944 and Hugh Cox, formerly Thurman Arnold's chief antitrust lieutenant, in 1951. O'Brian, seventy-one years old when he joined the firm, had served six Presidents from the time Wilson picked him in 1917 to head the War Emergency Division of the Justice Department through 1944 when he served as general counsel of the War Production Board. (In the former post he had hired J. Edgar Hoover as an investigator, a job which led to Hoover's half century as director of the FBI. This, O'Brian would subsequently rue as "something I prefer to whisper in dark corners. It is one of the sins for which I have to atone.") When his time came to return to his native Buffalo, O'Brian found the lure of Washington too great. He stayed with the law firm until his death in 1973 at age ninety-eight, although well before that time this strict, almost puritanical, man had come to be known as the Dean of the American Bar.

By 1950 the firm name, then Covington, Burling, Rublee, O'Brian & Shorb, seemed anomalous. Shorb had recently died and Rublee had retired. In 1951, to close the gates to future major domos who might want the status of name partners, O'Brian voluntarily withdrew his name from the firm title to permit it to revert to the name of the original founders, Covington & Burling.

The early fifties proved to be politically and financially sensitive years for C&B. Despite its rank as the bluest of blue-chip Washington firms, it did not escape the McCarthy era. Dean Acheson—perceived somehow as pro-Communist by those who saw Red everywhere—returned to the firm in 1953 after his controversial years as secretary of state. But he attracted "markedly less" business in 1953 as compared with when he had left in 1941, according to a C&B senior partner. Another firm partner in the 1950s was Donald Hiss, once law clerk to Justice Holmes and the brother of Alger. Because of this blood tie and the fact that Donald, like Alger, had served in the State Department in the 1940s, many anti-Communists (including Richard Nixon) continually lumped the two together. Whittaker Chambers accused Donald of being a Communist; other critics questioned his representation for the firm of the Polish Supply Mission in 1945—all without result. The firm rallied to protect Hiss from persecution. But some clients were upset. When Lehigh Cement found out that Donald Hiss was to meet with their trade association, they refused to attend the meeting. When another client suggested to C&B that it might be wise to drop Hiss and Acheson, the firm dropped the client instead. Only a personal apology from the client's president achieved its reinstatement.

Financially, Covington & Burling revenues noticeably dipped with the reduced activity of the Eisenhower administration. The New Deal that Ned Burling had professionally coveted, though not entirely gone, seemed a thing of the past. Firm billings dropped after 1953, and it was not until 1959 that the gross exceeded that of 1953. From seventy-nine lawyers in 1952, the firm fell to seventy in 1954, getting back up to eighty-five by 1957. There were, to be sure, some celebrated matters, such as the Steel Seizure Case and the du Pont antitrust cases (described in Chapter 4), but symptomatic of C&B's slippage during these years was its dependence on only two clients for more than 40 per cent of the firm's gross income.

Nineteen-sixty-one saw the advent of an administration promising to "do better," to shift the machinery of government into higher gear. The economy began a prolonged period of prosperity. Covington quickly recovered from its financial slump. Business boomed, and so did the size of the firm: from the approximately 80 lawyers it had taken some forty years to amass Covington grew in the next thirteen years to approximately 150. Overcrowding its Union Building offices, the firm moved *in toto* over Memorial Day weekend in 1969 to its present location.

But as will be seen, the transition has been more than merely physical, for Covington & Burling, apparently as immutable as the Washington Monument or Treasury Department, is today very much an institution in flux.

• *Dean Acheson,* of Groton, Yale, and the Harvard Law School, began his Covington career in 1921 by representing Norway in its $16 million claim against the United States for its wartime confiscation of Norwegian ships. Months of work culminated in six weeks of arguments in the summer of 1922. Apparently heady with excitement, the green Acheson at one point brazenly accused the defense of questioning the good faith of the purchasers and even the King of Norway. Halfway through his monologue, Burling passed a note onto Acheson's lectern which said, "Shut up." "The time for that had passed," Acheson later recalled; "I pressed on for want of an alternative." In the end Covington, Burling & Rublee's clients won a $12 million judgment.

In the 1920s Acheson fielded a wide range of corporate cases, arguing many in the Supreme Court. Toward the end of the twenties he began to work more in the area of international law, or as he called it, "interstate disputes." After his brief stint as undersecretary of the treasury in 1933, he was retained by the Federal Reserve Bank in New York to repel the attempt of the British-American Tobacco

Company to recover in gold what the bank held on behalf of the company. In 1939 he represented close-friend Felix Frankfurter at his confirmation hearings as a justice of the Supreme Court. After an appreciative Franklin Roosevelt appointed Acheson assistant secretary of state in 1941, he remained at the State Department for six years, heading the American delegation at Bretton Woods in 1944 and, as undersecretary of state, shaping the Marshall Plan after the war. In 1947 he again returned to C&B, eager to get back their now internationally famous international lawyer.

It proved a short stay, for President Truman selected Acheson as his secretary of state in 1949. Tall, courtly, imperious—"he looked like a Secretary of State sent over by central casting," Arthur Schlesinger, Jr., once wrote of him—Acheson's regal airs rankled opponents. It was not surprising that he became an inviting target during his four-year term for the anti-Communists of that period—"the Primitives," as Acheson came to call them. He fought often with Senator Joseph McCarthy ("He was a very cheap, low scoundrel. To denigrate him is to praise him") and he defended his friend Alger Hiss ("My friendship is not easily given, nor is it easily withdrawn. . . . I do not intend to turn my back on Alger Hiss"). The day after his resignation on January 20, 1953, Acheson returned permanently to the more insulated world of Covington & Burling, but not without some regrets. "To leave positions of great responsibility and authority," he said ruefully, "is to die a little. . . ."

He remained associated with the firm for eighteen more years, handling a variety of foreign and domestic matters. In one exotic international dispute, Acheson successfully persuaded the International Court of Justice in 1962 to declare that the sacred Temple of Preah Vihear on the Cambodian-Thailand border belonged to Cambodia—for which Cambodia paid Acheson $114,000. The then head of state, Prince Sihanouk, decorated Acheson "Grand Duke of the Royal Order of Cambodia." (Covington & Burling lawyers later were fond of telling how the prince, in a fit of appreciation, had announced that Cambodia owed its possession of the temple to Buddha and Acheson, but, add the C&B lawyers, Sihanouk had gotten his order reversed.)

In the mid-1960s, Dean Acheson began to reduce his C&B involvement,* other than to maintain his dignified presence at the firm and to pursue publicly his own personal interests. (But then, he never really loved the private practice of law, once archly admitting that "one of the blessings of Washington legal practice is that the clients are far away.") It was the public arena that continued to hold his attention. As a former and quite celebrated secretary of state, he of course had substantial influence over the foreign-policy establishment, but he exercised it in ways which at times dismayed even his admirers. In 1962 he advised President John Kennedy to bomb the Russian missile sites in Cuba; he endorsed Lyndon Johnson's handling of the Vietnam war and Richard Nixon's efforts to install an anti-ballistic-missile system.

Perhaps most troubling was Acheson's militant and continuous defense of antiblack colonial regimes, such as Portugal, South Africa, and Rhodesia. Waldemar Nielson, author and former president of the African-American Institute, has criticized the way Covington & Burling privately represented Portuguese and South African interests while Dean Acheson publicly traded on his stature to promote those interests, which he failed to acknowledge as clients. Former State Department official William Duggan remembers Acheson's advocacy at meetings of the department's Public Planning Council from 1962 to 1966: "He pled for a more businesslike approach, a more conservative approach with respect to the South African government and Rhodesia. Why was he being their axman, their defender? We specifically asked him whether he or the firm represented such clients, but he was evasive."

At this time C&B did represent South Africa, but not Rhodesia. Although such exploitation of public stature for private client is disappointing, it is unlikely that a mere client could persuade someone as strong-minded as Acheson to publicly defend reactionary regimes. No, Dean Acheson deserved to be taken at his word, for he believed in the regimes he defended.

---

* By 1969 Acheson had effectively retired from the firm, and gracefully refused a request for an interview. "You may attribute my disinclination to undertake the burden," he wrote in a letter, "in part to what I believe is a well-earned right at 76 to indolence, and, part, in Dr. Johnson's words, to "Ignorance, madam, pure ignorance.'"

• *H. Thomas Austern* is Tommy to his friends and enemies—and he has plenty of both. From a Manhattan ghetto, Austern went to New York University on a scholarship and then won the prestigious post of president of the *Harvard Law Review* in 1929. (When in Cambridge he will still occasionally march into the *Review* offices, open Volume 42 to the masthead, and pointing to the top say, "That's me!") He clerked for Justice Brandeis in 1930–1931 and then immediately joined Covington & Burling as its first Jewish lawyer. He became partner in 1936 and remained there for the next thirty-eight years.

He is sixty-nine, frog-voiced, bald, wears spectacles, and walks like a tottering bowling pin. His personality does not get him on "best-liked" lists. Austern is salty, gruff, demanding; he "eats associates for breakfast," said one junior lawyer at the firm, while another said, "Austern reminds me of Vince Lombardi." He has complained that one of the things that worries him the most is the "sloppiness" of young lawyers. But he does have his favorites, such as former associate Sally Payton, who is black. "I got a real kick out of seeing her do a bang-up job for the tobacco companies and the big corporations," he has said.

Austern has elevated blunt truisms and offhanded expletives into something of an occupational trademark. Should an associate do *pro bono* work on firm time? No, he says, let him instead get to the office at 6:00 a.m., not 9:00. At a meeting to discuss the extent of Covington's cooperation with this book, Austern asked the writer if he had read Brandeis's famous 1890 law review article "The Right to Privacy." No, but why do you ask? He answered, "Would you cooperate with the Kinsey Report?"

He is involved in few outside activities: sitting on the Overseers Committee at Harvard Law School, occasionally teaching a seminar at Harvard's or NYU's law school, joining an American Bar Association (ABA) antitrust section report with eight other corporate lawyers denouncing consumer class actions. Mainly, Austern's life is firm business. "He is perhaps the most important partner in the firm," said one C&B member, "and certainly the biggest business-getter and money-maker." Austern is the doyen of the food-and-drug bar in

Washington, having represented, among many others, the National Canners since 1931. "He's a lawyer's lawyer who will give you advice on what is legal, not what is moral or good policy for the public," said a colleague close to him. "But being a twenty-four-hour-a-day lawyer, he is not a good father, social theorist, or political philosopher."

Nor does he want to be. To Austern the highest accolade is "the respect of other lawyers. . . . It's like being a professional violin player who can play the hard passages really well; being good at it is very important, but when other lawyers ask you for advice on technique, that's the most satisfying." But one firm associate who has seen Austern play law speaks of his senior partner more wistfully than respectfully. "It's sort of sad that his greatest accomplishments include keeping Geritol on the market."

When Austern left C&B's management committee at age sixty-five in 1970, all in the firm personally signed a letter to him, reading in part: "Your place on the Management Committee can never be filled. It has been a place too large for ordinary mortals."

• *Peter Barton Hutt,* forty, said, "I hated Harvard Law School and finished in the middle of the class"—secure in the knowledge that a decade later, this earlier lack of distinction hadn't meant a damn thing. After law school he spent a year on a fellowship at NYU's Food Law Institute. Hutt, whose family has been in the retail dairy business since 1840, joined C&B in 1960, where he planned to stay two and a half years and then return to his home city of Buffalo. But Covington and Washington proved irresistible. By 1962 he was doing nearly all the firm's food work at the Food and Drug Administration (FDA); by 1967, after one of the quickest climbs within memory, he was made partner.

Hutt "loved" Covington & Burling—loved his tutelage under partners Paul Warnke and Tommy Austern, loved the responsibility the firm gave him, loved the freedom it gave him to do *pro bono publico* work. And his *pro bono* record was prodigious. In 1964 partner David Isbell asked him to handle a test case for the ACLU and the Washington Alcoholism Council against the D.C. alcoholism laws, laws which viewed alcoholism as more a crime than a disease. "Once into anything, Hutt is indefatigable," said a former colleague, Richard Merrill. Over the next few years Hutt invested an estimated two thousand hours on various alcoholism issues. By substantial after-hours work, he spent about as much time on *pro bono* cases as he did on billable clients, yet his billable hours did not lag behind those of other firm associates. He argued some court cases on alcoholism, including three of the most important involving the crime versus disease question: *Easter* v. *District of Columbia, Budd* v. *Madigan* and *Powell* v. *Texas* (in the Supreme Court). He also helped maneuver the District of Columbia Alcohol Rehabilitation Act through Congress and into law in 1967. Robert Burt, now a professor at Michigan Law School and then on Senator Joseph Tydings' staff, described Hutt's work. "Without his effort and tenacity, there would have been no legislation enacted," said Burt. "He solicited congressional support and capitalized on our interest by drafting speeches which Senator Tydings was willing to deliver and ultimately he even drafted the final committee reports [Senate Committee on the District of Columbia] on the bill." Which is not bad considering Hutt was not even on the committee staff.

Hutt's food lawyering, his *pro bono* work, his boyish looks and disarming openness made him a firm *Wunderkind* with a Washington-wide reputation. (There were, however, some dissidents. "A lot of people here are eager to shoot him down," said a law-firm associate in 1969. "He's too young; he's too successful too fast for a lot of the older lawyers around here.") His reputation and successes led to his selection in September 1971 as the new general counsel of the FDA. Consumer critics were not pleased. "Hutt's transmogrification from tying up the FDA's regulatory process for the benefit of manufacturers to becoming general counsel of the FDA," said *Science* magazine, "is a switch of some proportions, comparable to going from poacher to gamekeeper." Hutt did little to ease this problem when he refused, based on the Canons of Ethics, to reveal the names of corporate clients who could create future conflict-of-interest problems, and he continued this nondisclosure even after an ABA committee announced it would not be unethical to release the list. This greatly upset public-interest lawyer Anita Johnson, who wondered how the public could tell whether Hutt should take himself off future cases.*

Hutt believed that his food industry representation perfectly trained him for this post, since "you can get snookered by everyone in this agency unless you know what's going on." He finds his new work more exciting than C&B, though more taxing and frustrating.

> I've never worked so hard in my life. It's seven days a week, which keeps me from my wife and four children. . . . Working for the government has been the greatest shock of my young life. The whole government system is built to inhibit ingenuity, creativity, and hard work. . . . We have twenty-five lawyers in my office and we need three times that to do a good job. And we don't even have a law library!

Hutt plans on leaving in 1975, although he says, "I haven't decided where I'll go." But he does acknowledge that if you had to put money on it, he would probably end up returning to Covington & Burling—a place he still refers to, in conversation, by the collective "we."

Covington & Burling is a culture as well as a law firm, as much a community of tribal customs, hierarchical relationships and extended loyalties as the Trobriand Islanders, the Tasadays, or the White House.

The firm scoffs at such comparisons. It aims to project an image of proficiency and formality, an effort which only obscures the lurking humanness of the place. In 1960 a partner suddenly commits suicide. An eight-year associate fails to make partner and has a nervous breakdown; another rejectee considers it a major reason for his marriage breakup. Two partners have well-known drinking problems. Two firm associates get into a fight at a cocktail party over the ethics of representing a certain corporate position. A lawyer rolls around the office floor with his secretary one Saturday morning, as an imperturb-

---

* Also troubling critics was the fact that Hutt, who had represented the Institute of Shortening and Edible Oils, replaced William Goodrich as FDA general counsel. Goodrich—who had first urged Hutt to go to NYU's Food Law Institute, who had counseled Hutt to join C&B, and who recommended Hutt as his replacement— became the head of the Institute of Shortening and Edible Oils, with an office at the same building and on the same floor as Covington & Burling.

able John Denniston, stumbling upon their frolic, simply steps by them. While perhaps not Peyton Place, Covington & Burling is more than a brief-writing machine.

There are three classes of people populating this legal institution: partners, associates, and the clerical staff. The partnership runs the firm and the management committee runs the partnership—a method of governance Howard Westwood saw as "the method of democracy and the method of dictatorship essential to the most effective functioning of C&B's special kind of anarchy." The committee (currently composed of John Sapienza, Daniel Gribbon, Stanley Temko, Weaver Dunnan, and Edward Dunkelberger) meets weekly to sort out conflicts-of-interest, make hiring decisions, ensure that the bills are paid, and divide up among the partners the firm's approximately $12 million annual billings. (Establishing this authority is a formal partnership agreement, which is never seen by an associate. When one associate, up that year to make partner, was asked in an interview if he would feel free to ask to see the billings and the agreement of a partnership he might shortly join, he cast a blank stare and then nodded no.) The task of allocating partnership shares can be sensitive, since they range from about $35,000 to more than $200,000, depending on seniority, work output, and client-getting abilities. (Donald Hiss once urged a $100,000 ceiling on partnership shares, with the rest being distributed to associates; and Paul Warnke urged that all partners of the same general age level get the same share. Neither proposal was well received.) The pie is usually big enough to avoid embarrassing and open haggles, though there are some secret jealousies over the size of other slices.

This politburo rules over a domain of mostly Eastern lawyers from mostly large Eastern law schools. According to 1973 data, sixty partners had birthplaces in twenty states, with eleven coming from New York and no other state counting more than five. Thirty-one, or slightly more than half, came from Harvard and eight from Yale. Although largely Democratic, "most of the partners voted for Nixon," said a former firm lawyer. "These people spend so much time with business that, though they'll deny it till they're blue in the face, they tend to pick up the businessmen's ways and views."

Of sixty-five associates, seventeen are from Harvard, eleven from Yale and eight from Columbia. Perhaps some 10 per cent of the firm have clerked on the Supreme Court ("We really love to get those Supreme Court clerks," said Edward Burling, Jr.), and at least 80 per cent have worked on their schools' law reviews. The firm hires about fifteen lawyers a year and loses slightly less than that annually. Most come directly from law schools, where a network of Covington-bred professors or friends refer their better students to the firm. Yet there are some important exceptions to C&B's preference for hiring recent law graduates, such as John Lord O'Brian, Hugh Cox, Edwin Zimmerman. But, by and large, one becomes a partner at C&B vertically, not laterally.

Few associates are black or female. Covington & Burling has proven no worse on these issues than other firms, though no better either. In a city two-thirds black, it hired its first black secretary and messenger in the early 1960s. One solicitous partner had suggested at a partners' meeting that *other* secretaries might object to sharing toilet facilities with nonwhites, to which Acheson replied, "Where the hell do you think the charladies go to the pot?" thereby ending the dispute. It was 1968 when Covington took on its first black associate, Ty Brown, who had been only the second black Supreme Court clerk in the Court's history. By 1974 the firm had five black associates, though still no black partners.

Women have been C&B associates since at least the 1940s, but, as with blacks, there has never been a female partner in the firm's history. By 1974 Covington was down to only five women associates, or 3 per cent of the firm. One recent female graduate of the firm complained that women were "cubbyholed there, doing dribs and drabs of cases." For example, she said that there seemed to be specific slots reserved for women—in trusts and estates, tax, and food-and-drug law.

This problem surfaced embarrassingly in 1973. For longer than anyone could remember, a weekly firm luncheon had been held at the Metropolitan Club, where partners and associates would chat and listen to invited outside speakers—except that the Metropolitan Club refused to seat women, so firm females were excluded from these events. (When the firm met at the Metropolitan Club in 1966 to eulogize Edward Burling, Sr., upon his death, a C&B memorandum was circulated specifying that female lawyers and the wives of male lawyers could not attend.) When a female associate protested to a partner, he admitted he had never really thought of it before but would certainly see what he could do. The partnership put its head together and replied that unfortunately it could find no alternative lunch site to accommodate so many people. (One firm elder suggested an occasional ladies' day at another club, which did not impress the women.) There then appeared a small item on C&B in the September 1973 *Washingtonian* titled "Oink, Oink," for the firm's unliberated luncheon treatment of women associates. This prompted female law-school applicants to ask some obvious but unanswerable questions. The firm shortly thereafter announced that it would henceforth hold its weekly luncheons at the Sheraton Carlton Hotel. Covington is also trying to hire more women, "but the firm has taken a beating on this issue," observed one (male) associate there. "It's an open question whether the partnership are a bunch of chauvinist pigs, but at least many of the women think so. Others think that they simply treated women as lousy as they treated everybody else."

The Metropolitan Club flap raises the issue of social clubs generally, for to paraphrase a truism, you can tell where a person stands by where he plays. What clubs do C&B members belong to? "All the bad ones," answers a firm lawyer.

Although there are dozens of private clubs in Washington, the most elite are the Chevy Chase, Burning Tree, and Metropolitan clubs. Thirteen firm partners belong to the Chevy Chase Country Club, which had a "deplorable record" of discrimination against blacks and Jews, according to Maryland's Montgomery County Human Relations commissioner. It is difficult to obtain a membership list for the Burning Tree Club, which is almost exclusively a golf club, but at least five Covington partners belong. Women are not allowed as members or even as guests (although the wives of members can, by special arrangement, purchase gifts for their husbands at the club's pro shop). In 1968 the Montgomery Human Relations Commission considered that the club had a history of "discrimination against nonwhite, non-Christian guests."

The Metropolitan Club, baroque in its splendor at Seventeenth and H streets, in the heart of downtown Washington, is a favorite firm haunt. More than half of its partners are members, and for years C&B held its annual firm dinner (black-tie and stag) there. The club features a library, card room, bar, and facilities for Ping-Pong, sunbathing, and massage. But the main attraction is the dining room, where prominent lawyers, businessmen, and government officials can conduct business in a plush setting—that is, if the diner is a white male. In 1961 Robert Kennedy resigned in protest because, in a letter sent to the club's board of governors, which included firm partners J. Harry Covington, Jr., and Fontaine Bradley, "it is inconceivable to me, in this day and age, that the privileges of this club, which holds such a unique and peculiar position in the Nation's Capital, would be denied to anyone merely because of his race."

In the late 1960s some firm associates threatened to boycott firm meetings at the club because of its policies, and they drafted a letter to firm seniors saying, among other things, " . . . it does not reflect favorably on the firm to have it tacitly acquiesce—indeed, tacitly support—an institution which would, for example, not admit one of us · to membership because of the color of his skin." They were successfully dissuaded from their planned boycott by partners who argued that the firm was trying to change club policies by working within it. And in April 1972, in part because of Howard Westwood's prodding, the Metropolitan Club accepted its first black member, John Walker, a Washington Episcopal bishop. But lest anyone get the wrong impression, club president Philip W. Bonsal saw Reverend Walker's admission as "a very special case because he was a bishop." He added that, "no question of admitting women to the Metropolitan Club membership has come up so far."

This club history did not seem to concern the Covington members. When asked about this pattern of racial discrimination, one partner answered, "After all, they allow some Jews, and given Washington social clubs, that's a step forward. And it's been said," he continued, "that the only way to get into the Metropolitan if you're Jewish is to be a senior partner in Covington." Another firm partner was asked if it concerned him that his law firm subsidized a racist institution. "It never occurred to me while I was a member of the annual dinner committee," he said—then recovered sufficiently to add, "Well, doesn't the Kerner Commission say that we're all racists anyway?"

Despite the few blacks and women, and the firm's propensity for Eastern law-school superstars, C&B lawyers do possess a modest degree of diversity. Covington, Burling, and Rublee shared the common goal of a ranking corporate law firm, but they strove toward it with varying styles. The firm has boasted leading Democrats like Covington and Acheson and now John Douglas (son of Paul Douglas and a key figure in George McGovern's Presidential bid), but it also has contained once-leading Republicans such as Senator John Sherman Cooper and Edward Burling, Jr.

The firm at one time managed to house people as dissimilar as Armand Derfner, Sally Payton, and Brice Clagett: Derfner was a public-interest lawyer in the 1960s before there was such a category; he once showed client Jerry Rubin around a startled firm. He left in 1967 to affiliate with the Lawyers' Constitutional Defense Committee in Mississippi. Sally Payton, the first black *and* female firm associate, joined President Nixon's Domestic Council after having lunch with a persuasive John Ehrlichman. In the White House she worked on D.C. affairs, and commented, "The subjects I work on are close to my heart, and the President's instincts and my instincts are not very far apart." When a group of firm associates picketed the Pentagon in a 1967 antiwar rally, Brice McAdoo Clagett was there to *counterpicket*. Clagett is a patrician with an illustrious family tree, as he consistently reminds people. He lives in the three-hundred-year-old house of his Maryland ancestors and has spent long hours poring over family records on microfilm. "Brice is convinced," said a firm lawyer, reflecting a wider consensus, "that America should have a monarch and that he should be king."

The firm, then, is no monolith. C&B, certainly, is more varied than Wall Street firms or the Committee to Re-elect the President. Still, it is hardly catholic in composition. Sally Payton sees C&B as naturally suspicious of people "on radical trips because the firm isn't sure they're 'sound' lawyers"; you can adopt a different lifestyle if you win, she

added, but if you don't. . . . Some lawyers with special styles,
ambitions, and talents, consequently, do not stay within this institution. The Brice Clagetts become partners while the Armand Derfners
invariably leave for places more congenial to their public-interest
impulses. The firm may be too restricting for exceptional members
like a Burke Marshall, a Paul Warnke, or a Nicholas Johnson, all of
whom left C&B for the government, and none of whom returned. The
eight-year progression from associate seems to weed out institutionally
those individuals who are "unsound," or lack a needed devotion to the
firm and the private interest, or who have either too little talent to do
the work *or* perhaps too much talent for the confines of a 150-person
bureaucracy.

To understand why some rise like helium within the firm while
others drift away, the world of the Covington associate must first be
understood. Most associates join the firm for postgraduate training, to
learn the realities of practice by osmosis from legal veterans. There are
secondary motivations: a curiosity to see what big firm practice is
like; a need to be credentialed by a prominent association; the awareness that C&B is an effective springboard to other jobs; the expectation that it is a nice place to temporize while you decide what to do
with the rest of your life. And there is the challenge. "Ninety per cent
of the reason anybody goes there," said former partner Al Prather, "is
to prove he can make it with the Yankees."

The position's accouterments are pleasant. A fleet of typists, secretaries, messengers, duplicators, and office managers ensure that forty-
page briefs are perfectly typed overnight and delivered anywhere in
the country. There is elbow-rubbing with legendary lawyers and the
recognition that comes at gatherings when you give your affiliation.
Of course, there is also the opening $18,000 salary, plus an approxi-
mately $2000 annual increase.*

---

* Eighteen thousand dollars is a lot of money, but a new associate actually generates
some $57,600 in billings annually (assuming a fee of $30 an hour). Since it is
estimated that 40 per cent of a law firm's billings go to salaries for nonclerical staff
and to office overhead, a law graduate is producing about $34,000 in salary (60 per
cent of $51,600) but is being paid $18,000. The difference effectively subsidizes the
partners. Associates appeared unconcerned with this income transfer, emphasizing
instead the education they are receiving and the prospect that someday *they* might
be the system's benefactors.

But these rewards are not costless.

The income can create near Faustian problems. "You get trapped by the money," said one-time associate Henry Goldberg. "They get to the point where most just can't afford to leave, because they're living on their salary and bonus." As for the work load of the associates, former associate Neil Adelman thought it "ran the gamut from full to unreasonably full to impossibly full." Again, Washington practice is somewhat more civilized than that of the Wall Street sweatshops of decades past—Hoyt Moore of Cravath, Swaine & Moore enjoyed telling how "no one is under pressure. There wasn't a light on when I left at two this morning"—but it is still not a nine-to-five occupation. A March 18, 1968, "memorandum to all lawyers" made the point for any who might have forgotten it: "The tradition of the Firm is that whatever time is necessary to perform a first-rate professional job is spent, even if it involves night work or week-end work." An associate is expected to submit eighty billable hours every two weeks, although it is never made clear what happens if this minimum is not met. A number of associates emphasized how much freedom they had within the firm, although their claims seemed to resemble the coal miner's monologue in *Beyond the Fringe*. "It's quite interesting work, minin'. . . . Quite interestin'. . . . You do what you like for eight hours a day as long as you get hold of two tons of coal."

At times, work relationships and firm rules can be quite taxing. Some partners see the early years as a legal boot camp, building up certain desired habits of mind and character. Al Prather noted how "the kids are good and they know they're good. The first job is to smack them down. Show him he's a miserable wretch who can't write his name." There is learning by doing, but also education by intimidation.*

---

* When an associate suggested to senior partner Joel Barlow that the firm research a certain point of antitrust law for the National Machine Tools Builders Association—the implication being that the firm had neglected to do this before—Barlow sent the young lawyer a tart memorandum: "You have leaped without looking. You will learn that C&B could not possibly have a client for twenty-five years and not give him good advice on his major legal problem. . . ." Barlow's ridiculing condemnation went on for pages, and, worse, he sent copies of it to three other important firm partners. "Barlow was always doing that," recalled an associate who had worked closely with him. "He was always rubbing other guys down in order to build up his own ego."

Perhaps because the work is difficult and time-consuming, there is little philosophizing or socializing among associates. The talk in the office or at lunch focuses on the intricacies and content of their cases. There is a professional emphasis on *doing* rather than *judging,* as ethical and social issues are largely bypassed. But what is unsaid is not unknown. According to former associate John Murphy, "Everyone I knew at Covington, to the extent the subject was broached, fully knew that the rich were getting richer and we were helping this, and that this involved social costs, like, say, a functionally undemocratic legal system." Also, while main-line Philadelphia law firms have traditionally encouraged their members to work and play together in their own closed communities, the C&B associate appears more isolated, knowing well just a handful of peers in his or her corner of the office. This bigness and professionalism leads to institutional impersonality. To humanize this environment, some associates have recently begun to hold periodic lunches to meet each other more regularly and to relate on more than the level of the jurisdictional statements of their cases.

The problem, however, goes beyond impersonal atmosphere to the firm's rules. A certain formality is expected from its members. When a partner and client a few years ago saw an associate sauntering around the firm offices one Saturday morning in his tennis togs, they were appalled. Managing partner Newell Ellison then circulated a firm memorandum, saying in part: "It has been noticeable—*quite noticeable*—that many of us come to the office on Saturdays, Sundays and holidays not properly dressed for a dignified law office. We come in shorts, slacks without coats, shirts without ties, dungarees, tennis shoes, and otherwise in attire that is wholly unacceptable." (Emphasis in original.) Dean Acheson subsequently sent around a memorandum requesting that C&B lawyers keep their jackets on at all times during the work day.

There is, in fact, an official 100-page "Covington & Burling Office Manual" to instruct every lawyer and staff employee on firm rites and wrongs. "A working day of 9:00 AM to 6:00 PM is customary," it begins, and goes on to explain how to fill out time sheets for billable hours to the minute. The manual emphasizes confidentiality. "*It is a*

primary rule of the office that all work is to be treated as confidential.
Nothing is to be said, even to close friends or relatives, of any work
being done in the office. . . . The fixed office rule, which must be
obeyed is, 'Don't tell!' " (Emphasis in original.) Under "Office Eti-
quette" it says: "Conformance to the norms for correct behavior is
expected of all office personnel in the way of dress, manner and
speech. It should be remembered that the office is a place of business
and one must conduct himself accordingly."

All this is perhaps sufferable to those whose main goal is good
legal training. But that is not what every Covington lawyer obtains.
Low on the totem pole, "half of the guys get on an antitrust case for
four years and end up guarding the files," says ex-associate Timothy J.
May. Covington & Burling frequently handles huge cases requiring a
team of lawyers, with some seeing only a corner of the case but rarely
the courtroom or the client. Many lawyers there spend years as legal
squirrels, digging out obscure cases from the firm library for their
superiors. Richard Cappelli quit the firm after his work on the Peanut
Butter Case (see Chapter 6) because, as he said, "I was disgusted
with the kind of work I was doing."

> Not once during [the case] did I see a law, regulation or court
> decision, except when I would longingly peek over someone's
> shoulder, I was—Williams College, Columbia Law, law review,
> Stone Scholar, etc—a bag-carrier. Among other earthshaking
> responsibilities I analyzed hundreds of pages of FDA investiga-
> tors' reports; created enormous statistical summaries from these
> reports (I was wedded to an adding machine for three solid
> weeks); read and tabulated 2500 consumer letters and was chief
> protector of the IBM cards used for a Procter & Gamble survey
> of peanut butter eaters.

This experience is not unusual. Robert Bicks, a well-known New York
antitrust lawyer and former Antitrust Division chief at the Justice
Department, thinks "Covington & Burling destroys great minds by
making them overwork on trivia." Legal paraprofessionals increasingly
do such legwork in other firms. The New York City law firm of Paul,
Weiss, Rifkind, Wharton & Garrison, for example, has a general rule
against more than four lawyers on a case. The Cappelli syndrome is
not inevitable.

This problem eases over time, but does not entirely disappear. With so many legal stars in the Covington stratosphere, many younger partners do not even run their own cases or handle client contacts. Their peers in smaller firms do so as a matter of course, but in a 150-person firm, a middle-level partner is often the number two person on a case. "At C and B you aren't your own man, making your own print, until you're maybe fifty years old," commented a former firm associate who, spotting this pattern, left after two years.

Of any entering class of fifteen associates, three to four may make partner. People leave for varying reasons, but one is not that they are fired; the firm is far too genteel for that. Some cannot abide the trivia/tedium problem ("I disliked making partners happy rather than serving clients"); some find the work politically intolerable (such as the liberal associate who spent all his time representing the U.S. Chamber of Commerce); others want to be bigger fish in smaller firms or in a client's legal department; others accept attractive positions in government or teaching;* and a few simply want to get off the firm escalator: in the words of one firm dropout, "I didn't want to wake up in ten years and regret that the only decision I made was one of omission."

But some of course stay on in the hope of becoming partners. They stay because being a C&B partner guarantees wealth, status, and even power, where the mere fact of the Covington cachet gives its

---

* Covington has graduated many of its alumni into government service, who then became a helpful network of contacts for firm activities. (As Peter Hutt noted in an interview, "The alumni of C&B would make a hell of a law firm.") Beyond those mentioned, such as Dean Acheson and Hutt, some former firm lawyers who went into government (with the year they left the firm) include: Henry Fowler (1934), former treasury secretary under Lyndon Johnson; Gordon Rule (1947), senior civilian procurement specialist at the Pentagon; William Bundy (1951), Acheson's son-in-law and assistant secretary of state for Far Eastern affairs under Dean Rusk; Donald C. Alexander (1954), presently the commissioner of the IRS; Abe Chayes (1955), the legal advisor to the State Department (1962–1965); Burke Marshall (1961), head of the Civil Rights Division of the Justice Department under Robert Kennedy; Stephen Pollack (1961), also in charge of the Civil Rights Division; Nicholas Johnson (1965), FCC commissioner; Paul Warnke (1967), general counsel of the Defense Department. David McGiffert was undersecretary of the army, 1965–1969, and then returned to the firm; John Douglas was assistant attorney general in charge of the Civil Division of the Justice Department, 1963–1966, and then returned to C&B; Gerhard Gesell (1968) went on to become a celebrated federal district court judge. The firm has also turned out a large number of academics. At Harvard Law School alone, Dean Al Sacks and professors Abe Chayes, Roger Fisher, Jerome Cohen, David Shapiro, and Richard Stewart were all once with Covington & Burling.

members' words greater authority. In smaller firms one can make partner within three to four years, but the Covington & Burling partnership usually makes an up-or-down decision at the eight-year mark.

Who makes partner? The kind of unbending criteria that for decades prevailed on Wall Street does not apply to Covington & Burling. Sociologist Erwin Smigel described those who succeeded on Wall Street as "well-rounded men who are law review . . . who are Nordic, have pleasing personalities and clean-cut appearances, are graduates of the 'right' school, have the 'right' social background and experience in the affairs of the world, and are endowed with tremendous stamina." Instead, "the way to advance at Covington," said one associate, "is to work like a sonofabitch." Some associates simply grind their way into the partnership, the firm appreciating that someone willingly does the detail work. Other associates dazzle their way up, as obvious talent and reputation reinforce each other. Having a pleasing personality helps: "After all, who wants to work with a schnook?" said one associate. Part of the climb toward partnership involves pure luck: the firm might really need an international tax expert that year or may already be overstocked with good litigators. Thus, a mediocre international tax lawyer may beat out a crackerjack litigator.

Although nepotism was at one time an operative factor—the sons of both firm founders became firm members—today blood lines appear irrelevant. One's club memberships or social style are also irrelevant, firm members say. But at a minimum, if he refused to attend firm functions at the Metropolitan Club because of its racial and sex discrimination, or if he wore tennis clothes on Saturdays, or went jacketless during the week, it would not be unreasonable for the seven- or eight-year associate to wonder whether a key senior partner might be antagonized. Hence, there can develop an appreciation for Sam Rayburn's dictum that to get along you go along. There can be the tendency for an associate to seek out partners with clout who can best promote his or her candidacy. He studies the competition and tries to guess who will and who won't make it. Dreams are deferred and sacrifices endured to grab the partnership brass ring. As the months tick toward eight years, anxieties accelerate. Said one associate who didn't make it, "After eight years, a person doesn't come out whole."

The firm historically has not explicitly told an associate before his year of decision what his chances are, but supposedly there are clues along the way. Is his bonus—which can vary up to 25 per cent of his salary—high or low? Does he work on important cases or local wills; is there little or much client contact? Are his draft briefs marked up with unflattering comments or do they pass easily into final copy? Such tip-offs are supposed to tell him either to look elsewhere or hang around. "If he doesn't know [by these indicators]," said Paul Warnke, "he's too dumb to ever be a partner."

Which would mean 1972 was a very dumb year.

Fully seven associates were confident of their selection that summer, but only two got the all-important phone call welcoming them to the partnership. This "bloodbath," as it is known at the firm, sent shudders through C&B. Associates could talk of little else, some summer law students quit, saying, "We don't want to work for a place like this," and morale plummeted. The losers felt deceived and, unlike predecessors passed over, complained bitterly to firm partners—leading two of those rejected to be reconsidered and accepted a year later, in a departure from firm precedent.

Like governments, Covington & Burling is slow to change—except in crisis. The firm moves its luncheons away from a discriminatory club only when it has been publicly embarrassed. And it now better informs associates of their partnership prospects before their eighth year, but only in response to a minipalace revolt.

There is one continuing development, however, so obvious and crucial that not even a very traditional Covington & Burling can afford to be indifferent. Within five to ten years nearly all the first- and second-generation firm lawyers will be gone. Covington, Burling, Rublee, Acheson, O'Brian, and Cox are dead; those colorful curmudgeons of the 1930s—the Austerns, Gesells, Barlows, Westwoods—will have retired. Partners Paul Warnke, Al Prather, and W. Graham Clayton, Jr., left in the late 1960s.

As its founders die and New Deal partners age into retirement, a third generation of Covington lawyers slowly begins to grip the levers of firm power. The new firm leaders are not legal frontiersmen who worked in a young firm called Covington, Burling & Rublee and helped it evolve into prominence. Instead, they are more like organization men, less colorful though perhaps equally able men who have risen through the ranks of an institution with its own filtering mechanism. What effect will this loss of name talent and this new firm orientation have on Covington's clients and reputation in the Washington bar?

Some at C&B have a feeling of inevitability: the firm name will outlast any of its illustrious members, they say, as clients and lawyers have grown accustomed to the competence of an establishment called Covington & Burling. The firm has positioned itself for perpetual existence, much like a Department of Health, Education, and Welfare (HEW) regardless of who is its secretary. But others wonder. Donald Hiss candidly admits the problem, observing that the firm's 1973 offer to Senator John Sherman Cooper "was a deliberate attempt to get someone of the dignity and stature of Dean [Acheson]." He adds that the firm's size is a "devilish problem," which has begun to hurt recruiting, as some good law graduates have chosen to go elsewhere. "The larger you get, the harder it is to get good people."

As politicians tell us, name recognition and drawing power are essential *and* ephemeral, often as easily lost as gained. New corporate managers and general counsels may shift their Washington accounts away from a firm perceived to have lost its influential leaders in a town supposedly run by influence. That Covington's work quality may not decline an iota may count less than this illusion, for illusion and not reality can shape the legal market as it has the stock market. Given its structure and purpose, it is inevitable that the firm will continue to represent in general large corporate clients; but it is not ordained that, specifically, the National Canners will be as devoted to a C&B without Tommy Austern, or du Pont as committed to the firm without Gesell and Cox manning its antitrust barricades.

Great institutions come, peak, and decline, from the British East India Trade Company to *Life* magazine to the New York Yankees, and it is only in retrospect that we learn that moment in time when events conspired to undo institutional inevitability.

The Paradox
of Being Cutler

*The way I look at it . . . in a big firm it's a tough climb
to the top, but a mighty nice view if you can get there. I
don't want to get to the top in a small firm and find I still
can't see over the heads of the crowd.*

—*Richard Powell,* The Young Philadelphians

*Lawyers fall more into the category of politicians, civil
servants and jockeys—some of them are probably honest
[thinks the public], but how can you ever be sure?*

—*Lloyd Cutler*

To his admirers he is the model of the modern lawyer, but
his critics would sentence him to the eclectic chair.

He represents the American drug industry *and* the Lawyers Committee for Civil Rights Under Law, counsels the violence-prone
automobile industry *and* the President's Commission on Violence,
innovates in the civil liberties area *and* belongs to the discriminatory
Metropolitan and Kenwood clubs, and advocates a Justice Department more independent of outside pressures while he occasionally
lobbies it into submission.

"Lloyd Cutler is a strange man," said Joe Laitin, who has worked
closely with Cutler and is now an official in the Office of Management
and Budget: "On the one hand he's a corporate devil and on the
other hand he's a nineteen-thirties' liberal." Ben Gordon, staff assistant on the Senate Small Business Committee, says flatly that "when I
see Lloyd Cutler representing anybody, I know that it is not in the
public interest." Yet public-interest lawyer Charles Halpern respects

Cutler because "he does as much free work as any lawyer in town." Perhaps more than any other Washington lawyer, Cutler seems to epitomize that dilemma of the corporate liberal—a progressive promoting conservative causes . . . who can very suddenly reverse roles to do good works. He moves with the deftness of a chameleon between the boardrooms of corporate power and the anterooms of advocacy groups, as each comes to accept him as one of them.

The leading influence in the Washington law firm of Wilmer, Cutler & Pickering, Cutler, fifty-seven, spends the bulk of his professional life representing companies such as General Motors, IBM, CBS, and Kaiser Industries. But it is his public side that he prefers to expose, understanding well that the next legal generation will remember a Louis Brandeis but not a Tommy Austern. Consider, for example, Watergate—an episode in which Cutler fused his conflicting roles into a near populist performance.

When the name of Richard A. Moore surfaced at the Senate Watergate hearings—as special White House counsel he had personal knowledge of the Nixon-Dean conversations—he turned to his former college and lawschool classmate, Lloyd Cutler, for help. Moore's testimony was prepared at Wilmer, Cutler & Pickering and distributed to the press by Cutler's personal secretary. Although Cutler initially hesitated to accompany Moore during his televised testimony, he sat directly behind Moore "to show the flag." "And then I found myself having my hand shaken by John Mitchell [the prior witness] on national TV, to the horror of all my children," said Cutler, laughing. But he did not consider at all amusing Watergate Committee counsel Terry Lenzer's withering cross-examination of his white-haired and fumbling friend. (At one point Moore got sufficiently flustered to say, "I'll let my answer stand—whatever it was.") Cutler thought the grilling "overdone, without adequate prior notice, and it caused a net loss for the committee."

Another acquaintance, columnist Joseph Kraft, found himself inadvertently swept up by the Watergate current when it became known in 1973 that the White House plumbers had wiretapped his home and bugged him in 1969. Kraft spoke with Cutler, who was willing to provide legal assistance, the two having spoken previously on wiretap issues. Kraft asked him if he had represented Moore, and Cutler said no, that he was only lending friendly support. Kraft's syndicate did subsequently have Cutler represent him on wiretap-related matters, though without compensation. In addition, Kraft put Cutler in touch with CBS correspondent Marvin Kalb, who had also been wiretapped by the Nixon White House; again, however, Kalb did not take Cutler on as his lawyer in a Watergate matter.

Cutler's Watergate activity accelerated as the ball of campaign-funding illegality unraveled. In January 1971 he was the lead lawyer in Common Cause's lawsuit to enjoin corrupt spending practices by the two major parties in the next year's elections. "We owe Cutler a medal," said Common Cause's Tom Mathews. He participated on the Common Cause committee which approved of the momentous 1972 legal action to compel the Committee to Re-elect the President to disclose all secret contributions to President Nixon's campaign made prior to the public disclosure provisions of the 1972 campaign-spending law. Undoubtedly, Cutler is a serious hawk on campaign-spending reform, urging the public financing of political campaigns and, in a *New York Times* op-ed piece, and elsewhere, promoting the creation of a *permanent* special prosecutor to handle cases of political corruption. "Teapot Dome and Watergate," he has said, "are only the tips of icebergs floating around in political waters all the time."

But all this public activity collided with the dealings of a private client. For the pursuit of illegal corporate contributors led to, among others, American Airlines, a Cutler client. In April 1973 Presidential lawyer Herbert Kalmbach told American Airlines chairman George Spater that a list of corporate contributions made prior to the law's April 7 effective date, a list including American's name, might soon be disclosed. Spater informed Cutler who later informed Common Cause's John Gardner, a long-time friend, of his client's problem. The Washington lawyer then refrained from any further participation in the Common Cause enterprise and plunged into counseling his nervous client.

His advice was simple: come clean; a cover-up can only aggravate your problem. "I don't doubt that there are some lawyers who would have urged them to stay in the bushes," said Cutler; "we decided to urge them to come forward." Spater agreed. On July 6, 1973, with Special Prosecutor Archibald Cox nipping at the heels of firms who had illegally contributed funds out of corporate coffers, Spater issued a press release admitting American's illegal $55,000 contribution and describing a political shakedown: "I was solicited by Mr. Herbert Kalmbach, who said that we were among those from whom $100,000 was expected," wrote Spater, aided by Cutler. "I knew Mr. Kalmbach to be both the President's personal counsel and counsel for our major competitor [United Airlines]. I concluded that a substantial response was called for." John Gardner issued a statement commending Mr. Spater for his disclosure.

Cutler's strategy aimed to win the airline good will for its admission and to mitigate any criminal penalties. Toward this goal, he began phoning around Washington to drum up support. After Cutler spoke to his friend James Reston about corporate contributions, Reston produced a *Times* column urging firms which had made illegal gifts to admit their guilt. Cutler called *Washington Post* executive editor Benjamin Bradlee to elaborate on American's admission and his own role in the episode. Bradlee thought this excessive self-promotion, but the *Post* story did laud the press release's candor as "extraordinary" and described how "one of those instrumental in the American Airlines disclosure to Cox and his prosecutors was Lloyd N. Cutler, American's Washington attorney. He said that the company's lawyers and management 'agreed that it should be done as soon as any of us looked into the matter.' "

The publicity was all they had hoped for. Spater became the only chairman of a firm found to have made illegal contributions in the 1972 campaign who was not *personally* charged with breaking the law.* Cutler appeared to have snatched victory from defeat—almost. For in September 1973 the board of American Airlines deposed

---

* In addition, Cutler also privately persuaded Senator Sam Ervin of the Senate Watergate Committee not to publicly ask Spater where he got $20,000 of unaccounted-for funds which ended up at the Committee to Re-elect the President. Cutler said that he sought to protect from possible public ruin a minor figure who had committed a relatively minor transgression. "It was the only time we agreed to hold something off the public record," said one committee prober; "it was because of Spater's admission and Cutler's stature."

George Spater as its chairman. In addition, Cutler was dismayed that American's admission did not inspire a chorus of other corporate *mea culpas*. (By late 1974 a total of seventeen firms had admitted illegal contributions.) "There are many more in the wings who are just hoping they won't get caught," he sighs, adding quickly, "but we would have done it even if no one else had."

An earlier event, at least, had lifted any sagging spirits. Lloyd Cutler, ally of a close aide to Richard Nixon and of America's leading corporations, saw his name included on the White House's "enemies' list." And not just the two-hundred-name list (interestingly listed under the heading "Business") but the special twenty-person enemies' list. Cutler's affiliation with Common Cause's lawsuit appeared the major reason for this Democratic Emmy. Morale at Wilmer, Cutler & Pickering surged. But as someone there remarked warily—it may be great for recruiting, but how will it go over in the boardrooms? What did Cutler think of this event? "I don't like it," he said with a faint smile. Nodding in the direction of the White House three blocks away, he added, "There is an awful lot of power down the street."

Still, from the point of view of his career, Watergate was a "net plus" to Lloyd Cutler. Hardworking, hustling, and employing his contacts—Gardner, Kraft, Reston, and Moore were all personal friends; Archibald Cox was a former Cutler co-counsel on a communications case; the *Washington Post* is a client—Cutler managed to make his way prominently into the most important political event of the nineteen-seventies.

As far back as anyone can remember, in fact, Lloyd Cutler has been hardworking and hustling.

He is the son of a New York City trial lawyer who was a law partner to Fiorello La Guardia. Bright and precocious, son Lloyd graduated from Yale College at eighteen, in 1936, and from Yale Law School at twenty-one, in 1939. At the law school he worked his way to the top of his class and into the position of editor-in-chief of the *Yale Law Journal*. It was a period of political and intellectual ferment—internationally over war, domestically over the New Deal, and locally over Yale's school of legal realists. "It was a stimulating period," he remembers. "The left-liberal issue then was how to fight totalitarianism and whether we should enter the war. Unlike some of my isolationist friends like John Bingham and Sarg Shriver, I was an internationalist and felt the country had to be awakened. . . . Most of us felt in nineteen-thirty-nine that social reform was well under way; for the next ten to fifteen years the great reform issues were defense and helping Europe recover." Cutler continued, with more than a hint of pride, that "Yale was the radical law school of the nineteen-thirties." It was then that the Thurman Arnold/William Douglas/Charles Clark influence led the law school away from a conventional case-study method to a more functional analysis of *why* the law was the way it was.

Cutler's connection to Yale has been one of obvious significance. Between 1939 and 1942 a legal old-boy network arose to parallel Yale's now legendary intelligence community of the 1950s.* And he has remained close to Yale alumni affairs ever since, even spending six months at Yale in the fall and winter of 1973–1974 spearheading a major fund-raising drive and teaching a course called "The Limits of Regulation."

But back in 1939 he was about to enter professional life, with the twin goals of being "an effective responsible lawyer" and of someday earning, he hoped, as much as $10,000 a year. A lawyer who has worked with him thought Cutler was then "a young, aggressive Jewish kid from New York who wanted to make it big. But he was too smart for politics and lacked the connections to get into Sullivan & Cromwell." So instead he clerked for a year on the prestigious Second Circuit Court of Appeals for Charles Clark, who had just left the deanship of Yale Law to sit on the bench. "Charlie Clark was an important influence on me; he was very much the radical maverick on the Second Circuit at that time," said Cutler.

After his clerkship, he spent two years on Wall Street with Cravath,

---

* As a Yale law student, Cutler got to know future law partners such as Louis Oberdorfer and Marshall Hornblower, and future contacts such as Jonathan Bingham (congressman), Potter Stewart and Byron White (Supreme Court justices), Eugene Rostow (Yale Law dean), Richard McLaren (Antitrust Division chief), Frederick Beebe (*Newsweek*'s chairman), Sargent Shriver (Peace Corps director and Vice-Presidential nominee), William Scranton (Pennsylvania governor), Cyrus Vance (diplomat and negotiator), and Peter Dominick (senator).

de Gersdorff, Swaine & Wood, beginning at $2700 a year. (He applied to ten Wall Street firms and managed to obtain three offers, despite the prevailing anti-Jewish sentiment of the large New York firms.) Cutler liked Cravath, calling it "the most competent professional organization I've ever been in." Staying two years during which time he got married, he worked largely on railroad-reorganization issues. Again he made acquaintances that would endure—with young lawyer John Pickering, Cravath's Washington lawyer Richard Wilmer, and future Department of Commerce secretary John Connor. The firm was all business, and not very socially conscious. If you had asked to do public-service work on firm time in those days, recalls Cutler, "people would have thought you were a bit queer and didn't have enough to do." He left in 1942 for the war effort's Lend Lease program, a move which infuriated Robert Swaine. The Cravath senior partner complained that Cutler was leaving in the middle of the giant Western Pacific and Seaboard railroad reorganizations, which he said were as important to the war effort as Lend Lease, that he would have to train another young lawyer on this case, and that a fine legal mind loses its professional edge when it goes from New York to Washington. Cutler left nevertheless.

At Lend Lease he worked under its general counsel Oscar Cox, who was as well an assistant solicitor general. Among other tasks, Cutler participated in the *Ex Parte Quirin* case, involving eight German saboteurs who had come ashore on Long Island. Cutler went over to French North Africa in December 1942 as the deputy chief of an economic supply operation. He returned to Washington seven months later, considered but rejected the choice of a direct commission ("I was full of ideas about being a combat soldier"), and ended the war in a military intelligence unit in the Pentagon, where he rose to the rank of First Lieutenant. After the war he opted for a State Department desk job, as the assistant foreign-liquidation commissioner for Latin America, in order to get the "points" necessary to complete his service obligation.

The war over, an unforgiving Swaine made Cutler feel unwelcome if he tried to return to the Cravath firm. Cutler then joined his boss Oscar Cox and two others to form the new four-man Washington law firm of Cox, Langford, Stoddard & Cutler. It was to be a professional marriage of sixteen years. In the early period Cutler handled a series of plaintiffs' antitrust cases, where he argued against large networks he would later come to defend. In the McCarthy period he represented several clients on security issues before administrative agencies. Much of the fledgling firm's work involved clients with foreign interests, which had grown out of Cox's Lend Lease association. The Italian, Belgian, and French governments were clients. So was Edgar Kaiser and his far-flung empire of steel, cement, aluminum, ships, and cars. Cutler began doing substantial work for Kaiser, aiding businessmen to arrange for Kaiser's construction of aluminum plants for war production during the Korean war and arranging for the construction of Kaiser auto plants in Argentina and Brazil.

By the early 1960s, however, he felt cramped and restless in Cox, Langford, Stoddard & Cutler, which numbered fourteen in 1961. He and Cox had what Cutler calls "friendly disagreements," but other witnesses call less polite things—over firm size, growth, and associate advancement. The upshot was that Cutler and eight firm lawyers left to merge with most of the lawyers at the small firm of Wilmer & Broun, a group whose local practice and litigation complemented Cutler's growing national clientele and his lobbying efforts. The twenty-man firm was renamed Wilmer, Cutler & Pickering in 1962, and has remained so since.

There have been occasions when Cutler could have left the firm. Just when Wilmer, Cutler & Pickering was forming in 1962, George Ball, who was then undersecretary of state, asked Cutler if he would become the assistant secretary of state for economic affairs; he demurred because of the needs of his fledgling law practice. Then in 1965, Secretary of Commerce John Connor remembered his old friend Lloyd Cutler (who had gotten Connor his first government job in 1943), and tried to install him as undersecretary of commerce. This time Cutler was interested.

Reports then circulated that President Johnson would make a three-way appointment: Franklin Williams at the United Nations would become deputy director of the Peace Corps; Franklin Roosevelt, Jr., would leave the Commerce Department, where he was undersecretary, to fill Williams' place at the UN, and Lloyd Cutler would become undersecretary of commerce, replacing Roosevelt. President Johnson leaned toward Cutler because, according to columnists Rowland Evans and Robert Novak, he was "a Democrat with important connections among some of the President's oldest Washington friends. Furthermore, he was co-chairman of the special lawyers for Johnson committee that worked hard all fall to round up support for the Johnson-Humphrey ticket." An Associated Press wire story went so far as to headline: "Cutler to Get Commerce Post."

But the appointment fell through, embarrassing and distressing its subject. Reports vary on the cause. Evans and Novak claim that once Cutler's name leaked to the press, a secretive and sensitive President withdrew the appointment in anger. They wrote:

> Today sources close to the White House are privately complaining that Cutler himself leaked the news of his imminent appointment as Under Secretary of Commerce. The fact is, however, that, no man can agree to accept any high position in the Administration without confiding in literally scores of people—family, business partners, and close friends.

Consequently, Cutler has remained with the firm he created for its twelve-year existence, seeking to fulfill his goal of creating a great Washington law firm, "an all-around firm with people in it who could do anything and who would have the resources to do anything."

Wilmer, Cutler & Pickering is located around the corner from Covington & Burling, in a building so new that it was unfinished when the firm moved there in September 1973. Reflecting its client boom, the firm doubled in size between 1970 and 1974, as it now totals slightly more than ninety lawyers. (Two are in a London office, aiding American clients with foreign problems and foreign clients with American problems.) In 1973 twenty-four had come from Harvard, twelve from Yale, eight from Stanford, and the remainder from a variety of other major law schools. The firm is decidedly Democratic; there are ten female associates and three black associates. Unlike some firms that stress former government officials, WC&P recruits mainly from the law-school community, hiring about fifteen graduates a year. Nevertheless, the firm has its share of ex-government people. Louis Oberdorfer once headed the Tax Division of the Justice Department and Howard Willens was the first assistant to the head of the Criminal Division; former SEC chairman Manuel Cohen joined Wilmer, Cutler & Pickering in 1969 ("I thought it was the Tiffany of Washington law firms") and quickly multiplied the firm's securities and corporate work; Strategic Arms Limitation Talks' (SALT) negotiator and Republican Gerard Smith became "of counsel" in 1973, because, as one firm lawyer saw it, "it broadens the firm's political base by taking such a well-known Republican. But he is very much in the Cutler mold—Yale, formal, and very distinguished. The idea is that he will help our growing international practice."

It would be difficult to distinguish between Wilmer, Cutler & Pickering and Covington & Burling as to the kind of clients represented and the kind of work done. Both produce technically proficient work for the largest companies in the country for their appearances before Congress, the agencies, and the courts; both do a substantial amount of *pro bono* work for impecunious clients; both have bright young lawyers. "Maybe Covington commands more respect because they have been here longer," observes Cutler, but other than this concession to age, there are few admissions at WC&P about the superiority of other law firms. Among the lawyers there is an élan that has long inspired the sons of Eli: Harvard may be bigger, older, more famous, but surely not better.

On the other hand, there are some differences of style and organization. C&B has a sense of history and, in terms of its customs and decor, seems almost indentured to history. Wilmer, Cutler & Pickering projects modern. A racy red carpet covers its huge reception area, matching two large abstract red paintings. Black, low-slung, Scandinavian furniture fills the reception room and many of the offices. On the walls are abstract prints of indiscernible lines and swirling colors. There are two saunas (one for men, another for women). Young secretaries wear miniskirts and even pants, which would be considered heretical at C&B.

Covington & Burling has been a large firm for as long as most of its lawyers can recall. But Wilmer, Cutler & Pickering has ballooned into bigness almost overnight. Many of its attorneys still think as they did in the old days when all the lawyers could chat around a big table, but like a six-foot-four fifteen-year-old, WC&P is bigger than its experience can gracefully manage.

Yet it is struggling to avoid the impersonality and hierarchy of size. The firm is decentralized into four groups, each largely autonomous in taking on and staffing its own cases. Associates rotate frequently among partners and among groups. Once a year an associate is told by two partners in a formal "evaluation session" how he or she is doing. Every associate is paid the same as other graduates of his or her year in law school (with a few exceptions), and there are no discretionary bonuses. Perhaps once a year everyone in the firm meets on a Saturday to discuss firm direction and policies, and even associates air their views with the partners. (But if an associate asked to see the annual billings and partnership agreement, "we would say, 'You have to have some faith,'" said John Pickering.) A ten-man executive committee oversees firm policy. The firm partnership votes on the basis of one man, one vote, and no decision is made if there is what is considered a "substantial minority" against it. One recent innovative proposal was adopted by the partnership: a partner can take a six-month sabbatical approximately every ten years at full pay.

There of course remain two separate and unequal classes of lawyers at the firm—associates and partners. And though in the old days any associate who stayed the requisite number of years made partner, this is no longer true, as fifteen associates a year join the firm. So the young lawyers begin eyeing each other somewhat uneasily, and some firm members fear that the kind of tensions which Covington & Burling suffers may be inevitable at WC&P. For a law firm, though, Wilmer, Cutler & Pickering is making a serious attempt to democratize itself.

But like a China also bent on democratization, there is a *primus inter pares,* a cult of personality. There may not be large, brooding posters of his visage on the walls, but Lloyd Cutler dominates the firm he helped found. Like Mao Tse-tung, once a founding father, always a founding father. Former firm lawyer Russell Phillips sees

Cutler as "the quarterback of most issues and the coach of all," and another ex-firm-lawyer adds: "When he blows up, few in the firm can hold their own against him. When he gives orders to someone, the someone does it." Although the membership of the executive committee rotates annually, Cutler (along with Pickering) are permanent members. Richard Wilmer is eighty-one and largely retired; John Pickering spends more time than Cutler on internal firm administration. But it is Cutler who is the chief client-getter and -keeper, the firm's most visible public figure.

This notoriety, of course, has some institutional benefits. Clients and law graduates in search of a home, and unable to study all Washington firms, usually have heard of Cutler and hence Wilmer, Cutler & Pickering. Firm phone calls get returned. But the firm's democracy-plus-Cutler does create some problems. There are occasional flashes of partner envy—"Some of the partners are insanely jealous of him," said a former associate. Partners can find themselves carrying Cutler's briefcases to trials or hearings, which is unhealthy for those who hold themselves in very high regard. Firm morale, however, remains generally high, because "there is so much money coming in," said one lawyer there; in addition, Cutler makes an adroit and bona fide sacrifice, one mentioned in nearly every firm interview: he is said to take home far less of a partnership share than he could otherwise obtain as the organization's leading business-maker.

Today his clients include the auto, drug, and steel industries, where he represents the trade association of each. He also counsels Kaiser Industries, the Columbia Broadcasting System, American Airlines, and the United States Railway Association, the newly created federal agency to restructure bankrupt railroads in the Northeast. He has helped defend the House of Representatives against a suit by Adam Clayton Powell, and even acted as arbitrator in a dispute between the Rolling Stones and their former manager. But no longer are there plaintiffs' antitrust cases against big business, and although he admired Yale Law School and Charles Clark for being radical mavericks, it is difficult to consider Cutler one today. Like Abe Fortas and Tommy Corcoran before him, Lloyd Cutler is a graduate of the New Deal—who now recalls the rosebuds of his youth as he defends the kind of business the New Deal was created to control. Thus, *Fortune* has called him "the very model of a modern legal conduit," and in an article on lobbyists, the *Washingtonian* ranked him second only to Clark Clifford in a list of the "Kings of the Hill."

The American auto, drug, and steel industries: total assets, $90 billion. The House of Representatives *and* the Rolling Stones. An annual estimated income of $250,000. In the thirty-five years since Lloyd Cutler once dreamed about making $10,000, he has done very well indeed.

I sit waiting in Lloyd Cutler's spacious and modern eleventh floor office at 1666 K Street. A comfortable judge's chair rests behind a stylish and light brown oval desk. Eight "in-boxes" are filled, without a paper astray. The walls are covered with neatly shelved books and prints of old English court scenes. On a coffee table in front of a couch are arranged Tom Wicker's *Facing the Lions,* Shaw's *The Perfect Wagnerite,* and copies of the *Economist,* the *Annals of the American Academy of Political and Social Science, Foreign Affairs, Forbes,* and *Newsweek.* It could be the office of a corporate president, a cabinet secretary, a diplomat. Lloyd Cutler and John Pickering come in.

Cutler is an extremely careful man. In order to interview him in 1970, I first had to get an American Bar Association opinion declaring that it would not be considered unethical advertising or soliciting for him to accede to my request for an interview. As a condition to this second interview in January 1974, I agreed to check back with Cutler for accuracy any fact I planned to write about him. And at the meeting John Pickering—at fifty-eight a large, white-haired man of much bearing and dignity—sits as a colleague and witness, taking notes as I take notes.

Eclectic as a matter of substance, Cutler appears consistent and integrated as a matter of style. He is a fastidious dresser, today (a Saturday) casually decked out in a blue blazer, patterned tie, and gray slacks. (When asked why Wilmer, Cutler & Pickering had a two-man office in London rather than Paris, one firm lawyer half joked, "Because Lloyd likes English tailors better.") He has wavy gray hair and dark bushy eyebrows that may not dance like Sam Ervin's but can still punctuate a point. Five feet ten inches tall, Cutler is inching toward jowls and stoutness, although an energetic interest in tennis slows this tendency. After decades of national advocacy, his mellifluous voice has lost its hard New York edge; indeed, at times he is so soft-spoken that he is difficult to hear. There is friendliness in his demeanor, but not warmth; he appreciates jokes, but rarely makes them himself. "Like Abe Fortas, he is brilliant but aloof," said a fellow Yale graduate who knows both men well, "showing a superficial amiability but essentially removed and cold." Cutler projects a low-keyed confidence, a cool exterior.

With two glaring exceptions. First, while all else appears decorous poise, oddly flailing appendages betray a certain tenseness. As he speaks his fingers do a digital dance, waving in the air like some upside-down caterpillar. His feet twitch and jerk this way and that, as his elbows flap up and down, as if unconnected to his body. ("It is surprising given how much he's done," said WC&P partner James Campbell, "but he still gets nervous before an argument.")

And second, there is his temper. When critics such as Senator Gaylord Nelson, former FCC commissioner Nicolas Johnson, Congressman Lionel Van Deerlin, or Ralph Nader contest him, he blows up (as subsequent chapters describe). An interviewer begins asking increasingly sharp questions and an initially amiable Cutler suddenly dresses down his secretary for some minor error. When Berkeley law professor Stephen Barnett inquired if Cutler had disqualified himself from the Violence Commission's inquiry into the media, since he represents the media, Cutler replied archly, "I do not think it appropriate for you to question my ethical judgment in the matter." And when I inquired into Cutler's offer of legal assistance to Joseph Kraft during the Watergate episode, he glowered, said something inaudible, and added in a voice low with rage, "Mr. Green, that is the kind of question that would make me like to take you by the scruff of your neck and throw you out of this office."

Nor does Cutler like it when he is called a lawyer-lobbyist, an appellation whose political tinge he shuns. Thus, he has tried to dissuade at least two publications from calling him that. But it seems a fair label for someone as involved as Cutler was in the 1962 Kefauver-Harris Drug Act, the 1966 Traffic and Motor Vehicle Safety Act, the 1969 Newspaper Preservation Act, and the House Commerce Committee's citation of CBS for contempt of Congress.*

Personal criticism, personal challenge, or the designation of lobbyist: all obviously violate Cutler's genteel mien. Clients, of course, can be criticized for the positions they take, but lawyers like Cutler are unaccustomed to being held accountable for the views they promote in public. Even to be questioned about them apparently rubs like sandpaper on Cutler's lawyerly sensibilities.

Commandment IV: Interlocking Interests—One technique of corporate law is, in effect, to merge with your clients. Many lawyers sit on the boards of directors of their clients. Lloyd Cutler sits as a director on the board of Kaiser Industries and the Norfolk and Western Railway Company (a former client). William Hudson's 1973 study Outside Counsel: Inside Director *found that 1919 corporations in 1971 paid $157.5 million to 1182 law firms whose partners were directors of the companies. Defenders of this interrelationship argue that lawyers can better learn and understand the problems of their business clients as directors. But critics say that it compromises independence of judgment to be formally or financially tied to a client. Paul D. Cravath, according to his biographer, Robert Swaine, "early came to believe that in most cases the client is best advised by a lawyer who maintains an objective point of view [which] may be impeded by any financial interest in the client's business or participation in its management." One New York lawyer thinks that "any time a lawyer advises a corporation to do something that might embarrass or*

---

* Among others in the past few years, Wilmer, Cutler & Pickering has represented the following interests on Capitol Hill: J. P. Morgan and Company and the American Express Company on bills amending the Bank Holding Company Act; J. C. Penney on a variety of consumer legislation; Kaiser Industries; the National Corporation for Housing Partnerships; Yale, Stanford, and the Massachusetts Institute of Technology on tax matters; the American Basketball Association on its effort to merge with the National Basketball Association; the Dealer Bank Association, the Jonathan Development Corporation and Oil Investment Institute on various financial issues—as well as American Airlines, the Chronicle Publishing Company, the Automobile Manufacturers Association, the Pharmaceutical Manufacturers Association, and the American Iron and Steel Institute.

cast aspersions on the board, he is going to think twice about it if he is a member of that board." For similar reasons, the American Institute of Certified Public Accountants has prohibited its members from becoming directors of the companies whose books they audit.

As for lawyers in government, a veritable shuttle service conveys them in and out, a fact that has consternated even a usually mild Business Week: "Nowhere is there a greater potential for conflicts-of-interest than in Washington, where influence-peddling is a fine art and an honored profession. . . . Lawyers, bankers and businessmen are brought into government, serve for a while, and then go back to what they were doing before. Today's buyer becomes tomorrow's seller; the man who is a regulator today may be one of the regulated tomorrow." Occasionally such conflicts involve serious breaches of ethics: the Senate Permanent Subcommittee on Investigations condemned Roswell Gilpatric, former deputy secretary of defense, for the way he maneuvered a $6.5 billion Pentagon contract for the TFX fighter plane to General Dynamics, a client of the law firm he worked for before and after his government service; when FTC lawyer Francis Charlton left the agency for General Foods, he passed on to his legal supervisors there a confidential FTC memorandum detailing its cereals' case, in which General Foods was a defendant. Other examples of the lawyer/government shuttle are more routine: Joseph Califano, Jr., left President Lyndon Johnson's inner circle and vowed to avoid lobbying (in 1974 he refused to work against the Consumer Protection Agency bill); but other White House graduates made no such vows.

There is at least one palpable benefit to Washington lawyers who were government officials. As a Securities and Exchange Commission lawyer said of a phone call from Manuel ("Manny") Cohen, once SEC chairman and now a Wilmer, Cutler & Pickering partner: "You know, I still jump when he calls."

Ideologically Cutler sees himself as a liberal Democrat, because, he says, "I am left of center and am a believer in social change." He is a committed civil libertarian—proposing, during the McCarthy years, a system of civil-damage suits against those giving intentionally false testimony against individuals, recommending in 1972 to then treasury secretary John Connally a citizens' review board to watchdog the Federal Bureau of Investigation, and recently representing a news-man's group protesting the way American Telephone and Telegraph (AT&T) was turning over phone records to snooping prosecutors. At the same time, Cutler appears a strong believer in the business sector, telling author David Ignatius: "Business ethics among big firms, like IBM, etc., are very high—both in terms of personal ethics and corporate decisions. Most of the companies that have been around for a long time make a lot of money anyway, and have no need to cut corners. . . . Outside counsel and directors exert a great deal of ethical influence." This is a frequent leitmotiv—Cutler civilizing his clients, as with George Spater. He once described chief executives as people "who retire four years later and then a whole new generation of men from the engine plant must be trained about public affairs." Trained by Cutler. But has this faith in business ethics been shaken by the recent corporate crime wave over illegal campaign contributions? No, replies Cutler, citing an imaginative defense: "Those cases were exceptional because they involved a notoriously unenforced fifty-year-old law; consequently, there was pressure to violate the law from the *government*."

Lawyering at this interface of business and government, Cutler has developed a canny ability for negotiating the differences between these two sectors of society—which is why he is often called into the later stages of an antitrust case or a delicate congressional hearing. Just as he has tried to combine in himself the conflicting roles of private-interest and public-interest advocacy, so he seeks to harmonize conflicts between others. In this he is benefited by his polished demeanor, a logician's gifts, and an assumption that differences between corporations and the state result from good-faith misunderstandings, not venality. And he displays an appreciation of power, if not ingratiation to powerful people, that enables him to work well with the prominent. He apparently understands the benefits of knowing and massaging those who matter:

• In early 1970 the Yale Law School Association of the District of Columbia invited Dr. Henry Kissinger to address them in May.

Then occurred the Cambodian invasion, and some of the association's lawyers wanted to disinvite him. Instead, as a compromise, a question-and-answer session would follow his talk. Kissinger came, spoke, and threw it open to the audience. "Henry," began the first questioner, who continued on to ask a lob of a question apparently aimed at defusing the expected hostility. Some in the audience cringed at what they considered the first-name grandstanding. Later Kissinger asked one of his hosts who it was that had addressed him as Henry. "Lloyd Cutler," he was told, and Kissinger asked, "Who's he?"

• Also in early 1970 Cutler participated in a panel discussing "Justice in America." Karl Hess, a converted conservative, got into an argument with Donald Santarelli, assistant to then Deputy Attorney General Richard Kleindienst, over whether Santarelli had indeed, as reported, told a law student, "What we need in this country right now is a good dose of martial law. Frankly, we don't give a damn about an individual's civil liberties." During a heated exchange among Hess, the law student, and Santarelli, Cutler attempted to rescue the situation and a fellow panelist: "Let's get on to something more serious than whether or not Mr. Santarelli said or did not say something. Let's all assume we are honorable men." To which co-panelist and author Edgar Friedenberg replied, "I must certainly disagree with that. . . . I am certainly not prepared to assume that the personnel of the government or anyone else are honorable men."

• Back in the early 1960s, with the involvement of Cutler, a consortium of aluminum companies was meeting in New York City to arrange for the development of aluminum mines in Guinea. Covington & Burling's Donald Hiss, an international lawyer of some note, joined the group when one of the participating companies took him on as its counsel. At the first meeting he attended, Cutler rushed up to him and said that Hiss's participation was "great," as they had needed help. Another aluminum lawyer later told Hiss that Cutler's warm reception was odd for "he had fought your appointment for five days as unnecessary," since the consortium already had adequate counsel.

• When critics attacked Presidential counselor Daniel P. Moynihan for his much-criticized phraseology about black people (in the famous "benign neglect" memorandum), Cutler came to Moynihan's defense in a letter to *The New York Times*. "Ringing denunciations have their place in achieving necessary social change, but so also do dispassionate analyses of the underlying causes of social injustice and the creative development of remedial techniques and institutions."

• In June 1971 fifteen hundred lawyers met at the Washington Hilton for the "National Convocation of Lawyers to End the War"; on the speakers' platform were Eugene McCarthy, John Kerry, Robert Drinan, Pete McCloskey, and Ted Kennedy. Senator Kennedy spoke early and left the podium early. "And there was Cutler," recalled a Washington lawyer on the scene, "way on the other side of the room, casually working his way across to intercept Kennedy on the way out and pat him on the back as he was leaving; it seemed so painfully planned."

Taken alone these are small incidents, but together they reveal a lawyer who understands how to keep his fingers on the pulse of power. When combined with his Yale, Cravath, Lend Lease, and media contacts, his client list, his *pro bono* work, his negotiating skills, his dogged hard work ("Why, I don't think he can read a novel for fun without marking it up," said Tom Barr, Cutler's friend and a Cravath partner), and his sheer legal talent, Lloyd Cutler is today among the most prominent of Washington lawyers. It was a hard climb, achieved without the benefit of pedigree, family wealth, an important government position, or a single book (since 1939) or law-review article. His drive toward prominence has been fueled by an industriousness and ambition not noticeably lacking in a Julien Sorel, a Cash McCall—or a William Simon. "You've got to really want to be the best, to be number one, to get to the top," Washington attorney Victor Kramer said of his former classmate and acquaintance. "He really wants it."

Now that he has created a Wilmer, Cutler & Pickering, Cutler may well feel driven toward new goals. Although the undersecretary-of-commerce episode pained Cutler, in an interview he admitted that there are some government positions he could accept. Based on Cutler's recent speeches and articles on the Justice Department, a former firm lawyer is convinced that "he's running for the attorney generalship." One government official who has worked with him thinks Cutler "wants a big government job to finally sanitize him."

Even if he never makes it into government, Lloyd Cutler has made his mark. But what is it?

This paradoxical lawyer has left varying imprints. Among his colleagues and clients, Tom Barr considers him a dedicated attorney; a Frank Stanton and a James Roche no doubt think him an effective corporate lawyer; Edgar Kaiser probably sees Cutler as a damn good businessman; John Gardner appreciates him as a public-interest advocate; some firm associates admire him as a career model ("His meetings don't take a minute longer than they have to," says an impressed Ron Rotunda, former WC&P associate; "there is no idle chatter; he uses his time very effectively"). Cutler himself has the self-image of a client reformer, if not a people's lawyer. (When asked if he would ever become a full-time public-interest lawyer, Cutler declines, saying that he couldn't afford it and that he likes private practice.) On the other hand, congressional, courtroom, and agency adversaries make more harsh judgments in interviews, and do not confuse him with NAACP's Jack Greenberg or a Ramsey Clark. Instead, they perceive this Washington lawyer as an articulate special-interest spokesman who spends 90 per cent of his professional life opposing reforms like safer drugs and cars.

To resolve these contrasting views it is not enough to invoke metaphors like influence-peddler or to flash one's Common Cause membership card. To judge whether a Washington lawyer or a Washington law firm is a social credit or a social debit, it becomes necessary to examine closely its client work and public impact, to evaluate its quillets, its cases, its tenures, its tricks.

The Washington
Way of Law

Sentries of Monopoly

The antitrust field I think is an area where lawyers, perhaps without realizing it, come closest to the very limits of what is ethically proper. . . . On the defendant's side they are closer to the line in actually advising clients to cover up criminal activity. [Judging from] some of the essays I have read in the Antitrust Law Journal, *if you took out the word "antitrust" and substituted "prostitution" or "narcotics," you would think that the lawyer would be disbarred if he put into practice the views expressed.—Federal District Court Judge John P. Fullam*

The antitrust laws were conceived by lawyers, are prosecuted by lawyers, and are defended by lawyers.* More than in other governmental activities, Washington lawyers play a pivotal role in the antitrust process. But there is sharp disagreement about what that role is. One flattering appraisal sees them as private law-enforcers, counseling their corporate clients into obedience. Covington lawyer-author Charles Horsky wrote in his 1952 *The Washington Lawyer* that the antitrust bar encouraged ten times more compliance with the antitrust laws than the slender efforts of the federal antitrust agencies. Former head of the Antitrust Division of the Department of Justice Richard McLaren asserted that antitrust law "works because the private antitrust bar—well informed and highly perceptive—counsels compliance. It works because the antitrust bar has the courage to say to the client: 'No, you can't do that.' "

---

* In brief, the 1890 Sherman Act forbids price-fixing and attempts to monopolize commerce, and the 1950 Celler-Kefauver amendment to the 1914 Clayton Act prohibits mergers and acquisitions which tend to substantially lessen competition in any line of commerce.

On the other hand, says Thomas Kauper, head of the Antitrust Division in 1974, "Too often clients dictate to counsel their own view of antitrust values and legality." Judge Fullam apparently sees not profiles in courage but profiles in conspiracy, since defense counsel may "actually advis[e] clients to cover up criminal activity." This can take a variety of forms:

• *Blitzing. Fortune* has reported that one Washington, D.C., law firm advises its clients, "If you think the merger is going to be challenged, get it through quickly." For example, the first that the Antitrust Division knew about the *Washington Post's* acquisition of the old *Times Herald* was the morning after when they read about it in the *Washington Post.*

• *Looking Away.* "Yeah, price-fixing is rampant," said one defense counsel in an interview. "But if they do go ahead and get in trouble, they pay us fees to get them out of it"—an approach, as we shall see, Covington & Burling lawyer James McKay apparently understood well.

• *Politicking.* ITT saw virtually every relevant government official about its antitrust problems from 1969 to 1972, nor was this the first time political pressure had been exerted on an antitrust case. Sometimes the lawyers inspire the pressure, sometimes they are unaware of it, and at times they will fight it. An attorney from the Chicago firm of Sidley & Austin once called an Antitrust Division lawyer to warn that a client would improperly attempt to influence a case. An important public official would be calling the division lawyer (he did); but the law firm apparently wanted it understood that it had nothing to do with the client's misbehavior.

• *Access.* There are also the benefits that derive from the special access to the Antitrust Division enjoyed by some lawyers. "We know all the people down at Justice," said one antitrust counselor, with some candor. "I'm not talking about influence—we don't deal in that —but it's our business to know what those people are thinking, and we've got a book on every one of them."

• *Delaying.* This is so prevalent that FTC Bureau of Competition director James Halverson denounced it as a "specifically designated tactic" in an unusually stinging address before the Association of

General Counsel.* He threatened to "accumulate a portfolio on the actions of certain counsel" and to suspend or disbar from an FTC proceeding offending lawyers. J. Thomas Rosch, director of the FTC's Consumer Protection Bureau, agreed, accusing defense counsel of often holding on to requested and relevant material "until the eve of trial." This "may well result in unnecessary adjudicatory proceedings," he added, "and in unnecessary legal fees which inevitably flow from such proceedings."

• *Kitchen-sinking.* With millions at stake, lawyers and business clients think, Why not throw that proverbial plumbing fixture at an undermanned agency? So when Chicago District Court judge D. J. Fox, in a rare move, rejected a client's *nolo contendere* plea in 1968, Covington's response was "to bury the judge with paper," according to an Antitrust Division lawyer. A recently appointed and overwhelmed Fox relented, and, reversing himself, accepted the *nolo* plea. "He was scared by what they threw at him," confirmed a friend of the judge. The tactic was not novel to Covington. The late Thurman Arnold claimed that many defense lawyers deliberately bogged down antitrust cases "to wear the Government out." The result is incredibly complicated and extended litigation: merger cases now take an average of five years to resolve, and monopolization cases eight years.

• *Burnbagging.* It is not unknown for clients and counsel either to destroy subpoenaed evidence (which is criminal) or, more commonly, to periodically purge files of potentially damaging documents (euphemistically called a "document-retention policy"). The government understands this problem of disappearing data. A legal aide to an

---

* Halverson said: "While not intending to exhaust the means available for intentional delay of investigations, I would point to the following types of conduct which may be evidence of bad faith on the part of counsel: promises voluntarily to comply with document demands, in lieu of compliance with subpoenas, which are not promptly kept and were not intended to be kept; motions to quash subpoenas, the bases of which are boilerplate objections which have already been repeatedly rejected by the Commission; request after request to extend the deadline date for compliance with the subpoena, while no reasonable effort has been made in the document search. Litigation is also fraught with opportunities for inexcusable delay, e.g., making unnecessary motions to extend deadlines or to change pre-trial conference dates; and asking for subpoenas to be issued to third parties knowing full well that enforcement of them will probably be tied up in federal court, while little valuable evidence is expected to be forthcoming."

assistant attorney general for antitrust complained in an internal staff memorandum about "the increasing practice on the part of substantial business concerns [to] destroy documents periodically. . . .'. This writer is firmly convinced that in large part this [occurs] because of the advice of sophisticated lawyers." Nor is this tactic only used by disreputable shyster firms. After one former Covington & Burling associate discovered the Electronic Industry Association, a trade-association client, dividing up markets, a criminal offense under the antitrust laws, a C&B partner told him to burn the information. The partner even cautioned against writing the client a warning, lest the law firm become implicated.

Former Antitrust Division chief Donald Turner, while in office, chided the antitrust bar not so much for what they do as for what they don't do. As an antitrust enforcer in a sea of defense counsel, Turner came to appreciate those counsel who supported improved antitrust enforcement. There were not many. "The Antitrust Section [of the ABA] has rarely shown vast enthusiasm for pushing out the boundaries of antitrust," he complained in a 1965 speech. "Service to a client, even continual service to a client, does not prevent a lawyer . . . from taking positions on public issues in opposition to the views of his client." The concept of the public obligations of the private lawyer was perhaps best expressed by Randolph Paul in the 1950 *Harvard Law Review*. His comments about tax lawyers are equally apt for drug, food, auto, airline, or antitrust lawyers:

> The responsibilities of the tax advisor, *qua* tax advisor, may be said to end at the point of faithful attendance to his client's interest. But this is not, in my opinion, the end of the tax advisor's responsibility. He is a *citizen* as well as a *tax advisor*. He is more than the ordinary citizen; he is a specially qualified person in one of the most important areas of the public interest. His experience equips him with a peculiar knowledge of what is wrong with tax laws and makes especially valuable his objective opinion about what should be done—and sometimes what should not be done—to remedy defects. Special qualifications bring special responsibilities which may not be passively discharged.

In sum, these lawyer techniques and this lack of enthusiasm for antitrust enforcement have resulted, in large measure, in the historic ineffectiveness of the antitrust laws. No doubt the Sherman Act (and later the Clayton Act's prohibitions against anticompetitive mergers) has discouraged some monopolistic practices in our economy. But who would claim that eighty-five years afterward we have an effectively competitive economy? For the antitrust laws and antitrust enforcement have indeed proven, as Professor John Kenneth Galbraith said, to be a "charade." The combined budgets of the Justice Department's and Federal Trade Commission's antitrust efforts total some $29 million, or about as much as IBM alone is spending to defend itself against government monopoly charges. Like ants eyeing a rambling mastodon, these agencies must monitor a trillion-dollar-plus economy of more than a million and a half corporations; and some two hundred fifty firms have assets over a billion dollars. Yet only sixty cases a year are filed by the Antitrust Division, or about the same number that were being filed three decades ago.

The reality of a closed-enterprise system is decidedly different from the high-toned description of free enterprise invoked at corporate banquets. "Competition has survived," Walter Lippmann has said, "only where men have been unable to abolish it." Economists William Shepherd and Richard Barber have both calculated that monopolies and "shared monopolies" today control about two-thirds of all manufacturing in the country. This concentration results in higher prices for consumers. The FTC estimates, for example, that the cameras we buy are overpriced by 11 per cent and soft drinks by 7 per cent— which result in annual consumer overcharges of $403 million and $248 million respectively. Economic concentration can frustrate government monetary and fiscal efforts to checkmate inflation. And when *Fortune*'s top 1000 firm presidents were asked whether they agreed that "many [businessmen] pricefix," 60 per cent of the 110 respondents concurred. Yet in the entire history of antitrust criminal enforcement, there have been just four occasions when businessmen have actually gone to jail for antitrust offenses; and even though Sherman Act fines can go as high as $50,000 per violation, corporate fines averaged $13,420 between 1955 and 1965—which did not unduly discomfort those top five hundred industrials with average annual profits of $56 million.

Even before Dita Beard made antitrust a household word, economic concentration was a problem, as our corporate economy collectivized itself in the name of free enterprise. In 1967 the *Wall Street Journal* offered an appropriate, if somewhat exaggerated, scenario:

> It is the not too distant future, and the biggest financial news item of the day is the merger of General Motors Corp. into American International Consolidated Everything, Inc. The GM purchase completes AIC's acquisition program. It has now bought every company in the U.S. Apparently there was no competitive overlap involved and the Division gave it a premerger clearance.

Mention Lloyd Cutler's name at the Antitrust Division of the Justice Department and you invariably provoke both respect and suspicion. As will be detailed in later chapters, Cutler has represented auto, airline, and media clients against antitrust assaults on their size or behavior. Sometimes he prevails (the auto smog case) and other times he does not (the proposed American-Western airlines merger), but he lawyers with a skill and intensity that alerts those in the Justice Department, according to one of its lawyers, "to dig in our heels."

Cutler is regarded with some suspicion because he lawyers not only with much skill but with special access, and because he employs a cunning that led an Antitrust Division lawyer to remark, "When he proposes something, we automatically ask what's wrong with it." His access to Division hierarchy derived initially from his personal relationship with Donald Turner, who ran the Antitrust Division from 1965 to 1968. From 1951 to 1954 the two worked together at Cox, Langford, Stoddard & Cutler, and remained friends as well as ex-colleagues. And after Turner had left the division, Cutler retained him as outside counsel on a number of matters, including the American-Western merger and the Comsat (Communications Satellite Corporation) -domestic satellite proceeding at the FCC.

But during Turner's years at the Antitrust Division, Cutler had a virtually open-door status, according to one of Turner's young aides:

> He [Cutler] had much easier access to Turner than even the staff. . . . He played upon his contact deftly and excessively, and

benefited from it materially, since clients and potential clients found that if you wanted to get through, you should get Cutler. . . . But the staff knew they were being backdoored by Cutler and they resented it. The really amazing thing about this is that Cutler really didn't have to exploit the relationship, because he is really a good lawyer.

One former antitrust assistant attorney general complained that Cutler would tout his contact to his clients, saying for their eager consumption, "Well, I'll call Don on that problem." This former official disagreed with the Turner aide's high assessment of his boss's friend: "Cutler wasn't really anything before Turner came in," he said. "He made his name and got his clients by trading on his relationship with Don." While this harsh view may overstate the case, Cutler's intimacy with Turner did enable him apparently to harvest more antitrust clients.

Among other cases, Cutler persuaded Turner to settle the General Motors bus case, which had aimed to get automaker GM out of the competing bus business. According to a Senate Antitrust Subcommittee report, "In 1965, after nine years of protracted litigation, the Department disposed of the case by reluctantly accepting an innocuous consent decree (GM was allowed to keep its bus division), whose principal provisions were drafted, at least in part, by GM's antitrust attorneys." Subsequently, in 1967, Cutler helped convince Turner not to file criminal charges against the auto firms for an alleged conspiracy to retard the installation of antipollution exhaust devices.

As one example of the benefits of access, Cutler represented Von's Grocery in the relief stage of that famous antitrust case (in which the Supreme Court decided that a merger of Von's and Shopping Bag, with a combined 7.5 per cent of the Los Angeles retail grocery market, violated the Clayton Antitrust Act). Cutler and Arnold Lerman of his firm negotiated the relief with Gordon Spivack, director of operations at the Antitrust Division and perhaps the most admired graduate of the division in the past decade. Spivack insisted that the grocery chain agree within thirty days to divest 25 per cent of itself; if Cutler and Lerman disagreed, the percentage spinoff would increase to 33⅓ per cent. More than thirty days later, a Wilmer, Cutler & Pickering attorney called up for more information on the 25 per cent figure and was told by Spivack that the 25 per cent offer was canceled and it was now 33⅓ per cent, to increase to 50 per cent ninety days hence. More than ninety days later the firm desired to settle for 33⅓ per cent, but *per* the original arrangement, Spivack insisted on 50 per cent. At this point he and Cutler went to Turner's office to discuss their disagreement. Turner said that 38 per cent seemed a fair figure, because after the two firms involved merged, Shopping Bag received 38 per cent of the stock in the merged company. Spivack agreed that figure might be fair, but it was now unacceptable based on the progression of the prior negotiations—at which point a perplexed Turner announced that he and Cutler had already discussed the 38 per cent figure. It seemed that Cutler had gone over Spivack's head and implanted the 38 per cent figure in Turner's mind in a phone call. Spivack was miffed at Cutler's tactic—which succeeded when Turner accepted the 38 per cent figure.

When Turner left, Cutler lost some of his extraordinary access, but it may be that his firm did not lose much access at all. The evening of Richard McLaren's first day as head of the Antitrust Division in February 1969 he attended a party at the home of a long-standing Washington friend and former *Yale Law Journal* co-editor, WC&P partner Louis Oberdorfer.

*   *   *

Whatever Cutler's prominence as an antitrust counsel, Covington & Burling's antitrust contingent over the past two decades has dominated this subject area in names and cases. Gerhard Gesell, Hugh Cox, and, more recently, Edwin Zimmerman and Daniel Gribbon have been as influential as any other team of four antitrust counsel. This has led to an emulation effect, according to former partner Al Prather, who commented, "How C&B did antitrust work was influential over how other firms did antitrust work." The firm's Justice Department docket reads like a list of the most important civil and criminal cases in recent antitrust history: the 1956 du Pont cellophane case, the 1957 and 1961 GM–du Pont divestiture decisions, the electrical-machinery conspiracy in the early 1960s, the plumbing manufacturers' conspiracy, and the ITT imbroglio.

On December 13, 1947, the government charged du Pont with monopolizing the cellophane market. Although the case was filed in Washington, du Pont successfully got it transferred to the more congenial Delaware, where du Pont's influence is not insubstantial. There, in a 192-page opinion with 140 findings of fact, the United States District Court said that the giant chemical company did *not* control the cellophane market. This set the stage for a Supreme Court review on October 11, 1955, pitting an oratorical Gesell against government-lawyer Charles Weston.

"If the Court please . . ." began Gesell with an advocate's traditional deference to the nation's highest judicial tribunal. He then proceeded to tear into the Justice Department for dabbling in theories, not the "realities of the marketplace." "It is very easy to develop a theory of monopolization, I suppose, in any industry, if one can select a fact here, a half-fact there, a quarter-truth here, and put them together with theory and surmise," he told the justices, adding with some evangelical passion that "the whole history of du Pont's price since the time it got into this business in nineteen-twenty-three has been to reduce price, to reduce price, to reduce price, to reduce price. . . ." Gesell's essential argument was that although du Pont did control two-thirds to three-fourths of all *cellophane* sales, it only controlled about 20 per cent of the *flexible-packaging-material* market, and *that*, said Gesell, should be the relevant market for any monopoly analysis.

To support this approach he produced an intricate array of charts to prove that cellophane competed with foil, glassine, papers, films, and other packaging materials. Aside from imitating a Consumers Union testing laboratory, Gesell provided the justices with various packaging materials and wrapped products so they could see and feel the issue. (This prompted a usually stern and scholarly Justice Felix Frankfurter to blurt out, "I have bacon. Is that all right?")

Worth Rowley, then a government antitrust lawyer and now a prominent private practitioner, witnessed Gesell's performance. "I said to myself, 'Here is the world's greatest auctioneer.' He was so glib, so perfect, so persuasive. Weston was a brilliant and respected brief-writer, but in court was squeaky-voiced, straightforward, and not dramatic. Gesell put on a dog-and-pony show better utilized before a jury." But Gesell obviously did something right, as the Court in 1956 held 4 to 3 that du Pont had not monopolized the flexible-packaging-materials market. The three dissenters were incredulous. Justices Warren, Douglas, and Black wondered how cellophane could be so comparable and competitive with these other wrapping materials if it cost seven times as much. Government lawyers were aghast at the decision. But the Covington team of Gesell, Burke Marshall, and James McGlothlin had won what was to be, until the 1970s, the last major antitrust victory of a private corporation against the government in the Supreme Court.

This success did not surprise those who understood Gesell's talents and background.

The son of the noted Dr. Arnold Gesell, founder of the Yale Clinic of Child Development, he attended Yale College and Yale Law School. From there he went on to serve in 1936 as a special trial counsel to the newly formed SEC. He represented that agency in the Temporary National Economic Committee (TNEC) hearings as something of a muckraking investigator of the insurance industry, and later wrote the book *Families and Their Life Insurance*. Gesell joined Covington & Burling as a partner in 1941, and by the late 1950s had become a firm power. He was extremely hard-working (John Lord O'Brian once mused that "he never seemed to need as much sleep as most lawyers"), was a big client-getter (they loved his vivacity and charm, said one lawyer) and seemed to really like lawyering ("But are you having fun?" he would ask his associate Jim Hamilton). As a matter of style, Gesell—white-haired, barrel-chested, and somewhat chunky—would establish a key point and then pound it home with staccato statements and planned repetitions. He could, if necessary, adapt to the situation, remaining the calm and deferential advocate when the occasion called for it, yet behaving theatrically at other times.

Firm business alone could not satisfy Gesell. As his SEC crusading showed, he enjoyed public service as well as corporate service. "He's a liberal," one friend reported, "but he also has a lot of horse sense." At the requests of Presidents Kennedy and Johnson, he chaired the

President's Committee on Equal Opportunity in the Armed Services (1962–1964), worked on various bodies promoting court reform, and served on the governing boards of the St. Albans School and Children's Hospital. Still, after almost thirty years at C&B, according to former firm associate Gerald Norton, "he'd done it all in the private practice world—winning cases, making piles of money." So lawyers at Covington were not entirely shocked when in 1968, at age fifty-eight, Gesell was appointed by President Lyndon Johnson as federal district court judge in Washington, D.C. There he has compiled an impressive record of precedent-shattering decisions. He has held that the *Washington Post* could not be prohibited from publishing the Pentagon Papers case; members of Congress could not constitutionally hold military commissions; Special Prosecutor Archibald Cox had been illegally fired; the Senate Watergate Committee could not have five Presidential tapes; "national security" was not a defense in the case involving the plumbers' break-in of Daniel Ellsberg's psychiatrist's office; and, despite his years as corporate defense counsel, "voluntary" steel import quotas between foreign firms and the U.S. government violated the antitrust laws. "He was an activist lawyer," explained a firm member, "and now he's an activist judge."

In a second momentous Covington-du Pont antitrust case, Hugh Cox's mellow elegance replaced Gerhard Gesell's histrionics. In 1949 the government alleged that du Pont's purchase of 23 per cent of General Motors stock in 1917 was now anticompetitive, since this connection induced GM to favor du Pont's auto paints and finishings. Again the government lost in district court and again it appealed to the Supreme Court.

Factually, Cox had a difficult position to defend, for du Pont memoranda existed which indicated that the 1917 stock purchase did in fact aim to exclude competitors and lock up the large GM market. John J. Raskob, du Pont's treasurer at the time of the GM purchase, wrote in a memorandum: *"Our interest in the General Motors Company will undoubtedly secure for us* the entire Fabrikoid, Pyralin, paint and varnish business of these companies [GMs divisions], which is a substantial factor."* (Emphasis added.) Lammot du Pont wrote GM in 1922, "You really ought to buy from us. *We are a shareholder,* and you can be sure that we will give you the best possible treatment. We will give you a preference over other people because we do own stock." (Emphasis added.) Confronted with such obstacles, attorney Cox mixed disarming concessions with appeals to look at what actually happened between GM and du Pont, not what some du Pont executives hoped would happen. Of the Raskob memorandum, Cox told the justices in November 1956, "If I were in [the government's] shoes, I would emphasize it too." On the obvious closeness of the two corporations, he admitted that "looking simply at the two companies and looking at the stock relationship, seeing the people on the Board of Directors and on the Committees, and then looking at the volume of purchases, I think it is quite natural for someone to say, 'Well, there must be some relationship between these two things. It just seems reasonable.' " But he cautioned against substituting surmise for facts, and the facts, Cox stressed, showed GM did not favor du Pont.

Yet even on the facts Cox showed some modesty. "Now, I may be wrong about the facts in this case," he said in his summation. "Counsel sometimes are; but . . . I think [the case] should be decided on all the facts and not just part of the facts or fragments of the facts." Cox's efforts, however, could not erase the past—the incriminating inside memoranda or the fact that 93 per cent of du Pont's Duco paint sales went to GM. Nor could the Court. In 1957 it ruled that du Pont's relationship with GM violated the antitrust laws. "The inference is overwhelming," wrote Justice William Brennan, "that du Pont's commanding position was promoted by its stock interest and was not gained solely on competitive merit." This did not surprise Cox, since early in the case, according to business reporter John MacDonald, Cox admitted he had counseled Pierre du Pont that his firm would probably lose its case in the Supreme Court. But Pierre du Pont insisted on fighting the case "as a matter of honor" (and profits, it should be added, since du Pont reaped the investment's returns until it was ordered to sell off its shares years later).

For most, a Supreme Court decision would settle the matter. Not for du Pont or Cox. They devised a scheme whereby du Pont kept the GM shares (and its dividends) but denied itself many ownership prerogatives, such as voting and sitting on GM's board. The Justice Department objected, and Cox again in 1961 appeared before the Supreme Court exhibiting the Coxian soft-sell. He saw divestiture as merely a "symbolic ceremonial act." "Now, I concede the importance of ceremonial law, but I raise the question with the Court whether the injury to the shareholders that will be caused by divestiture can be justified in the name of ritual or ceremony." Justice William Brennan, for a 7–1 Court, in effect answered yes, and ordered once and for all that du Pont sell its now $3 billion worth of GM stock.

This du Pont eventually did, but not before hiring Washington lawyer Clark Clifford to reduce the tax costs of this huge transfer. Clifford and du Pont worked together in 1962 to produce special legislation that would tax the du Pont distribution of the GM stock to its shareholders at capital-gains rates rather than the higher ordinary income-tax rates. Their bill became law, saving du Pont hundreds of millions of dollars. Why had du Pont switched from C&B to Clifford in this stage of its dilemma? Said Clifford: "This was a complicated question involving not only Congress but also the Treasury and Justice departments, as well as a specialized knowledge of government. This was not in their line, but in ours. That's all."

Cox had lost his biggest case, yet his vaunted reputation and career were unaffected.

Originally from Iowa, and then Nebraska, Hugh Cox became a Rhodes Scholar at Oxford, then worked in Thurman Arnold's Antitrust Division from 1938 to 1943. Yeasty with recognized talent, he rose to become Arnold's indispensable lieutenant, representing the Justice Department, among other tasks, at the TNEC hearings. When Arnold became a federal judge, Cox had the opportunity to head the Antitrust Division. But a persistent indecisiveness about his plans discouraged even an admiring Arnold, and Tom Clark was appointed instead. Cox then went to England during 1943 to head a staff researching Germany's economic position. He joined New York City's Cleary, Gottlieb, Friendly & Cox in 1946 and went permanently to Covington & Burling in 1951, after acting as Donald Hiss's lawyer.

"He was the greatest practitioner of my time," according to Cox's onetime Antitrust Division associate Victor Kramer. "He had a perfect mind, unerring judgment and his written work was the best." He was an aristocratic, aloof, witty, erudite man, forever puffing on a very British pipe. He was also extremely quiet, almost diffident, "a mystery to all of us at the firm," an associate who worked closely with him recalls. Because of his imperious bearing and Olympian stature, all associates would call him Mr. Cox, never Hugh. He could also be impatient and curt. When asked his favorite hobbies by a reporter, Cox snapped, "I am tired of people who have little hobbies —they bore me." Yet he and his wife shared a passion for eighteenth-century furniture, which filled his two-hundred-year-old Georgian brick residence in Alexandria, Virginia.

Cox was extremely devoted to the firm, in his fashion. He cared nothing about office politics or rules, wouldn't attend management-committee meetings, and socialized little. But he did have clout there. When Cox announced he would not move to C&B's new modern office building unless his office had windows which would open, architects quickly redesigned his office to accommodate his wish. Once he did address a firm dinner, dryly poking fun at his partners in verse. Would he let the writer read his talk? Oh no, as it was "slightly jejune and certainly parochial." Would he at least be interviewed? No, again, because "when they were doing the early anthropological studies, my sympathies were always with the natives."

Childless, Cox spent most of his waking time on firm work. He was, especially, an antitrust expert; and his work was meticulous. An associate recalls how "we once spent two hours going over two sentences!" Another remembers how Cox would never delegate responsibility to an associate to prepare memoranda on a line of cases. Instead, he would read every case, while the young lawyer sat in his office to rebound Cox's ideas. At a firm luncheon once, Gerhard Gesell was holding forth on trial advocacy. Go for the jugular, he said, by pruning away secondary issues until the real issue stands alone. Fine, said Cox, unless your jugular point is lousy; and then you want the protection of lesser points. Vigor versus nuance.

On October 20, 1973, Hugh Cox died of cancer at age sixty-eight.

In 1960, it was the electrical-machinery conspiracy. That year the Justice Department indicted twenty-nine electrical-machinery firms and forty-five executives for price-fixing, bid-rigging, and market-splitting in what became the biggest criminal antitrust case in history. During the period of the cartel and conspiracies, some *$7 billion* of electrical-equipment sales were involved. As ably described in detail in John Herling's *The Great Price Conspiracy,* General Electric, the largest of the named firms, retained Gerhard Gesell as special counsel. Gesell's general goal was to persuade the government and the public that any crimes were those of a small group of disloyal employees, but certainly not those of the company. Although a corporation, of course, can only act through its agents, Gesell tightroped on the wire-thin difference between individual and institutional culpability. More specifically, he aimed to keep top management unconvicted and unjailed, and to avoid documentation on the public record which could benefit later lawsuits for private damages.

Gesell's first test concerned indicted GE vice-president Arthur Vinson. Four subordinates all asserted that Vinson had participated in conspiratorial meetings. They privately took polygraph tests, which corroborated their claims. Gesell wouldn't let his client take a lie-detector test because, among other reasons, the results would not be admissible in court. This tack cost Gesell and Vinson some publicity points, but they were nevertheless playing their hand well. Antitrust chief Robert Bicks did not want to risk the whole case over Vinson, his prominence in the GE hierarchy notwithstanding. According to John Herling, Bicks "realized that the parade of GE witnesses—some of whom were distinguished government officials—assembled by the company and Gesell might overwhelm an ordinary jury and obscure their view of the antitrust evidence." Rather than jeopardize a pretrial settlement, Bicks decided to drop the indictment against Vinson. This paved the way for a settlement of the GE case between the government and Gesell.

Both sides trooped into court in November 1960 to enact a rehearsed scene before Philadelphia District Court judge J. Cullen Ganey. The Vinson count was dropped. Gesell, representing GE's top management, then rose to speak: "Before pleading in this case, inasmuch as this is the only one of the cases involving General Electric where there have been any allegations concerning the company's board of directors, I would like to ask the government if they have a statement they wish to make" (Gesell knowing that they did). Government prosecutor Charles Whittinghill then read their jointly prepared statement:

> In response to the request of General Electric, the government makes this statement: The government has not charged and does not claim that any member of the General Electric board of directors, including Mr. Ralph J. Cordiner and Mr. Robert Paxton, had knowledge of the conspiracies pleaded to in the indictments, nor does the government claim that any of these men personally authorized or ordered commission of any of the acts charged in any of the indictments.

With this Gesell stood up and, with much satisfaction, addressed the court. "Your honor, with that statement, General Electric pleads guilty in this case." Gesell had secured his original objectives. No top GE official was convicted or went to prison. (The firm paid $437,500 in fines, or .01 per cent of its annual gross; some lower-echelon management, whom the government had cold, served thirty-day jail terms.) Gesell had kept the record barren of ammunition for subsequent lawsuits and had obtained a specific exoneration of GE's highest officials—which the firm later exploited to claim that it had pleaded guilty "only when it appeared that the company would be held legally responsible for what had been done by a few officers and employees, in spite of the innocence of the directors and top management."

Still, a combative Gesell had tiffs along the way—with co-counsel, with Judge Ganey, and ultimately with GE itself. In one court hearing, Gesell complained that the defendants were not jointly negotiating with the Justice Department because Westinghouse insisted on going alone to Justice, a remark which unnerved Bruce Bromley, Westinghouse counsel. "You were the one who refused to go to the Justice Department," he angrily said to Gesell. At another hearing Gesell defended GE's management by arguing that GE directive 20.5, which prohibited violation of the antitrust laws, "created the atmosphere and the standard under which those loyal to the company should have conducted their affairs. They were under no compulsion to go along [with illegal schemes]." Judge Ganey was skeptical. "Why were they doing that?" he shot back. "I don't know whether they got bonuses for advancement or anything else, but . . . if they were doing this meeting, making these arrangements, rigging prices, and having these allotments made, certainly I am not naïve enough to believe that General Electric didn't know about it and it didn't meet with its hearty approbation."

Since this view undermined GE's public posture that the case involved the derelictions of individuals, not of the company, Gesell could not let this pass. He addressed Judge Ganey about this "so-called organization-man theory," and heatedly reasserted that unlike other defendants GE had long had a specific policy against collaborating with competitors.

Finally, the Covington partner conflicted with GE over private lawsuits for damages. He had protected GE's legal position as much as any lawyer could have in the circumstances. So when he urged GE to settle damage claims quickly and generously, in order to avoid court-imposed treble damage payments, he expected that his client would agree. "In litigation he was urging them not to drag heels, put up phony defenses, or send out phony interrogatories," said Harold Kohn, the well-known plaintiffs' antitrust lawyer who represented some governmental authorities suing GE. But if Gesell finally felt conciliatory, GE did not. The firm and the lawyer permanently parted company, and GE retained instead Henry Sawyer of Philadelphia and White & Case from New York City. Afterward GE said simply that the new counsel were more experienced for the damages' stage. But among Covington lawyers and leading plaintiffs' counsel, it was common knowledge that Gesell had quit when his client failed to follow his advice. "GE wanted to litigate everyone to the bloody end and they expected Gesell to go along. He refused," recalls antitrust lawyer David Shapiro, "and they got their asses kicked in." One Covington partner recalls that Gesell had been "hurt by the falling-out. After all, he was a renowned lawyer who was used to clients' following his advice."

Eight years passed before another American businessman went to jail for antitrust crime, and again a Covington lawyer was involved, deeply involved.

"A trail of deceit, blackmail, and stupidity led some of them to jail," read a headline in the usually staid *Fortune* about the plumbing manufacturers antitrust conspiracy. In 1961, only six months after seven electrical conspirators had gone to jail, the Plumbing Fixtures Manufacturers Association (PFMA) met. After legitimate business had been dispatched, the member firms then set standards and fixed prices at rump sessions. Involved were fifteen manufacturers of bathtubs, sinks, and toilets doing over a billion dollars annual business. As a result, the bathtubs and toilets sold to home builders, and sold in turn to homeowners, cost $50 to $100 extra.

At the center of the controversy stood William Kramer, the young, thickly set, goateed executive secretary of the PFMA who had bugged some of the conspirators' meetings for self-serving purposes. When the PFMA threatened to fire and expose Kramer, he in turn threatened to release his tapes. The unpredictable Kramer instead left the country. Meanwhile the Internal Revenue Service was investigating him and came to his office looking for canceled salary checks, where they fortuitously found three of Kramer's secret tape recordings. With these the antitrust case clicked open like a safe. The Justice Department empaneled a grand jury. Kramer, tired of being on the lam and coveting official leniency, sent in sixteen more tapes and surrendered. In the summer of 1966 the grand jury returned eighteen indictments. Eight individuals, including Kramer, went to jail, and the PFMA was abolished.

James C. McKay has been a Covington & Burling partner since 1958. A general litigator for the firm, affable though nervous, he represented the PFMA throughout this episode. But he was far more than merely its lawyer. He and Kramer socialized together; Kramer, in fact, claims that he let McKay know about his group's dirty little secret.

On April 29, 1963, the PFMA held a formal meeting at the Georgetown Inn in Washington, D.C. That evening McKay phoned Kramer to call the get-together a "big coverup . . . a subterfuge . . . camouflage." According to Kramer, the members at meetings would discuss routine problems such as market expansion or research and development, but every so often someone would accuse the brethren of cheating in the price-fixing agreement. In a December 17, 1963, letter, three years before indictments were issued, Kramer wrote McKay, "The Association's chief concern—in fact, the basic foundation of its very existence—has been the fixing of prices and the limitation of competition." Trusting no one, Kramer secretly taped conversations with McKay.

> KRAMER: You know this has been going on before I ever joined the Association. Kelch [a conspirator], you know, Kelch has said many times that—
> MCKAY: Well he was talking about another industry.
> KRAMER: No, he's talking about this industry. He said why us bathtub people have all been in bed together for a long time and then Crane company came along and made this tub for the small fellows and we all fell out of bed.
> MCKAY: Yeah, well, that's probably true. O.K. Well, I hope they can continue to get away with it, ha ha, for your sake.

In another conversation, McKay said the following to Kramer:

> . . . of course, they violated the antitrust laws before; but they just—it hasn't been a successful violation. But this sounds like if this pottery increase is successful and also if they are successful in eliminating non-acid-resisting tubs . . . well, I think there's a fair chance that someone's going to squawk, that's all, and then you might have a grand jury and then you have subpoenas, and then you're in trouble, especially if those assholes are writing memoranda about this.

In a generally unnoticed court deposition by Kramer in 1970, and in a personal interview with him that same year, Kramer described McKay's situation in detail. His deposition under oath states that "Mr. McKay was fully aware of this conspiracy . . . and not only of the general scope of it, but also even [of] many of the details of the conspiracy, who was involved, what the meetings were about, where they were held, who attended the meetings, and what was to be discussed and decided upon. He was aware of price increases before they occurred."

McKay categorically denies all this. He says that no matter what the taped conversation indicates, he was not engaged in price-fixing.

"Hell, I'm not naïve. I at no time knew these guys were price-fixing."
He considers Kramer a practical joker whom he did not take seriously,
and whose character he seriously misread. "For some reason he had
it in for me," McKay says of Kramer. The Covington lawyer insists
that he periodically advised the association on the requirements and
penalties of the antitrust laws, and would conduct "antitrust audits"
of his client's files to see if anything illegal was going on.

That something spectacularly illegal was going on leads to one of
two conclusions. Either this diligent lawyer could not see the obvious
or he chose to ignore it. His taped comments to Kramer, however,
seem to indicate that McKay was put on notice in 1963 that his client
was probably violating the law. Yet McKay claims that he never
directly asked the PFMA whether they were criminally restricting the
market and fixing prices. Under these circumstances, his warnings
against antitrust crimes seemed to be either ritual, or sermons on how
to sin without getting caught.

McKay did not drop his disobedient and lawless client. He did not
go to the authorities. Rather, he remained as counsel, continuing to
earn his fees by warning his clients against what he either knew or
should have suspected they were doing. "McKay was just used," said
a plaintiffs' lawyer in later damages cases against the plumbing firms.
"He was just a front." Another lawyer involved in the plumbing litigation explained the cross-currents pulling at McKay. "Attorneys who
represent trade associations may have great difficulties if association
members feel it necessary to fix prices. When I run across it I tell them
to cut the shit out, that it's a violation of law. But a lot of pressures
can build up on you. It depends on the age and experience of the
attorney, the importance of the client to the firm, and the career of the
attorney within the firm."

For McKay, judgment bent to pressure—and a $5000 annual re-
tainer plus expenses. When Covington & Burling learned of this
episode, it was understandably anxious. It prepared elaborate briefs
and memoranda in his defense and assigned Gerhard Gesell as his
lawyer. Called before a grand jury on April 21, 1966—he had to
testify since he was granted immunity and since the PFMA waived
the lawyer-client privilege—McKay denied any knowledge of his

client's criminality and said that the first he ever knew about it was when he was asked it that day. In the end, McKay was neither indicted nor disciplined by the local bar. In fact, little of McKay's role in the plumbing case has ever previously been made public. Instead, he was mentioned in local newspapers as a possible candidate for a Washington, D.C., Superior Court judgeship in 1970. And he recently contributed a chapter on trade associations in an antitrust manual, where he wrote of such subjects as "Discussions at Meetings: Forbidden Topics."

Commandment X: Corruption—Watergate has educated many citizens about lawyers' ethics. The IRS reports that a higher percentage of lawyers are tax violators than are members of any other profession. Those who daily calculate how to find legal loopholes in, for example, the tax code, may find their moral sensitivities dulled as they slide from loophole hunting into actual illegality.

Not all lawyers fulfill Justice Cardozo's injunction that they must have "the punctilio of an honor the most sensitive." For example, they may tolerate or cover for antitrust crimes by their clients, or be conduits for illegal corporate money. In February 1956 a lawyer for the Superior Oil Company of California, seeking the passage of a bill to free natural gas rates, left $2500 in cash with Senator Francis Case (Republican, South Dakota); Case promptly exposed the incident and President Eisenhower vetoed the bill because of such "arrogant" influence. In 1971 lawyer-lobbyist Nathan Voloshen was convicted of fraud and perjury by using Speaker John McCormack's office on behalf of private clients. At a conference of corporate general counsels at Northwestern Law School in 1971, Mobay Chemical Corporation lawyer Robert Finch told the writer, "I've seen Pittsburgh law firms give envelopes with cash for delivery that day to the Sheraton [Hotel] for pickup by a Washington lawyer to grease the bureaucratic wheels." Was it perhaps just a retainer? "Hell, no. Straight influence-peddling. That's not the way Washington law firms collect their bills."

Lawyerly illegality, however, need not hurt one's business. Within a month after former SEC chairman G. Bradford Cook admitted that he had repeatedly lied under oath about the Vesco case, he announced he would open his own Washington law firm to represent corporate clients and to "act as a liaison for other law firms that don't have Washington offices."

For a corporation conceived in deception and lawlessness—it tried to confuse itself in the 1920s with the more recognized name of AT&T and entered into a cartel agreement with Ma Bell to divide up world telecommunications markets—ITT in its 1972 difficulties revealed a half century of impressive consistency. But ITT did achieve something of a breakthrough in 1972. Now everybody knows its name.

Covington & Burling represents ITT on many antitrust matters. C&B defends ITT's subsidiary Continental Baking, and defends it, and defends it, and. . . . For Continental, a $700-million-in-sales firm before its 1967 acquisition by ITT, has made a habit of being sued in antitrust cases. Based on SEC, Justice Department, and FTC records, and Commerce Clearinghouse trade cases, Continental Baking has compiled the following record: Between 1968 and 1971 it was sued at least fifteen times by private parties alleging antitrust violations, thus far winning one, losing two, settling three, with nine pending. In 1967 and 1968 the federal government brought seven antitrust cases against Continental, three criminal and four civil; the government won all seven. Unrepentant and certainly undeterred, ITT-Continental pleaded no-contest in 1972 to conspiring from 1966 to 1969 to fix bread prices in the New York metropolitan area. If there were a corporate "habitual offender" statute, Continental Baking would be out of business.

Covington's continuing representation of Continental Baking, owing to that company's activities before and after ITT's acquisition of it, has concerned some of the lawyers in the firm. One former associate reported:

> It is commonly assumed that the company has followed an intentional, conscious policy of engaging in such practices despite the antitrust laws, presumably on the theory that the potential benefits of this policy far outweigh the possible costs or other disadvantages of defending antitrust suits—particularly when the astute legal work of C and B, masterminded by John Schafer,

could tie up such litigation for years or result in an acceptable negotiated settlement.

This attorney then posed the professional and ethical dilemma:

> The obvious question was how Covington could continue to represent a firm purportedly engaged in continuing violations of the law. It was generally thought that under the terms of the retainer arrangement, Continental did not come to C and B for antitrust or business advice, nor did they want it; rather, the firm was retained only for litigation.

The law firm's two major ITT counsel are Henry Sailer and Jack Schafer III. Sailer, born in Peking, is considered a brilliant legal technician who could not care less about the firm's administrative problems. Schafer is a wiry, athletic-looking forty-eight-year-old partner who contributed to George McGovern's Presidential campaign in 1972. In his office is a large Sister Corita poster based on (ITT-subsidiary) Wonder Bread's slogan, "Helps build strong bodies in twelve ways"; there is another poster of a slot machine with the words "Grand Old Payoff" at the top, "Nixon's Hideaway" on the machine, and "ITT," "ITT," and "Dita Beard" filling the three slots.

Schafer and Sailer have worked not only on the active Continental account, but also on the ITT–Hartford Fire Insurance Company acquisition. In this they got some help in Hartford, Connecticut, from Joseph Fazzano. Exactly who is Joseph Fazzano? It is a question to which Covington itself would have liked a precise answer in 1970.

Fazzano was taken on that year as one of ITT's local Hartford counsel, a fact that appears nowhere in the public records of the case. His assignment was to persuade William Cotter, now a congressman but then the Connecticut insurance commissioner who had initial authority to accept or reject the ITT–Hartford Fire combination. He first turned down the acquisition on December 14, 1969, and later reversed himself, upholding it on May 23, 1970. Between these two decisions, Fazzano, a long-time friend of Cotter's, stressed the benefits of the acquisition in some fifteen personal phone calls and luncheon tête-à-têtes. Yet six months later, the counsel of record had still not heard of Fazzano. Henry Sailer of Covington admitted, "I don't know the man." The Hartford firm representing ITT—Day, Berry & Howard—also knew nothing of Fazzano's role. And the assistant attorney general of Connecticut, Frank Rodgers, openly.pondered: "They had the big one in Hartford [Day] and the big one [Covington] in the U.S. . . . . Why the hell did they need Joe Fazzano?"

Not one but two questions are raised: why Fazzano *and* what should Covington now do as formal counsel on the case? At best, their client had hired other legal counsel while regular counsel assumed that they were running the case. In fact, the *Hartford Courant* obtained a January 1969 memorandum from ITT senior vice-president C. T. Ireland, Jr., to Harold Geneen which urged the company to exert "inexorable pressure" to achieve the merger. At the worst, their client hired a legal fixer to get the merger approved while Covington & Burling performed legal window dressing. But to whatever degree, their client had apparently misled them during the conduct of legal proceedings.

It turned out there were a lot of things ITT forgot to tell Schafer and Sailer. For the Fazzano episode was not the only time Covington stuck to the technical work while others did the backslapping. There were, of course, the controversial ITT merger cases of 1971. Schafer and Sailer did accompany a contingent of ITT representatives—ITT director Felix Rohatyn, ITT general counsel Howard Aibel, Wharton School dean Willis Winn, and Columbia professor Raymond Saulnier —to a meeting on April 29, 1971, with Deputy Attorney General Richard Kleindienst. Rohatyn made the presentation, arguing that ITT must be allowed to keep its Hartford Fire Insurance acquisition in order to finance its cash-short French and Spanish subsidiaries, or else there would be a damaging ripple effect on the whole stock market. The Covington team then largely receded to the Antitrust Division, where they worked hard to hammer out a consent decree to settle the three major conglomerate cases brought against ITT. But it is doubtful they were told that their client was also working very hard. In a series of ex parte meetings, ITT brought its case to the attention of, among others, the President of the United States, the Vice President, the secretaries of treasury and commerce, and to many members of Congress. It attempted to donate a $100,000 *quid* to the planned San Diego Republican Convention for the alleged *quo* of

a favorable antitrust settlement. ITT also furiously shred incriminating memoranda after its activities came to light—activities which
should not require retelling here.

ITT director and lobbyist Felix Rohatyn has testified that he was
the first person told by the government that it would settle the merger
cases on terms ITT would accept. Rohatyn in turn told three others,
one of them being Henry Sailer, who had been negotiating its terms
for months. If Sailer had not previously known who ran the antitrust
show, the lobbyists or the lawyers, he knew it now. All ITT's shenanigans in this episode, admitted former C&B lawyer Gerald Norton,
were "a source of some embarrassment."

Perhaps even more taxing to lawyers of conscience were ITT's
involvement in Chile and its claim before the Foreign Claims Settlement Commission—neither of which specifically involved antitrust
matters but both of which posed ethical dilemmas for the participating
attorneys.

On March 21, 1972, ITT executives all around the country read
Jack Anderson's column with some horror. Based on inside corporate
documents, Anderson charged that ITT was involved in "a bizzare
plot to stop the 1970 election of leftist President Salvador Allende"
in Chile. This exposé prodded the Senate Foreign Relations Committee to create a special Subcommittee on Multinational Corporations
to study multinationals generally, and ITT in Chile specifically.

Hearings in March and April 1973 revealed how ITT—nervous
about its $160 million investment in Chile—attempted first to inter-
vene in the 1970 Chilean presidential election and then to disrupt
Chile's economy after Allende's election by seeking U.S. government
help in blocking loans and aid. ITT, again, had gotten in hot water,
but it was again up to Jack Schafer to keep it from getting publicly
scalded at Senate hearings. In meetings with the subcommittee staff
and senators, Schafer argued for executive (secret) sessions rather
than public hearings—a position all knew would persuade no one—
and then simply tried to present events in a light most favorable to
his client. Two weeks before the hearings were to open, however, ITT
suddenly realized that their Covington counsel lacked the kind of
political background essential to the hearings. So the company scram-

bled around to retain a lawyer with recognized credentials as an influential liberal Democrat to brief the company, as well as to approach the senators on the subcommittee, especially the liberal Democrats. Washington lawyer and former John F. Kennedy associate Myer Feldman was approached, but he said no, thinking the cause hopeless. But Washington lawyer and former JFK associate Fred Dutton said yes. This last-minute pitch did cause some chuckles among the senators at their executive sessions, and it embarrassed Schafer, who did not appreciate his client's underwhelming show of confidence.

At the seven days of public hearings, Schafer accompanied nine of the key ITT witnesses, including Harold Geneen. There is normally little accompanying counsel can do in these situations "other than to make sure the microphone is working and that the water pitcher is full," said Schafer. One major task, however, was to keep his witnesses from committing perjury. He would also occasionally interject to clarify a point ("Are you reading from the transcript, Mr. Chairman?"), to polish ITT's image ("As you know, Senator, we have produced every document that the subcommittee has ever asked [for], and we would be delighted to produce these"), and to buoy a sinking client. But the latter function became impossible after an irritated Senator Symington cut off Schafer during one triangular colloquy among Symington, ITT director John McCone, and Schafer. "It is fine you are here," Senator Symington disarmingly began, "but at this time we are not asking for the opinion of either the ITT or its counsel. . . . I would suggest that you let us question [Mr. McCone], and, in due course, we will have the people from the ITT before the subcommittee"—after which Schafer became predictably more quiet.

"He was decent in our dealings, without any sharp tricks," said a Senate aide about this Covington partner. "Once we interviewed two ITT guys and it was obvious they were lying. Schafer admitted they were, and got them to later change their stories." But Schafer's "decency" created an ethical dilemma when exercised on behalf of a gamy client. Another subcommittee aide described the problem.

> Schafer appeared to be being used, sort of like a spear-carrier. If he said he'd try to find certain documents, he would try. That the client may have burned them was not his fault. Also, we would find out things about his client that he wouldn't know.

When we first asked Schafer if he knew Geneen had offered money to the CIA, he said, "Christ, no, let me call my client." They let him play his legal game because they were playing their own game on top of him.

The lawyer talking paused and then shook his head sadly. "If they were my clients, I would have kissed them good-bye long ago." Schafer has made no such comment; instead, he has been content to tolerate the indignities of a client who failed to tell him the truth and who hired another lawyer—Fazzano—for the same task without telling him.

ITT's war claims also created a case to try lawyers' souls.

The forum was an obscure Washington agency, the Foreign Claims Settlement Commission, which compensates United States nationals for damage done to their property in the Pacific and in Germany during World War II. Since its creation in 1962, the commission has made more than seven thousand awards totaling over $335 million. The second largest claim ever presented before the commission was ITT's $78 million request for damages to fourteen of its German plants during the war. John Laylin, Brice Clagett, and Stanley Temko presented ITT's case, "which fills up at least one file cabinet, maybe more, of materials about the financial details of ITT operations," according to Wayland McClellan, the agency's general counsel.

ITT filed its claim in 1964, and Covington lawyers began to get impatient with what it considered bureaucratic creakiness. On January 24, 1967, Laylin and Clagett visited Chairman Edward Re to apply some pressure judiciously. As summarized by Chairman Re's memorandum to his files: "Mr. Laylin informed me that he was of the opinion that 'the Commission had issued instructions' that the ITT case was [to be] delayed. . . . The Chairman stated that a discussion of 'a delay' at this late stage of the War Claims Program was foolish since the program must be finally completed by May 17, 1967. Mr. Laylin asked if the Chairman would call in Mr. Rode [the commission lawyer preparing the case]. The Chairman indicated that this was completely unnecessary and that there was no need to notify Mr. Rode of any matter pertaining to the development of a claim assigned to him."

On March 27, 1967, the Foreign Claims Settlement Commission

awarded ITT $16,601,308 for losses to its German property, but the company objected that this sum was inadequate. Laylin et al. filed objections, and, following an oral hearing on May 3, 1967, the commission two weeks later agreed to increase its compensation by about $11 million to $27,004,394.

Yet what appeared to be merely a technical judgment on the evaluation of damages also contained a serious moral component. For as has been shown by internal commission memoranda, the files in the National Archives of the wartime Federal Communications Commission, and Anthony Sampson in *The Sovereign State of ITT,* many of the factories for which ITT received compensation had been turning out bombers for the German war machine, and during the war the *Germans* had compensated ITT for damage done to its plants by the *Allies!* Two of the damaged plants, the Focke-Wulf and Lorenz subsidiaries, which represented $20,800,000, or over 75 per cent of the final claim, were primary manufacturers and suppliers of German war material. In its decision the commission had reasoned that the ITT subsidiaries were controlled by the German government as "an enemy property custodian." But ITT was hardly the helpless victim of Nazi power; if anything, as Anthony Sampson has shown in detail, ITT's chairman Sosthenes Behn actively connived with the Nazis to secure a favored status for his ITT plants in Germany. If Germany had won the war, it would have been logical, if not predictable, for ITT to have sought compensation from the victorious Axis for damage done its plant by Allied bombing.

These unblinkable facts troubled the commission. In a December 20, 1966, letter sent to Walter Monogan, the attorney in charge of the General War Claims Division, the head of the commission's European office wrote:

> Apparently in view of his training in the United States and his mastery of the English language, [German lawyer Dr. Mailaender] was picked shortly after the visit of Mr. Clagett, of C&B, in Europe in May and June 1966 for the purpose of making a concentrated effort to compile the information and documents required to substantiate the claim. . . . Dr. Mailaender admitted that large payments were made to several claimants' subsidiaries by the German Reich authorities before the end of World War

II to compensate for war damage suffered and promote a quick resumption of the war production. The Focke-Wulf aircraft manufacturing company, for instance, received about 185 million [reichsmarks].

Shortly before the proposed award to ITT of March 27, 1967, commission staff attorney (and now general counsel) Wayland McClellan wrote to the then general counsel:

> There is only one issue which disturbs me and this does not go to the legality of the claim under the statute or the amount of the award.
>
> The record before the Commission on this claim indicates that the corporation referred to as "Focke-Wulf" was one of the primary manufacturers and suppliers of the enemy air force and the firm of "Lorenz" was likewise a chief supplier of German war material. The latter company was cited by the German Nazi party for its outstanding contribution to the war effort. In fact, it appears that the firm manager or principal officer was considered for treatment as a war criminal after the war. . . .
>
> The commission must be mindful of the possibility of critical analysis of its decisions in the future and therefore be made fully aware of the facts involved in these claims.

These considerations did not seem to affect the commission's final judgment. "The case was a perfect example of the nonadversary process in action," commented an ex-Covington lawyer familiar with the proceedings. "There was no one representing the public saying 'disallow!' or cross-examining ITT. The agency was very helpful to us, since all were on one side. Their job was to give away the money and our job was to get it." The forum and the issue, however, distressed this lawyer, who could not dissolve his queasiness by reciting the cliché that lawyers merely advocate but do not judge. "I'm a Jew and I was bothered by it. There they were killing my relatives. . . . The next thing would be to pay off the people who made the ovens, assuming they were damaged and an American company had built them. . . . It was one thing that made me realize my future lay elsewhere."

Du Pont sells off three billion dollars of stock. GE gets caught in the biggest price-fix ever. ITT-Continental ranks as perhaps the biggest fouler of our antitrust laws. Whatever Covington's role in these Justice Department cases, no one can doubt their significance. Which cannot be said of C&B's Federal Trade Commission cases. For their impact is seemingly trivial, and their unfolding often appears like scenes from a Beckett play.

Part of the problem lies with the laws enforced by the agency. Checking the authenticity of wool and fur products or analyzing whether a toothpick manufacturer sold his product at varying prices to local retailers can lead to unexciting enforcement. Even the Federal Trade Commission Act's injunctions against "unfair" trade practices has led the agency into many obscure crannies of industry, while leaving the structure of industry largely unchallenged. Part of the problem, then, is the agency itself—its priorities, its traditional sloth.

Much of the reason for a historically insignificant FTC, however, has been Washington lawyers, who play the agency as an expert violinist plays his instrument. Employed are all the techniques sketched above, from politicking to delaying to outgunning an undermanned agency—*especially* outgunning the agency. "[Thomas] Austern has the reputation of being an arrogant bully who treats government lawyers with contempt and uses political muscle," said a legal assistant to an FTC commissioner, and then explained why an Austern can succeed. "Washington lawyers are wily old veterans while fifty-five per cent of all FTC lawyers have been there two years or less. In combat our young people get outlawyered and butchered by experts knowing every trick."

Covington & Burling, like other FTC practitioners, has found itself an active participant in the kind of trivial, political, and procrastinating cases for which the FTC, at least until recently, has become well known. For example, Covington & Burling's Henry Sailer unsuccessfully represented the Campbell Soup Company in 1970 when the FTC accused it of putting marbles in its televised soup to make it look thicker and more appetizing. Or what of client Colgate-Palmolive, which shows how Rapid Shave shaves sandpaper on television, only it isn't sandpaper, but Plexiglas. A team of Covington lawyers under Austern argued that their product *can* shave sandpaper, but it was messy to work with on television; hence the Plexiglas. They lost in the Supreme Court.

A case more political than trivial involved Broadway-Hale's acquisitions of Emporium Capwell and Neiman-Marcus. West Coast–based Broadway-Hale was the nation's sixteenth largest department-store chain in 1966 when it attempted to acquire a third of Emporium Capwell, a $166-million-in-sales chain with ten stores in the San Francisco Bay area. Given the geographically similar market, FTC staff recommended that any settlement include divestiture of the two linked firms. But Austern, on behalf of Broadway-Hale, said that there should be no divestiture because Abe Fortas had won such a settlement in an earlier (though less anticompetitive) situation, Federated Department Store's acquisition of Bullock's Stores. Never one to be terribly subtle, Austern complained to an FTC lawyer that, "they got theirs," adding that it would appear to be political favoritism if a plugged-in Fortas succeeded where Austern failed. The commission permitted the acquisition.

Two years later Broadway-Hale wanted to acquire the prestigious Neiman-Marcus of Texas. On December 17, 1968, a majority consisting of commissioners Philip Elman, Mary Jones, and James Nicholson voted to deny the acquisition. The next day Commissioner Jones withdrew her vote and asked for further study. On January 23 the commissioners voted again, but the result was a 2–2 tie since Ms. Jones declined to participate in the vote. Before the merging companies could be formally notified about the tie vote, which had the effect of vetoing their merger, Broadway-Hale president and prominent conservative Democrat Edward Carter asked Chairman Dixon for an informal conference. Ms. Jones broke a speaking engagement to hear the arguments and cast the deciding vote in favor of the merger.

As Ms. Jones said to the *Wall Street Journal,* "I flipflopped all over the place and at one time I tried to duck." Some Washington critics attributed her vote to her desire to become the FTC chairman. A Republican, she was being pushed by a number of prominent sponsors, including Broadway-Hale lawyer H. Thomas Austern. According to the *Wall Street Journal* report, Ms. Jones argued that propriety did not prohibit her from discussing her ambitions with lawyer friends who happened to be involved in FTC cases. But she admitted, "Tommy has been helpful and encouraging." Little more is known about how Broadway-Hale and its lawyer got their merger through the FTC. As a dissenting commissioner, Elman pointed out that "no investigation was made by the Commission, no document subpoenaed. The Commission's findings generally . . . are predicated solely on materials submitted by the parties in an ex parte non-adversary proceeding, with no opportunity for cross-examination."

Finally, Covington & Burling has found itself, perhaps not inadvertently, in some of the most protracted and convoluted cases in FTC annals. In the *AMC* case, the FTC in 1945 ordered the Associated Merchandise Corporation to stop soliciting and receiving from manufacturers preferential quantity discounts and rebates. By *1968,* the commissioners were deadlocked on whether to settle or litigate. Then, to the delight of Covington attorneys Austern, Harvey Applebaum, and Randolph Wilson, the commissioners decided to drop the complicated case altogether on the condition that none of them would file a dissent!

An even older case is *Nabisco,* first begun on May 19, 1943. The issue was Nabisco's discount schedule on its products, which discriminated in price in violation of the Robinson-Patman Act. Covington first entered the case in the late 1940s in the person of Austern, and more recently has been represented by partner Randolph Wilson. The case was initially settled in 1944, but over the years the FTC complained about the inadequacy of Nabisco's compliance reports. Beginning in 1967 the agency and C&B struggled for several years over the issue of whether the court of appeals should hold Nabisco in noncompliance with the earlier FTC order. Finally, twenty-eight years after the original settlement, a court of appeals in 1972 ruled simply to reinstate the 1944 consent decree to cease and desist price and discount discrimination. Some commission lawyers blame the case's prolongation on antiquated rules and procedures built into the agency process. But Nabisco's lawyers requested twenty-eight extensions of time during the case, and insisted on litigating issues the commission was willing to concede, as over the question of whether the 1944 settlement was a "consent decree." An FTC lawyer on the case thought C&B's delays were intentional. "We had to prove what happened twenty-five years ago, and our witnesses were dead."

A Covington summer clerk bragged to a group of law students in 1970 that "Randolph Wilson has personally held up *Nabisco* for seventeen years. In their circumstances, that's winning the case." When he spotted this writer in the audience, however, he quickly added, "but the government delayed too."

This is true in most protracted litigation—like the continuing Geritol episode, for example, which former FTC chairman Caspar Weinberger would repeatedly refer to as "that horrible case." From 1959 to 1962 the FTC investigated the advertising of iron tonics. Geritol—manufactured by the J. B. Williams Company, which invented the phrase "tired blood"—was an obvious object of interest. Its annual advertising budget was then $4 million (today, it is $8 million). In December 1962 the commission formally charged that J. B. Williams misrepresented Geritol as helping more people than it did, since iron deficiency in men and in women in nonmenstrual years would not be alleviated by Geritol. (Geritol had been advertised on "To Tell the Truth," among other programs.) In the next decade a total of eleven Covington attorneys defended Williams against this charge (one associate spending most of a year and a half researching "iron deficiency" in medical journals). Over the next two years the commission held hearings on the technical issues raised in various cities—in Boston, New York, Washington, New Orleans, and Kansas City. C&B put on thirty-eight witnesses, at undisclosed witness fees, and the firm's brief required a 47-page appendix just to list all their credentials. The hearings accounted for over 5300 pages of testimony and over 400 pages of exhibits. One Covington associate involved called them a "traveling road show." "We went from one end of the country to the other quibbling about the merits of something that probably helps nobody but hurts nobody, but makes a lot of money for J. B. Williams," he added.

The hearing examiner ruled against J. B. Williams in May 1964, and in September 1965 a unanimous commission agreed. It found Geritol's advertising deceptive and ordered Williams to stop advertising Geritol as a generally effective remedy for tiredness and to start disclosing that the product was not effective for most tired people. Williams and C&B appealed but lost again in a sixth circuit court decision. But this did not end the case, for the commission staff found that Williams was not complying with the FTC's order. Rather than rapidly seeking penalties, the commission kept asking for more compliance reports, all of which confirmed its original conclusion. The case now bogged down, since Williams's general counsel insisted to its C&B co-counsel that all important decisions be cleared with company chairman Matthew Rosenhous, who was often unavailable in Florida with his ailing wife.

Eventually, on April 20, 1970, the Justice Department filed suit for $1 million in civil penalties for continued Geritol deception. The case again slowed after the lead Covington lawyer, James McGlothlin, suffered a heart attack in 1971. C&B lawyers Charles Horsky, John Vanderstar, and Michael Boudin (son of Leonard Boudin, attorney for Daniel Ellsberg and the Berrigans, among others) filled the gap. In January 1973 Judge Constance Baker Motley assessed $812,000 in penalties against J. B. Williams—a decision appealed by the Covington team. And in May 1974, twelve years after the FTC had first moved against Geritol, a court of appeals overturned Judge Motley's decision. The court adopted the C&B argument that its client had been unconstitutionally denied a jury trial, one required in a case where such high penalties carry criminal implications. By now, estimates Patricia Hynes, the lawyer in the U.S. attorney's office in New York City handling the case, J. B. Williams' attorneys' fees probably exceed any penalties that have been or will be assessed.

Why should a case with such a simple factual deception have taken, so far, a decade? Again, in the view of former FTC officials Robert Pitofsky and Basil Mezines, both sides contributed to the tedious pace. The commission, rarely pushing J. B. Williams forward and requiring yet more compliance reports when Geritol's continuing deception was palpable, earned the scorn it received. And a Covington lawyer candidly admitted that "that case is a good example of what lawyers can do. . . . As long as the legal fees are less than the amount Williams makes selling Geritol, our services are worth it to the company."

But beyond the apparent inefficiencies of all parties to the case is the futility, even irony, of the whole proceeding. It took ten years to end Geritol's claims that it cured tired blood, only to see this potion now being advertised by the slogan, "If you've got your health you have just about everything." And as if to prove that even corporations have a sense of poetic justice, on December 31, 1971, the J. B. Williams Company was acquired by Nabisco—a merger not merely of two firms but of two clients and of two cases with a combined age exceeding that of FTC chairman Lewis Engman.

The Drug World

For who would bear the whips and scorns of time,
The oppressor's wrong . . . the law's delay.
                              —Hamlet, *Act III, Scene 1*

The Pharmaceutical Manufacturers Association advertises that the industry's testing process is "long, tedious, and expensive." "If you were responsible for someone's child, father, mother," it concludes, "would you settle for anything less?"

Apparently the industry does. In the late 1950s pharmaceutical firms were touting combination antibiotics as was Dr. Henry Welch, the head of the Food and Drug Administration's Division of Antibiotics. It did not help promotion of these wondrous combinations when Welch was forced to resign after disclosure that he had received $287,000 from pharmaceutical sources while a public official; nor did it please the drug firms when their products were called "shotgun therapy" and "irrational" by the Council on Drugs of the American Medical Association—the overprescribing of two drugs instead of one in the hope that something would work. The industry's response was advertising, and more advertising. By the 1970s it was spending $1 billion annually for promotion—more than $3000 per doctor in the United States or four times its investment in research and development. The purpose, of course, is to sell drugs. But "a definite conflict of interest appears to exist," concluded a Senate Small Business Committee report, "between the supplier's goal of selling more drugs and the physician's interest in using drugs in a fully informed and rational way."

The industry appears to be winning. For nearly all unbiased studies

102

show us to be an overdosed society. The main reason for this, says Senator Gaylord Nelson, is that "drug advertising promotes excessive use." The National Academy of Sciences–National Research Council found that only one-fifth of all claims of therapeutic efficiency were clearly supportable. An estimated 3 to 5 per cent of all admissions to medical institutions and as many as 30,000 hospital deaths annually result primarily from adverse drug reactions. There are some 1.5 million adverse drug reactions annually, 70 to 80 per cent of which are preventable.

The drug industry is also the most profitable in all of American manufacturing, and it is not hard to understand why. As Senator Estes Kefauver saw the problem, "He who orders does not buy; he who buys does not order." This market quirk discourages smart buying based on low prices. Drug houses do not compete for lower prices to consumers, who don't order the drugs, but for higher prices to doctors, who do. They accomplish this by lavish advertising which persuades doctors to prescribe by brand name, not by equivalent generic name. But, concluded the FDA's Dr. Henry Simmons in 1973, "there is no significant difference between so-called generic and brand name antibiotic products on the American market." The differences in price, however, are dramatic: Carter-Wallace's Miltown costs $61.20 for 1000 tablets, but under the generic name of meprobamate it costs $4.95; Ciba's Serpasil is priced at $39.50 for 1000 tablets, but the price is $1.35 for geserpine, the generic equivalent.

More than brand-name promotion balloons the price of drugs. Consider Orinase, an antidiabetic drug marketed in the United States by Upjohn. The price to the druggist in Sault St. Marie, Michigan, is $82.68 for 1000 capsules; the price to the druggist in Sault St. Marie, Canada—a few miles away—is $6.63. Senator Nelson explains the difference: "Canada has a compulsory licensing system for drug patents to protect the public against price gouging." In this country we grant instead exclusive seventeen-year monopolies on patented drugs. Consumers, especially the old who need drugs the most, are consequently overcharged millions annually. So is the government, which wastes an estimated $750 million annually by its brand-name, rather than generic-name, purchases.

"If you say that just shows a lack of social responsibility," said Lloyd Cutler of charges of exorbitant drug pricing, "we disagree with you."

That the drug industry needs Washington lawyers is as predictable as is cynicism from Diogenes. For where there are lush profits and a federal agency able to depress them, industry eagerly employs Washington counsel to steer it safely by bureaucratic shoals. These lawyers "descend like locusts," in former FDA commissioner James Goddard's phrase, whenever the FDA tells a drug firm to stop some unapproved activity. "High-priced lawyers will spend hours in conference with FDA officials, haggling over the wording of promotional material, engaging in semantical arguments as to whether a certain section of government regulation does or does not give FDA the right to limit the companies' 'freedom' in a certain area," complained Goddard after he left his FDA post.

In the area of drug advocacy especially, Washington lawyers have an obvious impact on all consumers as well as on specific clients. To the extent that lawyers shape policy, they help determine which drugs enter our bodies and which do not. "Potential victims, far away from any policy judgment, are faceless," commented Dr. Robert McCleery, former special assistant to Goddard, "but the immediate losers are closer at hand—in your inner lobby. They are the sleek, suave, sophisticated, stripe-tied, sympathetic, sensitive representatives of business. . . . And they are reasonable men with reasonable suggestions."

One of these reasonable men is Lloyd Cutler. Whether as witness or negotiator or litigator, Cutler represents the Pharmaceutical Manufacturers Association—the industry's trade association, with 135 member firms and a $4.4 million budget—for fees reportedly up to $100,000 in a single year.

Among his earliest PMA labors was work on the 1962 "Drug Amendments." Senator Estes Kefauver's Antitrust Subcommittee had held years of hearings into the drug industry. They documented astronomical drug prices due largely to monopoly patent rights; and they showed how overpromotion and inadequate warnings—in 1959, 89 per cent of all drugs did not label side effects—caused unnecessary drug consumption and danger. The result of Kefauver's investigations was his drug bill, S1552. Its major provisions aimed to control prices by limiting patent rights to three years rather than seventeen, and by limiting the amount of permissible price markup to 500 (!) per cent; also required were greater disclosure of a drug's side effects and the labeling of generic as well as brand names.

The PMA was predictably worried and turned to Lloyd Cutler, among others.

Cutler decided early that it would be best to favor *a* bill, though not *this* bill, since, according to author and investigator Richard Harris, "history had shown drug legislation to have a way of getting stronger the longer it lay around Capitol Hill, so the chances were that if the companies succeeded in blocking Kefauver's bill, they would sooner or later get something worse." But all would not be sweet compromise. On the patent and advertising provisions of the bill, said one industry leader, "we mean to fight to the death."

The "fight" tactic turned out to be a private strategy session, held behind the back of Kefauver, the bill's sponsor, on June 8, 1962, in Senator Eastland's Judiciary Committee room. Around the big, wooden conference table in this august chamber were two legislative draftsmen from the Department of Health, Education, and Welfare, staffers from the offices of senators Eastland, Dirksen, and Hruska (all of whom opposed Kefauver's bill), and three PMA lobbyists, Cutler, Marshall Hornblower, of Cutler's firm, and Ed Foley. Cutler not only carried PMA's banner at this meeting but was also understood to be speaking for Senator Dirksen. "The presence of special-interest representatives in such a meeting is," according to Harris's view, "if not unique, rare, for ordinarily everyone prefers a little more discretion when it comes to suggesting where the power lies."

The meeting sought to implement Cutler's strategy: secure a PMA-approved weak bill to preclude more restrictive legislation. Bernard Fensterwald, then an antitrust subcommittee attorney (and later James McCord's lawyer), said that "Cutler was the unofficial director of the meeting, and he gutted the hell out of Kefauver's bill. After the meeting it was totally reversed." The revised bill had no provisions for price reductions or drug advertising, the heart of S1552;

it dropped the generic-name issue in the lap of the HEW secretary, without any guidelines on how to decide policy. *The New York Times* editorialized that "the drug reform bill has undergone drastic dilution" and attributed it to the (previously) secret meeting, which it called "a bizarre method of revision."

The PMA ploy might have proved ultimately successful but for a factor that no one could have anticipated: thalidomide. This drug, sold in Western Europe but not in the United States, caused pregnant women to give birth to deformed children. The 1938 Food, Drug and Cosmetic Act passed largely because of the national scandal over a drug inaptly named Elixir Sulfanilamide, an unproven mixture which resulted in 107 deaths. A usually prevailing lawyer-business alliance again found itself being swept along by the current of tragedy. It was only after the thalidomide disclosures that the White House, HEW, and many legislators coalesced to support a measure stronger than the Cutler revisions.

The PMA forces now met in a second private session. Added to the original group were Deputy Attorney General Nicholas Katzenbach, and the godfather of lawyer-lobbyists, Thomas ("Tommy the Cork") Corcoran. But as discussions began, two Kefauver aides, John Blair and Horace Flurry, accidentally stumbled upon the meeting. They quickly understood their find and observed that Cutler and the industry representatives "looked like little boys caught stealing apples from the store." Blair and Flurry, of course, stayed to watch and influence the action. The discussion focused on the testing to be required before a new drug could be marketed. The HEW representative, Jerry Sonosky, wanted a showing of efficacy by "preponderant evidence," which he thought put the burden of justification on the industry. Cutler insisted on a standard of "substantial evidence," which he hoped would put the burden on the government to deny the marketing of a drug.

Blair came up with a compromise solution, previously developed at the FDA: "adequate and well-controlled investigations, including clinical investigations, by experts qualified by scientific training and experience to evaluate the effectiveness of the drug involved." After much back-and-forth disagreement, Cutler agreed to the compromise.

Blair remembers Cutler's performance with an adversary's admiration. "Cutler is a skilled craftsman. No one knows better how to assess the effect of complicated amendments," he said. "You can't compare him and Corcoran."

Eventually S1552 was reported out of the Judiciary Committee and passed the Senate 75 to 0—but *without* any patent or price provisions, because of the effective and unalterable opposition of Eastland and Hruska. The administration still waffled on its support, choosing instead to back the weaker House bill.

Cutler and the PMA team now simply renewed their opposition in the other Chamber, believing the conservative House to be more responsive to their industry views. At hearings before Congressman Oren Harris's Interstate and Foreign Commerce Committee, Cutler accompanied no less than six industry witnesses, including Eugene N. Beesley and John T. Connor (his 1940 Cravath friend), then the presidents of Eli Lilly and Merck respectively. As committee members began pressing his witnesses, Cutler began increasingly to interject himself. At one point, exhibiting the logic of McCleery's "reasonable man," he summarized the industry's position:

> What we are saying in a capsule is that if there is a responsible difference of opinion among responsible clinicians, trained investigators, as to whether or not a drug is effective, the mere existence of a responsible difference of opinion, based on adequate and well-controlled tests, should be sufficient for the FDA to allow the drug on the market.
>
> The FDA's role should be to decide: Is there a responsible difference of opinion; and, if there is, they should let it on the market, even though a numerical majority or a preponderance of evidence, or whatever else you might call it, might still be on the side that the drug is not effective or not proven effective.

But Congressman John Dingell argued that "there is a great deal of difference between 'preponderance of the evidence' and 'substantial evidence' "—a point Cutler, having participated in the bill's formulation in the Senate, presumably understood well. Dingell continued to scrutinize the industry's representatives closely. After listening to the repeated sanctimony that the PMA was second to none in its concern for the public health, and after listening to Theodore Klumpp, president of Winthrop Laboratories, testify that he favored the bill except for a long list of objections, Dingell saw the strategy of being for *a* bill, but not *this* bill. "So for all intents and purposes," he said, "we have involved a situation where the Pharmaceutical Association is opposed to the whole bill." Cutler leaped to the rescue. "Mr. Dingell, I really respectfully, sir, do not feel that is a fair way to put the matter," he protested. ". . . it is hardly fair to us, because we have a few changes in language to suggest in a substantive proposal, that, therefore, we are against the proposal. We are not, sir."

Nor did Cutler fare much better outside the hearings, as his energy may have exceeded his judgment. One drug company lobbyist observed his work.

> The only big error he made was that just before the Harris committee met, he handed each member a fifty-page rewrite of the bill to bring it in line with what PMA wanted. Congressmen simply don't have the time or the staff help to get through a document like that. The way we ordinarily do it is to type up amendments—a sentence here and a paragraph there—on separate pieces of paper. We parcel them out among the different congressmen who are friendly toward us, and when the time comes, it's a simple matter for them to take the slips out of the pockets and offer them.

The House Commerce Committee did ultimately accede to the PMA opposition to disclosing side effects in drug advertising. It was a victory for the trade association, "whose representatives, Lloyd N. Cutler and Edward H. Foley," according to the *Washington Post,* "buttonholed committee members near the committee rooms" on the issue. At this Dingell moved from criticism to outrage. Seeing Cutler outside the committee room, he exploded: "I'm sick and tired of these pharmaceutical people. . . . They accepted something in the Senate, and now they come over here and welsh on it. If this goes on, I'm going to be forced to compile a dossier on what's happened and make a speech about it on the floor." In fact, Dingell organized into victory a rare House phenomenon: a successful floor fight. After giving examples of false and misleading advertising and its critical effects, the advertising-disclosure requirement was reinserted. Again the drug bill passed unanimously, inspiring the members on the floor to burst into uncharacteristic applause. Explained one member of the House press corps, "It's not often they're able to do something for the people."

All the while, Cutler, Corcoran, and Foley were impassively watching the proceedings from the House galleries. At the final vote, according to John Blair, "they looked like statues on Easter Island." Nevertheless, the drug bill was no Dunkirk for the PMA and their legal battalion—their war chest against the legislation costing an estimated five million dollars—since no provisions to limit the patent monopoly or pharmaceutical profits were included in the final legislation. Now, a decade later, in part because of Cutler's lobbying, drug prices are still exorbitant. But despite his best efforts, there are today stricter standards for the marketing of dangerous or worthless drugs.

For all his obvious effort on the 1962 Kefauver-Harris Drug Amendments, Cutler never did register as a lobbyist under the 1946 Lobbying Act—although PMA did. That law requires a person to register as a lobbyist if he gets paid more than five hundred dollars for efforts primarily attempting to influence legislation by direct communications with members of Congress. Helping write a proposed bill at the behest of senators, and "buttonhol[ing] Committee Members near committee rooms" would seem to fit easily under these requirements, but a search of both the Senate and House records failed to reveal a registration either by Cutler or his law firm.

The returns on Cutler's 1962 investment did not come in all at once. It took years for the real dividend to materialize: Cutler's familiarity in later court cases with a law he helped write. It was a headstart appreciated by his litigious clients.

"We hoped the 1962 act would require the industry to make a self-examination of their [pre-1962] products and begin complying," said William Goodrich, the former FDA general counsel for twenty years. "Instead, the PMA promptly sued us. . . . They ended up contesting everything affecting their vital interests." Lloyd Cutler and Covington & Burling were the lead industry lawyers in all the cases.

In *Abbott Laboratories* v. *Gardner,* the industry complained about the FDA regulation, established under the Kefauver-Harris amendments, which required that "every time" a brand name was used in a label or advertisement the generic name also had to be printed. Represented by Cutler and Gerhard Gesell, the drug firms argued that the rule would unnecessarily impair the readability of their ads and therefore obscure the difference between proprietary names. It presumably did not escape the industry's attention that the frequent use of generic names might also undermine the profitability of brand names.

The *Abbott Labs* case, however, turned on the procedural question of whether the drug houses had "standing" to seek a "pre-enforcement" judicial review of the legality of the rule. After hearing Gesell's oral argument, the Supreme Court said they could, and sent the parties back to the court of appeals for a decision on the merits of the case. But not before an unusual tongue-lashing by Justice Tom Clark, who wanted to throw the plaintiffs out of court right away. For those who assume that Court opinions are courtly etchings, read Justice Clark's dissent:

> The pharmaceutical companies, contrary to the public interest, have through their high-sounding trademarks of long-established medicines deceitfully and exorbitantly extorted high prices therefor from the sick and the infirm. Indeed, I was so gouged myself just recently when I purchased some ordinary eyewash drops and later learned that I paid 10 times the price the drops should have cost ...
>
> The Court says that its action in so sabotaging the public interest is required because the laboratories will have to "change all their labels, advertisements, and promotional materials . . . destroy stocks of printed matter; and they must invest heavily in new printed type and new supplies." I submit that this is a lame excuse for permitting the continuance of such a dishonest practice. Rather than crying over the plight that the laboratories have brought on themselves the Court should think more of the poor ailing folks who suffer under the practice. I dare say that the practice has prevented millions from obtaining needed drugs because of the price.

Perhaps chastised by this rebuke, but also aware that the 1962 law specifically provided for an "every time" rule, Cutler and Gesell negotiated a settlement entirely satisfactory to the FDA: every time the brand name was *prominently* featured (and at least once in each column where it was not), the generic name had to be printed in type at least one-half as large. For results measured in half inches, Washington power lawyers often earn their retainers.

In the 1969 *PMA* v. *Finch* case, Cutler opposed the FDA's high standard of clinical testing required for pre-1962 drugs. He argued in his brief that the FDA had no rule-making authority under the 1938 food and drug act and that this rule required "the burdensome and expensive task of conducting large numbers of clinical investigations . . . on all pre-1962 drugs that have not previously been the subject of extensive clinical testing of that nature." Since the act and its legislative history are replete with instructions to do just that, answered the FDA's brief in a passage appropriate for Cutler, "they are seeking to gain a point in court that they lost in the Congress."

Cutler and a team of his young associates went to Wilmington, Delaware, to argue the case before Judge James Latchum. But since he had been previously occupied with other legal business, Cutler had only minimally reviewed the legal issues just prior to his court appearance. "We pumped him and briefed him that night and the morning of the argument," marveled a former firm lawyer, Frank Lloyd. "We would say something once, he would absorb it, and we'd move on to something else. He is a very talented lawyer and a quick studier, with a monomania for the law." In court, Cutler won the *procedural* point that FDA had failed to follow the proper process under the Administrative Procedure Act in creating the rule in question, but he lost the key *substantive* point that the FDA had no authority to promulgate any rule. So the FDA simply reinstituted its proposed rule by executing the proper procedure. When Cutler and the PMA went back to court on the merits of the rule, this time Judge Latchum upheld the FDA.

In 1969 Cutler was also involved in the *Panalba* case, described subsequently in detail. Here he made a supplemental but important contribution, discussing the legislative history of the food and drug act, a chronicle in which he had played so prominent a part. The following exchange should be read with the knowledge of the second "secret meeting" of 1962:

> THE COURT: When did that "adequate and well-controlled tests" standard come into the regulations?
>
> MR. CUTLER: It is part of the legislative history of the statute, your Honor, and was brought along into the subsequent regulations issued by the FDA shortly after 1962. The major purpose of the substantial evidence requirement—and I draw your attention to that phrase "substantial evidence" as distinguished from "preponderant evidence"—and the legislative history is very clear on this, was to establish that, particularly on this issue of effectiveness, there was not to be any official authoritarian U.S. Government medical dogma as to what doctors would prescribe. . . .
>
> In other words, if there was a disagreement among experts as to whether a particular drug is effective, the drug was to go on the market as long as some of the experts thinking that it was effective were qualified experts, and so long as they based their judgment on adequate and well-controlled tests. And that was to be true even if those experts were a minority of the total number of experts that had looked at the drug.

Cutler argued that a drug could be marketed if some experts thought the drug useful, even though most experts thought it was dangerous. (At one time, it should be remembered, some doctors thought that leeching and bleeding had curative powers.) Thus industry would have the right to market a drug *unless* the government could very clearly show that it was dangerous—a possible argument but one, as John Blair and John Dingell could attest, Cutler had already lost.

In late 1962 Attorney General Robert Kennedy found himself indirectly negotiating with Fidel Castro for the return of 1113 expatriates taken prisoner during the Bay of Pigs invasion. Since the invasion, of course, had become a synonym for failure, the administration was eager to recoup what it could by a humanitarian exchange. Castro's ransom price was $53 million worth of drugs and chemicals, medical and surgical equipment, and baby food. To raise this, the administration looked to the pharmaceutical companies for contributions in kind.

Helping Kennedy organize the proposed exchange was Louis Oberdorfer, his assistant attorney general in charge of the Tax Division and a former and future law partner of Cutler's. It was therefore natural for Oberdorfer to approach Cutler, PMA's Washington representative, about the possibility of contributions by the drug companies. Cutler thought that a deal could be arranged. But suspicious of the government seeking gifts, he listed the problems to be resolved before his clients could become committed. Haynes Johnson describes these in *The Bay of Pigs*:

> He made it clear that in order to do the job the companies would have to be able to work together without fear of subsequent antitrust or other action. And, he pointed out, because of the unfavorable public and political image of the drug manufacturers stemming from Senator Estes Kefauver's investigating subcommittee in 1960 and 1961, the companies would need some assurance from the administration that they would not be attacked because of their participation in the prisoner exchange. *They also would have to be assured that they would not be required to disclose their cost and markup data in order to secure a tax deduction.*

It is understandable why firms would want to be free from antitrust charges if they joined together in this common effort initiated by government; so is the requirement that the sums donated be deductible as gifts, thus passing on some of the cost to the government. Therefore on December 11, 1962, the IRS issued a ruling that contributions of merchandise would be deductible at a value measured by the lowest wholesale catalogue prices at which the manufacturers customarily sold their products—a ruling common to all industries. But *only* the drug industry has as large a discrepancy between costs and even the lowest wholesale price. The taxation truth is that, because of this high markup for drugs, some manufacturers could reap a windfall gain as the tax benefit exceeded the actual cost of the product. The operation of this oddity is simple: If it costs $1 to make the drug, and if it sells for $4, then the company can deduct the $4 from their tax base, realizing an actual tax saving of about $2 (i.e., 48 per cent of $4). They therefore would have spent $1 and "saved" $2, for a $1 profit. To avoid such self-gain, the administration urged the contributing firms to give away any "profits" to charity (which Merck and Company did . . . to the Merck Foundation). In fact, Merck netted $300,000 after taxes on their contribution and Pfizer reportedly netted $120,000.

The deal was successfully completed after Kennedy had met with drug- and food-industry representatives, and Cutler, in mid-December. The attorney general reassured the drug officials, who feared that the industry might somehow be criticized, that the sight of prisoners returning to the United States would blunt any skepticism. But ten years later it became impossible to blunt the skepticism of new revelations, when they eventually became public. In his *Kennedy Justice,* Victor Navasky describes how more may have been exchanged for drugs than prisoners:

> Of more than sixty contributing firms in the Cuban prisoner exchange, almost every one was at least under antitrust or FTC investigation. At the time thirteen were actually defendants in antitrust actions, twelve in FTC actions and seven in both, for a total of eighteen different companies as defendants. As Jack Rosenthal, then an assistant in the Public Information Office, put it in a memo, . . . "Nothing to crow about here. I suppose a quiet death is the best answer."

In the same year as the Cuban-prisoner exchange, the Colombian government entered into an agreement with McKesson and Robbins, the largest American drug wholesaler, to buy drugs under their generic names. By avoiding the heavy promotion and advertising costs that swell the price of brand-name drugs, McKesson was selling chloramphenicol, for example, for 3 cents a tablet whereas it sold for 30 cents a tablet under its brand name in the United States; antibiotic pills went for 3.6 cents a tablet but sold for 29 cents a tablet here. It was both making a reasonable profit and helping resolve the dilemma of Colombian President Lleras Comargo: "I can understand why my people cannot have new cars, television sets, and other luxuries and can only eat meat at infrequent intervals, but I cannot understand why they should be deprived of life-saving drugs because these are priced out of the reach of more than 80 per cent of the Colombian people."

The arrangement may have been good news for poor Colombian peasants, but it was not for the PMA and American drug firms. The McKesson effort drastically underpriced their own sales in Colombia. And it threatened to do the same in other Latin countries then negotiating with McKesson, and in the United States as well once it became obvious how easy it was to sell generically at a profit. The initial retaliation was undertaken by "about a dozen American manufacturers," according to Bernard Nossiter, "who formerly supplied McKesson with raw materials [but who] have refused to sell any for the firm's cut-rate program." The American firms took other measures, including political pressure against McKesson's plans in other Latin American countries and a barrage of propaganda against generic drugs, directed to American doctors. McKesson's chairman of the board, Herman Nolen, said he was "alarmed at the extent and severity of the concerted attack against the generic program."

Enter Lloyd Cutler in an effort to resolve and escalate the problem at the same time. A confidential meeting was held in Washington on January 14, 1963, among the top officials of the PMA, five domestic drug companies, the South American analogue of PMA (AFIDRO), and Cutler. After Dr. Austin Smith, president of the PMA, opened the meeting by cautioning all members against discussing price matters, owing to the antitrust laws, the conversation quickly focused on the best way they could collectively block the McKesson efforts in South America. The AFIDRO representative urged "a government-to-government appeal" to discuss legislative enactment, supporting his view with two nonpocketbook arguments: "the generic plan was not viable and . . . would most probably collapse in one or two years for lack of adequate capital, know-how, equipment, etc."; and secondly, "this would have grave political consequences as the Communists would blame such a development on the proverbial 'Yankee Imperialism.' " (But Yankee Imperialism, like beauty and politics, is in the eye of the beholder. To the *Washington Post*, "the efforts of certain American pharmaceutical manufacturers to prevent the distribution of low-priced drugs under generic names in the Republic of Colombia seem likely to prop up anti-American charges of Yankee Imperialism.")

Cutler then summarized the problem and offered "a constructive counter-proposal," according to the internal memorandum of the meeting. It involved sending some unpatented generic compounds to the Colombian government, combined with "U.S. government support *stimulated* by PMA on the one hand, and renewed intercession by AFIDRO with the Colombian government, on the other." This tactic, said a Senate investigator, meant a lobbying effort to get our government to discourage the McKesson-Colombian plan. In fact, Dr. Smith supplemented the Cutler proposal by noting that "one possibility would be an approach to Mr. [Teodoro] Moscoso, the United States official of Puerto Rican descent in charge of the Alliance for Progress program in Latin America. (It was noted that Mr. Moscoso comes from a drug-industry background.)"

Within six months the Colombian government had discovered and publicized the AFIDRO-PMA alliance, leading Senator Maurine Neuberger to denounce it as a "shocking conspiracy by drug manufacturers to prevent one of their members from furnishing low-cost drugs to the impoverished citizens of Colombia."

The PMA and Cutler had been publicly embarrassed about their private affairs for the second time within a year. But the industry was not without a rebuttal:

> The drug makers have simply exercised a legitimate right to petition for the redress of what they regard as grievances. PMA officials further contend that lower priced generic drugs won't reach enough people to make a substantial difference. They also argue that selling drugs by their chemical names damages the property rights that the makers have built into their patents.

Another rejoinder was made by PMA official Walter Wein, who thereby proved that the *Weltanschauung* of a Jay Gould and an Andrew Carnegie was gone but not forgotten: "A better way is for the Colombians or any country to raise their income so they can afford more drugs, foods, clothing, and other basic staples."

Free speech and free enterprise are common defenses for American business interventionism abroad; ITT also saw itself as merely redressing its grievances when it tried to buy the support of the Central Intelligence Agency for its Chilean misadventure. But beyond acknowledging that the First Amendment permits such arguments to be made, there is little more to commend them. For beyond procedural defenses are substantive effects. What were the actual results of PMA's activities and Cutler's lawyering? Cutler doesn't think about it, said Senator Gaylord Nelson's drug aide Benjamin Gordon, who thought that the ultimate consequence of PMA's opposition would be the denial of necessary drugs to hundreds of thousands of South American peasants. "Like a bomber who drops his bombs and doesn't see the result, Cutler doesn't worry about the result of his role," said Gordon.

When Cutler—whose firm, as has been mentioned, receives substantial PMA fees—was asked years later in an interview what had finally happened in Colombia, he said, "I don't know; you see, I was only outside counsel to PMA."

Cutler is often called upon to help the drug industry in congressional testimony—an event which can be either as prearranged as the thousandth running of a Broadway play or as dramatic as the most contentious cross-examination. The Senate Small Business Committee's continuing hearing on drugs at times approached the latter level during its forays into the pricing and advertising practices of the drug industry. During the 1967 hearings Senator Gaylord Nelson of Wisconsin—so bothersome a drug opponent that the industry spent upwards of $90,000 in an unsuccessful effort to unseat him in 1968—was pitted against Dr. Leslie Lueck, the director of quality control for Parke, Davis and Company, and against Lloyd Cutler, his lawyer.

Cutler prepared his witnesses before they took the stand and interrupted them when he sensed trouble. He fulfilled his life-preserver function during the testimony of PMA's economic experts, four academics hired for a total of $34,000 to argue why drug prices were so high.

> SENATOR NELSON: . . . Under what economic theory would you justify vast price discrepancies between two licensees of the same product, neither of whom did the research, both on the same continent, with adjoining borders. Why is the Canadian Government paying $2.60 for tablets [of chloropromazine] and the American Government $32.60 a thousand[?]
>
> DR. [PAUL] COOTNER: . . . If there were no differences in costs or quality you would have to find something else to explain it if you could. . . . If they are identical products then I think it would require some explanation.
>
> MR. CUTLER: Mr. Chairman, Professor Cootner is clearly not qualified to answer on this and perhaps I am not either. But I do know some of the factual assumptions put into your question are not correct. I do know, for example, that Smith, Kline & French did a very large part of the research needed to prove that thorazine would be useful as a mental illness drug. That Smith, Kline & French did a very large part—in fact all of the U.S. work, necessary to prove the safety and efficacy of that drug and put it through the new drug approvals of the Food and Drug Administration.

Cutler's performance was smooth and impressive, leading him later to assure his pharmaceutical clients, in the privacy of a Senate office building elevator, that "we really showed them today." All chuckled. Yet all was not smoothness at the hearings. Cutler again found himself increasingly intervening between client and committee as a well-versed staff pressed his witnesses. After one questioner challenged his assumption that recent lower prices indicated a competitive industry (rather than one formerly afflicted with monopoly profits), Cutler exploded:

> MR. CUTLER: You have convinced me, if I needed any convincing that no fact presented can make an impression on this committee.
>
> SENATOR NELSON: Just a minute. . . .
>
> MR. CUTLER: I am sorry, Mr. Chairman, I withdraw that remark.

Then came the chloromycetin controversy. The drug was effective for most prescribed infections but also carried a high risk of death for certain users. Based on statistics from the California State Department of Public Health, Morton Mintz, *Washington Post* reporter on consumer and drug affairs, estimated that about 666 users of chloromycetin died in the 1950s. Dr. Albe Watkins testified how he gave his own ten-year-old son chloromycetin after being assured of its safety. The child died within two weeks, both from unstoppable bleeding and the gradually disintegrating effects of gangrene. In a letter to the company, Dr. Watkins said, "I might have done better had I taken a gun and shot him—at least he wouldn't have suffered."

Because of such tragedies—not to mention the passage of the 1962 law encouraging more candid advertising and labeling—Dr. Lueck of Parke, Davis admitted that he would not run ads that lacked adequate warnings; he acknowledged that he believed the present advertising requirements were justifiable. Nelson then suddenly produced an advertisement appearing in a British monthly journal, the *Lancet,* which promoted chloromycetin *without* indicating the side effects. Although the then current American advertisement for this drug contained about 1300 words of caution and warnings—included because of FDA compulsion—the British ad contained not a word of warning. Ironically, both ads appeared in one publication, the *Lancet,* which had an American edition as well as an English edition.

Murmuring swept through the interested audience. "No warning at all in that ad. How do you explain that?" asked Nelson. At first unable to reply, Lueck finally stammered that they met "the legal requirements of whatever country we distributed our products in. . . ." Cutler sensed a sinking client. "Mr. Chairman, I think you will find that the point you are developing is true of every ad in this magazine, which is a distinguished magazine of the British Medical Society and I assume it meets all of what they consider to be appropriate requirements."

Senator Nelson flashed an anger uncharacteristic at Senate hearings:

> SENATOR NELSON: . . . [This] sure shocks me. What the witness says is we will meet the standards of the country where the drug is sold. That means, of course, there is not a single underdeveloped country in the world that has any defense against the exploitation of their people for profit by an Ameri-

can corporation who does not warn them of the serious, mighty serious, possibly fatal consequences here. . . .

MR. CUTLER: . . . This is a British Medical Society. The British doctors are sophisticated doctors. Just as sophisticated as the doctors in this country. This meets all their requirements. . . .

SENATOR NELSON: Any company, drug company or any other kind of company, that would do that, I would be pleased to indict on moral grounds. Your testimony is that you will meet the standards of the country in which you are advertising, not the standards of safety which the witness has testified is a proper standard, the proper ad which gives this warning that is put in ads in this country. But in countries where the people do not know any better, where the country is not protected by laws, you will tell us that you have no compunction about running an ad that will fool a doctor, as you did in California in 1961.

Nelson went on to describe the travail of Dr. Watkins, concluding, "I should think you people would not be able to sleep."

Cutler complained about Nelson's free-swinging criticism of "a company that brought you some evidence you have been asking for," and he three times repeated his objection that the subcommittee had surprised his witness (and himself) with unexpected questions. Nelson retorted with an open-ended invitation for Cutler to return with the "proper" witnesses, which he never did. The chairman then summarized the day's hearings by turning pointedly to Cutler: "It shocks me that you do not even blush. . . . If this is the standard of ethics by which the industry operates, I tell you, you fellows are in for some sad trouble. I do not think this country will stand for it."

Nelson's assault had clearly unsettled Cutler. One spectator chortled and said: "It was the first time I saw the whites of Lloyd Cutler's eyes. A lawyer like that doesn't like to be embarrassed." A Parke, Davis attorney later recalled that Cutler was upset because "it was one of the only times that *he* was a witness." Worse, Cutler no doubt considered himself an innocent witness. He was a lawyer, for God's sake, not a corporate official. If Colombians did or didn't obtain drugs due to his client, it was not for him to know. When asked, three years after the Nelson exchange, whether Parke, Davis still failed to advertise side effects in Great Britain or elsewhere as thoroughly as it advertised them in the United States, he answered, "I don't know." But was he not even curious? "Yes," was his one word reply.*

*   *   *

Covington & Burling is also one of the leading legal architects of pharmaceutical-industry policy, although it focuses far more on the FDA than does Cutler. The firm devotes a clutch of its top lawyers to drug work, including Tommy Austern, Stanley Temko, Herbert Dym (Yale College '56, Harvard Law School '60, Covington partner '69), and formerly, Peter Hutt, now general counsel of FDA.

Covington's drug clientele includes Merck and Company, Parke, Davis, Squibb, American Cyanamid, Eli Lilly and Company, Abbott Laboratories, Miles Laboratories, and Upjohn. With these many well-known clients, C&B lawyers perform many chores—from preparing clients for general congressional hearings, consulting on charges of deceptive advertising (Miles Laboratories' Alka Seltzer has come under attack because it fails to say it contains aspirin, which causes bleeding in many people, especially those with ulcers), to advising on criminal charges (Abbott Laboratories and five of its present or former officers were indicted on May 29, 1973, in a case involving the sale of allegedly contaminated intravenous fluids in 1970 and 1971; the indictment was later dismissed).

It is the FDA and Upjohn, however, which seem to command most of C&B's attention.

---

* In 1971 the State Department criticized Parke, Davis for marketing chloromycetin in Latin America without labeling its "serious and fatal" side effects. A comparison of U.S. and Italian chloromycetin labels that year also showed significant differences. The former's package insert warned that "serious and fatal blood diseases could result." But the Italian package insert read: "The fact that therapy with chloromycetin is remarkably without secondary reactions is very significant. . . . In the few cases in which reactions occur, these are generally limited to slight nausea or diarrhea and their severity rarely requires suspension of treatment." To this Parke, Davis replied in 1971, as it had in 1967, "We are conforming to the specifications [of the various countries where chloromycetin is sold]."

In 1972 Warner-Lambert acquired Parke, Davis, but the policy toward differential disclosure of adverse side effects did not change. As of mid-1972, the Italian labels lacked the contraindications listed on the American label. Warner-Lambert board chairman Stuart K. Hensley said it would be unwise to arouse "Yankee go home" feelings by labeling otherwise abroad, since each host nation should assume responsibility for adequate labeling. Again, a dose of Yankee imperialism to ward off a case of Yankee imperialism.

For example, consider the drug Orinase, and Gesell's and Temko's defense of it. Orinase is an effective oral antidiabetic drug manufactured by Upjohn. But it also has fetricidal (fetus-killing) and teratogenic (fetus-deforming) effects. The Food, Drug and Cosmetic Act requires such a "contraindication"—that it is obviously dangerous for pregnant women—to be listed on the drug's labels. This warning appeared on the label of the Orinase bottle, but it was *not* included in the 1965 *Physicians' Desk Reference (PDR)*, a book surveying the effects of all prescription drugs which is sent free each year to some two hundred thousand doctors in the United States. "As a practical matter, physicians do not have the full disclosure insert [which accompanies each bottle of a prescription drug] available in their offices at all times when prescribing drugs," said the FDA. "They rely on reference books, most principally *PDR*." Thus, if important contraindications are omitted from the *PDR*, the result could be fatal. Each drug company is responsible for the content of their drug descriptions in the *PDR*.

To the FDA this omission was criminal—"as major a defect as one can commit in this area of law," according to the FDA's Dr. Robert McLeery. In March 1967, on the recommendation of the FDA, the Justice Department indicted Upjohn for its alleged mislabeling under the Food, Drug and Cosmetic Act—in a case which would illustrate why it is so difficult to hold corporations criminally culpable.

The FDA as early as September and November 1963 were quarreling with Upjohn over the exact language of the Orinase label. The FDA's medical advertising branch determined that Upjohn knew enough about Orinase's dangers in late 1963 for them to be included in the 1964 *PDR*, not to mention the 1965 *PDR* a year later. But it was not until 1967, two years after the first acknowledged omission, that Upjohn was indicted. FDA general counsel William Goodrich blamed delays in his office. Gesell immediately after the indictment wrote Harold Shapiro of the Justice Department's criminal division asking that the case be dropped. "Upjohn has an outstanding record as an ethical house," he said, a claim with no apparent relevance to the immediate issue of mislabeling. On that Gesell made three defenses: first, Upjohn didn't know that the FDA's labeling requirement extended to drug descriptions in the *PDR;* second, Upjohn did try to put the warning in the 1965 *PDR* but a low-level employee failed to deliver the relevant clause to the publisher; and third, there was "no evidence that anyone was injured because the [warning], added by Upjohn to *PDR* copy of 1966, at the request of FDA, did not appear in the 1965 *PDR.*"

These reasons did not impress Goodrich when Shapiro, shortly after getting Gesell's letter, asked him if the case should be dropped. To the FDA the disclosure requirements of the law clearly applied to the *PDR.* If the omission was really just a staff oversight, wondered Goodrich, why didn't Upjohn correct it in one of the four later *PDR* supplements that year? And the food and drug act does not require for prosecution the "intent" to avoid full disclosure—a will-o'-the-wisp in a corporate complex. The question for criminal culpability under the act is: did they make full disclosure or did they not?

Pretrial motions on the case began to be argued in March 1967 before Michigan District Court judge William W. Kent. For a year he weathered a blizzard of C&B motions, supporting memoranda and supplemental memoranda (e.g., "Defendant's Reply to the Government's Supplemental Memorandum in Opposition to Defendant's Motion to Strike Surplusage"). These filings put off a decision until April 1968 when Kent supported the government on all points of procedure, but could not bring himself to subject a drug defendant to the icy winds of a criminal trial; so, displaying much judicial inventiveness, he threw them a coat: for the government to prevail it had to show not only Upjohn's guilt, but also that its action against Upjohn was typical FDA policy. This requirement exists nowhere in the act in question nor in standard criminal law, but rather sprang full-blown from the judge's brow.

It was now three years after the original alleged offense. The FDA and Justice scoured about for medical witnesses to sustain Kent's additional requirement. Apparently, it could not meet this demand, for on January 2, 1969, the government dismissed the case. It did wrest from C&B's Temko this concession—"Mr. Temko is prepared to state to the Court that the 1965 *PDR* did not contain all of the required warnings and precautionary information, that the pregnancy warning was omitted through a company mistake, that all of the labeling deficiencies have now been corrected, and that Upjohn will continue a company policy of using the full page insert of information in *PDR*." Nice, but hardly rewarding in light of the original indictment and original FDA fervor in the worth of its case.

The capitulation was a victory for Gesell's and Temko's tenacity and an embarrassment for the FDA, which privately blamed its failure on the Kent ruling and the cumulative effects of delay. The agency had great difficulty in finding doctors willing to testify about something that had happened four long years earlier and that had been corrected by the company anyway—all of which merely aggravated most doctors' disinclination to get on, as they saw it, any drug industry "enemies' list." The delays of the FDA, the delays caused by C&B, the burdens imposed by (as we shall see) a business-oriented judge, the difficulties of assigning criminal blame in an institution, such as the corporation, which diffuses accountability—all of these worked against successful enforcement.

Commandment IX: Delay—"Delay is just another word for injustice," it has been said, "and the massive traffic jam in our courts spawns one judicial accident after another." Because, to paraphrase a legal proverb, justice delayed can be profits retained, capital lawyers may engage in their own form of work slowdowns: the Commerce Department is trying to draft regulations making pajamas more flame retardant, or a merger has been completed and the Antitrust Division wants to break it up, or a profitable drug may be hazardous and removed from the market by the FDA. Lawyers, trained to find a problem in every solution, can hold off such agencies for months or years. This is ironic, since the commissions were created, in part, to expedite justice because court adjudication was considered too slow. But small budgets,* a high caseload, and procedural obstacles have been carefully exploited by private lawyers in no particular hurry.

---

* Some people may view the problem of economic regulation as giant bureaucracies steamrolling over helpless regulatees. This is far from the case. The total budget for the six major regulatory agencies (FCC, ICC, SEC, FPC, CAB, FMC) was $132,-315,000 for fiscal year 1973, which was some .05 per cent of the federal budget. Their total manpower was 7246.

It is a problem so apparent that even its perpetrators feel brazen enough to acknowledge it. Ex-judge Bruce Bromley, a senior-senior partner at Cravath, Swaine & Moore, has said:

> *Now I was born, I think, to be a protractor. . . . I quickly realized in my early days at the bar that I could take the simplest antitrust case that Judge Hansen [Antitrust Division chief] could think of and protract it for the defense almost to infinity. . . . If you will look at that record* [United States *v.* Bethlehem Steel] *you will see immediately the Bromley protractor touch in the third line. Promptly after the answer was filed I served quite a comprehensive set of interrogatories on the Government. I said to myself, "That'll tie brother Hansen up for a while," and I went about other business.*

One Washington lawyer saw it as "natural for lawyers to drag out litigation if they think it's in their client's interest. They often consciously calculate that if enough continuances are brought, the adversaries will either tire or die." But does this violate your ethical obligation as an officer of the court by abusing the judicial process? he was asked. "You are only obliged to play the system to the maximum advantage of your client," he replied.

Perhaps Covington's most important recent drug case involved Upjohn's Panalba—a matter of such controversy that Upjohn's local Kalamazoo law firm, its house counsel, a PMA lawyers' committee, Lloyd Cutler, *and* Covington & Burling all joined forces. C&B's lead lawyer was Temko, a joking and gregarious man, as intense and scrappy on the tennis court, say friends, as he is in court. Others view him as a relentless and aggressive advocate, "a classic example of a guy who does whatever his clients want him to do," said a former firm member.*

This was a criticism fully tested by his Panalba experience. A combination antibiotic taken for various infections, Panalba was com-

---

* Temko, as lawyers say of certain arguments, can cut both ways. When Mary Gardiner Jones was being considered as an FTC commissioner in 1964, Temko realized her consumerist orientation might do damage to his corporate clients; so he lobbied against her at the White House. After Jones was nominated and confirmed, however, Temko let it be known that he was partly *responsible* for her nomination.

posed of 250 milligrams of tetracycline and 125 milligrams of novo-biocin; and "it has been for several years among the twenty most frequently prescribed drugs in the United States" said Stanley Temko in 1968. It was Upjohn's fifth largest seller, grossing $18 million a year, some 12 per cent of the firm's domestic income. It was pre-scribed 750 million times by twenty-three thousand physicians in its twelve-year history.

Panalba was first marketed in 1957, before the 1962 Drug Amendments threw the burden on the manufacturer to show by "substantial evidence" that a new drug was efficacious as well as safe. It took six years for a government-sponsored study of Panalba to be completed. But in September 1968 a thirty-man panel of the National Academy of Sciences–National Research Council finally reported its findings on Panalba: "Ineffective as a fixed combination."* The actual dangers of Panalba were significant. By late 1969, the FDA file had 110 reported adverse cases: blood dyscrasias (19, with 8 fatalities), gastrointestinal disturbances (20), skin rashes (12), oral problems (12), liver disturbances (4, with 1 fatality), and miscellaneous (43, with 2 fatalities). By March 1970 there were 12 reported deaths tied to Panalba. Yet the actual harm is best estimated by multiplying the number of individuals treated by Panalba, 47,500,000, by the percentage estimated to have contracted each of the diseases listed above. Therefore, it is estimated by the FDA that 475,000 consumers have contracted blood dyscrasias (1 per cent), 9,250,000 have had hypersensitive reactions (20 per cent), and 475,000 have undergone liver disturbances (1 per cent) from ingestion of Panalba.

The Panalba issue, however, soon became one not of the rights of

* This conclusion was based on three findings: First, it proved *less* effective to take the combination rather than its constituent parts, since the two drugs restricted the activity of each other; this had been apparent in Upjohn tests as early as 1960, tests that remained undisclosed in Upjohn's files. Second, the novobiocin component of 125 milligrams was too small a dosage to achieve whatever novobiocin could accomplish. Therefore, third and most significant, the "novobiocin appears to add nothing to it [Panalba] except risk to the patient," according to the 1968 FDA commissioner Dr. Herbert Ley, Jr. The chairman of the NAS-NRC panel investigating Panalba, Dr. William M. M. Kirby, observed that "novobiocin was marketed as a single drug for a few years by Merck, who then dropped it because of its undesirable characteristics and lack of wide acceptance." Although Merck, a Covington client, dropped novobiocin, Upjohn, another Covington client, included it as surplusage along with a wholly different drug, tetracycline.

victims but of the rights of Upjohn—which refused to discontinue sale of the drug after the FDA, on December 24, 1968, announced its intention to decertify Panalba. Instead, Upjohn got a 120-day delay from the FDA. During this hiatus Commissioner Herbert Ley sent an inspector to collect Upjohn's own files on Panalba. The result: the inspector found eight reports attesting to Panalba's ineffectiveness and hazardousness, data which by law Upjohn should have submitted to the FDA by 1964.

Based on this uncontradicted crush of evidence, as well as a March 26 memo from the FDA's Bureau of Medicine which reiterated that Panalba was unsafe as well as ineffective, Commissioner Ley on April 30, 1969 informed HEW secretary Robert Finch that he planned to decertify and recall all Panalba stock.

On May 1 Commissioner Ley announced his decision to a meeting of Upjohn representatives, including Ray Parfet, Jr., Upjohn's president, Dr. Fenimore Johnson, an Upjohn scientist, Gerald Thomas, the firm's general counsel, and Stanley Temko. Temko criticized the proposed action as "terribly extreme," emphasizing that "we have not anticipated your drastic and shocking call for a cut off by May 31," and adding that "combinations are important products to the practice of medicine." The Covington counsel then gave his basic rationale for disagreement: "If there was a large incidence of side effects, the drug wouldn't be as widely used. . . ." The meeting ended with Ley giving Upjohn until May 5 to decide whether they would voluntarily comply with the order.

Temko's arguments fell on skeptical FDA ears. More surprising than any FDA suddenness was its six-year delay, since 1962. Upjohn should hardly have been surprised at this development, since it had known from at least 1960 that Panalba was less effective than tetracycline taken alone. And Temko's tautology—that Panalba is good because it's used—was contradicted by the promotional reality of the medical industry. Explained Dr. William Kirby:

> The answer lies I think in the education provided for by the drug companies, otherwise known as advertising, including elaborate displays in medical journals and at medical meetings. . . . Doctors do not like to admit that they are influenced by adver-

tising, but it seems to me that the facts speak for themselves. These expenditures would not be likely to continue if they did not bear results.

Thus, Panalba is not valuable because it is prescribed, or vice versa; it is prescribed because—according to the best independent scientific views, such as those of the NAS-NRC—the very company which points to use creates that use by massive advertising.

Over the first weekend in May, Upjohn and Temko decided to fight the withdrawal of Panalba from the market. On Monday, May 5, two hours before the scheduled meeting with Ley, Upjohn officials, led by counsel Temko, met secretly with Secretary Finch and Undersecretary John Veneman. The meeting was arranged by Congressman Garry Brown of Kalamazoo, Michigan—who also conveniently was a name partner in Ford, Kriekrod, Brown & Stanton, Upjohn's Kalamazoo law firm. Two hours later this same contingent met Ley, William Goodrich, and FDA deputy commissioner Winston Rankin, never telling these officials that they had just gone over their heads to meet with Secretary Finch.

Though Temko's arguments were the same at both meetings, it was with the secretary's people—where there were no FDA staff present to rebut his contentions—that Temko succeeded at least for a time. Finch and Veneman pressed Ley to permit Upjohn a hearing *before* decertifying Panalba, precisely the delay Upjohn was seeking. On May 9, at 9:30 a.m., Finch formally ordered Ley to hold this hearing. But by 3:00 p.m., Finch had reversed his earlier decision. According to general counsel Goodrich, Secretary Finch in the interim had been enlightened about the dangers that Temko had omitted to mention concerning his client's product.

On May 27, in its home city of Kalamazoo, Upjohn filed suit before, again, district court judge William W. Kent, to prevent the FDA from decertifying Panalba without a hearing. Kent granted a temporary restraining order to allow time for a decision. The struggle over Panalba now moved into court in an attempt by Upjohn, as drug investigator Don Gray of the House Intergovernmental Relations Subcommittee saw it, "to achieve by legal manipulation what it could not prove by scientific judgment."

Temko, Cutler, and Goodrich argued the case on June 20. The basic issue in *Upjohn* v. *Robert Finch, et al.* was whether the FDA could take Panalba off the market prior to a hearing. The plaintiff wanted a hearing since otherwise *Upjohn* would allegedly suffer "irreparable injury." The FDA, on the other hand, feared that during lengthy hearings *consumers* of Panalba might suffer irreparable injury. The demand for a hearing seemed misinvoked (a) where there did not appear to be an issue of fact, the weight of scientific evidence being so clearly against Panalba and (b) where the legal burden was on a firm to show that a drug was as valuable as claimed, not on the government to prove that it was not.

Judge Kent ruled for the FDA on the major point of law in his July 10 decision, saying that the 1962 Drug Amendments did not entitle a party to a hearing. But then this local judge of thirty years' standing repeated his Orinase performance, ultimately deciding in Upjohn's favor based on what he called "the principles of equity." He criticized the namelessness of the members of the NAS-NRC, approved of Upjohn's promise to conduct the necessary tests within two years, and minimized the medical danger, an issue he had earlier specifically said he would not consider. Consequently, Judge Kent restrained the agency from enforcing its May 15 order until it had ruled on the many objections filed by Upjohn. These were filed exactly thirty days later (the legal limit) in the form of fifty-four medical articles on Panalba's supposed fitness.

Given the competing scientific and legal merits of the case, Panalba's critics could not understand how Judge Kent could apply his notions of equity to favor Upjohn and Temko. A month after the decision, however, one palpable explanation appeared. It became public that Judge Kent was the chairman of the Kalamazoo Science Foundation, a tax-exempt organization with its major stock holdings in drug companies. It had held Upjohn shares until 1965, and four of the foundation officials had prominent Upjohn connections: the foundation's treasurer was the treasurer vice-president of Upjohn; the foundation's secretary was the research director for experimental chemistry at Upjohn; and two other former officials were once employed by Upjohn. Judge Kent could not be reached for comment.

"Temko was as annoyed as could be," confided a Covington attorney on the case.

Kent's ruling required the FDA to grant Upjohn an "oral presentation" to see if a fuller hearing was necessary. Little new was learned at the "presentation," other than that another man's death had been linked to his use of Panalba. But at least Temko revealed how closely he identified with his client's plight: "I say, and this is a flat statement, that I find it impossible to understand how fair-minded and disinterested men could say that reasonable grounds have not been presented in this case for a hearing. That is a very strong statement. It is one I feel most deeply." On September 19 the FDA again announced that it would stop the sale of Panalba thirty days hence. And again, nearly thirty days later, Temko appealed for Upjohn. He was joined in the court of appeals by Cutler, representing the PMA, since other combination drugs were threatened by the Panalba controversy.

Finally, on February 27, 1970, a three-judge panel for the U.S. Court of Appeals for the Sixth Circuit unanimously overruled the Kent opinion, holding that the FDA could move against Panalba without a hearing since there was a health hazard involved. Upjohn and the PMA appealed to the Supreme Court to stay the order, but on March 10 the Court refused their request. And on March 19, legal appeals being exhausted, Panalba was finally ordered off the market.

C&B's advocacy in this case had taken the form of requests for delays, filing papers on the last day of deadlines, and the struggle for a full-blown hearing, although there was no bona fide scientific dispute. Goodrich, as a result, had strong feelings about the case: "The whole thing was a farce, they're fighting for delay." His conclusion proved to be more than the expected hostility of a legal adversary. For, according to a C&B source, there exists a 100-page memorandum in the firm's files which spells out in precise detail how to delay the Panalba case as long as possible.

The benefits of delay are apparent. The gross receipts for novobiocin alone in 1968 were only $200,000, as compared with the $18 million for Panalba. As Dr. William L. Hewitt of the University of California estimated in Congressional testimony, "the net theft from the public is approximately $12 million, since the cost of tetracycline is one-third that of tetracycline and novobiocin." In other words, for every month more that Panalba remained on the market due to Covington lawyering, the company grossed approximately $1.5 million. In the fifteen months that Panalba stayed on the market after the FDA first threatened to remove it, Upjohn grossed $22.5 million from the drug. At the same time, based on the documented frequency of adverse reactions, thousands of customers unnecessarily suffered harmful side effects from their use of Panalba.

In a market economy that produced an Elixir Sulfanilade and a Corvair, such a lure not infrequently overwhelms judgment. Contrary to the view of John Locke, private vice does not invariably result in public virtue. Dr. Ley saw the problem as a conflict "between commercial and therapeutic goals." It was a conflict that concerned *Washington Post* reporter Morton Mintz. "In a struggle between public interest and special interest, in which the stakes are needless exploitation, injury, and even death to helpless patients," he asked of a Panalba situation, "can American institutions function reliably to protect the public?"

Still, it is one thing that Upjohn succumbed to the sirens of profits. That's business. But Covington & Burling? The firm—which was, after all, outside counsel, not house counsel—could have urged its client to forgo this conflict because of inevitable consumer injury, especially after Upjohn was shown to have measurable evidence damaging to Panalba in its own files. As EC7-8 of the lawyers' Canons of Ethics suggests:

> A lawyer should bring to bear upon this decision-making process the fullness of his experience as well as his objective viewpoint. In assisting his client to reach a proper decision, it is often desirable for a lawyer to point out those factors which may lead to a decision that is morally just as well as legally permissible. He may emphasize the possibility of harsh consequences that might result from assertion of legally permissible positions.

In fact, one C&B lawyer on the case did suggest this to Temko, who rejected it. Later, after Panalba had been outlawed, this lawyer sighed that he "thought it was a mistake to bring the lawsuit."

Thought for Food:
On Peanut Butter
and Other Treats

*They have no lawyers among them for they consider them
as a sort of people whose profession it is to disguise matters.*
—*Sir Thomas More,* Of Law and Magistrates, 1516

"You are what you eat" is a popular refrain of *Whole Earth Catalogue* devotees, though not necessarily of the American food industry. Health, it is assumed, is for the doctors. But corrective medicine can be more costly and tragic than preventive medicine. Food is as biologically intimate a product as any, and affects our long-range health as much as any—something which even food manufacturers are coming to realize.

Americans today consume an average of approximately five pounds of additives per year, things such as flavor enhancers, preservatives, colorings, and processing aids. Reports show that some additives over time may damage the human fetus, increase vulnerability to cancer, or increase genetic mutations. One study linked additives in foods and beverages to hyperactivity, a serious disorder afflicting children. For reasons like these, the FDA has removed cyclamates and fourteen other additives from the market since 1960.

Looking at the American diet, Dr. Jean Mayer of Harvard University sees us as a nation of "nutritional illiterates." Perhaps our most dangerous food problem is the increasing trend for American children to consume a diet high in calories, sugar, fat, and salt. Most physicians and nutritionists believe that such diets increase the likelihood of heart disease in later life. The United States Department of Agriculture's Human Nutrition Research Division studied the benefits of all Americans receiving optimum nutrition, and suggested there might

132

be a 50 per cent reduction in infant and maternal deaths, three million fewer congenital birth defects, a 25 per cent reduction in heart and vasculatory deaths, and a 25 per cent reduction in cancer deaths.

Food manufacturers may skimp on nutrition but not on what they charge. Federal Trade Commission data indicate that seventeen selected food industries may be collecting monopoly overcharges of at least $2.63 billion annually. One reason is economic concentration, as the top four firms in the baby-food industry control 95 per cent of the market, in the ready-to-eat-cereal industry 90 per cent, in the chewing-gum industry 90 per cent, and in soft drinks and bottling 89 per cent. A second reason for overcharges is advertising, which leads to "product differentiation" and market power. The industry spends some $3 billion annually—General Foods alone had a $150 million advertising budget, or five times as much as all levels of government spend on human nutrition research—for such informative consumer tips as "'mm good," "lip smacking, whip cracking, patty whacking" and "anyone can be a Frito Bandito." Or, from Procter and Gamble, there was the Jif "Mountain of Peanuts."

The ad had been very effective. Children played joyously on a "mountain of peanuts" as a picture of Jif peanut butter, manufactured by Procter and Gamble, hovered nearby. The message was clear: good peanut butter was made from lots of peanuts, and Jif was a terrific peanut butter.

But the Food and Drug Administration found out differently in 1958. FDA investigator Sidney Weissenberg discovered that Jif contained at least 20 per cent of a Crisco-type base (another P&G product) and only 75 per cent peanuts, a lesser proportion of peanuts than the products of all other manufacturers. The issue in 1958 seemed hardly a pressing national concern. But the average American was eating an annual 5.6 pounds of peanut butter, which was not always what it was made out to be. Also, the FDA had a law to uphold; it had been charged by Congress to establish "Definitions and Standards of Identity" for food products in order to "promote honesty and fair dealing in the interest of consumers." The agency, therefore, decided to issue a peanut-butter standard to require the listing of all necessary and optional ingredients so that when consumers bought something called "peanut butter," that is just what they got, not peanut spread or peanut grease.

It took fully seven years for the issue even to get to an FDA hearing, mostly because the agency was closely contested on every move by a hostile peanut-butter industry. They protested that a 1959 FDA proposal to require that peanut butter be 95 per cent peanuts and 5 per cent stabilizer would make the product too thick, sticky . . . and expensive to produce. By July 1965, after years of negotiations, tests and more negotiations with the industry, the FDA relented somewhat. The new proposed standard was 90 per cent peanuts and 10 per cent optional ingredients. *But* there was also a 3 per cent limit on hydrogenated vegetable oils (also called lard) as an optional ingredient, a restriction that upset Procter and Gamble, since it was and is the largest manufacturer of these vegetable oils. And the 90 per cent minimum upset the Peanut Butter Manufacturers Association, which wanted a minimum no higher than 87 per cent.

A peanut of an issue? Not to H. Thomas Austern, who treated the FDA hearing with the seriousness and attention of a Darrow contemplating evolution.

As lawyer to Procter and Gamble, he knew that the difference of a couple percentage points in this food standard meant millions of dollars to his client. One of Covington's lawyers on the case said of Austern, "His capacity for work is prodigious. Perhaps his greatest asset as a lawyer is his attention to detail. Absolutely every facet of the peanut-butter case was explored in the minutest detail."

There was more to Austern's lawyering than attention to legal detail. For he was unofficial chairman of the FDA bar in Washington —and he acted it. "He was always standing up, swaggering, leaning back and forth, pulling his pants up," observed an FDA official of Austern at the hearings. With one veteran FDA witness, he enjoyed the following cross-examination:

> Q: . . . do you recall where that phrase "honest and fair dealing in the interest of consumers" comes from?
> A: It comes from Section 401 of the [Food, Drug and Cosmetic] Act.

Q: You don't happen to remember who suggested that to
    Congress in 1938, do you?
A: I have been told that a young attorney by the name of H.
    Thomas Austern suggested that.
Q: I just wanted to test your historical interest, and I cannot
    suggest who the attorney was.

A light moment. But it was not so funny when he periodically complained off-the-record to FDA officials that "Coke got theirs; why
can't we get ours?"—referring to the way a cooperative FDA had not
insisted that Coca-Cola put its caffeine content on its label. The FDA
officials sternly ignored his badgering. But he didn't seem to get the
message. Another time, Austern privately called the peanut-butter
hearing examiner, William Brennan, in an effort to get a continuance,
and was admonished that such a contact was unethical. (An FDA
regulation now specifically forbids such ex parte communications.)
"The agency used to be small and informal," Brennan said later, "and
some oldtimers, such as Austern, haven't gotten out of the habit."

Austern acted bigger than life at the hearings, certainly bigger than
a mere hearing examiner, opposing counsel, or opposing witness. For
example, when Brennan announced at an October 4 prehearing conference that the hearings would begin November 1, Austern vigorously protested that it was an "impossibility" that he and his witness
could be ready in time. "Do you vote?" he asked Brennan. "I am
advised November 2 is also Election Day, which is a legal holiday.
Are you going to deprive my witnesses of their franchise, as well as
me of some other things?" He then elaborated his complaint, along
with a threat:

> I think it is outrageous that on this amount of notice that we
> should be asked to start the hearing. . . . I can't protest too hard
> that this is not only unprofessional, it is an imposition on counsel
> and I think the agency is acting in what I would regard as a high
> handed fashion and I have no restraint in saying that to the
> [FDA] Commissioner or to the [HEW] Secretary.

This complaint seemed overdrawn; after years of negotiations, the
November 1 date could hardly have taken him by surprise, especially
since the hearing date had been twice postponed. And he knew that

his witnesses could easily be prepared by the time the government finished presenting its extended case. Brennan rejected his request.

It was not only the hearing examiner that Austern treated like a summer clerk. There was also the FDA's opposing counsel, Michael Foley. The hearings were difficult for him. Young, inexperienced, and alone, Foley was pitted against twenty parties of record, represented by seasoned practitioners of the food and drug bar. Austern did not make it any easier for him. When Foley went to Austern's C&B office to work out some prehearing stipulations, Austern dismissed his two associates on the case and got down to business. "Listen Mike, if you are going to be stubborn, I can make trouble for you. I have the commissioner's [James Goddard's] ear"—to which Foley answered, "Go fuck yourself."

Neither lawyer emerged from this meeting with added respect or tolerance for the other. At another prehearing conference, Foley gave Austern only a limited list of the exhibits he would introduce, since the Covington lawyer had offered no list in return. Shortly thereafter Foley received a note from Commissioner Goddard's office asking why Austern had complained to Goddard personally that Foley was "concealing facts" and "had not done his homework." The young FDA lawyer was never given a chance to rebut these charges, which he first learned about in a memorandum saying that a meeting had already occurred between Austern and his superior.

Finally, Austern had to deal with the only consumer representative at the hearings—which he did with considerable professional hauteur. Ruth Desmond, the founder and president of the Federation of Homemakers, is a good-natured and persistent grandmother from Arlington, Virginia, who wanted peanut butter to have as many peanuts and as *little* hydrogenated vegetable oil as possible. But H. Thomas Austern is a persistent lawyer employed at that time to obtain as *much* hydrogenated vegetable oil as possible; and he does not like lay people in agency proceedings. As early as 1947 he had written: "Any person [in a hearing] may object, cross-examine, and, unfortunately, argue. The exciting discovery that one need not be a lawyer to cross-examine is too tempting; a secretly harbored conviction, that but for fate another Erskine was born, can be gratified."

The intervening eighteen years had apparently not mellowed the food and drug bard. For Austern consistently patronized and harassed Mrs. Desmond. Early in the proceedings he said to her, "Now our problem here, and I know that you have no affection for lawyers and I respect that . . . ," at which point she shot back: "My grandfather was a famous lawyer. I have respect and love for them. Maybe not food lawyers, but lawyers." Throughout the hearings he would say things such as, "When I read her document—sincerely appreciating that it was done without the assistance of counsel—and really nobody should act as his own lawyer," or "For the benefit of those present who haven't been tainted by a law school education . . ."

Beyond harassing banter there was intimidation. As with Brennan. As with Foley. Austern spent an unusual amount of time asking Mrs. Desmond about her group's tax-exempt status. It is unclear why private counsel would investigate the tax status of an intervening consumer group in a food-standard proceeding—other than to try to discourage such individuals from participation. Also, shortly before she took the stand as a witness, reports Mrs. Desmond, Austern privately cautioned her about the risks to herself and her federation that would result from perjury or libel. Such advice has a way of throwing cold water on candid testimony.

Another witness was George Mechling, the president of a small peanut-butter firm disagreeing with the industry line. He told how he refused to testify the first few times the FDA invited him because "several people" in the peanut-butter industry "indicated that it would be desirable not to testify" and said "it would certainly not be helpful to the position of the peanut-butter industry." Austern was impatient and distressed with this imputation. "I don't need anybody to admonish me on what are professional ethics," he said. "I am not involved in this. I had nothing to do with it. But since you are directing this broadly to every lawyer in this room I would like to say. . . I have a lot of ideas as to what is a proper and improper way to run a hearing, but I will reserve those to an appropriate time."

When he got down to the issues at hand—the 90 per cent peanut-butter standard and the 3 per cent hydrogenated oil maximum—Austern, as is his reputation, was painstakingly deliberate and careful about everything going into the record. Everything every witness said was carefully and s-l-o-w-l-y probed. How do you know consumers want to know the ingredients in peanut butter, he asked an FDA official? Because of letters we've received. Where are they? Exhibit 11-A. Can you cite me one specific letter? There are 2300 letters entered; the second one before me says, "Any substance other than peanuts and salt should be stated on the label." O.K., but what does "substance" mean to you? And so forth, and so forth. (Later a C&B lawyer on the case would privately say, "Jif labeled its ingredient as hydrogenated oil without indicating the new material. For obvious reasons P and G didn't want its customers to know that a derivative of cottonseeds was in their peanut butter.") When the chief of the FDA's Food Advisory Branch testified, Austern demanded that he bring in and identify all the consumer letters that might have shaped his conclusion—all 20,000 of them.*

Why such "unmerciful" diligence? It is second nature to a meticulous Austern; it builds up a record to file appeals; and it can wear down government lawyers or at least delay the day of decision—during which there is no 3 per cent encumbrance. "Perhaps one [strategy] was to browbeat the government into submission, but I can't say that with confidence," commented Richard Cappelli, a C&B lawyer working on the case. "Certainly there is something suspicious about a 24,000-page hearing transcript and close to 75,000 pages of documents on a case involving peanut butter."

The hearings covered four acrimonious months. Covington & Burling had three lawyers working full time before, during, and after the hearings ("I was immersed in peanut butter seven days a week, twelve hours per day," and Cappelli). Numerous other industry law-

---

* But Austern did not always measure up to his own stringent standards. When he introduced the results of a 24,000-person consumer-attitude survey—"We are very proud of this survey," he said—Foley asked Austern for all the original questionnaire replies. Turning to a co-counsel, Austern answered ". . . I want to cooperate with him [Foley]. Because I think, goodness knows, he has been taxed unmercifully in giving us what we need, and we may be taxed in the same fashion." But Austern later had to admit that the originals "had been lost in some warehouse since 1962." Foley could not resist an Austernian riposte: "It seems a shame to have had such a tremendous survey and then to lose the questionnaires. Someone would not be 'proud' of it." But at least Foley did not complain to C&B's management committee that Austern "had not done his homework."

yers were involved, especially Vincent Kleinfeld for the Peanut Butter
Manufacturers Association and Earl Spiker on behalf of Swift and
Company's Peter Pan. Although the hearings began seven years after
the FDA launched the peanut-butter inquiry, it took five more years
for the final FDA order to become effective, industry court appeals
delaying its final implementation. Elapsed time: twelve years. The
results read like the epilogue to Z:

• Mike Foley left the FDA in July 1969 to work for Abbott
Laboratories, a Covington & Burling client also represented by
Tommy Austern.

• Richard Cappelli fled C&B because of his peanut-butter work to
teach at the University of Puerto Rico.

• Tommy Austern continued to give speeches complaining that
"hearings often go on interminably" and warning law students to avoid
arrogance in their work: "Even though you went to Harvard Law
School," he told a Harvard audience, "never condescend . . . nor politic, nor threaten, nor go over the administration's head."

• The FDA successfully issued the 90 per cent peanut-butter minimum that the manufacturers had fought.

• Procter and Gamble, however, of all the intervening firms, got
what it wanted: the final peanut-butter standard promulgated in July
1968 and effective in April 1971 did *not* have the 3 per cent limitation on hydrogenated nonpeanut oil.

But precisely how Austern managed to defeat the 3 per cent standard is still something of a mystery. After the hearings Brennan proposed a standard that recommended it. When his ruling came out of
the FDA wringer, however, the hydrogenated-oil maximum was
missing. Foley says that FDA official Ben Gutterman admitted that
the final decision was based on material other than that in the record
but wouldn't state *what* material. Said one FDA lawyer close to the
case:

> Since it nowhere appears on the record why the change occurs
> and since the examiner is rarely overruled on such a determi-
> nation, there must have been an ex parte conference where he
> [Austern] convinced them of the lesser standard. Probably he
> told them that they didn't want the bother of having to contend

with him on appeal when they had other issues and companies [i.e., those fighting the 90 per cent standard] to deal with.

Austern had won the war, but the FDA may have won the procedural battle. In 1966, the FDA completely revised its rules regarding hearings. It added two new sections: one required all those involved in hearings to conduct themselves "with honor and dignity and observe judicial standards of practice and ethics" and "not indulge in offensive personalities, unseemly wrongdoing, or intemperate accusations or characterizations"; the second section required that a public record be made of the substance of any conversation between an official of the FDA and private individuals concerning matters involved in the public hearings.

Commandment V: Preferential Access—Access in Washington ranks somewhere between a valued asset and a sine qua non. *Dean James Landis in his 1960 report on regulatory agencies to the President-elect complained about "the existence of groups of lawyers, concentrated in Washington, itself, who implicitly hold out to clients that they have means of access to various regulatory agencies off the record."*

The privilege of being able to get through to government decision-makers can be obtained if you were once a powerful official, if you represent an important client, if you have a friend in high places—in a House subcommittee report, Congressman Morris Udall charged that Mudge, Rose, Guthrie & Alexander were chosen as counsel to the underwriters for a Post Office bond issue because of their association with, and access to, former firm lawyers like Richard Nixon and John Mitchell—or if you have bought the prerogative. "The Republican dinner this year [1969] cost five hundred dollars a plate, the Democratic dinner one hundred dollars," said a Washington lawyer, "and lots of lawyers in Washington have to pay that kind of money to keep the wheels well oiled for their clients, that is, to stay on friendly terms with the power centers."

None of this seems to bother one Washington veteran, who thought that "everybody gets somebody who is supposed to know somebody, so they all cancel each other out." Nor does preferential access concern Harvard law professor Abram Chayes, a former C&B lawyer *and State Department legal advisor: "Sure they wine and dine government officials, but what's wrong with it? . . . You must have a sense of history about this and what has been done in the past. In England the judges and lawyers used to ride circuit together, sharing the same hotel room. It unified the profession."**

Though the peanut-butter controversy commanded an undue amount of resources and attention, Tommy Austern and Covington & Burling did not earn their reputation on peanut butter alone. Their food industry advocacy is long-standing and broad-based. They represent or have represented not only Procter and Gamble but also Campbell Soup, ITT's Continental Baking, Foremost Dairies, Green Giant, the Institute of Shortening and Edible Oils, the Milk Industry Foundation, Nabisco, the National Brewing Company, Topps Chewing Gum, the Vitamin Products Company, J. B. Williams, the United States Brewers Association, American Can, and the National Canners Association.

Covington & Burling lawyers perform in various ways for these various groups. At the most general level, they can write articles discussing issues of client interest. Here is Austern, for example, lampooning an FDA proposal for nutritional labeling at a food-industry briefing: "I wonder whether the label of any food can effectively be converted into a nutritional handbook to be read in the bustle of supermarket shopping with one or more children tugging on Mama's dress."

There is also the situation of counseling of clients in matters of business judgment. A few years ago the United States Brewers Association had a problem. Heavy beer drinkers in Canada had contracted a strange heart disease tentatively traced to a cobaltous salt additive

---

* The use of preferential access became a subject of judicial inquiry in the unusual case of Georgia lawyer Robert Troutman against the Southern Railway. Southern got Troutman (who had roomed with Joe Kennedy, Jr., at Harvard) to see President John Kennedy four times in order to argue why the ICC should *lower* Southern's grain rates due to the efficiency of its "Big John" boxcars. Kennedy, his staff, and the Justice Department agreed, the latter joining with Southern in court to oppose the ICC. But Southern ungraciously refused to pay Troutman's bill of $200,000. It claimed he had not performed legal services and that it was against public policy to enforce a claim for political influence. A court disagreed, saying it was legitimate to use influence to gain access to argue one's case, so long as sinister influence did not later substitute for argument on the merits of the case.

found in their beer. The Canadian beer firms immediately ceased their inclusion of cobaltous salt in their beer. What, wondered the United States Brewers Association, should its position be? C&B strongly urged the group to voluntarily withdraw this food additive, and within a few days the 100-member association had agreed. When the FDA banned the additive in 1966, the industry had for months already ceased production of it. C&B's motives may have been noble, but, said Richard Merrill, one C&B lawyer on this case, the firm may have suggested the action because the brewers "couldn't tolerate the PR impact this story would have on their customers."

Covington lawyers also help prepare food clients for congressional or executive hearings that affect their interests. In one hearing, C&B focused less on a food client's product than on the human conditions of its production. The American Can Company, with a subsidiary there, runs Bellamy, Alabama, as a company town. In April 1968 the United States Civil Rights Commission held hearings in Montgomery, Alabama, into alleged racial discrimination by American Can. It seems that the company presided over segregated schools, swimming pools, and public bathrooms; all the company-owned homes of white employees had running water and bathrooms but only 7 per cent of black-employee homes did. Prior to the hearings, Covington's Jerome Ackerman, a forty-seven-year-old partner representing American Can, tried to dissuade the Civil Rights Commission from holding public hearings because of the "sensitive" issues involved and the possible "adverse reflection" on the company. This appeal predictably failed. But a more unusual tactic soon appeared. Plant officials called a special meeting of all firm employees the night before the hearings were to begin. At the meeting, plant manager Hugh C. Sloan read a letter prepared by Ackerman:

> . . . One of the things we expect the Commission to ask us is whether the company housing situation at Bellamy will be changed. Right now we are not sure what we will be able to do because of the cost and other problems.
>
> The recent Open Housing Law may force us to stop renting any houses to either white or colored employees in the near future, if it is not possible for us to make changes.
>
> All possibilities are now being considered. No final decision has been reached. . . .

The discovery of this letter left Howard Glickstein, then general counsel of the commission, livid. He considered it a clumsy attempt to intimidate federal witnesses by hinting that future housing hung on how and whether any of them testified at the next day's hearings. Assistant general counsel George Bradley thought that "the letter had a great deal of effect. The white employees blamed the black employees for all the trouble." Two witnesses did come forward (and both then left the company within the year). But afterwards Glickstein took the unusual step of visiting C&B senior partner Charles Horsky to protest Ackerman's role. "The company representation was so negative; they were resisting us the whole time," said Glickstein in an interview, adding that Ackerman "acted the way a lawyer representing a Mississippi sheriff would have been expected to act . . . not a lawyer from a highly reputable law firm."

Because of the nature of this civil-rights dispute, one Covington law clerk refused to work with Ackerman on the case; and Civil Rights Commission officials considered asking the D.C. Bar Association to discipline Ackerman, but eventually dropped the matter after they and American Can worked out a compliance settlement.

Although its counseling may vary, Covington's forte, as its peanut-butter success showed, remains its FDA practice. There it wields the handy combination of both experience and clout.

The FDA's vitamin hearings tested this combination. The Standards of Identity for Vitamins was a huge proceeding, the hearings alone lasting two years, 1968 and 1969. The FDA alleged that it was unnecessary and dangerous to ingest an excessive amount of certain vitamins and that some claims by vitamin manufacturers were false. The half-billion-dollar-a-year vitamin industry appeared not to be taking any chances when its own health was at stake. There were a total of 104 participants in the hearings and some thirty active lawyers. Covington had the largest contingent, with between two and seven lawyers there every day, including Herbert Dym, Paul Hoff, and Joseph Vining (representing the PMA and Squibb), Richard Herzog (representing the NCA and National Biscuit), Eugene Lambert (representing Abbott Laboratories) and senior partner Charles Horsky (representing the PMA).

Again, more interesting than what C&B argued was how they argued. The firm persistently challenged whether a senior FDA staff member, Sidney Weissenberg (also the Jif investigator), qualified as an "expert" witness. Weissenberg had been instrumental in drawing up the proposed vitamin regulations and was an unfriendly witness for the vitamin companies. After testifying for fifty-one straight days and being constantly grilled about his opinions and competence by C&B, he and Robert Anderson, the FDA lawyer in the hearing, settled on a little ploy to divert the industry's attack. Anderson asked Weissenberg if he had ever been consulted by industry lawyers on labeling requirements. Yes, he answered, and among others who sought out his "expert" advice were some four C&B clients *and* Tommy Austern of Covington & Burling.

Although Austern was a counsel of record in the hearings, he had not actively taken part—until he appeared a few days after the Weissenberg exchange intent on clearing, as he saw it, his firm's good name. He carefully cross-examined Weissenberg on each of their unextraordinary consultations, probing the time, issues, and extent of each meeting. He concluded with this (unsuccessful) appeal to the hearing examiner: "May I ask . . . that there be expunged from this record all references to individual lawyers or law firms on what happened at any individual conferences? . . . As far as what he said about my operations, I did not much care. But it is important professionally."

Anderson, thinking Weissenberg's revelation harmless, could not understand Austern's sensitivity. But the C&B contingent apparently disagreed. After the episode, one firm lawyer walked over to Anderson and said simply, "You're stunting your growth." It was a not-so-veiled threat that distressed Anderson. "Listen, I'm not going to stay here forever," he said, "and where do you think I'll go [later] with my expertise? To industry or these very law firms. I try not to let it affect my argument, but it is something which stays in the back of your mind."*

Nor was this all, complained Anderson. The C&B team would contact his witnesses without telling him, and would prolong cross-

---

* Today Anderson is a lawyer with the drug firm of Richardson-Merrell in New York City.

examination in order to slow down the proceedings. "There are conscious efforts to delay the hearings," he said. "It is a recognized technique since every day the regulations don't go into effect is another day of sales." The result was a 31,000-page dinosaur of a transcript, and a decision, after a decade of FDA study and hearings, that high-potency doses of vitamins A and D could only be taken by prescription. But the C&B phalanx did defeat the proposal which had most worried its clients: a label warning consumers that most people get all the vitamins they needed from their normal diet.

Covington's FDA food advocacy, and particularly Austern's, does not appear to command the professional respect that Austern says is the great goal of great lawyers. There were ex parte appeals to political higher-ups and the constantly articulated threat of such appeals, intimidation of government lawyers, intimidation of witnesses, and delay for delay's sake. To a certain extent, Austern succeeded in these tactics. "He had a great deal of influence in this agency. This agency is running scared of Tommy Austern," said one FDA official and Austern-watcher. Why? Because, he continued, the FDA leadership over the years have been involved in many compromises on close, controversial cases; and Austern knows where the bodies are buried. ("Coke got theirs; why can't we get ours?"). Just as a cornerstone of J. Edgar Hoover's power at the FBI rested on the awareness that he might have a file on *you,* Austern's power rests on his inside knowledge, so that agency officials may tread warily when confronting him.

But such machinations can meet resistance. One FDA hearing examiner (they are now called judges) is extremely suspicious of any Austern or C&B argument, checking every citation and assertion on his own—and finding some "erroneous or misleading." Former FDA commissioner Rankin (the one who deleted the 3-per-cent hydrogenated-vegetable-oil maximum) spoke generally when he castigated the food and drug bar to an industry group in 1969. "Your attorneys have helped make a mockery of the procedures for getting food standards," he said, subsequently elaborating his point:

> There is endless repetition of testimony, witnesses saying the same thing over and over. When several industry lawyers are in-

volved, they won't get together and let one of them do the cross-examining. Everyone has to speak. They'll ask for a recess of weeks to study documents that are put into evidence, even though the documents were available in advance. . . . And appeals to the courts at every stage: you set a hearing date, they ask a postponement, you deny it, they go to court. They seldom win, but everything stops while it is argued.

Austern himself claims to dislike this whole process, calling it "legislation by litigation." In fact, there are alternatives to food standards, standards which have the potential to frustrate new competition and new foods if definitions remain rigid. One alternative is to require strict labeling and grading of all food products, giving the consumer enough information at the point-of-purchase to decide whether he or she wants peanut spread, peanut brittle, or peanut butter. Austern, however, opposes greater labeling disclosure. He has consistently opposed them since he helped defeat Rexford Tugwell's attempt to get more accurate labeling into the 1938 Food, Drug and Cosmetic Act. During that battle, he exhorted his National Canners' clients "to sell the idea to other canners and to his representatives in Congress that this bill should not be permitted to pass. Don't try to do this by writing letters. It is a selling job that you have on your hands. You must go out and talk to people." Today he looks instead to a system of fewer government inspections and few public proceedings—what with all those bothersome consumer intervenors and feisty young FDA lawyers, and on the public record no less!* He has written that the FDA would do well to begin initiating the institutional secrecy characterizing the CIA and the Pentagon. "It is, of course, no secret," Austern has also written, "that the real questions in formulating food standards are not scientific or technical but ultimately economic and political." Thus he prefers a regime of more industry-agency collaboration to privately work out any necessary safeguards. As in the old days, when it was easier to disguise matters.

* On behalf of the National Canners, in 1962 Austern testified on Capitol Hill against a provision of the then-pending food-and-drug bill which would have authorized increased FDA inspections of cannery factory and equipment. A refusal to, in his words, "permit such unlimited ransacking of the files of a private business" would be a *crime*, he protested, quoting James Otis in 1777 against granting power that would "place the liberty of every man in the hands of every petty officer."

The Law of Smoke

I know you lawyers can, with ease
Twist words and meanings as you please;
That language, by your skill made pliant,
Will bend to favor every client.
                                        —John Gay

The heralded 1964 *Report of the Surgeon General on Smoking and Health* should hardly have come as a surprise. As early as 1604 King James I of England denounced smoking as "a custome lothesome to the eye, hatefull to the nose, harmefull to the braine, dangerous to the lungs" (although this view did not keep him from accepting import duties on Virginia tobacco). And in March 1857 the British medical journal the *Lancet* reported: "On the respiratory organs, [tobacco] acts by causing consumption, haemoptysis, and inflammatory condition of the mucous membrane of the larynx, trachea, and bronchae; ulceration of the larynx; short irritable cough; hurried breathing. The circulatory organs are affected by irritable heart circulation." But it was with the publication of the 1964 report—the product of a prestigious ten-person panel, screened by medical and tobacco people—that the link between smoking and health gained legitimacy and currency. Its conclusion: "Cigarette smoking is a health hazard of sufficient importance in the United States to warrant appropriate remedial action."

In the ten years since that pronouncement, no medical or scientific group in the world has disputed this conclusion. At least sixty-four have confirmed it and other researchers have elaborated the point. Former surgeon general William Stewart and Dr. E. Cuyler Hammond

147

of the American Cancer Society have both warned smokers that there are three hundred thousand cigarette-related deaths per year. The death rate for lung cancer is fifteen to thirty times greater for smokers than for nonsmokers, for oral cancer four times greater, and for chronic bronchitis and emphysema seven times higher. The death rate for coronary heart disease is 70 per cent higher for male smokers than for male nonsmokers. A twenty-five-year-old man who does not smoke has a life expectancy of 73.6 years; his peer who smokes two packs a day or more can expect to live 65.3 years, or some eight years less.

Tobacco smoke can also be dangerous and irritating to nonsmokers. One study showed that low exposures to carbon-monoxide concentrations—of the kind given off by cigarettes—can result in poorer performance on psychomotor tests, impaired visual discrimination, and physiologic stress in heart-disease patients. In another test 70 per cent of nonsmokers, when exposed to smokers, experienced eye irritation. Wayne State University researchers found that respiratory illnesses occurred twice as often in young children of parents who smoked at home as in those of parents who did not. Babies of mothers who smoke during pregnancy are about twice as likely to be aborted, to be stillborn, or to die soon after birth as babies of nonsmoking mothers.

"No one has ever convinced me that smoking is a hazard," says H. Thomas Austern, who chain-smokes Chesterfields.

In 1958 the major growers—firms such as Liggett and Meyers, Philip Morris, P. Lorillard, R. J. Reynolds—created the Tobacco Institute, Incorporated, a lobbying public-relations group with an undisclosed budget. "On the power chart of the pressure lobbies," columnist Marquis Childs wrote of this organization, "the Tobacco Institute rates not far behind the gun lobby, which is the untouchable top." The political emphasis of its operations emerges from the people chosen to head it: from 1958 to 1962, George V. Allen, former director of the United States Information Agency; from 1966 to 1970, Earl Clements, a former Kentucky senator and Lyndon Johnson ally; and from 1970 to the present, former North Carolina congressman

Horace Kornegay. The Institute's major mission is to rebut criticisms of the tobacco industry and to avoid bothersome regulation. This they were able to do without undue stress—until the surgeon general's report of 1964.

The surgeon general's report led to a Federal Trade Commission proposal to require health warnings on all cigarette packages and in cigarette advertising—a requirement hardly compatible with their promotional theme of romantic frolic. So, as an immediate response to the FTC move, the Tobacco Institute retained Abe Fortas, of Arnold, Fortas & Porter, and Covington & Burling's H. Thomas Austern.

The push for health warnings had been a bold move by a usually yawning FTC, but the commission had been jogged awake by health critics and the surgeon general's report. In reply, Austern and the Tobacco Institute argued that the FTC lacked authority to issue such a rule. Austern made his case diligently at the FTC's 1964 hearings, citing statutory language and legislative history. But the commissioners, also lawyers, became irritated by arguments they came to regard as contrived.

Austern's tactic was indeed a risky one, for only twice in history have congressional delegations of administrative power been overturned. "Lawyers who try to win cases by arguing that congressional delegations are unconstitutional," Kenneth Culp Davis has observed, "almost invariably do more harm than good to their clients' interests." Tobacco Institute leadership now agree, as one of their former members put it, that "this approach was a mistake. It just got the FTC hostile for the next round in 1969. Austern just failed to give us options." Two FTC commissioners were later asked how they would have reacted if the industry had voluntarily reduced its TV advertising 50 per cent. "They said they would not have insisted on a TV ban [on advertising] as they did later in 1969," said this former Institute spokesman.

As one chronicler of these 1964–1965 events, Ailee Fritschler, saw it, the industry's "opposition, although not well founded in prevailing opinions of the law, served to cast doubt on the Commission's authority and to make it clear that, should the Commission promulgate its proposed rule, there would be months of uncertainty as the issue was fought out in Congress, the courts, or both."

As it turned out, Austern's effort proved only a diversionary measure. The issue was ultimately fought out and resolved in Congress. (Austern did try to lobby several Commerce Committee staff people. But when they complained to Tobacco Institute officials that he was nagging and harassing them, Austern was recalled from the legislative arena.) Because the House Interstate and Foreign Commerce Committee was stacked with sympathetic southern-tobacco legislators, Congress proved a far more hospitable place to the industry than the FTC. Managing the congressional offensive were the savvy Fortas and former senator Clements—both of them blessed with a mentor in the White House (in Clements's case, the tie to Johnson was almost familial, as his daughter was Lady Bird Johnson's social secretary).

The congressional outcome was an unusual rebuke to the FTC. The Cigarette Lobbying and Advertising Act—duly signed by President Johnson on July 13, 1965—pre-empted the authority of the commission. The bill prohibited any federal or state agency from further regulating the tobacco industry for four years and it required a mild package (but not advertising) warning: "Caution: Cigarette Smoking May Be Hazardous to Your Health"—a warning which, by informing the smoker of the risk, also helped absolve cigarette firms in product-liability suits. "The bill is not, as its sponsors suggested, an example of congressional initiative to protect public health," wrote a critical Elizabeth Drew; "it is an unashamed act to protect private industry from government regulation."

But the law's protection did not guarantee perpetual immunity, as subsequent activities in the FCC, the courts, Congress, and the FTC were to show.

First to challenge the tobaccomen was the Federal Communications Commission.

On June 2, 1967, in response to a petition by a young New York lawyer, John Banzhaf, the FCC ruled 6–0 that cigarette commercials came within the scope of the 1949 Fairness Doctrine, since they expressed a point of view on a controversial subject of public importânce. Television stations therefore had to donate "roughly approximate" time for reply to antismoking groups, such as the American Cancer Society. This time was later officially determined to be the equivalent of one antismoking ad to every three cigarette ads.

The cigarette and network firms fought this ruling as if it were an economic Armageddon. By the time the case got to court, the constellation of legal luminaries gathered by industry was dazzling. Among others on the briefs, there were Howard Westwood, Ernest Jennes, Edgar Czarra, and Herbert Dym of Covington & Burling; Paul Porter, Abe Krash, and Daniel Rezneck of Arnold & Porter; and, almost inevitably, Lloyd Cutler. On behalf of the Tobacco Institute, Covington & Burling led the way by filing a petition for rehearing. This the FCC rejected on September 8, saying: "There is, we think, no question of the continuing obligation of a licensee who presents such commercials to devote a significant amount of time to informing his listeners of the other side of the matter—that however enjoyable smoking may be, it represents a habit which may cause or contribute to the early death of the user."

The decision triggered an unusual chain of events. Although C&B represented the tobacco people, Arnold & Porter were lawyers for the National Association of Broadcasters (NAB), who of course had an intimate pocketbook interest in the whole broadcasting-advertising issue. But the smoking alliance decided that the NAB, for reasons of standing and reputation, rather than the Tobacco Institute, should appeal the FCC ruling; and C&B's lawyers, especially Howard Westwood, were simply considered better technical lawyers than Arnold & Porter's. So there occurred one of the more interesting trades of the legal season: for purposes of this case, the NAB acquired Covington & Burling as its law firm and the Tobacco Institute got Arnold & Porter.

Although the FCC announced its decision on September 8, it hadn't made available any copies of the opinion—and such copies are usually required to file an appeal. But John Banzhaf, who had handled his own case, understood whom he was up against. To compensate, he hurried to Washington on a Saturday morning to appeal the FCC decision to the District of Columbia court of appeals. He *formally* appealed because the FCC only gave him "significant time" not "equal time" to air antismoking advertisements. In fact, he *actually* appealed because the appellant gets his choice of circuit courts and the District of Columbia circuit was far more liberal than Covington's expected choice, the fourth circuit in Richmond, Virginia, the heart of tobacco country. Covington later did appeal to the fourth circuit on September 13, the same day the FCC finally made copies of its opinion available.

Angry and chagrined at Banzhaf's procedural coup, Covington worked to dismiss the D.C. circuit petition and remove it to the fourth circuit. They argued that Banzhaf was actually defending, not appealing, that he wasn't a party in interest, and that because of the "unique and unprecedented aspect of a race to the courthouse . . . he began running before the starting gun had sounded." Covington exhibited its pique when firm-lawyer Edgar Czarra refused to agree to Banzhaf's request for more time in the preparation of his briefs on this point—a not unreasonable request, since Banzhaf was but a single attorney opposing ten law firms.

The D.C. circuit eventually allowed Banzhaf and his appeal to stay in its jurisdiction. It did this after hearing Banzhaf refer to the *Midwest Television* v. *FCC* case, in which Covington's Ernest Jennes did *exactly* the same thing as Banzhaf did here: lacking the FCC opinion, Jennes quickly appealed a decision that seemingly held in his client's favor, in order to locate himself in a favorable circuit court. Czarra in court appeared dismayed to find himself undone by his firm's own actions. Ultimately, after hearing the legal arguments on the merits of the case, the court upheld the FCC ruling.

Meanwhile, the industry's four-year congressional time-buy was running out, and it again had to face the problems of cigarette advertising and warnings. As before, the industry's lobbying was led by Earl Clements (Fortas having gone on to better and worse things). "When you have a guy like Clements, on a first name basis with most senators," said a former C&B associate, "you wouldn't want Austern to handle your communications with the Hill." Austern the lawyer; Clements the lobbyist and publicist. It was a standard bifurcation of responsibility, with C&B merely serving as the legal arm of the political body. But this raises the difficult issue of whether lawyers can or should ethically compartmentalize their advocacy, and not assume responsibility for client advocacy from which they are carefully insulated. Involved is a contradiction of clichés: Does the right hand not know what the left hand is doing? Or does one hand wash the other?

At the least an Austern should be curious about some of the Tobacco Institute's political and promotional forays. In 1967, two years after the first round of hearings, it was discovered that all doctors and professionals who had publicly criticized the surgeon general's report had been solicited by the Tobacco Institute. Their testimony had apparently been typed on the same typewriter, and most had been paid large fees by the institute. This surprised the Senate Commerce Committee, which had assumed that the professional opinions they had heard were unsullied by any financial ties to business.

At the 1969 hearings, when Tobacco Institute chairman Joseph P. Cullman III solemnly testified at a House Interstate and Foreign Commerce hearing that "the tobacco industry has been for many years and it continues to be profoundly conscious of questions raised concerning smoking and health," he failed to mention two examples of this consciousness. Three years before the institute had circulated, without identifying itself, one million copies of a *True* magazine prosmoking article that was written by a sportswriter and later employee of the institute's public-relations firm.* Nor did Cullman mention how the institute had hired Rosser Reeves, the public-relations tycoon, to write protobacco speeches for willing doctors and to pay sympathetic reporters one thousand dollars a week to write on preselected topics and to publish the results in their own journals.

By 1969 it had become obvious that the Senate Commerce Committee, no bastion of Southern tobacco interests, would no longer

---

* An FTC report describes the incident: "It would seem to be fair comment to say that the acts of retaining a free lance writer specializing in sports articles to write an article dealing with medical facts; promoting the acceptance of the article in *True Magazine* [sic] and then advertising excerpts therefrom favorable to the cigarette industry before a newspaper audience to read the article; failing to disclose in such advertising that tobacco interests, not *True Magazine*, phoned and paid for the advertising; posing as *True Magazine*, before the Am. Med. Assoc. and posing as the editors of *True*, before [eventually over a million readers] . . . are not the acts of an industry either confident of its facts nor solicitous of its reputation."

prohibit the FTC or FCC from cigarette regulation. Afraid of losing too much television revenue too precipitously (cigarette commercials at that time accounted for one-eighth of all television-ad revenues), the NAB proposed to phase out all smoking ads by 1973. The Tobacco Institute was at first furious at a concession that undermined their earlier arguments. But upon realizing that antismoking ads on television and radio hurt them more than their own commercials helped them, Cullman trumped the broadcasters by proposing to end all broadcast advertising by late 1970. Congress then passed a law requiring just that, which in turn angered NAB president Vincent Wasilowski. "It's no great sacrifice on [the tobacco industry's] part. . . . They will save $200 million with the full knowledge that consumption of cigarettes will not decrease." (Actually, the industry didn't save quite that much. Instead, they shifted mediums; between 1970 and 1971 they more than doubled their newspaper/magazine advertising budget, going from $64.2 million to $157.6 million.) The bill also required a new package label—"Warning: The Surgeon General has determined that cigarette smoking is dangerous to your health."

Throughout this congressional debate, the FTC was again holding its own proceedings on the smoking issue. Seeking a stronger warning than Congress eventually accepted, the commission referred to the evidence and reasoning of the 1967 Public Health Service report: "To say that smoking 'may be hazardous' is to ignore the overwhelming evidence that cigarette smoking is clearly hazardous to health." And it was based on the logic of inherently deceptive advertising, as best expressed by Dr. William Stewart, former surgeon general:

> In a reasonable world, any product which is both habit-forming and dangerous would be promoted with the greatest care and responsibility, if it were promoted at all. Cigarettes are that kind of product. . . . It is to our mind indefensible that cigarettes should be advertised, in a context of happiness, vigor, success and well-being, without even a hint appearing anywhere that the product may also lead to disease and death.

Tommy Austern's defense was sophistic and surprising: since everyone knew smoking was dangerous, he said, there was no need for health warnings to protect the consumer. Because this argument astonished Commissioner Philip Elman as he heard it *and* the Tobacco Institute when they found out about it, an extended reference to the transcript is appropriate:

> AUSTERN: The data I shall endeavor to summarize demonstrates that the current public awareness of the hazard in cigarette smoking is now potent.
> ELMAN: You mean to say everybody knows that cigarette smoking is dangerous to the health?
> AUSTERN: Yes, I will take it on that issue, sir.
>
> •   •   •   •
>
> AUSTERN: I suggest to you that the current public awareness of the hazards of smoking is potent . . .
> ELMAN: Are you going to proceed now on the premise which you hoped you convinced the Commission upon, that everybody knows that cigarette smoking is dangerous to health and may cause death from cancer and other diseases?
> AUSTERN: Precisely. There is such widespread public awareness of the hazards of smoking that the three bases that were advanced in that statement [proposed 1964 rule] are no longer valid.
>
> •   •   •   •
>
> AUSTERN: I suggest, Commissioner Jones, anyone not deaf and blind can today not be unaware of the hazards.
> ELMAN: If everyone knows that it is the position of the industry then just having it included in advertisements does not add to the knowledge of everybody, does it? Is that what this is all about?
> AUSTERN: I would be very happy to pass this on to my clients.
> ELMAN: I think you are making this proceeding really a little silly, if you present the controversy and the questions as we are dealing with in that form. I think there is really something substantial at stake here.

An article in the next day's *New York Times* by John Morris quoted the statement that anyone "not deaf and blind" today knows it's a hazard, and continued: "This was the first time that a tobacco industry spokesman had conceded any link between smoking and health." This reference took up about 15 per cent of the length of the entire article, whose headline, "FTC Challenged on Cigarette Ads," did not highlight it.

Nevertheless, Austern took umbrage and wrote the *Times'* James

Reston a five-page letter denouncing the article as "grossly inaccurate ... irresponsible ... misquoted ... out of context ... misleading ... completely inaccurate." The letter was aimed more at Austern's clients than at Morris or Reston. "There's no doubt about it," said an industry lawyer, "Tommy was scared they would fire him." For the cigarette manufacturers were furious that Austern had admitted the unmentionable: that smoking is dangerous.

To withdraw statements "misspoken" in public is a difficult task, as Austern uncomfortably discovered. First, he claimed that what he actually said to Commissioner Mary Gardiner Jones was "anyone not deaf or blind can today not be unaware of *charged* hazards." In fact, he was heard to say by those in attendance, "unaware of the hazards." Austern then criticized Morris's conclusion that he had admitted a link between smoking and health. "Inability to penetrate a legal argument is one thing. Reportorial distortion of a factual presentation, however inadvertent, is another," he wrote Reston, with more apparent application to himself than to Morris. Austern also denied saying more than two sentences in Morris's "interview"; actually, Austern spoke to Morris for five minutes, as a witness to these events, Stanley Cohen of *Advertising Age,* later confirmed. Finally, Austern contended that the article underplayed his point about FTC jurisdiction and overplayed his secondary point about the hazards of smoking. Yet anyone who heard or read the hearing's proceedings quickly realized that Austern did emphasize smoking's hazards, with the jurisdictional point getting briefer mention at the end—an order of priority he now seemed to regret.*

Austern then tried to change history a second time, in this instance with some success. He petitioned the FTC to allow him to alter his remarks as transcribed at the hearing. He claimed that the FTC reporter (like John Morris and everyone else at the hearing) had incorrectly heard and reported what he said. Austern claimed to have

---

* In his spacious C&B office looking out over the White House, Austern has the following quotation from Lewis Carroll's *Through the Looking Glass* featured prominently on his wall:

"When I use a word," Humpty Dumpty said in a rather scornful tone, "it means just what I choose it to mean—neither more nor less."

"The question is," said Alice, "whether you *can* make words mean so many different things."

listened to a trade reporter's tape recording which allegedly confirmed that he used qualifiers like "charged" or "asserted" whenever he discussed the dangers of smoking. But repeated attempts by the trade reporter to get the tapes returned, in order to check them against Austern's claim, failed. The Covington seigneur added that of course he had meant to say "asserted," a contention Elman rejected out-of-hand. "His whole point was that there was no need for a rule since 'we all knew it was dangerous'; the whole discussion was senseless if he meant 'asserted' danger." Considering the matter merely one of professional courtesy, the full commission allowed Austern to change the transcript. So despite a public bungling unworthy of a first-year law student in moot court, this Washington lawyer was still able to squeeze out of his dilemma by carefully applied appeals and belligerence. Elman, however, dissented in strong language:

> Changes should be made only to accord with what was actually said, not with what counsel later on thinks he should have said. . . . The question is whether we should allow retrospective doctoring of what in fact was said at the hearing, on both sides of the bench. The Federal Trade Commission, with its traditional concern for truthfulness and honesty, should be the last agency to tolerate any relaxation of the standards of accurate reporting.

The commission's act of clemency notwithstanding, Austern had clearly tripped in his own verbal tango. His ultimate difficulty, like the Tobacco Institute's, traced to the uncompromising denial that smoking actually was dangerous. But this public posture was not ordained, as Robert Wald indicated. Wald, the soft-spoken and thoughtful founder of Wald, Harkrader & Ross, then represented P. Lorillard and Company. He later explained his personal lawyer's ethic, one which contrasts with the "hired gun" approach embraced by many in the corporate bar: "In matters of public health and safety, a lawyer's role becomes more critical. If he sees a conflict between his client's interest (as the client views it) and the public's, he has a responsibility to broaden his client's perspective." Wald therefore thought some compromises would be in the interest of the industry and the public. "It is inevitable that TV advertising is going to end, one way or another. . . . The industry should have been making out an orderly withdrawal with the Congressional staffs and the agencies. Warren Magnuson and Bob Kennedy offered them some chance. Instead, the sentiment is to fight this down to the wire."

Austern could not broaden his client's perspective, perhaps because his own was so narrow. Nor is such an alternative mere star-gazing. The Tobacco Institute's intransigence on the danger issue led Hill & Knowlton, its public-relations firm, to drop it as a client.* The liquor industry voluntarily refuses to advertise over the airwaves. Wald's firm in fact did argue for the liquor-industry alternative to its cigarette clients. Arnold & Porter privately agreed but was not willing to go along publicly; Covington & Burling rejected it outright. "If these three firms had stood together on this one," one sympathetic tobacco attorney lamented, "we could have gotten the change."

The April 1, 1970, Public Health Smoking Act again usurped FTC authority to issue some of its intended regulations, but not all of them. The commission wanted cigarette advertising to disclose tar-and-nicotine content and to carry an even sterner warning than Congress required on cigarette packs; namely, "Warning: Cigarette Smoking is Dangerous to Health and May Cause Death from Cancer and Other Diseases." Death. Cancer. These were the scare words the industry couldn't abide. Representing it in extended negotiations with FTC lawyers were Austern and Horace Kornegay, the Tobacco Institute's president. One FTC lawyer recalled their negotiating sessions:

> Austern would be unbelievably overbearing, trying to intimidate staff lawyers *and* bureau chiefs. He's the Bobby Riggs of the law business, a hustler who trys to rattle you with all his Austernisms. He would tell [Robert] Pitofsky [former FTC head of the Bureau of Consumer Protection] that he didn't think there was anyone on the FTC who could handle such a big case against

---

* The Institute's problem was described by the *Wall Street Journal:*
But a tension developed between the agency and the Institute . . . the agency is said to have wanted to take a "positive" approach to the health controversy, conceding that smoking may in some cases be harmful but emphasizing the steps cigarette companies are taking to resolve the problem. . . .
Tobacco company lawyers, however, prevented Hill & Knowlton from carrying out such programs because they felt the campaigns would impair defenses against damage suits from cigarette smokers or their families. . . .
Because the lawyers prevailed, Hill & Knowlton's activities were limited to issuing defensive statements critical of health evidence and supplying pro-smoking literature to those who requested it, industry sources say.

him. Then he suddenly turned to me and demanded to know what I meant by my quizzical look. "You're like my students; I can't tell if you understand or not." And then Kornegay, a soft-spoken and polite Southerner, would try to work out something. A real Mutt and Jeff routine.

Although they were still unwilling to admit that smoking was dangerous, the industry did want to avoid the publicity and exposure of major public hearings. Thus, they decided, in effect, to switch rather than fight. In 1971 the domestic tobacco companies began to disclose tar-and-nicotine content in their advertising. In October 1972, as the settlement of an earlier FTC complaint, printed cigarette advertisements would henceforth contain the same warning that appeared on their packages. Like Pyrrhus's enemies, the industry came to understand how to win by losing—here by conceding small territories to keep the castle inviolate. Explained Allen Brauninger, the drafter of the FTC tar and nicotine standards and of the advertising regulations:

> They were masterful, getting delays and making the best of every situation. Only a small percentage of all smokers really care about tar and nicotine; they care about taste. And once the warning was on the package, its appearance on ads didn't matter much. The warning talks about "the Surgeon General has determined," which is wordy and, well, he's just a government bureaucrat and we all know about government bureaucrats. But it doesn't say that smoking causes death and cancer, that it has fatal consequences. The industry's gradualistic approach has conditioned the public to weak ads, so now I don't think anything will work.

Commandment III: Reconnaissance—"There are no secrets in Washington," said Washington lawyer-lobbyist Thomas Corcoran, with perhaps some understatement, "but there is such a thing as a three hours' head start. . . . All law is power and the law changes as the power balance changes. You work with your client so he won't be colliding with the government, so he will be running with the current, not against it." For example, Gulf and Western retained Washington counsel to watch out for legislation that could affect any of that conglom-

erate's many divisions. "There's just more going on there," fretted one G&W executive. Their lawyers will read the press releases of an agency, its reported decisions, an industry trade journal, a legal reporter. They will keep up contacts within the agency and keep book on new appointments. They practice pre-emptive law. For a legal world where agencies have so much discretion to make decisions (broadcast licenses are issued "in the public interest, convenience and necessity") and where a change in personnel can mean a change in policy ("the law changes as the power balance changes"), keeping a client informed is essential, tedious but essential. It is far preferable to avoid problems than to sue after they occur.

Representing a client with as inherently hazardous a product as tobacco has rankled some in Covington & Burling. Austern may be a true believer, but others are not. When the firm assigned associate Sally Payton to work on the appeal from the 1967 FCC order, she decided to tell Howard Westwood that for personal and political reasons she could not participate in the case. (Once in his commanding presence, however, she could not register her objections, as personal conviction accommodated institutional expectation.) In 1969 a summer clerk from Harvard, Virginia Coleman, refused to do research on a tobacco-related issue. And even Joel Barlow, a crusty senior partner not known for his concern over antisocial clients, was heard by a C&B lawyer to mutter, "I don't see why we have to represent those bastards."

But the firm does represent them, and not half-heartedly either. "At one time or another almost all of the permanent law clerks worked on tobacco problems," observed a law clerk in 1970. Their job, under supervision, was to predict and pre-empt potential trouble areas. For example, C&B and the industry were very concerned about state regulation subjecting cigarette manufacturing and distribution to the vicissitudes of varying and tough local laws. So Richard Merrill had a team of clerks in 1969 study the growing number of states proposing to place special taxes on the gross receipts of cigarette advertising. Christopher Buckley at the same time was sending a memorandum to the attorney general of Colorado successfully arguing that a legislative proposal to change the burden of proof in cigarette-liability cases was unconstitutional. Two firm attorneys were trying to change language in the *Third Restatement of Torts* which was considered damaging to the liability of cigarette manufacturers. And a slew of other clerks worked on a top-priority "massive legal memorandum," prepared in anticipation of an industry campaign to pre-empt completely state cigarette taxation by a scheme of federal taxation—a memorandum whose time has not yet come.

Drew Pearson once accused Covington & Burling of trying to discover a way to deprive the American Cancer Society of its tax exemption because of its political activities. Richard Stone, formerly with the firm and now in the solicitor general's office, vigorously denied the charge. Someone had mentioned it in jest, he said, and a naïve associate began work on it. "Do you really think our firm would do something like that?" he asked rhetorically. Apparently at least one associate did.

Finally, there were two Austern gambits, ones to surprise even his worst critics. Few assume that the world of Washington, Esq. is strictly governed by Marquis of Queensbury rules. But to Austern legal rules appear inconveniences, as he confuses client success with legal ethics.

In an arena where information reigns, Austern yearned to get the annual Public Health Services' (PHS) smoking data as soon as possible —perhaps even before its parent department, HEW, did. In the public-opinion arena of charge and answer, the shorter the rebuttal time the better for perennial rebutters like the Tobacco Institute. Consequently, Austern sent former C&B law clerk Jim Costello on a special assignment. Costello has told how he went to the PHS's National Institute of Smoking and Health in Bethesda, Maryland, to get then-undisclosed government data from a friendly C&B contact. He then traveled to another location in Bethesda to make copies of the material before returning them to the PHS contact; after this, he went home. Costello followed this plan for four days, he has said, getting material from a woman in her early twenties. The first day alone he reproduced a few hundred pages. But although the assignment was supposed to last two to three weeks, it was terminated without explanation after four days. They were "really scared of getting caught," said a law clerk.

Second, there is the computer. For the data-lorn such as Austern, a computer programmed with everything ever written on the subject of smoking and health was logical and, in retrospect, inevitable. Under the aegis of Austern and partner John Denniston (who can't stand anyone smoking in his presence), Covington & Burling since 1967 has operated such a supercomputer, mysteriously referred to in firm memoranda as "the 3i." Its purpose is to provide a near instantaneous reply to any public statement critical of their client's interest. But Austern also treats it as his toy. He will occasionally show it off to special visitors who are asked to raise a topical tobacco issue, and who then receive in response a rapid printout.

Why is this nonlegal entity operated by Covington & Burling, attorneys at law, rather than by the Tobacco Institute? Because Austern can claim it as his "work product" to keep the computer data from being legally "discovered" and used by an opposing party in litigation. Former associate Joseph Vining warned Austern in a memorandum that such a brash tactic could never convince a court. Nevertheless, Austern decided to retain the retrieval system under Covington's control, thereby exploiting an ethical privilege as a propaganda front. But by so doing he lays waste the bifurcation theory that supposedly shields Washington lawyers like himself from their client positions. For it now appears that he is less a good soldier than a commander-in-chief, helping organize the industry's public relations.

Austern and the Tobacco Institute; the Tobacco Institute and Austern. Like the animals and men in the last line of *Animal Farm,* they have grown so alike it is difficult to distinguish one from the other.

Car Counsel

Listen, Mr. Green. There is one point I want to make clear: we believe in the arguments that we make.—Lloyd Cutler

It has often been said that Americans are having a "love affair" with the automobile, or indeed that they are wedded to those sexy vehicles. This may have been true a half century or half decade ago, but no longer. For much of the public has effectively filed for a divorce on grounds of physical cruelty and expense.

In July 1973 an unnamed American established an inadvertent milestone and became the 2 millionth person killed in a car accident in our history—2 million people is more than twice as many as have died in all foreign wars combined; a record 56,056 died from auto accidents in 1973 alone. More than 1 hundred million Americans have been seriously injured in the past half century. The National Highway Traffic Safety Administration has placed the societal cost of 1971 motor-vehicle accidents at $46 billion—much of which cost existing technology could have avoided. A former General Motors engineer has shown how a car could be built for only $500 more than it costs today and "would be virtually fatality-proof in crashes up to fifty miles per hour." Yet Detroit did little about auto safety until forced to do so in 1966 by an impatient Congress.

In 1966 Lloyd Cutler wrote that "American cars—whatever their shortcomings—are among the world's safest . . . the automobile industry has made commendable progress in many aspects of automobile safety." To a reporter in 1969 Cutler said, "There are no more ethical companies in terms of business honesty than Kaiser or General Motors —despite [what critics see as] their social obtuseness."

163

The price paid for a car is not the only price paid: air pollution caused by motor vehicles, concludes the Office of Science and Technology, results in at least $6 billion annually in damages. Breakthroughs in engine and/or emission technology have come not from Detroit but Germany (Wankel) and Japan (Honda). It has been said that when the 1970 Clean Air Act was passed, Japan hired engineers, and Detroit hired lawyers.

General Motors, with annual sales of some $36 billion, produces more than one-half of all American cars. The largest three American firms—GM, Ford, and Chrysler—account for 83 per cent of all sales and 97 per cent of domestic-car sales. Professor John Kenneth Galbraith has said that the American automobile industry "is cited more often than any other as the classical manifestation of oligopoly." (When GM replied that it lacked market power, the Harvard don observed that for such a statement to "come from a wills and deeds lawyer in the most remote boondock would be surprising.") A Federal Trade Commission study reports that the industry's concentrated structure permits it to overcharge consumers $2.49 billion annually, or about $240 per car.

Lloyd Cutler had done work for the auto industry before 1966. In the mid-fifties, for example, he helped Kaiser Industries arrange to build auto plants in Argentina—a delicate negotiation involving financing by the Agency for International Development and an Argentine tariff monopoly for Kaiser. A decade later he occasionally advised General Motors which local defense lawyers to retain on the many product-liability cases filed against it. But if it is crisis that draws two people even closer together, Lloyd Cutler and General Motors really got to know each other in 1966, the year Detroit had a blowout.

In 1965 Senator Abraham Ribicoff's Executive Reorganization Subcommittee began holding hearings on auto safety, although the auto industry did not seem to share the subcommittee's concern. "If the drivers did everything they should," said Harry F. Barr, a GM vice-president, "there wouldn't be accidents, would there?" John Bugas, a Ford vice-president, later argued before the Senate Commerce Committee that *no* regulation was necessary, since the industry could regulate itself (a view which prompted Senator Maurine Neuberger to reply, "I say, 'Ha-ha' "). These views reflected the corporate hubris of being a (then) $40-billion-a-year industry and the only major transportation industry free of government regulation.

But by early 1966 the industry was backpedaling from Ralph Nader's *Unsafe at Any Speed* and GM's now well-known investigation of Nader. After much of the damage was done, Cutler registered as a lobbyist in April for the Automobile Manufacturers Association (now called the Motor Vehicle Manufacturers Association of the United States). "Lloyd Cutler was hired to pick up the pieces," observed White House advisor Joseph Califano, then deeply involved in the drafting and passage of an auto-safety bill. Columnist Drew Pearson agreed, but with a different emphasis:

> The smartest thing the Detroit motor moguls did in the auto safety hearings was to hire Lloyd Cutler as their attorney. Cutler is a close friend of Secretary of Commerce John T. Connor [formerly a president of the Merck drug house, and on the board of directors of General Motors] who will be entrusted with enforcing the safety standards if and when Congress writes them. Connor thought so highly of Cutler that he wanted to appoint him Undersecretary of Commerce.

The industry obviously needed a face-lift, and Cutler surgically provided it. As with the 1962 Drug Amendments, he and his clients realized that sentiment favored some auto-safety bill; they worked to make it as painless as possible. The Cutler impact was immediately noticeable to Paul Sitton of the Commerce Department, one of the initiators of the legislation: "Suddenly Bugas in the House was saying that he recognized the problems and the need for some legislation. He was really saying, 'We'll love you to death.' At the same time Cutler was meeting with us and saying, 'Let us sit down like reasonable men. . . . The industry are not criminals.' "

Cutler admirers see this performance as an example of the Washington lawyer's "civilizing" his corporate clients. And Cutler—along with Theodore Sorensen of New York's Paul, Weiss, Rifkind, Wharton & Garrison, who specially counseled GM president James Roche—did mellow their client's more outrageous posturings. But critics see this talk as simply a more genteel and circuitous route to the same destination: the weakest safety bill possible. "Lloyd would come over every day with new amendments to dilute the bill," said Sitton. "They were consistent, persistent attempts to undo the public purpose of the act." Paul Halpern, a political scientist writing a book about these events, said that "the AMA and Cutler told the press that they favored a bill when, in fact, they were trying to undermine it."

Whatever one's opinions about his purpose, Cutler's methods and arguments were clear. He enjoyed an easy access to the principles involved—in the White House, in the Commerce Department, and in the Congress. He saw Califano four times at the White House on the pending bill. Said a Commerce Department aide, "Whenever we got a letter or call from Cutler it was always returned promptly." And he spent a month talking to Secretary of Commerce Connor and general counsel Giles ("although," said this commerce aide, "he never got through with them since Boyd [Alan Boyd, then assistant secretary for transportation] and Sitton were really running the show"). In Congress he and associates lobbied the Senate Commerce Committee's staff intently, inundating them with scores of suggested amendments. Cutler also tried some cross-fertilization. He got another of his clients, Edward Kaiser, personally to call Senate Commerce Committee chairman Warren Magnuson on the bill. (In a later interview Cutler said that Kaiser Industries had an interest in the proposal since they produced jeeps in the United States. But when a Kaiser lobbyist was asked what interest his firm had on the auto-safety legislation, he said, "We had none.")

Some of Cutler's many arguments, in summary form, follow:

1. The AMA emphasized that safety standards should be set with the cooperation of the Vehicle Equipment Safety Commission (VESC), a multistate agency set up to develop similar standards. Cutler outlined the reasons in an unsigned memorandum to various senators:

> *Why VESC is Essential to the Federal Safety Program*
>
> 6. The states have a vital role to play in the field of vehicle safety—in developing and enforcing safety standards. . . . Accordingly, improved vehicle safety through the adoption of safety

standards requires a joint cooperative effort between the federal government and the states.

7. VESC is plainly the best mechanism for achieving this cooperation. . . .

10. We live in a *federal* system of government. . . .

But the VESC, first authorized by Congress in 1958, had taken four years to establish itself, had no full-time staff until early 1966, and had issued one safety standard in its history—a guideline on tires just as Congress was about to pass a tire bill. Paul Halpern wrote that "This wide attempt to sabotage the bill was so obvious that the AMA was literally laughed out of the hearing room." Califano agreed. "Cutler wanted to turn over the standard-making to these state safety groups," he said, "but further investigation showed VESC to be an industry shell, and they knew it."

2. Cutler initially made a series of other proposals, such as: different standards for different types of cars; a lead time of two years after the auto firms agreed on an improvement; any safety feature was to be, in the words of a Cutler memorandum to House Commerce Committee chairman Harley Staggers, "consistent with . . . efficient designing, engineering, and manufacturing practices, and with innovation, progressiveness and customary changes in the industry." All these would limit and slow down governmental authority to insist on minimal performance standards, and all but the first were rejected by Congress.

3. The original bill provided for a civil penalty of $1000 per substandard car, which the AMA feared could reach "staggering proportions." They proposed, instead, that there could be "some maximum limit," and that they believed "$100,000 for any related series of violations [was] a sufficient deterrent." (General Motors' net profit is $250,000 per *hour*.) The final bill had a ceiling of $400,000.

4. The industry sought an antitrust exemption to be allowed "to cooperate reasonably" in the safety area. The potential for mischief in such a legislative precedent dissuaded the bill's sponsors from accepting the AMA suggestions. The industry had hoped that such a congressional exemption would shield them from a potential (and later actual) antitrust suit for suppression of antipollutant exhaust devices.

5. Elizabeth Drew, writing in the *Atlantic Monthly,* commented on another of Cutler's amendments:

> For example, the Secretary of Commerce would not be about to order the industry to install a safety device which could not be made [according to Cutler's proposal]; yet to write into the legislation that he should not do so would burden the Secretary with the proof that a proposed device could be made, create more arguments, more delays, and more grounds for legal challenges that could postpone the setting of standards for years.

6. Cutler and the industry successfully fought to keep criminal penalties for willful safety violations out of the bill. At first Cutler did not strongly oppose them, believing such penalties unenforceable. But following losses on many of their amendments, Cutler and client considered criminal sanctions an issue that could not be compromised. Cutler argued generally that most statutes are either civil or criminal, that there was no incentive willfully to violate the law, and that his clients were surely not criminals (although the law would apply to hundreds of manufacturers and dealers, businessmen whom he could not ethically underwrite). Among others, Senator Vance Hartke disagreed with this view on the Senate floor:

> The simple question before us is whether or not we are going to subject a person who knowingly and willfully violates this act to criminal penalties. To ask this question is to answer it. The position that such a person be exempted from criminal penalties is indefensible in law, reason or morality. . . . It is a poor precedent to set in a policy of favoritism. Criminal behavior is criminal behavior whether done on a dark road or behind a corporate organization.

His colleagues, however, having already imposed the first serious legislated restrictions ever on the giant auto firms, shied away from rubbing salt into the wounded industry. The criminal provisions were defeated in committee and on the Senate floor. (Sometime after this provision was dropped, Cutler was talking to Ralph Nader about the problems of punishment and confinement in the system of criminal justice. "Now there's a problem," emphasized Cutler, "that you should look into." "It's easy," was Nader's reply. "Abolish criminal penalties.")

The Senate Commerce Committee favorably reported on an auto-safety bill on June 21, 1966. Majority Leader Mike Mansfield, in an action reflecting the issue's popularity, scheduled a floor vote for June 24. With only two days to prepare the necessary report, a harried Commerce Committee staff sat Cutler in one room and Nader in another and ran the committee print by each separately, since they represented the two sides of the controversy. Cutler was even allowed to draft two paragraphs, describing the industry's safety record, in the final committee report.

That summer the Traffic and Motor Vehicle Safety Act passed both Houses of Congress unanimously, and was signed into law by President Johnson. It created an agency to establish performance standards for cars and to require auto manufacturers in certain situations to send out "defect letters" to customers warning them about car defects.*

For this effort, Cutler earned substantial fees, and some substantial critics, too. Michael Pertschuk, as Senate Commerce Committee general counsel, observed Cutler throughout the entire episode. "He is clearly a very skilled advocate and a real technician at drafting amendment after amendment. He's a genius, but an evil genius. The role Lloyd Cutler plays reflects poorly on the legal profession since it is ex parte advocacy. It is not in the best tradition of the practice." And when a reporter asked Ralph Nader his view of Cutler's performance, he replied, "Mr. Cutler succeeded as a lobbyist but failed as a lawyer."

Not surprisingly, Cutler is sensitive to such criticisms. A year later in a speech before the Federal Bar Association, he complained that "the entire subject of traffic safety has too often been portrayed . . . as a fifteen-round world championship bout between the government —wearing white trunks and a white hat, and the automobile industry, wearing black trunks and a black hat." He later asked Pertschuk to

---

* When the infant National Traffic Safety Agency (NTSA) got GM to send out its first defect notices in late 1966, Cutler attempted to persuade the agency not to make these notices public because they contained trade secrets and were exempted from the reach of the Freedom of Information Act. NTSA's head, Dr. William Haddon, Jr., came under substantial pressure to keep the letters secret, but Senator Warren Magnuson resolved the issue by obtaining the notices and releasing them himself. A Haddon aide recalled that "Cutler was furious, absolutely livid. He called Haddon and gave him hell," Cutler assuming that Haddon had given Magnuson the materials.

give to Nader, without further comment, a copy of Canon 17 of the Canons of Ethics—the one which frowns on one lawyer criticizing another.

Commandment VI: Lobbying—An estimated 80 per cent of the largest U.S. companies either employ law firms or have set up their own offices for lobbying purposes. At the executive and regulatory agencies, some Washington lawyers ply the halls daily for their clients in off-the-record meetings with officials. Immediately after his resignation in 1969, FDA chief Herbert Ley complained about the "constant, tremendous, sometimes unmerciful pressure" from the drug lobby and predominantly its lawyers. One case where private meetings led to success was the favorable settlement of the AT&T–Western Electric antitrust case in 1956, when AT&T's lawyers met with Justice Department lawyers to hammer out an agreement in the quiet conviviality of hotel rooms in White Sulphur Springs, Virginia, and in Florida.

The Cliffords and the Corcorans also lobby Congress. (So do former members of Congress, as 124 of them—including many lawyers—have registered as lobbyists in the past twenty-five years.) Lawyer-lobbyists insist that they carefully avoid using influence— except, it seems, when it is necessary. An aide to the Senate Finance Committee described how the lawyers do it: "First they would try to convince us how fair it was for them to have a special exemption to some general tax provision added to the bill in committee. If that didn't work, they would urge that their company was being ruined by some unfair provision. Finally, they would start telling you how much business they were doing in your state."

Lobbying Congress can be quite creative. Abe Fortas, after his departure from the Supreme Court, persuaded a local minister to call a senator on a bill. The senator realized Fortas was behind the call, and hung up. Or consider the case of Tommy Corcoran (who once stunned a luncheon of Covington associates by blandly asserting that when big money is at stake, politics controls the law, not the other way around). Corcoran recently represented a drug firm seeking to water down a pending consumer-product-safety bill. He conscripted Rowland Kirks—who as chief administrative officer of the U.S. courts is directly responsible to Chief Justice Warren Burger—and the two visited House Majority Leader Carl Albert to complain that the bill would clog the courts in ways the chief justice wouldn't like. Unfortunately for them, Burger had never expressed such an opinion and knew nothing of their visit. He was reportedly not pleased.

Political lobbying by lawyers raises several problems. Lawyers are presumed to make legal arguments in public; but Congress is a world of politics and secrecy. To the extent lawyers have employed political arm-twisting in unpublicized visits, they may have violated traditional professional obligations. Former Canon 26 (a new professional code was promulgated in 1969) thought it "unprofessional for a lawyer so engaged [in legislative activities] to conceal his attorneyship, or to employ secret personal solicitations, or to use means other than those addressed to reason and understanding."

In 1967 the auto issue shifted from safety to smog.

California for years had been poisoning itself, exhausting such volumes of pollutants from its millions of automobiles that a carpet of smog had settled comfortably into the valleys of its large cities. Whereas the Environmental Protection Agency has estimated that auto pollution accounts for 52 per cent (by weight) of all air pollution, the figure reaches 90 per cent in California. The state's attempted solution: an amendment to the pending Air Quality Act of 1967 to readily permit California to set stricter exhaust emissions controls than had the federal government. This "California Waiver" was a bipartisan effort, introduced in the Senate by conservative Republican George Murphy and in the House by such California liberals as John Moss and Lionel Van Deerlin. The Senate bill passed with this provision intact and with little opposition.

It was in the House that Lloyd Cutler and Detroit accelerated their opposition to a proposal which—since California accounts for some 10 per cent of all auto purchases—could disrupt car design and production. The obvious goal was to defeat the Murphy amendment in the House Interstate and Foreign Commerce Committee, and then pass the Air Quality Act with a less effective California clause.

Cutler worked often with Thomas Mann, the former undersecretary of state and then the president of the Automobile Manufacturers Association; his access to the drafting stage of legislative history was again extraordinary. In October 1967 he sent Congressman John Dingell an unsigned memorandum, which was in turn circulated to industry supporters on the House Commerce Committee. The memorandum boldly took the form of a proposed House committee report, which Cutler hoped the committee would adopt. It urged hearings before the secretary of HEW to prove "compelling and extraordinary conditions," stringent testing procedures to document this need, and the finding that any enforcement procedures be "technologically practicable and economically feasible." Cutler also argued that it would be more efficient and rational for Washington, not the states, to set emission standards. Thus, while Cutler was a devout states-rights advocate when promoting VESC the prior year, he now had transfigured into a pragmatic federalist.

Why was the AMA memorandum secretly circulated among certain of the committee members? "They didn't want to be tied so closely to the drafting of the bill," asserted Austin Hogan, a legislative aide to a California congressman who managed to obtain a copy of the document. "To show that the special-interest group drafted the bill within the House Commerce committee would have been devastating." Nevertheless, the committee acquiesced to Cutler's suggestions and substituted the so-called Dingell amendment for the Murphy amendment. The two Californians on the committee, Congressmen Van Deerlin and Moss, were the only dissenters.*

But a floor fight seemed likely, as the entire thirty-seven-man California delegation wanted to reinstate the jettisoned "waiver"

---

* Representative Dingell is a person usually attentive to consumer problems; e.g., his work on the 1962 Kefauver-Harris drug bill. But he also represented a district in Detroit. This conflict and his resolution seemed to weigh on him, as did characterizations such as Drew Pearson's that he was an "auto industry lobbyist . . . guided by Lloyd Cutler." Three years later, Dingell was asked about the purpose of his amendments. "I wanted uniform standards throughout the country," he heatedly replied. "Phoenix has problems, so does Denver and New York City. I wanted one uniform standard." His inquirer, Larry Silverman, of the Center for Study of Responsive Law, then asked whether the Automobile Manufacturers Association agreed with this purpose. Dingell shouted, "Listen, sometimes you have to walk with the devil to get what you want," and stalked away.

provisions of the Murphy amendment. Cutler and Mann now walked the halls of the Hill. "He [Cutler] was spending night and day there," observed Joe Pollard, a Los Angeles lobbyist. "Whenever I would walk into an office, he would have just left."

One office Cutler walked into turned out to be one he should have walked by. With a lobbyist's courage Cutler went to see Congressman Van Deerlin of California, yet with a lobbyist's wile he brought along with him another client, Kaiser's representative in Washington, Walter Phair. Phair happened to be a friend of Van Deerlin's, and Kaiser had a large shipbuilding plant in San Diego, Van Deerlin's district. The meeting was a half hour late in starting due to a floor vote, with Cutler making it obvious he was annoyed at the delay. Finally, he, Phair, and John McLaren, Van Deerlin's administrative aide, drove over to the House in Kaiser's chauffeured car to meet Van Deerlin. McLaren later mused over the situation: "The effective lobbyist is a friendly, easy-going guy. It is just no way to win your point by being abrasive and snappish, letting one know your time is very valuable, and then by driving around the Hill in a *chauffeured* car."

The meeting flopped. Cutler was angry at being kept waiting and Van Deerlin was angry at the pressure implied by the presence of the representative of a powerful constituent. The incident led Van Deerlin to deliver a denunciation on the floor of the House (in the *Congressional Record* it was entitled "The Great Detroit Smog Caper"):

> For far too long, the automobile industry, swaggering through our House office buildings with highhanded lobbyists—some of them paid up to $100 an hour—has sought to impose auto management's selfish interests over the judgment of the American public. . . .
>
> Detroit wants a bill that will reduce controls to a minimum. And just as Detroit's carpetbaggers sought to destroy Ralph Nader, they now seek to smash the police powers of the states in a vital field of health and safety.
>
> I invite colleagues to join in rolling back the pall of smog these slick operators have sought to spread through this legislative Hall—to prove with their votes next week that Detroit is not the capital of the United States.

Phair later laughed about the "one-hundred-dollar-an-hour" fees lobbyists were paid; they were, he said, closer to two hundred dollars an hour.*

Eventually, the California delegation's floor fight succeeded. After thousands of letters from California had poured into Washington, the Murphy amendment, introduced on the floor by Congressman Moss, was resubstituted for the Dingell amendment by a vote of 152–58. The House then passed the entire Air Quality Act of 1967, 362–0. President Johnson signed the bill into law two weeks later, saying, "Either we stop poisoning our air—or we become a nation in gas masks, groping our way through dying cities and a wilderness of ghost towns."

Beginning in 1964, the Justice Department had been collecting data on an alleged conspiracy among the Big Four automobile manufacturers to suppress the development of exhaust-control devices which would minimize auto pollution. The investigation focused on "product-fixing," a vanguard interpretation of Sherman Act price-fixing strictures; and, given the auto's contribution to air pollution, it involved the health of all Americans, car owners and non-car-owners alike. The industry was noticeably concerned. As mentioned, Cutler had sought to attach an antitrust exemption to the 1966 Auto Safety Act to cover and condone the very type of cooperation at which the investigation was aimed. Not only was this not an idea whose time had come, but the contrary idea, that it be declared criminally illegal, was considered by a federal grand jury a year later. The grand jury heard a tale of industry collaboration to ensure that antipollution devices would be a long time coming. The minutes of an AMA 1955 meeting discussed how the car companies wanted to be sure that "no one company should be in a position to capitalize upon or obtain competitive advantage over the other companies in the industry as a result of its solution to this problem." One incriminating memorandum re-

---

* In an interview Cutler again said that the Kaiser representative appeared because of Kaiser's interest in this legislation. Van Deerlin and McLaren, however, stressed that at no time did Cutler or Phair discuss the impact of the bill on Kaiser Industries, and both understood Phair's presence to be a "whipsaw" tactic. Phair, a personal friend of Van Deerlin's, later admitted that he had been "embarrassed" by his participation in the meeting.

counted a talk a du Pont representative had with a Chrysler engineer in 1961:

> While admitting that favorable publicity would result, he was very forceful in telling me that if this was done Chrysler would be severely chastised by the rest of the Industry. *He reminded me that the AMA agreement says that no one company will gain any competitive advantage because of smog,* and that Chrysler was a relatively small cog in the industry. *He indicated that Ford and GM were calling the shots.* . . . . [Emphasis added.]

This and other evidence led the Antitrust Division team on the case to conclude:

> We are convinced that we have shown the grand jury and are in possession of evidence to prove beyond a reasonable doubt the existence of an industry-wide agreement and conspiracy among the auto manufacturers, through AMA, not to compete in the research, development, manufacture and installation of motor vehicle air pollution control devices for the purpose of achieving interminable delays, or at least delays as long as possible. The cross-licensing agreement was used as a cover and focal point of the conspiracy.

The grand jury agreed. In December 1967 it wanted to indict for conspiracy General Motors, Ford, Chrysler, American, the AMA, and eleven prominent officials of the Big Four.

Despite the magnitude of the alleged harm and the findings of the grand jury, Antitrust Division chief Donald Turner did not want the grand jury to bring criminal charges. Two years later, Turner wrote Ralph Nader:

> Without going into detail, which would not be appropriate anyway, I will note only that the joint research venture among the auto companies, though in my view unlawful (as the later civil suit charged), was not in the category of "per se" offenses, and that most of the alleged restricted agreements were arguably ancillary to the joint undertaking. I will not pretend that a reasonable man, particularly if he had a more evangelical approach to antitrust than I have, could not have decided differently, but that hardly indicates that the presentations of the companies' lawyers played a decisive role.

In a subsequent interview, Turner added that he thought he would have gotten convictions out of a Los Angeles jury, but that he didn't want this result in a case involving such a new theory.

Turner's successor (and now C&B partner), Edwin Zimmerman, did bring a *civil* suit against the Big Four and the AMA in the waning days of the Johnson Administration, on January 10, 1969. "Industry fought that tooth and nail," recalled former attorney general Ramsey Clark in an interview. "We had three separate meetings on it. . . . Cutler was at the meetings [as AMA's counsel] as was Ross Malone [for GM], whom I knew. It seemed that he was sent to make an *ad hominem* appeal." This time it didn't work. The complaint alleged that the companies, acting under the auspices of the AMA, had suppressed research, development, and application of pollution-control devices through the technique of a cross-licensing agreement; furthermore, the complaint charged that the agreement prohibited any firm from gaining a competitive advantage from developing antipollution devices and that at least on three occasions—in 1961, 1962, and 1964 —the companies attempted to delay installation of such control equipment.

Wilmer, Cutler & Pickering set out to obtain for the defendants a consent decree—an agreement settling a case where the defendants admit to no wrongdoing but promise never to do it again. One diversionary effort was made by Howard Willens of the firm, who tried unsuccessfully to convince officials at the National Air Pollution Control Administration that the cross-licensing agreement in question *aided* the effort to develop an efficient antipollution device. But the firm's main effort was to obtain a consent decree to settle the case without an adjudication of guilt, without publicity, without a decision which would be prima facie evidence for later plaintiffs in treble damage suits, and which would impound all the evidence collected in the Justice Department investigation.

Intense argument and persuasion by Cutler of the new Nixon Justice Department followed. It was of such persuasiveness that one Justice Department lawyer involved on the case (disagreeing with John McLaren) called him "hands down, the best lobbyist in Washington." By early September 1969 there were rumors of an imminent consent decree. "If these charges are true," wrote nineteen congress-men to Attorney General Mitchell, "the American people have a right to be fully informed of this outrageous corporate callousness by a full and open trial of the issues involved. . . . But we fear that the entire incident will be covered over by a legal deal arranged between the Department and the AMA's Washington counsel." A full and open trial, however, was precisely what the industry wanted to avoid. Candid industry memoranda revealing its anticompetitive collabora-tion could only have been publicly embarrassing.

The government too wanted a consent decree. The Antitrust Divi-sion's $10 million budget in 1969 was dwarfed by its assignment to monitor the corporate economy, and consent decrees saved it time and money—especially against an adversary as formidable as the auto companies. So negotiating sessions between Justice and Cutler con-tinued, in secret and without any public participation or scrutiny. Trade-offs conceded and arguments made could have been legal or political, economic or personal. But since fungus grows in unlit places, no nonparticipant could ever be sure.

On September 11, 1969, the department's and the industry's needs came together, and the Antitrust Division's Richard McLaren an-nounced that a decree along the lines sought by Cutler had been negotiated. The reaction from Congress, consumers and municipal-ities, eager to sue to recover air-pollution damage, was immediate and negative. Numerous interested parties sought to intervene in the district court proceeding to approve the decree, but they were denied the legal standing to do so. J. Lee Rankin of New York City, then that city's corporation counsel and earlier the U.S. solicitor general, expressed their frustration. "I feel this is one of the gravest cases in the history of this country in the antitrust field," Rankin said. "This involves not only price-fixing but the health of our people."

Cutler opened his argument before the district-court hearing on the consent decree by noting that "this is the first case that has ever been brought against an industry for trying to solve a public-health problem. . . . I want to return to the importance of getting on with the job of making progress in pollution, the job of scientists achiev-ing a major breakthrough." The judge agreed and upheld the decree as a final judgment. Nicholas von Hoffman, columnist for the *Washington Post,* was not happy:

> Eastern man, clubman, genteel man, but sharp and combative for all his good manners and politeness . . . Mr. Cutler had all the precedents; all the citations were over on his side because, for 70 years, all the money, all the most adept legal brains have gone into shaping and warping the law so the judge would say he was awfully sorry there was nothing he could do about the smog.

This episode also displeased seventeen law students from George Washington and Georgetown universities who, under the auspices of Ralph Nader, picketed the Washington offices of Wilmer, Cutler & Pickering. They carried signs reading, "Deadly pollutants are overcome by lawyer's ethics, not lawyer's retainers," and "Lloyd Cutler & General Motors. More air pollution for your lungs." A resolution they drew up stated, among other things, that

> WHEREAS, law students are taught that a public trial is a cherished right under the United States Constitution, not a process to be avoided by backstage, secret negotiations between highly paid attorneys and the Government, WHEREAS, law students are taught that the attorney is the keeper of his client's conscience and that the public is the lawyer's first client. . . .

The statement concluded that the firm should advise the AMA to seek an open trial on the allegations. If the AMA would not agree, the firm should sever its relationship with its client.

Unlike, for example, business firms and governments, lawyers are unaccustomed to being picketed. The novelty of this tactic, as well as its content, outraged Pickering and Cutler. The former got into a shouting match with the picketing students. Cutler, in a press release, said:

> Today's picketline is a prime example of McCarthyism—1950 style. The late Senator from Wisconsin also believed he had a divine monopoly on knowing where the public interest lies. His zeal led him, as it now leads Mr. Nader, to assail his fellow lawyers for defending the targets of his attacks. We defended some of Senator McCarthy's victims. In appropriate cases, we intend to continue defending clients who are attacked by Mr. Nader.

Cutler and the students also had a verbal exchange. *The New York Times* reported that "his hands trembled as he spoke," as Cutler told the picketing students they were "practicing McCarthyism in reverse. You are trying to drive lawyers away." Nader dismissed the McCarthy reference as overwrought. "There are such a cluster of obviously significant differences between these pickets and McCarthyism that only a lawyer's myopia can miss them," he said. "He [Cutler] understands neither free speech nor the enormous disease consequences of his client's pollution."

The picketing and the issue raised by it upset the firm's associates: just how *were* they serving their client—and the public? What was the lawyer's obligation in this conflicting area? "Like a lot of white liberals when challenged," explained one firm associate, "we were asking: why us, why not go after the bad guys?" Another firm lawyer admitted that many of the associates thought Cutler had seriously overreacted, and few liked his phrase "McCarthyism in reverse."

An unusual firm-wide meeting was quickly called. Cutler admitted that his antagonism at such criticism had been building up over a three-year period, and that he could not help venting it against the students, whom he thought did not fully understand the issue. Cutler discussed how he had defended people against McCarthyism and now felt as they must have felt: the victims of unjustified personal attacks. The meeting also focused at length on the kinds of interests which the firm represented or refused to represent because of a potential client's antisocial behavior. Cutler admitted, for example, that the firm had declined to help a gun manufacturer oppose gun-control legislation. Legislation to avoid death by guns was apparently different from legislation to avoid death by cars.

"The picketing was all that was on his mind," recalls Russell Phillips, then a firm lawyer. Beyond his press release, Cutler considered releasing a list of some of the firm's *pro bono* work as evidence that they were lawyers who had executed their public obligations. Such a list was sent essentially in response to a later Harvard Law student questionnaire. He called a Washington reporter to check if his newspaper was going to run an additional story on the incident; and he phoned Congressman Robert Eckhardt of Texas to thank him when the latter publicly criticized the students. Finally, he called John Mac-

Kenzie of the *Washington Post* to explain further his remarks at the picketing. "No, he doesn't regret his charges," MacKenzie said later, "he's only upset that he didn't make his point clearer."

Lloyd Cutler's automobile lawyering is not limited to off-the-record efforts in the Justice Department and Congress. As leading industry courtroom advocate, he again demonstrates the synergistic rewards of litigating issues under a law he helped shape.

The 1966 act, as Cutler's lobbying had sought, only required that defect letters for defective cars be sent to car owners, not that cars themselves had to be recalled. Even a letter was too much for GM in 1969 when the National Highway Safety Bureau (NHSB) wanted it to send defect letters to the owners of certain 1960–1965 GM trucks with defective wheels. GM claimed that the wheels would break only if the truck were loaded down with a camper; the NHSB had examples of wheels collapsing in normal use. With two class actions pending based on such collapses, GM was not eager to confirm any defects by a warning letter. The NHSB, for its part, was more than willing to avoid the expense and difficulty of an unprecedented evidentiary battle with the balking manufacturer. On October 9, 1969, they agreed on a settlement by which GM would replace the wheels on 50,000 of the 200,000 trucks, but not the other 150,000.

Unfortunately for both the company and agency, an NHSB engineering study was uncovered which showed wheel defects in *all* the trucks, not just one-fourth of them. Under pressure from a lawsuit by public-interest groups, represented by lawyers from Arnold & Porter and the Center for Law and Social Policy, the NHSB admitted its earlier agreement with GM was a "compromise."

GM was biding its time, waiting for the agency's final decision to compel the defect letters on all the trucks. When it came on November 4, GM, represented by Cutler, offered what one judge called "a reply of sorts": it filed suit in Delaware on November 6 to get a pre-enforcement review of the legality of the NHSB order. An opposing lawyer explained: "Delaware has as much relationship to this suit as does China. They're just 'forum shopping.'" The industry's lawyers claimed it sought the "calmer atmosphere" of Delaware, which is a very civil way of admitting the conventional wisdom of corporate lawyers: sue in Delaware because Delaware law and courts are usually kindly disposed to business interests.

Circuit court judge Caleb Wright listened to Cutler and others argue why they were in Delaware and why GM shouldn't send out those defect letters. But on December 21 Judge Wright dismissed the industry's case, effectively sending everyone back to the District of Columbia where the NHSB had itself filed suit. He concluded that the pending issue did not affect GM's current business, since it no longer sells trucks with the wheels in question. Therefore, Judge Wright added, "GM's counsel's allegations that present sales would be adversely affected by a defect notification is somewhat incredible to the Court. . . ."

"GM then swamped the government with paper," said a lawyer familiar with the proceeding back in the district court in Washington. "Discovery requests and more discovery requests—it goes on and on. They play on the fact that U.S. attorneys are very busy and can't keep up with their docket and make this task more difficult by filing technical and voluminous objections. And every day the truck owners are not notified is a day lost." Finally, on June 13, 1974, Judge Oliver Gasch ordered GM to send out the letters because "the uncontradicted evidence establishes that the wheel fails unpredictably and catastrophically in large numbers." Fining GM $100,000 for its negligence, Gasch added that "this case has been dragged out for a number of years, partly due to the action of the parties. . . . It is time that the consumer should be informed [of the safety-related defect]." Undaunted, Cutler quickly appealed Gasch's decision. The court of appeals ruled four months later that while it was deciding whether to order GM to send out the defect letters, the auto giant at least had to notify the truck owners about the fact of Judge Gasch's opinion. Elapsed time since the NHSB had ordered effective defect letters sent: four years.

Cutler is also involved, predictably, in the private antitrust suits resulting from the Justice Department's smog-conspiracy case. Many states, municipalities, and consumers were seeking compensation from the auto industry for damages caused by polluting cars. Some plaintiffs sought "original jurisdiction" in the Supreme Court in early 1972 to require the Big Four to "retrofit" all their cars with antipollution exhaust devices. In his half-hour Court argument, Cutler warned that his clients were even struggling to meet the 1975 and 1976 emissions deadlines of the 1970 Clean Air Act. "But if, on top of our obligations to meet standards on new cars, which none of us have yet figured out how to do, this Court, or any other court, would impose on us a substantial retrofit obligation, amounting to some billions of dollars on the production of 50 million units for that purpose, it might have a very substantial effect on the EPA program." His argument found a receptive audience in Chief Justice Warren Burger, who relieved himself of a Coolidge simplicity, "Aren't we all polluting the air in some way?" The Court eventually told the plaintiffs to file their cases in district courts, not the Supreme Court.

Since that ruling Cutler has won two smashing victories in civil suits over the smog issue. First, a court of appeals denied states, cities, and individuals the right to collect any damages since they weren't commercial enterprises, as required by the antitrust laws. This procedural ruling may have saved Cutler's clients hundreds of millions of dollars in eventual damages. Second, and even more important, district court judge Manuel Real refused to order Detroit to retrofit used cars with antiexhaust devices—what Cutler had claimed would be a $1 billion proposition. Judge Real criticized the automakers for their "less than spectacular" effort against pollution, and the way they "somewhat reluctantly undertook to alleviate the public pressures against smog by conduct that occasionally bordered on the legerdemain." But he concluded that the relief sought by twenty-eight states and numerous local authorities "go beyond the power of this court to grant." Plaintiff's lawyer David Shapiro was disappointed, saying that "the judge just wasn't going to go through a four-month trial." WC&P lawyers, on the other hand, attribute their success to Cutler's advocacy. During the first day of argument, Cutler took the position that Section 16 of the Clayton Act aimed to restore competition, not compensate victims. Judge Real initially seemed unimpressed, and co-counsel afterwards tried to persuade Cutler to drop this line of reasoning. But he plunged ahead with the same argument in more detail the next two days, this time with success. "He had the judge in the palm of his hand," marveled one firm lawyer, "and after the argument Ross Malone and the other co-counsel rushed up to pat him on the back because they knew they had won."

In a third litigation, Wilmer, Cutler & Pickering is representing Ford against the Department of Transportation's (DOT) proposals for the installation of "air bags." Air bags inflate to the size of two pillows 4/100 of a second after a car accident and form a protective cushion between motorists and the steering assembly, the windshield, and the instrument panel. They therefore prevent the "second collision" of driver against car interior, which is when most injuries and deaths occur. The idea is that when a car stops dead, the passengers won't.

By the late 1960s NHSB (which was renamed the National Highway Traffic Safety Administration in 1971) wanted a substitute for, or complement to, lap and harness seat belts. When worn they proved quite safe, but they were then worn only about one-seventh of the time. The agency looked to a "passive restraint system" such as the air bag, one which could provide protection without requiring the driver to do anything. It had been first explored, then dropped, by Ford and GM in 1957 and 1958 respectively. Subsequently, non-auto-industry innovators showed the air bag to be a valuable life-saving device. "Tests have proven conclusively that the air bag is superior to a harness restraint system," concluded the agency. "Baboon tests at speeds up to 60 mph indicated that these subjects could withstand this type of crash without injury with air bag restraints. Conversely, tests using an Air Force harness system resulted in death to about 50 per cent of the subject baboons at crash speeds of 55 mph." It was shown that the air-bag system cost the manufacturer only about fifty dollars to install. So in July 1969 the NHSB proposed a Motor Vehicle Safety Standard which would have required the auto firms to install air bags in all new model cars by January 1, 1972.

In a rare industry division, GM favored this approach (in part because it had developed far more experience and know-how about air bags by 1969 than had its competitors), but Ford, Chrysler, and American were opposed. Their insistent opposition succeeded in obtaining three DOT delays in the proposed date of implementation. And in May 1971 they (but not GM) filed suit. Representing Ford were both Lloyd Cutler and John Pickering, as well as two firm associates and a Cincinnati law firm. Their brief argued that air bags were less protective than seat belts, had been faultily tested, and were beyond the authority of the agency.

The case was argued on April 20, 1972, before the sixth circuit court of appeals in a typical public interest–private interest battle. Lowell Dodge, then head of the Center for Auto Safety, described the scene: "The court was divided into two halves, one for the government and one for industry. I wish I had a photograph to display the difference. There were two inexperienced and nervous government lawyers against easily twenty industry lawyers, with Cutler in the middle." Pickering made Ford's oral presentation (after furious bartering with the other plaintiffs, he got thirty-nine of the sixty available minutes). It was Cutler, however, who sat at the defense team's nerve center—listening, taking notes, passing on notes, tête-à-têting with Pickering, coordinating all troops, a legal general behind the front lines.

Few battles are conclusively decisive, and neither was this one. Like a judicious Solomon, the court agreed with Ford, Chrysler, and American that NHTSA's test dummies, and hence tests, had been "unobjective"; therefore it delayed any standard until new tests were run. But, on the other hand, the decision stated that the agency *did* have the authority to require the installation of such new technology. "There is no suggestion in the Act that developed technology be in use by an automobile manufacturer or that any given procedure be an established industry practice prior to its incorporation into a federal motor vehicle safety standard," the decision said. "If the Agency were so limited, it would have little discretion to accomplish its primary mission of reducing the deaths and injuries resulting from highway accidents." The court subsequently went on to comment that the Automobile Manufacturers Association had tried to attach an amendment to the 1966 legislation to require such "developed technology"; the court added that "we must decline to write into the Act the very same suggestions which Congress declined to write into the Act."

Although they lost this key contention, the American (and foreign) auto men did secure a delay in the date of air-bag installation. The industry had put off for a fourth time the final deadline for air bags (the new deadline is the fall of 1976). But the delay had a deadly cost, best understood by a simple though persuasive syllogism: real-world crashes of experimental cars with air bags showed that some drivers would have been killed if their cars had lacked air bags; these delays, then, effectively prevent millions of passengers from the benefits of air bags; therefore, thousands of people will needlessly die in auto crashes. The Department of Transportation estimated in August 1974 that equipping all cars with air bags would save 15,600 lives a year and result in one million fewer injuries.

Industry objection to air bags fits easily into a long tradition: when a health or safety breakthrough threatens industry investment and planning, it is opposed. It is as predictable as a law of physics: shatterproof windshield glass, functional bumpers, seat belts, antipollution exhaust devices, and air bags were all initially fought by the automakers. And leading the battle against the last two devices was Lloyd Cutler, who in the executive, congressional, and judicial branches of government exploited his considerable talents to avoid or delay these life-saving advances. Lawyers in such circumstances often escape culpability for the societal consequences of their acts by pointing out that they were merely following client orders. Cutler, however, cannot and does not use this rationale. Rather he argues that if air bags were prematurely installed in 1974 models, and they misfired, it would generate consumer hostility. Like many arguments, this one appears plausible; it is not for nothing that Lloyd Cutler earns some $250,000 annually. But his argument is unpersuasive because even GM had decided the air bag was workable, and in 1972 was planning to offer fifty thousand new cars with air bags beginning in the fall of 1973.

What is good enough for GM engineering should be good enough for Cutler. But he supported instead a client (Ford) who didn't believe in air bags, even though his other client (GM) did. As Lloyd Cutler once said with firmness in an interview, he believes in the arguments that he makes.

Planes and Trains

If the CAB didn't exist the airlines would have had to invent it, and as a matter of historical fact—they did.
—*Secor Browne, former CAB chairman*

For Icarus they weren't such friendly skies, but things have improved since his famous fall. Today more than 70 per cent of domestic intercity passengers who use common-carrier facilities travel by air; the number reaches 96 per cent for those who travel between the United States and abroad. For this the major American air carriers, with assets of some $13 billion, earned about $194 million after taxes in 1973.

Yet the assurances of United Airlines to the contrary, the skies are not invariably friendly to consumers either. First, there is the danger, as one airplane defect can involve many lives. Though the risk of death per mile traveled is far less than for car-driving, there is still risk, dramatic risk. It is the rare passenger who has never contemplated the hazards of flying as he or she whizzes by the clouds at 600 mph. In 1970–1973, 523 passengers lost their lives in crashes of domestic air carriers.

Second, airline practices do not always show concern for consumers. For example, a 1973 Civil Aeronautics Board study of "interline" tickets (those involving tickets on more than one airline) revealed that fully 21 per cent of the fares had been wrongly calculated, with the vast majority favoring the airlines. Airline critic Reuben Robertson has said that CAB statistics show that over five hundred thousand people holding tickets have been "bumped" off U.S. domestic flights in the past five years. In April 1974 *The New York Times* reported that "federal agents say they have uncovered evidence of an extensive, systematic air travel kickback scheme in which millions of dollars in illegal rebates have been secretly funneled by airlines to travel agents."

Third, there is the cost. A trio of observers have estimated that air fares could be reduced dramatically if there were price competition in this industry. For example, whereas the regulated (interstate) New York City to Washington shuttle (230 miles) costs $29.64, the unregulated (intrastate) Los Angeles to San Francisco plane trip (340 miles) costs $18.25. Air carriers therefore price themselves out of the market for many Americans, and at least 50 per cent of the U.S. population have never traveled by air.

The major reason for such high fares is a Civil Aeronautics Board sympathetic to the desires of the companies it regulates. Since its creation in 1938, the CAB has not certified any new national (non-regional) carriers; the original eighteen, however, have been permitted to shrink to eleven via mergers. It has never seriously investigated the international and domestic air cartels which establish price (the International Air Transport Association and the Air Transport Association) and it tolerates such anticompetitive practices as airlines' meeting to eliminate flights reciprocally on common routes. Peter Passell and Leonard Ross, when describing CAB chairman Robert Timm, saw the irony: "An ex-farmer who proclaims his faith in 'free enterprise' . . . he has called for more mergers, restrictive agreements and federally enforced price hikes to ensure the airlines a more generous profit."

In the mid-thirties American commercial aviation seemed hardly ordained for success. Air crashes, managerial ineptitude, loss of governmental postal contracts—the industry was clearly in trouble. In an effort at joint recovery, existing air carriers created a trade group, the Air Transport Association, in January 1938. They installed as chairman the dynamic Colonel Edgar Gorrell, a leader of American combat aviation on the Western Front in World War I. He in turn searched about for a lawyer to help salvage commercial aviation. Referred to a growing law firm known then as Covington, Burling,

Rublee, Acheson & Shorb, Gorrell remembered what followed: "Judge Covington assigned Mr. Westwood, of that office, to help me, not alone because of his knowledge of legal draftsmanship and his excellent ability as an attorney, but also because he was for some time law clerk to Mr. Justice Stone." Westwood—then just twenty-seven, a self-described socialist, and a member of the bar for only one year— threw himself into his new assignment. He soon "determined that the industry required, above all else, a legislative charter for its permanent economic regulation similar to the ICC regulation of railroad and motor carriers." Concluding that the only thing worse than government regulation was price competition—Gorrell kept calling it "cutthroat competition" to show what he thought of it—the two set out to secure government regulation.

They found a receptive executive branch, with President Franklin Roosevelt partial to government-business collaboration. Gorrell and Westwood, however, had to labor hard to persuade a skeptical Congress. Proposals to create a federal aviation agency to control rates, routes, and entry, writes Westwood, met stiff opposition from the Department of Commerce and the Post Office; these departments considered the proposals monopolistic. But the great flier and the young lawyer saw them as essential and testified so before both House and Senate committees. Gorrell told the House Commerce Committee in 1937 that "the great field of transportation, and the convenience of the public, may actually be subjected to a more serious threat from unbridled and irresponsible competition than from any danger of monopolistic control."

He elaborated his vision of a closed-enterprise system for the airlines: "We commend the principle of regulation dealing only with the fundamental matters of certificates of commerce and necessity, rate regulation, adherence to tariffs, supervision of accounts, and control over mergers." Westwood added in testimony that there should be "grandfather clauses" permitting the eighteen existing carriers to keep their routes automatically but requiring *new* competitors to prove their fitness. Thus did these advocates seem to support the thesis of historian Gabriel Kolko that economic regulation is desired by business rather than imposed by the public.

During testimony Colonel Gorrell carefully repeated that "the airline industry is not here initiating legislation," only giving its views. This was false modesty, indeed, for as it later came out, Gorrell and Westwood helped *write* the controversial legislation. In early 1937, at the Carlton Hotel in Washington, industry people, Interstate Commerce Commission officials, congressional aides and Howard Westwood met at nights and on weekends to produce an aviation-regulation bill. Missing were representatives from the Post Office and Commerce departments, the two agencies favoring competition over regulation. The Carlton group's final product evolved into the law creating the Civil Aeronautics Act of 1938. "It must be recognized that Congress does not lead in settling questions of public, political or economic policy," the American Legion's legislative section would sagely observe years later. "Legislation is literally made outside the halls of Congress by groups of persons interested in legislation, mainly with economic motives, and the deliberative process constitutes a sort of formal ratification."

Commandment VII: Law-writing—Members of Congress have an Office of the Legislative Counsel to draft bills, but this office is overworked and only knows what it is told. Consequently, burdened and weary legislators at times look to an expert lawyer to lend a hand. "Perhaps he can prepare helpful questions, or lines of questions that may be asked during the committee hearings," wrote Covington & Burling attorney Charles Horsky in The Washington Lawyer *(1952). "Possibly he can be useful in composing a committee report. Or, assuming that the bill has reached the floor of either house, he may assist a member of Congress in preparing a speech for their common position." For one example, Horsky's own law firm in the mid-1960s persuaded the House Small Business Committee to hold hearings on machine tools for the sake of its machine-tool clients. The committee finally agreed, as Covington drafted the statements of all the "independent" witnesses, wrote the committee's questions, and prepared the witnesses with answers.*

Outside lawyers can also draft actual language in legislation, a category Horsky omitted. H. Thomas Austern and the 1938 Food, Drug and Cosmetic Act; Howard Westwood and the 1938 Civil Aeronautics Act; Clark Clifford and the 1962 tax legislation concerning du Pont; Lloyd Cutler and the 1962 Drug Amendments and the 1966 Traffic and Motor Vehicle Safety Act—in each case, Washington lawyers were present at the creation.

Consider, for example, the dealings of two Covington lawyers in the arcane world of international law.

Senior partner John Laylin, on behalf of the American Mining Congress, drafted a pending bill to permit American mineral interests to exploit the ocean floor without regard to a proposed UN-sponsored, multilateral treaty to treat seabed resources as being jointly owned by all nations. Laylin not only inspired this legislation as a private lawyer but deftly promoted it as a public advocate, as he sits on influential panels such as the Committee on Oceanography and Treaty Law of the American Bar Association and the Committee on Deep Sea Mining of the International Law Association—influential panels whose members supposedly speak their disinterested minds. For this the six-thousand-member Federation of American Scientists has criticized Laylin. They have said that "the American Mining Congress bill is simply a special interest bill drafted by special interest lawyers," and, in reference to Laylin among others, have attacked "the pressure placed on the State Department not only to permit industrial interests to serve on the U.S. delegation to the Law of the Sea Conference but also to give their personal opinions to other delegations even when those opinions are at variance with the U.S. negotiating position."

When the Commerce Department had to write regulations for direct foreign investment, they turned to an advisory committee of some fifteen private lawyers and accountants to do it for them. During Christmas week 1968 the group helped draft regulations substantially increasing the amount certain firms could invest abroad. Prominent among this group of "advisors" was C&B attorney John Ellicott. According to an economist at the Office of Direct Foreign Investment, Ellicott represented clients before that office while serving on the committee. It is not every Washington lawyer, and none from proverbial Peoria, who can write the laws that affect the clients who pay him.

For most of the past forty years, Howard Westwood has been a leader of Covington & Burling and of the Washington aviation bar, despite (or perhaps because of) his infectious way of charming by alarming.

A self-professed maverick from the Midwest, Westwood, sixty-five, enjoys wearing his string tie to black-tie formals. Originally a socialist, Westwood campaigned for Norman Thomas in 1932—"and by God I thought he was going to win!" He attended Swarthmore and then Columbia Law School, clerked for Chief Justice Harlan Stone, went to the firm in 1934, and became a partner in 1936. "I addressed everyone, young and old, as Comrade," he recalls with amused pride, "and whistled the 'International' as I tramped the corridors." It is somewhat difficult to comprehend why a socialist would labor for such a bulwark of American capitalism, but in fact Westwood has been able to try out a version of his philosophy. In part because of his efforts, the airline industry has proved a major example of corporate socialism in America.

Westwood has developed a substantial *pro bono publico* reputation. He was chairman of Washington's Neighborhood Legal Services Program, sits on the Board of the National Legal Aid and Defenders Association, assisted in the legal struggle to stop the Office of Economic Opportunity from its attempted self-destruction in 1973, and helped break the color barrier at the Metropolitan Club by inviting a black judge, William Bryant, to lunch there. His other nonfirm passion is the Civil War; his office is strewn with Civil War *objets d'art*, books, and furniture. (A favorite Westwood ploy in interviewing applicants in his office is to mention a fictitious Civil War battle to see if he can nudge the interviewee to talk about a nonexistent event.)

Because of such pranks and his no-nonsense candor, associates quake before him. Yet they keep coming back for more assignments. Why? John McKenna, who worked with Westwood at C&B, thinks that "Covington has people who are very good, and some who are more than very good, like Westwood. He's incredibly imaginative, seeing things others simply don't, which is the sign of a great lawyer." Under that tough carapace, Westwood reciprocates the feeling and reveals his devotion to Covington & Burling: "It is this firm's proudest tradition," he said at an annual firm dinner, "that in the young lawyers is its strength, that in his [sic] development, in his assuming responsibility, in his seizing the reins the firm is made great and its greatness preserved."

Westwood has this kind of reverence for the firm and has contributed significantly to its growth and rank. In the three decades after the 1938 aeronautics act, C&B's aviation department hummed with activity. Teams of counsel under Westwood's direction represented the largest airlines in the country when they appeared before the CAB he had helped to create. Route awards, rate filings, freight operations —the firm fielded most phases of CAB work.

Three CAB cases involving three different clients exhibit the type of tasks Covington & Burling performed for their airlines.

Covington and Westwood defended the interests of American Airlines in the huge Southern-transportation case in the 1950s. The issue: what airlines should fly between certain cities in the Southern tier of the United States and the West Coast? Because of its "grandfather" award in 1938, American had obtained a monopoly on air traffic from the Northeast to the Southwest and from the Southwest to Los Angeles, with Dallas as the "hub." People in Florida or Georgia who wanted to go to California would go to Dallas via a small Southern carrier and then from Dallas to Los Angeles via American, since only American flew this route.

This plum was the envy of other airlines, who began complaining to the CAB that they wanted a slice. Although the airline industry is essentially a noncompetitive cartel, there can paradoxically be keen competition to obtain the lucrative routes. As early as October 1943 Braniff applied for a route from Dallas to the West Coast; in 1949 this proceeding expanded to include the question of Dallas-Southeast traffic as well. At this point Covington successfully urged American to adopt an affirmative strategy to protect its Dallas-to-California monopoly. American proposed an "interchange" with Delta and National to allow a single plane, shared by all three, though under American's aegis, to fly between the Southeast and California. In 1951 the CAB approved this plan, with one commissioner dissenting because the interchange "contrives and extends a monopoly [American's] over one of the heaviest route segments in the country."

But by the mid-fifties this compromise began disintegrating. Delta and National yearned for their own single-carrier service from Florida to California. With traffic expanding, the city of Dallas wanted more carriers to California. And Houston's civic pride led to its demand for a direct route to the West, rather than one going through the Dallas hub. Both Dallas and Houston filed for new routes to the west in 1956. Competing for these profitable routes and the Southeast-to-California direct routes were Braniff, Delta, Eastern, National, and TWA, as well as smaller regional airlines. "It was obvious to all in 1956 that it was only a matter of time before new competitors over the Dallas to the West route would be certified," said a former C&B lawyer on the case, "and it was obvious to most people that American had no real chance to obtain the larger prize of a single-carrier transcontinental route." American's monopoly, one of the few remaining from the 1938 days, seemed slated for extinction.

But the big issue was *when*. "Each month we could preserve American's position," admitted this Covington lawyer, "meant savings [revenues] to the airline of three to four million dollars." American was therefore in no hurry to push the proceedings along. In an interview one former CAB commissioner compared American's position with that of "a winning card player, looking out the window instead of dealing while the losers cry, 'Deal!' "

As one key stratagem, C&B moved in 1958 to consolidate all the pending route cases into one "Southern Transcontinental Service Case." Two years earlier American had *opposed* consolidation; now opposing counsel termed American's switch "an eleventh-hour effort which fully reveals its selfish private interests—even to the extent that it requires a complete reversal of position." Attorneys for the city of Dallas, which stood to lose needed passenger service by any delays, were even more sweeping in their charges:

> American Airlines has, throughout this proceeding, tried to delay consideration of the need for competitive service between Dallas and the West. . . . It took a year to bring [this case] from a prehearing conference to the Examiner's hearing. It has taken two years to bring it to its present stage, when it is approaching decision. Barely two weeks ago American again tried to stall

consideration by a motion to "supplement the record," which it well knew would require a reopening of the proceeding and additional hearing and argument.

The cases were consolidated into what *Aviation Week* called in 1959 "probably the last of the great domestic route contests." It wasn't until March 1961 that the CAB issued its decision. Delta and National were awarded transcontinental routes between Florida/Georgia/Alabama and California; the CAB gave Eastern Airlines the route from Dallas to Florida instead of authorizing American's expansion to Florida from Dallas. Former C&B lawyer J. William Doolittle wrote that these awards cost his client, American Airlines, some $50 million annually.

American had lost, in the long run. But in the short run Covington & Burling had helped hold off the day of decision for five years, which earned American (at $50 million annually) an impressive $250 million in revenues. For this and other tasks, American has paid Covington some staggering fees: $340,102 in 1958, $332,078 in 1959, $324,595 in 1960, and $316,613 in 1961.

In the *very* long run, however, it was C&B that lost out with American. For in 1964, after decades of mutual satisfaction, American and C&B parted. That year Covington partner Al Prather, who had come to handle most of the American account, left to form his own law firm with fellow C&B lawyers Gerald Levenberg, Ky Ewing, and Edwin Seeger. When Prather told American's then general counsel George Spater that he intended to strike out on his own, Spater said that American would go with him. It was rare enough for a Covington partner to abandon such a prominent position, but to cart off one of the firm's largest clients as well . . . It became the talk of the 1964 legal season. This hardly pleased Westwood and others at C&B but there was little they could do other than wish the departed all the best.

To Western Airlines, Covington and Burling was more than just its Washington counsel. Howard Westwood sat on its board of directors and held five hundred shares of its stock worth some $18,000; he was also a long-time friend of Western president Terrell Drinkwater.

In 1967 C&B associate Ernest Kaufman left the firm to become Western's vice-president for regulatory affairs. So when a takeover of Western was attempted in 1968 by entrepreneur Kirk Kerkorian, C&B and Western's anxious management mobilized to repel him.

Kerkorian made a tender offer to Western's shareholders of forty-five dollars a share when it was selling at thirty-six dollars. For many shareholders, this was tempting bait. By the end of 1968 Kerkorian held 1.4 million shares and $6.2 million worth of convertible debentures, which if converted gave him control of 30 per cent of Western's common stock. Adding insult to injury, he had obtained an unsecured loan of $68 million from the Bank of America to finance his takeover bid—the bank having been Western's principal banker for twenty-three years. In a firm in which no one shareholder held even 5 per cent of the stock, 30 per cent clearly gave Kerkorian operating control of Western. And it was unlikely he would reward or retain the management and the lawyers who had tried to turn him away.

Unable to prevent Kerkorian's stock success, Westwood, Peter Nickles, and William Allen of Covington turned to the CAB for help. On February 28, 1969, they filed a petition arguing that Kerkorian could not hold such substantial stock or sit on Western's board of directors without prior CAB approval. The CAB, they noted, must review airline acquisitions when made by someone *already* engaged in a "phase of aeronautics." Covington's briefs claimed that the fifty-year-old industrialist controlled an air carrier called Trans International Airlines, that he owned an aircraft dealer and an air-taxi service, and that junkets for patrons of his Las Vegas hotel and casino were the equivalent of an airline service. Westwood's brief hinted at the, well, unsavoriness of Kerkorian, who provided "air transportation and accommodations to selected patrons of the Flamingo who have substantial credit ratings and are known to enjoy gaming, called, in gaming parlance, 'high rollers.' " High rollers! Would you sell an airline to this man?

Kerkorian answered that he controlled nothing (not even Western, which was a little silly) and that he could buy legally into Western Airlines without the CAB's approval.

The CAB was not the only theater in this war. Kerkorian sued

Western in Delaware in February 1969 to get the company's shareholder lists in order to solicit proxies. On Capitol Hill Westwood testified before both Senate and House committees in support of bills to require prior CAB approval for the acquisition of a controlling interest by *any* person; Westwood, with a chutzpa a Kerkorian could only admire, even urged that the bill be made retroactive to December 1, 1968, so as to frustrate one Kirk Kerkorian. In addition, C&B lawyers and clerks pored over SEC records and magazine articles in an attempt to find material on stock dealings to discredit Kerkorian. "The partners were very anxious about the whole issue," said one law clerk. "Whenever we would come back from researching, they would immediately come into our offices and ask if we had found anything."

Covington apparently enjoyed a privileged access to the SEC process. Another law clerk reported that Westwood visited SEC chairman Hamer Budge, a friend, to warn him about possible misdealings by Kerkorian. "Lawyers were extremely tense as they awaited Kerkorian's filing of his proposed board," said a C&B member. "I called the SEC three times a day and even though I reached the SEC within a half hour of the filing, [C&B lawyer John] Ellicott was already there. He said he knew someone at SEC who called him as soon as the filing came in."

Covington had at least eight lawyers and law clerks working full time on the Kerkorian matter for the first three months of 1969. But all this, as it turned out, was wasted motion. On April 2, 1969, the CAB dismissed Western's request for a declaratory ruling because of insufficient evidence to support its charges that Kerkorian controlled firms involved in air traffic. On April 24 Western's management and Kerkorian reached a compromise which allowed the latter nine seats on the twenty-one-person board of directors. That same day Howard Westwood, after serving four years, resigned as a member of Western's board. Covington & Burling lost the Western Airlines account. Terrell Drinkwater resigned as chairman on May 31, 1970, and was succeeded by Kirk Kerkorian.

An airline client that C&B still represents, to the distress of some firm associates, in South African Airways. In 1968 and 1973, Covington helped SAA obtain two route certificates from the CAB. The 1968 proceeding was very routine. SAA—owned by the government of the Republic of South Africa, and operated as a governmental department—wanted a route for passengers, mail, and property between Johannesburg and New York City through Rio de Janeiro. Brice Clagett, Peter Nickles, and Cary Dickieson of Covington presented SAA's case to the board, their brief concluding: "Nor can there be any doubt that the proposed service is in the public interest." The CAB agreed 5–0, and President Lyndon Johnson—Presidents having final say over the granting of international routes—approved of the award on November 7, 1968, a mere four months after the application had been filed.

South Africa's 1973 application was anything but routine. The airline wanted a Johannesburg-to-New-York-City route via Sol Island and Las Palmas. But intervening in this proceeding was the fifteen-member Black Congressional Caucus, represented by the Lawyers Committee for Civil Rights under Law. They complained that South Africa was a racist country discriminating against black passengers and whose airline, as a result, did not deserve this route award. Clagett strongly objected to this intervention. He argued that "the alleged interest of the petitioners is based on political opposition towards the Government of the Republic of South Africa rather than on any matters involving air transportation. Petitioners alleged interest is founded on such matters as . . . 'the perpetration of colonialism and racism in Africa.'" Clagett especially protested providing any evidence concerning the internal affairs of the South African government. Yet, the administrative law judge in the case, Ross I. Newmann, allowed the Black Caucus to intervene in the proceeding and allowed the introduction of some evidence on the issue of SAA's alleged racial discrimination.

During the April 9, 1973, CAB hearing, it came out over Clagett's objections that the cafeterias and toilets at SAA terminals were segregated by race, but the restrictions only applied to *local* blacks, not *foreign* blacks. Also, of fifty-three SAA American employees, only two were black, and both were clerical workers. Undaunted, the Covington brief insisted that "the record is completely clear that no discrimination or segregation is applied to United States citizens traveling in foreign air transportation or, indeed, in domestic air travel in South Africa." (But black Americans should be able to quickly produce their passports to distinguish themselves from local blacks, for local policemen are neither color-blind nor genealogists.)

The case troubled the CAB commissioners, but they ultimately took the safe course by dismissing considerations of race as irrelevant. Their task was to assay an applicant's transportation capacity, not "the full range of facilities which may be used by U.S. citizens visiting a foreign country." The board added: "Such evaluation would necessarily inject the Board into the complex and delicate diplomatic questions affecting relations between the United States and a friendly foreign nation." Accordingly, the commissioners approved SAA's route request in early September 1973. On September 28 President Richard Nixon ratified their decision.

This was not Covington's only effort to ward off SAA's critics. During and after the first route proceeding, the New York State Division of Human Rights charged that "the Government of the Republic of South Africa, of which SAA is an instrumentality, has pursued a policy of racial discrimination in the disposition of applications for visas to such persons because of their race or color." The agency claimed jurisdiction over this foreign carrier because it flew in and out of New York's Kennedy Airport. South African Airways, with Brice Clagett as counsel, subsequently hauled the Human Rights Division into court to argue that New York State law did not apply to a foreign air carrier. And in 1970 the New York Supreme Court agreed.

SAA and C&B had prevailed, though at a price. Some associates refused to work for SAA, complaining intrafirm about Covington representing, on an ongoing basis, a racist client. Five associates met with the management committee to explain their concern. "They were very vague about it," reports one of the associates about the committee. "They said it was up to each individual lawyer, although they did draw a line and say it would be difficult for the firm to represent Nazis." At one firm meeting partner Robert Owen also objected to this client, which did not sit well with Dean Acheson, occasional defender of similar colonial interests. At a dinner in his house, Acheson "disapproved rather strongly to Owen's objecting to the case," recalled a C&B member there.

The problem is more difficult than for a Chase Manhattan Bank or a Polaroid that merely invest in South Africa. Since SAA is part of the South African government, Covington gets paid by, works directly for, and helps promote the interests of South Africa's apartheid regime. This does not upset Brice Clagett, an aristocratic Tory who has made it obvious to fellow lawyers that he does not particularly like black people. But Peter Nickles is a different story. He was one of the five associates to petition the management committee on SAA. He is a serious liberal sincerely dedicated to *pro bono* work as well as to his corporate clients. In 1968 Nickles represented the interests of a government which oppressed black people. In 1969 he became the chairman of the Neighborhood Legal Services Program (NLSP), a legal-aid society that combats the oppression of black people.

A contradiction? There are two polar views. On the one hand, lawyers, both corporate and American Civil Liberties Union lawyers, argue that a client is a client is a client, that Nickles was just doing his job as a professional. "Hell, I'm a lawyer, not a reformer," Covington partner John Laylin stressed to Joseph Goulden when discussing this case. SAA "got a little choosy about who[m] it would issue visas [to], as is its right. . . . But that isn't our business. I don't give a second thought to the matter." On the other hand, some see the issue not so much legally as politically and personally. Politically, what would NLSP's black clientele think if they realized that their defenders of today had toiled for their oppressors yesterday? One former C&B lawyer said, "There are certain fundamental principles to which this nation is committed, morally and legally, and here we were, trying to uphold an abominable violation of them." And personally, is there any canon of ethics that mandates that someone must devote part of his professional time helping those who live on the backs of black people?

By 1974 Covington & Burling's airline work had devolved to this: American Airlines, gone but for some minor chores; Western Airlines, gone; Panagra Airways, once a client but now merged into Braniff Airways, an Arnold & Porter client; South African Airways, an unloved client, but still a client. C&B had earned $139,184 from American in 1964; but by 1966 Prather, Levenberg & Seeger received $159,406 in American fees and Covington received so little the CAB did not report it. Whereas Western Airlines paid Covington $278,102 in 1969, its payments fell to zero in 1970. When a firm loses some $400,000 annually in fees, even when the firm is Covington & Burling, it is noticed.

There is occasional other air-travel work. The firm represented Beech Aircraft at a National Transportation Safety Board inquiry into a crash killing fifteen; it sought (unsuccessfully) a zoning change to permit a Washington-to-Baltimore helicopter route; and it represented the industry in CAB proceedings on the "mutual aid pact," which provides for intercarrier payments in case of a strike. But for a law firm with a partner who wrote the aeronautics act and counseled airline chairmen in the major proceedings of the past decades, this is small potatoes indeed. It may not reach the epic dimensions of a a *Buddenbrooks*, but Covington & Burling's airline representation—for reasons not entirely within its control—is the small story of the rise and fall of a part of a law firm that had once breathed the Olympian air of lawyering at the industrial pinnacle. It is part of the story of Covington & Burling in flux.

*   *   *

Covington's loss has been Lloyd Cutler's gain, for today he is one of American Airline's legal confidants. His counseling in the illegal-campaign-contributions case has been mentioned, but there are other instances of American conscripting Cutler to aid it on major industry issues. Take the proposed merger of American and Western airlines in 1970. This combination of the second and eighth largest domestic carriers would have created a firm with more than a fifth of the national airline market and combined revenues of $1.6 billion. Western Airlines wanted an injection of American Airlines money to buy a fleet of new, wide-bodied aircraft. American's chairman George Spater—predicting that American's pretax profits would jump $50

million after the merger—looked longingly at Western's leisure market
to Hawaii, Mexico, Las Vegas, and the Pacific Northwest. To ensure
this conclusion, Spater and Cutler launched a lobbying campaign impressive even for the well-traveled corridors of Washington agencies.

The strategy was simple: visit all agencies affecting transportation
to urge a common governmental position on the merger before the
CAB. Spater would make the personal appeal, and Cutler the legal
follow-up. A *"Fortune* 500" chairman; a prominent Washington lawyer. A one-two combination.

On November 5, 1970, six weeks before the parties formally filed
petitions at the CAB, Spater and J. Judson Taylor, Western's president, met privately with four of the five CAB members to tell them
of the upcoming filing. Spater made this announcement, urged the
agency to expedite their proceedings, and then moved quickly beyond
announcement to advocacy of the merits of his case:

> SPATER: Since we are not at the moment able to file a formal
> agreement with you, rather than have you get the information
> second hand we thought we would tell you everything we know
> about the arguments....

> > •   •   •   •

> SPATER: Now on some of the items you are interested in, accord-
> ing to our computations the size of the two companies will be
> less than that of United....

> > •   •   •   •

> TAYLOR: We believe the merger with American is not only in
> the public interest, better for the traveling public, but also for
> our shareholders and employees.

> > •   •   •   •

> GILLILAND (CAB vice-chairman): I think maybe as a matter of
> caution I better observe that although I realize the statements
> are made in the utmost good faith, that perhaps some things
> have been said that relate to the merits of the merger and
> those are things that we sooner or later will have to pass upon
> and we will have to forget what has been said on these points
> when the issues have come into focus before us eventually,
> although we appreciate the spirit in which these things have
> been said.

SPATER: I might say this, that I would regard what we said here
as in the nature of pleadings, and—
GILLILAND: Perhaps that is the way we will regard them.
SPATER: So we have no contention, I mean everything I said—
GILLILAND: I don't want to imply that we think of anyone having
been guilty of an impropriety here.

Gilliland's diplomatic caveat notwithstanding, he effectively told
Spater and Taylor that the commissioners would have to "forget"
everything they said. If such ex parte contacts occurred *after* the
merger's formal papers had been filed, the meeting under CAB regulations would have been clearly unethical if not corrupt. That it occurred shortly *before* the papers were filed, in an obvious effort to influence the thinking of the case's ultimate judges, did not reveal
respect for the spirit of the CAB's ex parte rules, or for the letter of
the rules either. It was Spater himself who conceded that he saw his
appearance as part of his case, saying "we would not have come before the Board except in the nature of submitting preliminary pleadings." Senator Lee Metcalf later mused about this meeting: "Now if I
could have the ear of the judge a month before I filed my case in
court, I think that I would be delighted to retire from the Senate
and practice law."

Shortly thereafter Cutler went with Spater to meet with Richard
McLaren, then assistant attorney general in charge of the Antitrust
Division. Spater denied that Cutler and he asked Justice not to oppose
the merger, although two months later the division did receive a
thirty-page memorandum supporting the merger from, jointly, Wilmer, Cutler & Pickering; Prather, Levenberg; Ernest Kaufman (for
Western); and Donald Turner as a consultant.

Saying hello to the CAB and the Antitrust Division were not
Spater's and Taylor's only activities of the week. They also made their
now ritual "courtesy call" on Peter Flanigan, President Nixon's liaison
with the business community and the regulatory agencies ("the man
who calls the aviation shots for the White House," according to *Airline Management*) and on Charles Baker, an assistant secretary at the
Department of Transportation (DOT).

Helping shape DOT policy on airline mergers, Charles Baker occupied a pivotal position in this controversy. Consequently, he received a key Cutler memorandum on January 5, 1971. Cutler argued that the DOT's legislative history looked to that agency as a unifier of executive-branch transportation policy. The government should speak with one voice before the CAB, said Cutler, and the DOT should be that voice. This message came to be reiterated by the American team, but it failed to persuade the trade press. William Henzey of *Airline Management* thought the DOT's fuzzy authority "makes it a target to be used by those who want to make end runs around the CAB and other transportation agencies." Said *Aviation Daily:*

> A DAILY analysis of the document concluded that it fails to establish legislative goals for such a DOT role in transportation mergers in general, and for airline mergers in particular. Nevertheless, in a negative sense, it has been successful. It has frustrated the Department of Justice's antitrust division in its efforts to oppose the American-Western deal.

It was in early 1971 that Spater combined his eagerness to gain approval of his pet merger with a misjudgment that led to his downfall two years later. In February he heard rumors that the White House opposed the merger. "So I went to [Secretary of Commerce Maurice] Stans—I had known him in another connection—asking him if he could find out whether it was true that the White House did oppose, to let me know if that was the case." Shortly thereafter, with the American-Western merger delicately pending, Spater met twice with Herbert Kalmbach to discuss campaign contributions to the Committee to Re-elect the President. Kalmbach asked for $100,-000, and Spater eventually and illegally gave $55,000 of corporate funds. (Later, before the Senate Watergate Committee, Spater was asked whether the pending merger "play[ed] any role in [his] decision to contribute this money to the Committee to Re-elect the President?" Spater answered, "I think I was motivated by a host of fears, and as I explained, it is impossible for me to add up, tabulate, all of the items that went into it.")

On March 24, 1971, Spater and Cutler met with Secretary of

Treasury John Connally. The next day Cutler wrote the secretary "with further reference to your meeting yesterday with Mr. George Spater." Connally received the entire package: Cutler's memo urging a unified executive-branch position, Cutler's memo to the Antitrust Division asserting the merger to be procompetitive, and Cutler's memo arguing that the merger was consistent with an earlier Presidential directive.

Why Connally? He had long-standing ties to American and especially to C. R. Smith, for many years president and board chairman of American. He was also the chairman of an ad hoc cabinet committee on the financial problems of the airlines. In addition Connally was a well-known proponent of the benefits of big business. And, of course, he had power to spare with an admiring Richard Nixon, who would have the ultimate say on this airline merger.

Spater's and Cutler's drumfire succeeded in inspiring transportation summitry. All their meetings and exhortations crescendoed into an unprecedented July 29, 1971, parley attended by Attorney General John Mitchell, his assistant Antitrust Division chief Richard McLaren, Secretary of the Treasury Connally, Presidential assistant Flanigan, DOT secretary John Volpe, his general counsel John Barnum, and Charles Baker. They met, said Mitchell, to see if they could agree on "an overall administration position."

It turned out that they couldn't. The Antitrust Division opposed the merger as anticompetitive and without "any significant cost reductions." The DOT exhibited a lukewarm affection for the merger because "the benefits of the merger are in even balance with its detriments." The CAB staff opposed the combination. They thought it might trigger other mergers and argued that it was contrary to CAB policy to allow two profitable air carriers to merge.

At the earlier CAB hearings in June 1971, George Spater had lavished praise on his merger, but exhibited the recollection of a Watergate Committee witness. When asked if he and Taylor had met November 5 with Baker, Spater denied it, although Taylor later acknowledged their get-together. When asked if American representatives had requested the Department of Justice not to oppose the merger and if American had submitted written presentations to DOT for the merger, Spater said no; of course the answer to both inquiries was yes, as Cutler could have told him. When asked by a union counsel what other meetings or conversations (other than with Flanigan, McLaren, Baker, and the commissioners) there had been between American Airlines and other representatives of the United States Government concerning this merger, Spater replied, "I can't recall any others." He then joked that he may have spoken to an air controller sometime. But the next day consumer lawyer Reuben Robertson, of the Aviation Consumer Action Project, reminded him during cross-examination of his conference with John Connally. Spater appeared stunned that Robertson knew of that meeting. Oh yes, Connally. We talked "about a great number of things affecting the airline industry and I am sure the merger was discussed." Cutler later said in an interview that after Spater's first day of testimony, he reminded Spater of his meeting with Connally. But until Robertson's unexpected disclosure, American Airlines and Cutler did nothing on their own to formally correct the false testimony.

Other parties to the proceeding were neither so bland nor so benign as Spater about this network of contacts. The Air Line Pilots Association filed a motion requesting a special hearing into all the American-Western politicking in Washington as well as locally around the country.* Lawyer Lee Hydeman of Continental Airlines criticized all the ex parte contacts as permitting "no opportunity to cross-examine." Hydeman thought there should be some sort of notification process about such hidden contacts so that other parties could talk to the same officials.

A million dollars in legal and lobbying fees later (Cutler's firm alone received $141,229 from American in 1971, according to CAB records), American and Western lost their case at the CAB. By a vote of 4–1 the commissioners rejected the proposed merger as disruptive to existing routes, anticompetitive, and hence not "consistent

---

* For example, the Seattle Chamber of Commerce at first recommended a neutral position on the merger. Spater sent a letter to the Seattle chamber's executive committee promising an employment increase of two hundred for Seattle if the merger was consummated. Thus enticed, the executive committee then overruled its transportation committee and put the Seattle Chamber of Commerce on the record as favoring the merger.

with the public interest." Spater had "overplayed his hand," said a lawyer for a competing airline. "He got the right doors open but failed to convince the right people that the merger was necessary." Al Prather, who handled most of the CAB hearing, afterwards lamented the role Cutler had played. "I thought it was dumb to take him on," said Prather in an interview. "It could only, of course, attract attention and critical consumer advocates. And it did."

The problem, ultimately, was one of content not access. But the special access Spater, Taylor, and Cutler enjoyed leaves a question unanswered: is this the best way to formulate transportation or merger policy? Before Senator Lee Metcalf's Senate Subcommittee on Intergovernmental Relations, Reuben Robertson answered no. "It is hard to see how proper decision-making could possibly take place in this kind of pressurized environment. The public can only lose when important proceedings continue to be undercut by extraneous, off-the-record influence." Cutler quickly answered that this was "an entirely erroneous conclusion." He said that the law looks to the DOT to coordinate transportation policy, including mergers; it is therefore not unusual for merger applicants to try to win over the DOT and other executive agencies. Apparently it is not unusual; but is it sound?, *Washington Star-News* reporter Steve Aug asked. "The intensive lobbying surrounding the American-Western merger—while not unlawful—raises questions of propriety. Lawyers associated with the matter point out that everybody does it—although not always at the highest levels of government—but one major difficulty is that such contacts provide government agencies with a one-sided view."

*   *   *

If American and Western Airlines have ceased to generate cash for Covington & Burling, the Penn Central Transportation Company has proven a gravy train for the law firm. And because Penn Central is prone to spectacular misadventure, C&B's activities have not been limited to routine route applications before the ICC.

One corner of the Penn Central story involves Executive Jet Aviation (EJA). It is the kind of case study business-school professors throw at their students to show how inane and intriguing American capitalism can be. But to law school professors it poses the dilemma of how much obedience a lawyer owes to a wayward client.

Created in 1964 by retired Brigadier General O. F. Lassiter— something of a combination of Bernie Cornfeld and King Farouk— EJA was an air-taxi company competing with corporate aircraft. Lassiter interested the Pennsylvania Railroad Company (not yet merged with the New York Central) to buy 57 per cent of EJA for $5 million through a wholly owned subsidiary, the American Contract Company. But EJA's modest purpose of shuttling corporate executives soon gave way to bigger plans. Lassiter collaborated with high Pennsy officials to create a "World Operating Rights" program. This grand design required the acquisition of several foreign carriers to form a world-wide air capacity. In all, the Pennsylvania sunk $21 million into Executive Jet, some of it for planes and some of it for Lassiter. The high-living brigadier general made up for all those years of Air Force austerity by spending $887,000 of EJA's and Pennsy's money on himself—a Manhattan apartment, a bedroom and sauna at EJA's Columbus, Ohio, headquarters, and huge traveling expenses for a fleet of comely girl friends.

But there was one problem with all this. Section 408 (a) (5) of the Federal Aviation Act specifically forbids the control of air carriers by railroads. EJA and Pennsy were well aware of this problem. Investigators of the House Banking and Currency Committee found this August 1969 memorandum in EJA's files: "The transaction was handled in this way [nonvoting stock] because of the fact that rail carriers, under the law, cannot become involved in the operation of air freight service. The whole project was undertaken, however, in the hope that Executive Jet would expand into the freight area and at some future date laws might be changed so that Penn Central would move in."

While waiting for a future law to erase their present illegality, EJA did not let the CAB know about its control by the Pennsylvania through the American Contract Company. But Pennsylvania's lawyers, Covington & Burling, *did* know about these shenanigans. On March 31, 1965, Hugh Cox told his client that the law specifically prohibits railroads from acquiring airlines. The Pennsylvania, through its assistant general counsel David Wilson, then displayed its appreciation of Cox's counsel by soliciting another legal opinion to legitimize what it was going to do anyway. Wilson sought out Bruce Sundlun, who happened to be the general counsel of Executive Jet Aviation, the firm depending on the railroad's money for survival. "As I explained to you, we would like to have an opinion covering the matters in question in order to permit us to consider the nature and extent of our relations with EJA in the future," wrote Wilson to Sundlun, concluding like a man with something to hide: "For reasons of policy, we would prefer that none of these questions be taken up either formally or informally at this particular time with the agency [CAB] or any of its staff people if our identity would have to be disclosed."

Sundlun obliged with the expected letter of exoneration. In an August 4, 1966, letter, however, Hugh Cox again warned that "if the CAB were to find that EJA was controlled by the Pennsylvania, it would undoubtedly not approve the acquisition of the supplemental air carrier since it would view the transaction as an acquisition by the Pennsylvania and the requirement of the second provision of Section 408 (b) of the Federal Aviation Act could not be met."

Nevertheless, with the panache and obstinacy of a salmon swimming upstream to its death, EJA pushed ahead with its plans to acquire Johnson Flying Service, a small Montana company with a valuable certificate as a supplemental carrier. But at the required CAB inquiry an opposing attorney stumbled across the fact EJA had neglected to mention: that the American Contract Company, EJA's controlling shareholder, was in fact controlled by the Pennsylvania Railroad Company. With this their house of intrigue began to collapse.

It is documented that Hugh Cox knew of his client's derelictions. A key CAB lawyer and investigator on the case thinks that other C&B lawyers also knew of the EJA-PRR tie although it was hidden from the CAB. In this situation Covington could have told its client: we will not participate in a plan to deceive the CAB; you pay us for our advice; you ignore our advice; good-bye. Instead, loyalty perhaps overwhelming wisdom, Messrs. Westwood, Clagett, Charles Miller,

and Chris Little appeared on January 23, 1967, on behalf of the
Pennsylvania and the America Contract companies to argue diligently
but unsuccessfully that the Penn Central was just another EJA in-
vestor. This failed to persuade either the hearing examiner or the
commissioners. In June 1967 the CAB disapproved of EJA's acquisition of Johnson Flying Service because Penn Central controlled the
acquirer. The CAB ordered a divestiture.

When further hearings in 1968 revealed the full sweep of EJA's
illegalities, the CAB decided that more than merely divestiture was
necessary. On October 14, 1969, the agency, with Westwood giving
his approval, settled all of the remaining issues. EJA promised to
stop violating the law with its illegal purchases of various air carriers;
Penn Central put all its EJA stock in a liquidating trust, to be disposed of by March 1971; for thirteen separate law violations, the two
firms were fined a total of $70,000 (PC, $65,000; EJA, $5000).
Although this was the second biggest fine in CAB history, it pre-
empted the far larger fines and jail sentences for perjury convictions
that CAB lawyers thought they could have won in court if there had
been no settlement. For a client noticeably lacking candor and verac-
ity, Penn Central had done well with Covington & Burling.

Cutler's railroad work spans three decades, from his involvement in
the Western Pacific and Seaboard railroad reorganizations in 1941
and 1942 to his representation of the U.S. Railway Association
(USRA) in 1974. The latter client is a federally financed corporation created by Congress to design a new Northeastern rail system
and to help finance its construction. Cutler's assignment is to defend
the act creating USRA against the claims of creditors, who say that
any reorganization which fails to fully satisfy their claims is an unconstitutional taking of property without just compensation—an
assignment not without some controversy.

Several Capitol Hill critics wonder why a private law firm is handling this case in the first place. The defense of the U.S. Railway
Association potentially involves billions of taxpayers' dollars in the
form of appropriated subsidies. Given such a public responsibility, it
is not clear why the Department of Transportation did not create a
special group of government lawyers to defend this government body

—which if nothing else would substitute reasonable government salaries for large legal fees to a private law firm. When the Department of Justice (for obviously different reasons) found it could not and should not prosecute the Watergate defendants, a Special Prosecutor's Office was chosen to represent the government, not, say, a law firm such as Covington & Burling.

There are also Cutler's alleged conflicts of interest in this episode. He is a director of the Norfolk and Western Railway, which will be directly affected by the result of the USRA contest. Several of its lines may be directly competing with those lines that emerge from USRA reorganization of existing Northeast track, and the Norfolk and Western may buy some of the surplus Northeast rail lines which USRA puts up for sale. Also, on May 3, 1971, Cutler accompanied the chairman of the Morgan Guaranty Trust Company to a House Banking and Currency Committee hearing which inquired into massive sales of Penn Central stock shortly before the railroad's 1970 bankruptcy. Morgan loaned the railroad $25 million in 1969 and would like to get its money back—a goal directly affected by the USRA litigation.

Cutler denies any conflict. He notes that both the government and Norfolk and Western were aware of his activities and neither objected. And he argues that his Morgan Guaranty work involved an issue different from any Penn Central issue in the present case. "It would be almost impossible to find lawyers who are in firms of any size," Cutler remarked in August 1974, ". . . in which one of your other clients didn't have some interest in the Penn Central. The question is whether we've worked for them in that interest. We haven't."

Woody Price and Bennet Gellman aren't so sure. Price, legislative aide to Congressman Brock Adams of Washington, the chief congressional author of the reorganization bill, asks not so rhetorically, "Why didn't Cutler simply resign his directorship and end the conflict?" Gellman, counsel to the House Banking and Currency Committee, thinks that Cutler's Morgan Guaranty and USRA representations involve a direct conflict of interest. "Everything is a different issue if you compartmentalize far enough," he said. "But Morgan Guaranty considered itself at that 1971 hearing a participant, due to its stock-

holding status in Penn Central, in the failure of Penn Central. Now
Morgan has sued USRA for one hundred cents on their dollar."

Despite this controversy, the lawsuit is moving inexorably toward
a final Supreme Court resolution on the constitutionality of USRA. As
the case winds its way through the legal labyrinth, Cutler earns $132
an hour for his time—and his firm billed USRA $268,146 for its first
four months' work in 1974 by Cutler and others.

A nice guy. That's what everyone tells you about Charles Horsky,
and it's no coincidence that Leo Durocher's famous aphorism comes
to mind. In a firm of strong-willed, unshy lawyers, the unassuming
Horsky has much respect but little power. "He's too nice a guy to be
a firm leader," said one firm ex-lawyer, "and he has no independent
client base."

Horsky, now sixty-four, like so many of Covington's senior partners, went to Harvard Law School. He then clerked for Judge
Augustus Hand in 1935, and joined the firm in 1937. Unlike a
unilinear Austern, Horsky has had many interests outside of Covington & Burling. He was an assistant prosecutor at Nuremberg in
1948 and wrote *The Washington Lawyer* in 1952, a graceful though
generalized account of Washington practice. It was a period of wide-
spread governmental and legal corruption, giving rise to the epithet
"influence peddler"—a connotation Horsky aimed to counter. (How
has Washington law practice changed in the twenty years since his
book? "Not a hell of a lot," answers Horsky.) In 1961 President
Kennedy appointed him a Presidential advisor for national-capital
affairs. In a then mayorless Washington, this post had substantial
impact. Yet this soft-spoken, pipe-puffing lawyer managed to irritate
nearly the whole range of the District's political spectrum. Horsky
fought often with conservative members of the House District Committee, who saw him as too progressive on city issues. On the other
hand, Senator Wayne Morse complained that he had bungled Home
Rule legislation and his efforts to influence local appointments, and
urged that Horsky be fired. Horsky resigned in January 1967, to be
succeeded by another former C&B lawyer, Stephen Pollak. The *Washington Evening Star* reported at the time that "White House sources

said that Pollak has been told to remain out of the limelight and not take as active a public role as did Horsky."

Today Horsky sits on the board of governors of the Unified District of Columbia Bar Association, is a member of the American Bar Association's committee on the federal judiciary (he was instrumental in getting the ABA to find G. Harold Carswell qualified to be a Supreme Court justice), and occasionally teaches at Virginia Law School. And he is the firm's lead lawyer on the huge Penn Central bankruptcy proceedings. EJA, however messy, had been just a boil on Penn Central's decaying body. But when Penn Central collapsed in 1970, the biggest bankrupt in American corporate history, its trustees would turn to Covington & Burling and Horsky for salvation—and for one of the largest legal efforts in American corporate history.

Stuart T. Saunders, former chairman of Penn Central, was the hard-driving man who steered the Johnson administration and the ICC into approving the merger of the Pennsylvania and New York Central railroads in 1967, the largest rail merger ever. For this, Saunders won the William Penn award in Philadelphia in 1968, *Saturday Review*'s "Businessman of the Year" award the next year, and the praise of *Time* magazine: "It was Saunders, the lawyer-turned-railroader, who convinced the Interstate Commerce Commission and the Justice Department that both public interest and private good would be helped if two troubled rivals were allowed to operate as a unit, instead of continuing and wasteful competition."

Instead, there was to be a continuing and wasteful monopoly, as Stuart Saunders discovered the accuracy of John Kennedy's observation that success has a thousand fathers but defeat is an orphan. For the Penn Central merger failed: the financial costs of the actual merger (some $75 million), the diseconomies of merging, the incompatibility of their computer systems, insider trading, irresponsible management, somnolent directors, and a dramatic shortage of cash converted Saunder's success into a bankrupt corporation on June 21, 1970. The corporation had lost $430 million in 1970 alone. On June 12, 1970, Stuart Saunders resigned as chairman, and *Time* made no mention of the fact.

Now began the bankruptcy proceedings. The railroad itself had a staff of twelve lawyers handling the more mundane problems. But Covington & Burling was one of three law firms specially retained by the Penn Central's trustees to figure out how to satisfy clamoring creditors yet keep the trains running. The trustees assigned C&B to work out reorganization problems generally and the railroad's relations with the New Haven line, a major creditor, specifically. Paul, Weiss, Rifkind, Wharton & Garrison of New York City had the job of selling off Penn Central's substantial Manhattan holdings; and Philadelphia's Blank, Rome, Klaus & Cominsky assisted on real-estate matters.* Yet including all the attorneys for Penn Central, the creditors and various intervenors, there were some proceedings involving more than a hundred lawyers. "This is a lawyer's dream," commented one SEC lawyer to Israel Shenker of *The New York Times.* "It's like peeling an onion. For each skin of the onion you need a new lawyer."

Covington's Penn Central team included Charles Horsky, Edwin Zimmerman, Brice Clagett, John Vandestar, Philip Stansbury, five other lawyers, and three paraprofessionals. Their assignment was to figure out how the Penn Central could be reorganized under Section 77 of the bankruptcy code. This issue spawned some fabulously lengthy and complex proceedings. By 1974 the case docket had grown to eighty volumes, some 60,000 pages which, when stacked together, were thirty-three feet high. On February 12, 1974, presiding judge John Fullam issued his 1465th court order. Covington & Burling's assignment required it to reconcile recurrent liquidity crises, union featherbedding and strikes, lost boxcars, 26,000 creditors with claims of $3.3 *billion,* and the basic question of whether a bankrupt utility could use its assets to finance its daily operating expenses without first satisfying

---

* There were many other law firms working on different parts of the case; Mudge, Rose, Guthrie & Alexander, for example, Richard Nixon's and John Mitchell's former law firm, tried to get a federal bail-out loan. A *Los Angeles Times* story uncovered Penn Central board minutes in which Stuart Saunders had said that Randolph Guthrie was "close to [the] White House" and had "been influential in negotiations over a loan." Guthrie denied this. But the appearance of influence-peddling stood out like a drunk at a wake. It became an embarrassment to both the corporation and the administration. "Who hired Guthrie?" DOT secretary John Volpe was quoted as saying. "End it now, with publicity." Guthrie remained Penn Central's lawyer, but the federal loan never materialized, being successfully blocked by congressional forces led by House Banking Committee chairman Wright Patman.

its creditors. There were not many possible resolutions to these problems: either the railroad would become self-sustaining after a reorganization, would receive massive federal aid, would be liquidated, or would be nationalized.

On February 15, 1972, the Covington team prepared a key trustees' document, "Report of Trustees on Reorganization Planning." Charles Horsky's brief answered an optimistic yes to the question of whether Penn Central could feasibly be reorganized. *If* the railroad could abandon unnecessary track, cut down on superfluous personnel, and charge adequately to cover passenger service, said the trustees and Covington, then a reorganization of Penn Central would succeed. Nationalization? God no. "The bill for it would be billions of dollars. It would embalm present inefficiencies and inadequacies. . . . We have developed an alternative to nationalization which requires simply tough, spartan, private self-discipline."

By the time of the ICC hearings in mid-1973, however, their projections were decidedly less rosy. "The Penn Central trustees maintain that, absent massive external financial aid, there is no likelihood that the debtors' rail operations can achieve any significant earning power." And in September 1973 the ICC concluded that the trustees' reorganization plan was inadequate.

On that count it was back to "Go" for Penn Central and Covington. But in terms of fees, the law firm was already streaking beyond Park Place and Boardwalk. It earned $113,611 from Penn Central in 1971, a whopping $890,633 in 1972, and $301,000 in 1973. It has been getting $80 per partner hour and $50 per associate hour. Precisely because C&B knew they would have to make their hourly fees public in this case, say some observers, they charged such relatively modest rates. The firm has garnered these huge fees for the kind of plodding workmanship that characterizes its lawyering. "They're not people who move things along," said a prominent East Coast lawyer in some disgust as he faced off with C&B in a Penn Central matter. "They don't tell you what time of day it is without consulting their clients or holding a firm meeting."

The problem is not only Covington particularly but proceedings like this generally. One SEC lawyer explained that "there's an enormous amount of duplication and make-work in bankruptcy cases. One lawyer writes a memo, numerous others review it, forty firms study it, and everybody petitions for compensation." Said another observer: "It's common to spend $10,000 worth of time pursuing a matter involving $2000 worth of case" (a point of view which once led an appeals court to protest the prospect of "the debtor emerging from bankruptcy only to reenter it after the lawyers are paid"). One ICC law judge, John P. Dodge, calculated what would be a reasonable hourly charge by comparing government and private lawyers and factoring-in overhead and profit; he came to $39 an hour, or one-half of the fee charged by Covington partners. ICC commissioner Kenneth Tuggle defended C&B by asserting the firm "turns them away at $125 an hour," a statement which baffled partner John Vandestar. "We have to turn away business because of potential conflict of interest," he said, "but that's the only basis. I've never heard of the $125 fiction. The statement is, of course, ridiculous."

There is something circular about the lawyers' role at a bankruptcy proceeding: they help distribute to creditors the bankrupt's assets, which rapidly decline because of the large fees of the lawyers. "I feel very strongly that it's a mistake to allow this sort of procedure to be handled as though it were litigation between private parties," said Professor Vern Countryman of Harvard Law School, "to look to lawyers representing large private interests for assistance in the reorganization and then to compensate them out of the estate for their services." But the head of Penn Central's legal staff, Robert Blanchette, doubted that "there is a basis in fact for cramming a public-service orientation on a law firm. A lot of these firms do a substantial amount of work for indigent clients and legal-aid work. Why should they charge the Penn Central less than they charge a normal client?"

The ICC, however—with the legal authority to reduce attorney's fees in railroad bankruptcies—to an extent disagreed with the presumed answer to this rhetorical question. For at least a three-month period in 1973 the ICC knocked down Covington's request for fees by 25 per cent, from $126,347.50 to $95,000. On September 4, 1973, the agency took time to reduce one C&B request for compensation from $3270 to $2747 because "the sum sought is not justified in light of the evidence of record at this time, particularly in view of debtor's current financial condition."*

Controversies and fees aside, one thing is clear: Cutler and Covington may not affect *where* Americans travel, but they help determine *how* they get there. Cutler with cars, Cutler and Covington with respect to airlines and-trains—Washington lawyers affect the design, safety, routes, and costs of much of American transportation. Americans are paying above-competitive rates for their air transportation because of the work of wily Washington lawyers. Paraphrasing Secor Browne (who was paraphrasing Voltaire), if Washington lawyers didn't exist, the transportation industry would have to invent them. And who can say they couldn't have counseled even Icarus to safety?

---

* Penn Central is, to be sure, Covington's most interesting and lucrative railroad client, but not its only one. The firm represents Southern Railway in a variety of tasks, for which C&B earned $216,158 in 1971 and $114,698 in 1972. For those who think Washington superlawyering involves only great national issues, consider the description of one Southern Railway assignment by firm lawyer Allen Dougherty: "Tax research on deductibility of railroad grading which has been abandoned but not destroyed. Southern had a spur line to a mine which ran out." More than merely representing Southern, Covington has staffed it. Southern's president, W. Graham Claytor, Jr., once law clerk to Justice Brandeis and Judge Learned Hand and now one of the dominant voices in American railroading, was a firm partner until his switchover in 1969; other former C&B lawyers working in Southern executive and legal positions include Peter Craig, Earl Schramm, and formerly John McKenna.

The Media Lawyers

*It's the old cry of the administrator saying, "please for-
get your clients and make my administration more
effective." Utter nonsense. . . . I have news for Dean
Burch: I'm going to try a case in a way that is best for
my client and take advantage of every rule that's
there.*

—Washington lawyer quoted in
The Washington Monthly

When Spiro Agnew and Nicholas Johnson were both
clobbering television in the early 1970s, some neutral observers concluded that the networks must have been doing something right. They
were.

The Average American Adult watches television about twenty-five
hours a week, or roughly nine years of his or her life. Network news
shows have consistently gotten higher credibility ratings than either
the print media or the President. And television has proven the most
effective advertising mechanism in the history of American business.
"Television is not so much interested in the business of communications as in the business of delivering people to advertisers," said TV
critic Les Brown. "People are the merchandise, not the shows. The
shows are merely bait." Head & Shoulders, Scope, feminine-hygiene
sprays—who could doubt that television can overnight make success
stories of products which so personally affect us?

But there are reasons why television cannot shake off former FCC
chairman Newton Minow's appellation of "wasteland." Among the
reasons are industry structure and industry programming.

217

Structurally, ownership of many media outlets is concentrated in a few hands. Some 80 per cent of all television stations receive the bulk of their programing from just three networks. Newspapers own 25 per cent of all television stations, with 34 per cent of the total TV audience and a majority of all stations affiliated with the Columbia Broadcasting System and the National Broadcasting Company. Pyramiding their control, chain enterprises by 1967 owned half of all the newspapers and three-fourths of all the television stations in this country. For one example, the Radio Corporation of America owns five VHF, two UHF, seven AM and seven FM stations, as well as book publishers, record companies, defense firms, and the NBC network. And, with their licenses renewed nearly invariably by the Federal Communications Commission every three years, television stations in major markets earn 90 to 100 per cent return on tangible investment annually. In 1972 the pretax profits of the three television networks was $111 million, an increase of more than 100 per cent over 1971; in 1973 it was $184 million.

With so few networks supplying such lucrative outlets, nearly all programing is aimed at the same mass market. It is the market of Middle America, not of minorities, intellectuals, the right, or the left. "Competition" between networks proceeds by imitation, not innovation: a good cop show spawns eight bad cop shows. At times TV conformity can careen into corporate censorship, as the Smothers Brothers, Joseph Papp, or many "blipped" talk-show guests can attest. So we are left with the daily gruel of *Hee-Haw* and *Hawaii Five-O,* interrupted by an occasional treat such as *Long Day's Journey into Night*. And when a potentially competitive technology such as cable television comes along, it is stymied by a Federal Communications Commission sensitive to a broadcast clientele protesting that cable will reduce its profitability. And cable will, as electric-light bulbs did to whale-oil lamps and as cars did to horse-drawn carriages.

The media estate has an obvious dual impact. There is its economic importance. The revenues of the ten largest broadcasting organizations and ten largest newspaper groups total about $15 billion. But of far greater significance is the informational if not cultural impact of this industry. The print and broadcast media are, for most Americans, their windows on the rest of the world. Television network news shows, for example, nightly inform 50 million viewers what is going on.

Although the impact of the media is apparent, there is understandable concern about who should control this spigot of information and entertainment. As media critic A. J. Liebling put it in 1960, "Freedom of the press is guaranteed only to those who own one." The first amendment assumes a "multiplicity of tongues," as Judge Learned Hand once said, but multiplicity can become uniformity if a few groups control much of the media. Who should own media outlets, newspapers, and televisions, and who should have access to them? Newspapers may predictably arrive every morning, and the networks appear every evening at the effortless flip of a dial, but the determination of media ownership and access can be as Byzantine as astrophysics.

Which is why lawyers loom so prominently in this industry. They are trained to decipher and advocate. Lawyers, above all else, are communicators, verbal gymnasts who can pirouette through an argument while others stumble. As they wend their way through Congress, the FCC, the Antitrust Division, and the courts, they are the megaphones for the "media barons" in Washington. These clients, not unexpectedly, have as their prime objective continued profitability, yet this purpose creates an incentive to *limit* diversity and competition in this industry. If there are more stations to choose from, revenues for existing ones decline. The lawyers' role, then, can be quite influential. For to the extent that Washington counsel promote the monopoly control of a few major media centers or frustrate communication technologies promising an information cornucopia, they indirectly shape what all Americans read and view. And, at the head of the line of lawyer-shapers, is Lloyd Cutler. He and his firm represent or have represented Comsat (Communications Satellite Corporation), CBS, the Chronicle Publishing Company, the *Los Angeles Times*, the *Washington Post*, James Reston, and various broadcast stations.

Cutler's Comsat connection began with that organization's birth in 1962. It was a difficult beginning. At issue was a then novel public-private communications corporation, proposed by the Kennedy administration and opposed by a coalition of Southern populists and Northern liberals who thought this public enterprise should not tolerate any private exploitation. The battle continued for months, with American Telephone and Telegraph lobbyists (that company would own much of the "private" component of the corporation) making the argument for industry. The bill providing for Comsat broke through a filibuster by the first successful cloture vote since 1927, and soon became law. It would be 50 per cent owned by private communications carriers (AT&T, ITT, RCA, for example), who would elect six of the fifteen members of the board of directors. This control—the supposed competitors now jointly controlled international communications—spurred Senator Estes Kefauver to denounce the result as "the biggest giveaway in the history of our nation."

Cutler was subsequently selected to draw up the by-laws of Comsat. He obtained this account for several reasons: he was close to Philip Graham, wartime friend, publisher of the *Washington Post,* and the man selected chairman of the incorporators; another incorporator was Edgar Kaiser, Cutler client and *aficionado;* and Comsat needed someone of many skills to coordinate testimony and statements with a variety of agencies. Cutler accepted the assignment not merely because Comsat was a valuable client to add to the rolls, but also, said then Senate aide Herman Schwartz, because "he wanted to improve his image at a time when it was a bit shabby"—the 1962 Drug Amendments struggle having recently ended.

Together with J. Roger Wollenberg and Marshall Hornblower of his firm, Cutler drafted the articles of incorporation and the by-laws of Comsat. He was proud of his handiwork, pointing out that the articles contained conflict-of-interest and disclosure standards not required by the satellite act so as to ensure that none of the six "public" directors were associated with communications carriers. (This enthusiasm seems genuine but misplaced, since the communications carriers already had adequate influence with six directors, and the "public" directors were, in any event, big businessmen or corporate lawyers.) The company began issuing stock in 1964, with the long range goal that such a hybrid organization would become a prototype for other government-industry enterprises; and in fact, the concept was later duplicated by the President's Housing Commission, in which Cutler was to play a key role.

Today, Comsat's own legal office—totaling twenty attorneys under the direction of David Acheson (Dean's son and a former C&B lawyer)—handles most of their routine work, with Wilmer, Cutler & Pickering assigned special corporate and regulatory matters. For example, the firm is representing Comsat at the FCC's Domestic Satellite proceeding, where the issue concerns who will orbit our first domestic satellite. For labors such as this, the firm earned $134,000 from Comsat in 1966, and $382,084 in 1972.

Far more time-consuming than Comsat for Cutler in recent years have been CBS and the San Francisco Chronicle Company—clients that have retained his services in court, the FCC, and Congress. A brief survey of these involvements indicates how good Washington lawyers, like good football players, are triple threats:

• In 1967 Cutler argued a case for CBS before the seventh circuit court of appeals which became the landmark *Red Lion Broadcasting Co.* v. *F.C.C.* decision. At issue was whether the FCC's 1949 Fairness Doctrine, especially its "personal attack" provisions, could constitutionally compel a licensee to provide reply time to someone who was personally attacked "during the presentation of views on a controversial issue of public importance." Cutler entered the case after the record had been established at FCC hearings. To bolster his position, he appended to his court submission a "Brandeis-brief" of numerous examples when the Fairness Doctrine allegedly inhibited the open discussion of conflicting views. The FCC's office of general counsel was upset when Cutler introduced material into the hearing record after the hearing had ended, which did not permit the FCC an opportunity to rule on the examples cited. "Sure I was mad," said Henry Geller, then general counsel of the commission, "but yet it was a tough, clever move. He really puts out 100 per cent."

With considerable respect, however, Geller commented on Cutler in court: "Prior to the CBS brief, we had an easy time handling the NBC and RTNDA [Radio and Television News Directors Association] briefs, but the CBS one gave us fits." The brief and reply briefs— amounting to more than two hundred pages, signed by five Wilmer, Cutler & Pickering lawyers—again emphasized that stressed that a personal attack doctrine would chill zealous newsbroadcasting by keeping off the air controversial figures who might provoke reply-time requests. Having lost in the appeals court, the government appealed to the Supreme Court. Cutler was extremely eager to argue the case before the Supreme Court—an apogee all lawyers, but especially Washington lawyers, reach for. But Cutler lost out to another legal eminence, Archibald Cox, then just a Harvard Law professor toiling for RTNDA. Eventually the High Court, by an 8–0 vote, turned down Cutler and Cox, noting that the Fairness Doctrine "enhance[s] rather than abridge[s] the freedoms of speech and press."

• Another courtroom appearance involved the momentous Justice Department lawsuit in 1972 charging that each of the three major networks, by production or syndication of aired programs, gained anticompetitive and unfair advantages over other distributors and producers of TV entertainment; in other words, the Justice Department argued that control over the distribution of air time should not lead to control over production and programing. The antitrust action threatened network control over programing, a prospect the networks viewed with horror. Understanding that the best defense is a good offense, the networks announced the Justice Department lawsuit even before it was filed in order to get their side of the case out to the public first—a pre-emption that visibly irritated the Antitrust Division.

In court the three networks selected Cutler to argue their joint motion. "When really big money is on the line," said Frank Lloyd, formerly of WC&P, "they call in Cutler."

The networks wanted the case dismissed because supposedly ongoing FCC proceedings would be considering the very same issue of who had access to the airwaves. In addition, the networks' lawyers charged—in an ironic adaptation of a frequent approach taken by radical lawyers on behalf of political defendants—that the lawsuit had been politically motivated by an administration which aimed to "get" the media. (A solicitous Cutler, however, did first pay a courtesy visit to Antitrust Division officials to forewarn them about this argument and "to assure them that we expressly disclaimed any challenge to the good faith of anyone in the Antitrust Division.") Appealing to "judicial statesmanship," Cutler also tried to persuade the judge to infer that the FCC had "primary jurisdiction" over this issue and warned that antitrust cases such as the networks case took an average of eight years to resolve. The latter argument was accurate but audacious: protracted proceedings in antitrust cases are often caused by dilatory corporate counsel, who can then cite the self-created delays to justify dismissal to ease the court's burdens. Bernard Hollander of the Antitrust Division thought this was all nonsense and urged the court to get on with the merits of the case (which is still pending). "We are losing time," he complained in court.

• Cutler's CBS work, of course, took him to the Federal Communications Commission—"a quixotic world of undefined terms, private pressures, and tools unsuited to the work," according to Newton Minow. In an administrative predecessor of the Justice Department's antitrust case, the FCC's "50-50" proceeding in the summer of 1969 sought to forbid a station from running network-produced or network-syndicated shows for more than 50 per cent of prime evening time. Cutler, representing CBS, came prepared with an array of multicolored charts, produced under contract with all three networks, by the Boston consulting firm Arthur D. Little. Expensive consulting study or not, it was later discovered that Arthur D. Little's data were seriously incorrect, significantly understating the amount the networks dominated local prime-time programing. Cutler, whose presentation heavily relied on the original data, subsequently apologized to the FCC.

Cutler's oral testimony on the "50-50" issue emphasized that there were not enough non-network sponsors around willing to assume the production costs and risks of new shows, and that, anyway, CBS was producing high-quality shows. Following an otherwise polished performance, he became unsettled by Commissioner Nicholas Johnson's critical questioning:

COMMISSIONER JOHNSON: I think if I were paying writers per week what many novelists expect to get from a year or two of

> endeavor, that you might be able to produce something which might be somewhat different from the series shows that we now get. . . .
>
> MR. CUTLER: The only reason we don't is we are too dumb or callous, is that your point?
>
> COMMISSIONER JOHNSON: I am asking the questions.
>
> MR. CUTLER: I am sorry. . . .

Later in the hearing Johnson repeated his point, and Cutler again bristled; if Johnson were running the networks, he retorted, presumably all would be fine. The commissioner slowly leaned forward and said, "I don't have to reply to that, do I?"

"Why flare up so at Johnson?" wondered Johnson legal aide Tracy Westen. "The answer, I think, is that they resented his ventilating a 'closed system.' Broadcast attorneys and broadcasters themselves are used to having the game all to themselves. When one person comes along and starts raising objections (in a very dramatic and public fashion), they get upset. It's not that they're afraid they're going to lose the issue or case; it's that they apparently resent having to answer questions at all. For years and years, they have simply had the same mutual concert of interests with the FCC and have never been challenged or embarrassed in public."

• Between 1969 and 1973, the *San Francisco Chronicle* and its television and FM station KRON entwined Wilmer, Cutler & Pickering in both the FCC and Congress. KRON was facing a serious license challenge by a local group at the commission, both because of the *Chronicle*'s alleged concentration of media ownership in the San Francisco area and because KRON had clumsily investigated its challengers by private detective—an embarrassing fact that became public. In 1966 Cutler had helped salvage something for GM in parallel circumstances and the *Chronicle*-KRON group hoped he might do the same for them. Cutler dispatched WC&P partners Dan Mayers and Dennis Flannery to represent KRON on the antitrust aspects of the license-renewal proceeding. (The WC&P team was only one of five law firms retained by KRON; they were opposed by one San Francisco lawyer, Charles Moore, working on a *pro bono* basis.)

Cutler himself was quite occupied by the *Chronicle*'s other problem.

The paper faced a $250-million antitrust treble-damage action for an allegedly illegal joint-operating agreement with San Francisco's only other daily newspaper, Hearst's *Examiner*. Just that year the Supreme Court in *Citizen's Publishing Co.* v. *United States* had decided 7–1 that such joint newspaper ventures—involving price-fixing agreements and territorial restrictions—were clear violations of the Sherman Antitrust Act.

One proposed bail-out for the *Chronicle* took the form of the "Newspaper Preservation Act," first introduced in the Senate by Arizona Senator Carl Hayden in 1967. His bill aimed to overturn legislatively the *Citizens Publishing Company* case by exempting newspaper joint ventures such as the *Chronicle*'s from the antitrust laws. The lobbying for this "poverty program for the rich," in Senator Philip Hart's words, was extremely heavy in both houses. One California congressman protested specifically about "the way the *San Francisco Chronicle* treated [Congressman] Jeff Cohelan. . . . He didn't get a word in the *Chronicle* all through his campaign, and they had supported him editorially and covered his other campaigns."

In November 1969 the Senate Judiciary Committee voted 8–6 to support the newspaper exemption, but there was no provision for retroactive immunity to get the *Chronicle* off the hook. Cutler attempted to get an amendment exonerating *past* collusive behavior read back into the bill by urging senators Eastland and Hruska to have the subcommittee vote again, since three members had been missing in the 8–6 vote. "He was willing to corrupt the entire process for his client's singular benefit," observed one Senate staff person involved in the controversy, "for no future committee vote would be secure unless *all* the committee members were present. Yet it didn't matter here anyway, because the three votes he thought he owned, he didn't."

Another attorney in Wilmer, Cutler & Pickering lobbied the office of judiciary committee member Senator Edward Kennedy—this lawyer-lobbyist had previously aided various Kennedy campaigns—to argue that the *Chronicle* should be retroactively exempted. The WC&P attorney also gave the Kennedy staff a helpful tip: since Al Kramer, financed by the Robert F. Kennedy Memorial, was opposing KRON at the FCC, Senator Ted Kennedy, it was suggested, should be careful to avoid even the appearance of a conflict of interest. For this influence-peddling based on "frivolous arguments," in the view of the Kennedy staff, the Cutler colleague was gently shown the door.

The judiciary committee's bill did not make the exemption retroactive for any private suits filed. In a dissenting opinion to the committee's report, Senator Roman Hruska protested that omitting a retroactivity provision was "unreasonable and unfair." In fact, according to Berkeley law professor Stephen Barnett, opposing counsel in the *Chronicle* lawsuit, Cutler's firm helped Hruska write the dissent. As it developed, the *Chronicle* interests proved completely successful. The House of Representatives bill threw out of court any case then pending against joint operating agreements, including the *Chronicle*'s. And on July 15, 1970, a weary Senate went along with this legislative absolution.

In correspondence with Stephen Barnett, Cutler minimized his role in the legislative battle, considering it only "incidental to our principal services as counsel on the antitrust aspects of the [FCC] renewal proceeding." The firm registered as a lobbyist, saying only that it was "generally in favor of the bill" and that it had received "usual fees for legal services based on time involved." But a lawyer with the Senate Antitrust and Monopoly Subcommittee saw Cutler's performance as far more essential and intricate.

> First, Cutler did it in such a way that the press couldn't figure out what was really going on since it was complicated; [thus], the retroactivity provision was under-reported. Second, he got around the constitutional point of a bill of attainder, since it was only the result of *procedural* changes that plaintiffs were excluded.

The Chronicle Publishing Company did well by Wilmer, Cutler & Pickering. It repelled a lawsuit by a special act of Congress. And at the FCC, in a May 3, 1973, decision, KRON was permitted to retain its broadcasting license.

• In February 1971 CBS's "The Selling of the Pentagon" portrayed the promotional excesses of the Defense Department. The show was a popular success, except at the Pentagon. There, top brass protested that CBS had deceptively edited film and transcripts in an effort to tarnish their department. The Pentagon often has a receptive audience on Capitol Hill, but Harley Staggers, chairman of the House Interstate and Foreign Commerce Committee and long hostile to the networks, was especially intrigued.

In this country it is one thing for the media to investigate the government, but quite another for the government to investigate the media. Staggers saw the issue as one in which the representatives of the people were holding a user of the public airwaves accountable for deception; CBS on the other hand thought that the First Amendment protected it, as it did the press, from interrogation by the government. On behalf of CBS, Lloyd Cutler told a House Commerce Committee hearing on April 20, 1971, that his client was unable at that time to turn over the film recordings and "out-takes" subpoenaed. After some testy fencing with Congressman William Springer (Republican, Illinois), Cutler asked the committee to reconsider its request and to give CBS more time to formulate their final response. "I think that you are in contempt of Congress now," said Chairman Staggers, "but I would say we will give you ten days in order to answer this."

A week later Wilmer, Cutler & Pickering gave their legal opinion that the network should not comply with the subpoena. "The First Amendment's guarantee of the freedom of the press applies to the broadcast medium as it applies to any other journalistic medium," read the WC&P legal memorandum, "and this subpoena is an unconstitutional abridgement of that guarantee." That done, events moved inexorably toward a showdown.

On June 24 Cutler returned with Frank Stanton, the CBS president, and *both* were put under oath by a no-nonsense committee.* The mood was serious and exchanges curt, as the panel would not permit Cutler to speak at all on behalf of his client. At first the committee told Cutler he could only "consult with [his] client and then he will give the answer," but even that began to irritate a tense Staggers.

---

* Public-interest-communications lawyer Al Kramer wondered about Cutler's role here: "Why wasn't Roger Wollenberg of Wilmer, Cutler & Pickering, an incredibly competent lawyer for CBS, not considered competent to go to the Hill? Cutler is the man who has political weight and it clearly impresses some congressmen when he is there."

"Your attorney can keep whispering all he wants to now," he told Stanton during one discussion, "because he is not here to advise you and put words in your mouth, he is here to give you your constitutional rights, but I notice he has been whispering in all these things." Then Chairman Staggers got down to the business at hand:

> THE CHAIRMAN. Have you brought the materials with you which were called for by the subpoena of May 26?
>
> DR. STANTON. No, sir, Mr. Chairman; I have not.
>
> THE CHAIRMAN. Since you are the president of CBS, are the materials requested in the subpoena subject to your control so that if you wished you could have brought them here today?
>
> DR. STANTON. Yes, they are.
>
> THE CHAIRMAN. Is there any physical or practical reason why these materials have not been provided?
>
> DR. STANTON. No, there is not.
>
> THE CHAIRMAN. Is your decision not to bring with you these materials made with full knowledge of the possible action that may be taken against you for your refusal?
>
> DR. STANTON. Yes, I do.
>
> THE CHAIRMAN. Does the decision not to provide the subpoenaed materials reflect a decision of the management of CBS?
>
> DR. STANTON. Yes, it does.
>
> THE CHAIRMAN. So that the record may be clear on this point, speaking as the chairman of this subcommittee I hereby order and direct you to comply with the subcommittee subpoena and to provide forthwith the materials therein described. What is your response?
>
> DR. STANTON. I respectfully decline.
>
> THE CHAIRMAN. At this point, Dr. Stanton, it is my duty to advise you that we are going to take under serious consideration your willful refusal today to honor our subpoena. In my opinion you are now in contempt.

Shortly thereafter the committee did recommend to the full House that Dr. Stanton be held in contempt of Congress, something which the House has never denied a requesting committee. But then, no House committee had directly taken on the American media. Advised by its Washington counsel to concentrate on Congress since it could lose in court, CBS vigorously fought its contempt citation. And in a staggering reversal of deference to its chairmen, the House refused 226 to 181 to hold CBS in contempt.

Afterwards, a glum Congressman Springer said of the media-lobbying, "I haven't seen anything like this in years." Another member told how he had been pressured by a slew of local media, adding: "I was contacted by a lobbyist I've known for years. He told me he had been lured by CBS lawyers to see if he couldn't win me over. It wasn't very subtle." Cutler himself visited the House leadership, each separately—Wilbur Mills, Gerald Ford, Hale Boggs, and Carl Albert. He persuaded the powerful Mills not only to vote against the contempt citation, but to speak out against it—a rare stance for one committee chairman to take against another. "That was the big stone in the avalanche," Cutler said of the Mills move; "we didn't really expect to win, and we didn't have the two leaderships until the day before the vote. But after Mills, the leadership opposed the citation."

A spokesman for Wilmer, Cutler & Pickering told Robert Sherrill, reporting for *The New York Times,* that yes, he and his firm had talked to some congressmen, "convincingly in a couple of cases, I like to think." But this spokesman protested when this was called lobbying. "We were just giving our legal opinion. If you want good lobbyists, you don't come to us. We are very poor at that."

Cutler's communications work does not always involve clients. His power and prestige in the fifth estate of Washington lawyers depends in part on his reception in the fourth estate, the world of the Washington press corps. It is a world he knows well, because of his many media clients and his thirty years in the capital. Cutler is therefore not a novice when it comes to utilizing the media to serve his many interests. "The amount of power this man exercises is enormous," said Joe Laitin, the former director of information for the violence commission. "He can call Graham [Katharine Graham, publisher of the *Washington Post*] and suggest an editorial on something, and then it appears; I can make dozens of calls and nothing happens." A prominent Washington reporter concurs: "Any lawyer who doesn't try to use the press to his and his clients' advantage is short-sighted. Cutler knows how to deal with the press."

One media authority who seeks out Cutler's advice, since Cutler is his personal attorney, is James Reston of *The New York Times.* While the *Times Magazine* was considering a critical article by Judith Hennesse on Washington law firms, Cutler told Reston he didn't think much of it; it never ran. "Reston will at times say 'Lloyd Cutler thinks this or that,'" when a legal issue comes up, said one *Times* veteran reporter. Nor does Cutler merely wait for the phone to ring. His calls to city-desk rooms after American Airlines admitted its illegal contribution, and his words of explanation following the picketing incident have previously been discussed. John MacKenzie of the *Washington Post* was impressed by the number of hours Cutler spent with him trying to get coverage for the violence commission.

Since he understands the media, Cutler knows not only when to embrace it but also when to avoid it. In May 1967 the highway administrator of the Department of Transportation called all the auto-company presidents in to a meeting at his office to discuss some pending issues. A crowd of reporters waited in the press room to ask the presidents questions, but they never got the chance. "Led by Cutler," said one eyewitness, "they dashed into an elevator, where they were packed in like sardines"; the presidents escaped, with the press in hot pursuit. Six years later Cutler was sitting with client George Spater before the Senate Watergate Committee. During a break in the testimony, reporters approached Spater with questions. Aware that offhand comments during relaxed moments can be damaging, his lawyer was overheard to say, "Come on, let's get you away from the press"—as Cutler led Spater away.

Not every reporter is impressed with Cutler's media sophistication and/or manipulation. One *Newsweek* writer was appalled when Cutler opened an interview by casually mentioning his closeness with "Fritz" and "Kay"—respectively Frederick S. Beebe, the chairman of *Newsweek*'s board, and Katharine Graham, whose Washington Post Company owns *Newsweek*. It was, thought the writer, sheer name-playing and subtle intimidation. Another journalist recalls how she interviewed Cutler for an article on Supreme Court justices. Cutler implored her not to mention his involvement in the piece. "But he then ran and told some justices I was writing a critical piece!"

*   *   *

Commandment VIII: Inundation—With expenses often unlimited in cases of vast dollar importance, Washington lawyers can send the

paper flying and overwhelm agencies. Paid by the hour, some lawyers may be tempted to inflate fees ("big briefs are more to snow the client than snow the agency," said one attorney). Some counsel have an obsessiveness with thoroughness and continually fear they may have left out some telling argument. Or, more commonly, inundation may be a tactical judgment—as will be seen in Covington's media advocacy. One Covington & Burling alumnus remembered that "the intent of a lot of discovery is to break the other side financially," and another reported that a C&B partner once emphasized that "when we file a brief at the FCC, it should go to the bottom of the stack for two years." A third concluded that "we presented long arguments [at the FCC] knowing that we'd lose. But the bigger the pile, the more time bought at a place like the FCC. . . . The purpose is obstructionism while the client continues to make a profit."

Antitrust cases especially fall victim to a litigious death. Cases with thousands or tens of thousands of pages of depositions are not rare. One Arnold & Porter lawyer recalled how he was one of the five firm counsel who lived for a year in a Chicago hotel representing one railroad in an antitrust case with sixty railroads, each with its own lawyers. "What kind of society pours so much money and talent down the drain like this?" he asked.

Covington & Burling's communications contingent, among the firm's biggest at fifteen lawyers, is led by Ernest Jennes, Charles Miller, Edgar Czarra, and, occasionally, Brice Clagett. Until his death in 1973, Hugh Cox had done some work for AT&T, the world's largest corporation, for which AT&T paid $112,121 in 1971 and $96,462 in' 1972. (Although the price was steep and the talent substantial, AT&T did not invariably follow Cox's lead. In a complex court proceeding in mid-1973, fifteen plaintiffs charged AT&T with illegally refusing to provide mobile telephone service to users of a certain mobile device. Given AT&T's other worries, it did not seem a particularly large or important case, and Cox agreed to settle on terms acceptable to the complaining parties. But a hitch developed which embarrassed a usually imperturbable Cox: AT&T refused to accept the negotiated settlement and told him instead to prepare for trial. Subsequently, a contrite Cox invited opposing counsel to lunch to apologize.)

The firm has represented some clients from the print media, such as Drew Pearson, Evans and Novak, and the *Kansas City Star*. But by and large the C&B communications practice focuses on broadcast clients, including the National Association of Broadcasters (NAB), the Association of Maximum Service Telecasters (AMST), the American Newspaper Publishers Association, the CBS affiliates, the Post-Newsweek stations, Metromedia, and the Corinthian stations.

Covington today finds itself at the ramparts of a continuing legal struggle between networks and independent producers, between networks and cable, between big stations and small stations, and at times between the industry and the FCC. Its mission: to maintain the existing broadcast monopoly. Three relatively complicated FCC proceedings illustrate the C&B role:

• Brice Clagett joined Lloyd Cutler and four other law firms in fighting the "50-50" proposal, which came to be called the Prime Time Access Rule. Opposing the united front of these six law firms was attorney Earl K. Moore for the National Citizens Committee for Broadcasting. He took up only 6 pages of the 382-page hearing transcript to favor some form of a prime-time-access rule because "we think it is inherently wrong that any small group should control access to the minds of the American public and should determine who may speak and what he might say."

On behalf of the CBS affiliates, Clagett revealed a certain creativity by arguing that to give independent producers a greater role in television programing would deny the *networks* their First Amendment rights. "If the network had to go hand in hand with the advertisers to supply programs," he also wrote, "the advertisers would use the artificial leverage this would give them to drive down the price of network time." Artificial? The benefits of equal, arm's-length bargaining between suppliers (advertisers) and retailers (networks) is a cornerstone of a competitive, free-enterprise system—a system many corporations and their attorneys defend in theory but shun in practice.

At various points throughout his testimony, Clagett was unable to respond to a commissioner's question other than with the admission, "I'm not familiar with the details." His inexpertise was obvious, and it raises the basic question of why a Washington lawyer argues nonlegal, industry issues. There is, again, that oral grace of lawyers that their corporate clientele often lack. Former C&B associate Richard Merrill added that "lawyers don't usually talk unless they fear their clients will say worse things." And there is the usual transference of respect and legitimacy to a client in an agency proceeding when he is represented by a Covington & Burling, or an Arnold & Porter, or a Lloyd Cutler.

The FCC eventually split the difference between opponents and proponents of the measure. Instead of opting for a "50-50" rule, they voted 5 to 2 to divide up prime time 75-25, or three hours network to one hour for local programing—which freed up one half hour additionally each evening, since independent programing already consumed an average half hour a night. But even this compromise did not sit well with the industry. It sued to overturn the ruling as "arbitrary." Fully forty-seven private attorneys, including Lloyd Cutler and Brice Clagett, worked on the case for the networks. It was all a waste of money as the court of appeals upheld the commission.

• The existing FCC multiple-ownership rules limit the absolute number of broadcast licenses anyone may own, restricting the owner to no more than seven television licenses, seven AM licenses, and seven FM licenses. These rules also prohibit the common ownership of two stations in the same medium (TV, AM, or FM) having overlapping signals. The proposed "one-to-a-market rule" in the late 1960s went further: it would prohibit common ownership of *any* two stations—TV, AM, *or* FM—in the same market. (The proposed rule was only prospective, not affecting existing ownership patterns.) This proposal, said the FCC, was necessary for two antitrust reasons: TV, AM, and FM were now sufficiently interchangeable to be directly competitive; and a combined owner can exploit his advantages over the single-station owner (e.g., volume-advertising discounts if placed in more than one medium).

Representing eight local TV and radio stations, Covington & Burling filed briefs opposing this rule. They called it a "drastic departure from policies followed for a quarter century"—which was true, and which was precisely why the FCC had proposed it. Ed Czarra's brief was based on the premise, as it had to be, that there was no monopolization of the broadcast industry by the networks. "Of course, the present number of 'voices' could be increased somewhat if the proposed rules were to become fully effective"—a fatal admission if the need is shown for more, not less, competition.

In all, 116 parties, some representing as many as twenty stations each, filed statements totaling thousands of pages in opposition to the proposed rule. Four parties filed twenty-three pages of comments favoring it. In the internal FCC memorandum summarizing all 120 submissions, fifty pages are devoted to the industry position and three are allotted for the nonindustry position. "This is the normal situation," observed Tracy Westen, then a legal aide to Commissioner Nicholas Johnson. "Whenever an issue is raised which affects the broadcasters, we get overwhelming data from them and hardly a peep from the public." This obvious imbalance has implications for industry lawyers, trained to argue without compromise a client's position in an adversary proceeding. But these are not, it is obvious, adversary proceedings among equal contestants. To assume so is to permit elephants to dance among the chickens.

• The commission requires that each TV and radio station reapply for its FCC license every three years. Nevertheless, licenses have become, in practice, a continuous monopoly, reissued automatically after three years with very, very few exceptions. But the exceptions—WHDH in Boston, Massachusetts, and WLBT in Jackson, Mississippi—encouraged the broadcast industry to seek more protection for their $3 billion investment.

A sympathetic FCC proposed on April 11, 1969, to reduce from ninety days to seventy-five days the amount of time a challenger has to file a competing application after a licensee has filed his application. This would put additional pressure on inexperienced groups to come up quickly with the complicated proposals essential to a successful competing application. As the United Church of Christ, which had long fought the exclusion of blacks from TV programing, said in its submission: "It should be emphasized that public groups seldom can afford Washington attorneys who have immediate access to Commission facilities or who can devote unlimited resources to preparation of filings."

This organization was one of two opposing the rule; 168 broadcast-ing parties favored some version of the proposal. Ernest Jennes ar-gued for twelve CBS affiliates. His brief urged that the time differential should ultimately be *zero*. Jennes could not see any "sound practical or policy reason for according a new applicant the procedural ad-vantage of a filing date that is seventy-five days later than the filing date required of the renewal applicant." He thought that any serious applicant must make "an independent extensive and meaningful sur-vey . . . *before* the renewal application of the broadcasting licensee it seeks to replace is due." But an existing licensee, of course, has a leg up on potential challengers in terms of information, experience, resources, contacts, and counsel. Not everyone, as the Church of Christ brief emphasized, can retain a Washington law firm or a slew of law firms to prepare an overwhelming application financed by the lush profits broadcasters receive from their market-insulated mo-nopoly. The purpose of a ninety-day or even a seventy-five-day time lag for challengers is to equalize an unequal situation. But the in-dustry's arguments had their desired effect. The FCC established the cut-off time at *sixty days*, a time period neither discussed nor debated. Commissioner Johnson bitterly dissented: "The paucity of reasoning in the majority's opinion unavoidably suggests that there *is* no 'public interest' justification for reducing the public's filing time. It can only be understood as an out-and-out concession to the *industry's* interests."

Ernest Jennes enjoys telling young associates, "Call me Ernie," and correcting them when they say they work for him. "You don't work *for* me," he says, "you work *with* me." But his associates are not easily fooled by this burst of populism. They report him to be a stern boss, who works long hours, demands long hours in others, and con-siders *pro bono* work an indulgence. A new associate in 1968 asked if he could work on a draft-card case, and Jennes scowled and said, "No, not until you get your sea legs"—on cable-television issues. One lawyer who worked years for Jennes remembers him as "quite a task-master. On most matters he exercises very close supervision. And the worst thing about it is—he's usually right! But he likes rubbing your nose in the ground."

He attended Yale College (1935–1939) and Yale Law School (1939–1942). Jennes joined Covington in 1945, working with Howard Westwood on the American Airlines account. He became a partner in 1953 and has been doing a variety of communications work ever since. One industry colleague describes him as "extremely knowledgeable and very quick. But his mind moves quicker than his mouth, and sometimes his mouth falls behind. He is not a very quiet guy." A former Covington attorney explained what he thought was the source of Jennes's energetic efforts for communications clients. "He is totally committed to everything he does. He thoroughly identifies with his clients, so that when you sue them, you sue him. . . . This has one drawback: at times he lost his judgment and perspective. A good lawyer has to be able to put himself in his opponent's shoes, to 'feel' the opposing arguments, understand them, and then work out a defense. To Jennes, cable TV is the devil."

It is also the devil to his major clients, the Association of Maximum Service Telecasters, a trade association of 160 VHF television stations in the top hundred markets. This group's name is as euphemistic as the Department of *Defense* or Orwell's Ministry of *Love*. If one uses words according to their meaning, AMST should more realistically stand for the Association of *Minimum* Service Telecasters or be called AMPT, the Association of Maximum *Profit* Telecasters. For its goal has always been to ward off competition, limit supply, and hence boost its own profits. AMST was created in 1956 to contain the threat UHF stations posed to its VHF members. Today, with UHF rendered inconsequential by a series of FCC and industry moves, the association's avowed purpose is to restrict the growth of cable television, which by bringing in distant signals through underground cables threatens local stations economically. A former C&B communications lawyer called AMST "one of the most reactionary trade associations there is; it is opposed to everything that will increase competition with major TV stations."

Ernie Jennes has been AMST's chief lawyer since its creation in 1956 when he and other attorneys literally auditioned for the job. (Each gave a ten-minute speech to the AMST board on what the trade group should do; Jennes won.) Today, he spends up to 50 per cent of his time on this client, and exercises an unusual influence over its policies. "The AMST board doesn't decide what it does and then call Jennes and Lindow [AMST executive director]," a CATV (community antenna television) lawyer has said; "the process is just the reverse." A veteran Washington communications reporter went even further: "In terms of the real power of the broadcasting lobby, you've got to look to Ernie Jennes and Sol Taischoff [editor of *Broadcasting* magazine]; they are the big guns of the industry, influencing policy, not the lesser-grade types at the NAB."

With Jennes leading the way, the AMST won a substantial victory with the issuance of the FCC's "Second Report and Order" of March 8, 1966. This ruling froze all pending CATV license applications, and required an FCC hearing whenever a cable operator attempted to import distant signals into the top hundred markets. A CATV applicant then had the extraordinary burden of showing that no potential harm could occur to an existing television station in the relevant market.

The FCC, perhaps realizing the impossibility of this burden of proof, began waiving the hearings on applications by CATV companies—actions which angered AMST. So in May 1967 the top officers of AMST, plus Jennes, visited separately four FCC commissioners— Rosel Hyde, Robert E. Lee, Kenneth Cox, and Nicholas Johnson—to complain about the waivers. Jack Harris, president of AMST, made the major presentation, except to Commissioner Johnson, because, as Harris later wrote the FCC, "I had not previously met Commissioner Johnson; Mr. Jennes, who had, made the statement. . . ." (It is not clear what knowing a commissioner has to do with making an economic or legal presentation; of course, Jennes had known Johnson when Johnson had been an associate at Covington in the early sixties.)

CATV representatives hotly complained about these ex parte meetings when they were uncovered. If nothing were untoward, they felt, why didn't the AMST simply file its comments on the record? One cable firm, Multivision Northwest, petitioned the FCC to disqualify from certain CATV proceedings those officers and members of AMST who participated in the meetings. Another cable group, Tele-vue Systems of Conroe, Texas, complained that "the AMST delegation was composed of imposing, impressive, distinguished, affluent, prominent, forceful and persuasive persons engaged in representation of the economic interests of some of the most prominent and influential mass-media interests in the Nation. Petitioner further knows that fully sixty percent of the AMST delegation visiting the Commission were then *currently* and *directly* interested in those matters then in adjudicatory status before the Commission involving Conroe, Texas." The FCC denied these requests, but acknowledged that "CATV hearing proceedings are subject to the ex parte rule, . . ." and that these general discussions would have an obvious impact on specific proceedings. Therefore, "parties to a restricted proceedings are 'subject to higher standards and have a special responsibility' with respect to the discussion of general policy matters when those matters relate to restricted proceedings in which they are participating."

In sum, the decision upheld AMST and Jennes on their right to lobby the FCC on *general* policy, but reprimanded them for lobbying on policy affecting cases where they had a *specific* interest.

Jennes and AMST, in fact, *did* have specific interests at stake. Jack Harris's Houston station, KPRC, was then involved in a CATV waiver proceeding. Jennes also represented some San Diego stations in specific CATV contests, with one case then pending before the courts and the other pending before the FCC. And third, the materials the AMST group left with each commissioner alluded to the penetration of "a major Pennsylvania market" (which turned out to be AMST station WGAL) by "several major independents from New York and Washington."

Jennes was chagrined by the whole episode. He told one C&B lawyer, "I wouldn't advise anybody to do anything dishonest." But the firm was upset about Jennes's predicament, fearing the FCC would move against him personally. Covington even got senior partner Charles Horsky to represent Jennes before the commission. "It was a very big deal," recalls Henry Goldberg, who worked with Jennes from 1966 to 1971. "He spent a lot of time worrying about it. He was upset that those he considered sleazy cable operators were accusing *him* of impropriety, that those pots were calling his shiny kettle black." As a former C&B communications lawyer saw it, "Jennes probably got too close to the line, but those CATV cases sure changed after the meetings." Following the AMST visit, the FCC stopped granting waivers to CATV groups. And within a year the commission had imposed a second and yet more restrictive freeze of CATV applications, excluding cable, not only from the top hundred markets but from smaller markets as well. Sol Schildhouse, former head of the FCC's Cable Television Bureau, attributes this decision in part to the AMST-Jennes ploy.

Jennes, then, has managed to exploit two institutional weaknesses at the FCC. First, there is an obvious one-sidedness in groups petitioning the agency. The Washington communications bar lists 760 lawyers defending network and broadcasting interests but only 6 lawyers representing viewers and challengers.* And second, there is a casualness, an informality at the commission which can permit the personal, ex parte exhortation. In the 1950s it was widely known that politics played a large role in the granting of licenses. Though such influence is no longer so blatant, its aroma lingers on. (The abuse of access, however, has its limits. In the early 1960s, a senior Washington lawyer, once a regulatory commission member himself, approached his legal adversary, FCC lawyer Asher Ende, prior to an afternoon commission hearing. Ende was told, "I just had lunch with the chairman and he said that you should stop that line of inquiry." A surprised Ende then informed his opponent that *he* had just had lunch with the chairman, who had said no such thing. To which the lawyer shrugged, "Well, you can't win them all," and sauntered off.)

One-sidedness and an ethical sloppiness are only part of the entire context of broadcast regulation—a context that favors lawyers such as Jennes and Cutler. Broadcast lawyers lobby the White House when commissioners are to be appointed to the FCC. Commissioners well understand that if they become too antagonistic to broadcasting in-

---

* An FCC worried about this palpable disparity of resources surveyed fifteen of the major law firms practicing before the commission in 1971. They were asked if they would represent public groups against a broadcast station in FCC proceedings, assuming of course no conflict-of-interest. Only two firms, Arnold & Porter and Arent, Fox, Kinter, Plotkin & Kahn, said yes; the others, including Covington and Cutler, thought they could not. The task force's confidential report explained the disinclination: "The problem is one of client relations and credibility as a representative of broadcast interests. . . . Vigorous representation of a public interest group, possibly establishing precedent damaging to the broadcaster-client, would tend to damage the attorney's credibility as a representative of the client's interests."

terests, it is highly unlikely they will be reappointed (compare Nicholas Johnson with four-termer Robert Lee). They also can be grilled by congressional subcommittees on their views, answering hostile questions prepared by broadcasting lawyers who feed them to senators and congressmen. These attorneys can also feed material to trade press— *Broadcasting* magazine, for example, and to the White House. Broadcasting supporters can do all this far more easily than their critics because they have the numbers and the information. And since administrative law in Washington usually turns on empirical evidence (the relevant legal standards being inexact), and since the industry controls the data about itself, there is an inevitable regulatory tilt toward the regulatees.

By combining C&B's ability to overwhelm their opponents, his own preferential access, and his noticeable abilities, Jennes has become a powerful communications lawyer with an impact on clients and non-clients alike. Clients understand well his role in their continued profitability and broadcast control; but television viewers probably do not understand how their channel selection has been limited by a lawyer they've probably never heard of.

WHICH WAY?

There Ought to Be a Lawyer

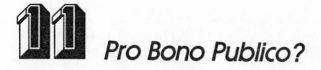

Pro Bono Publico?

> *To the extent that law firms already operate as the makers of public policy—with regard to the operation and design of the legal system, and with respect to official governmental policy—then direct conscious involvement in public interest work is essential if law firms are not to be the unwitting perpetrators of institutional injustice.*   *—Jean and Edgar Cahn*

Lawyers, especially Washington lawyers, have a long history of occasionally representing the unrepresented—*pro bono publico* it is called, "for the public good." John Adams defended a British captain of murder charges arising out of the Boston Massacre, Charles Evans Hughes represented five socialists denied their seats in the New York Assembly during the 1920s Red scare, and Samuel Liebowitz defended the Scottsboro Nine in rural Alabama. In Washington, Abe Fortas earned his salary as a corporate-counselor, but he won his popularity by his memorable defense of an indigent defendant in *Gideon* v. *United States.* John Lord O'Brian received wide tribute because of his government and civic service, not some railroad reorganization.

Such performances, however, are still the exception in a profession largely assuming that justice results from private lawyers representing private clients for a fee. The invisible hand of legal Darwinism will ensure fairness, the lawyers imply. This school of thought argues that the dichotomy between public interest and private interest is unfair; lawyers representing their corporate clients in the legal marketplace, it is said, also serve the public good. For these lawyers, nonpaying work

243

is at best extracurricular time during nonoffice hours for the local symphony or legal aid. "Yes, I believe in *pro bono* work," Tommy Austern told an audience of law students, "but on the attorney's own time; I don't believe in forced charity." Only forced work for paying clients.

Austern's views are decidedly not those of Wilmer, Cutler & Pickering. In recent years this firm, like many others in Washington, D.C., has increased its public-service work. Its projects range from fighting a proposed New Orleans riverfront expressway that would have marred the historic French Quarter, to consulting an urban renewal agency, to the development of a "new town," to the representation of indigents. This development stems in part from Lloyd Cutler's orientation. However protean his efforts for his business clients, Cutler has invested much of his considerable skills in public enterprises. Public-interest lawyer and private-interest lawyer, Common Cause and the Corvair—both merge in this oxymoronic man. But it is the mantle of public advocate that Cutler seems to relish, understanding well the Fortas/O'Brian legacy, and perhaps reflecting some small sense of penitence.

Still, the fact that a law firm or lawyer does *pro bono* work is not the end but the beginning of analysis. Because it is now considered legal chic, *pro bono* work can become merely self-serving or token activity. As a percentage of firm resources, how much *pro bono* work is done? Is it built into the law firm's structure or merely random events? Do senior partners expend their influence on behalf of *pro bono* clients as they would for business clients, or does this work mostly devolve to the younger associates? Do firms contribute time or money? Do non-paying cases aim to correct generic injustice in our society, or do they merely service individual grievances? As answers to these questions can vary greatly, law-firm *pro bono* work can vary greatly.

It was 1963 and official illegality shrouded the South. Local law-enforcement officials harassed black school children, black "trouble-makers," and white civil-rights workers; sometimes they did worse than harass them. In response, President John Kennedy called together 250 prominent attorneys, Cutler among them, to create an organization to find counsel for victims of official hostility. The result was the Lawyers Committee for Civil Rights Under Law, and Cutler became the group's first secretary. He participated heavily in its organizing process: he sent firm associates and well-known lawyers South to handle civil-rights cases; helped raise money; made calls from his home to compile a list of attorneys to oppose Alabama governor George Wallace; and even used his connections with his client, the Automobile Manufacturers Association, to get the committee free use of some cars. The group's organizers "represented the conscience of the bar, or at least represented its quest for manhood and identity," wrote Raymond Marks in his seminal work *The Lawyer, the Public and Professional Responsibility*. "The lawyers' committee was an establishment version of the Abraham Lincoln Brigade. Mississippi was their Spain, and the returning lawyers had become not only changed men but folk heroes to some of their colleagues. . . ."

The lawyers' committee took root and branched out, and by 1969 had worked on an estimated 850 to 900 projects. In *Alexander* v. *Holmes County Bd. of Education* Cutler signed a committee brief—drafted at his firm—criticizing Justice Department laxness in enforcing Title VI of the 1964 Civil Rights Act against segregated Southern schools. Cutler (1971–1973) and Louis Oberdorfer (1967–1969) have recently served as co-chairmen of the lawyers' committee—a fact that is not without some irony. While the committee was promoting the tough enforcement of Title VI of the Civil Rights Act against recalcitrant schools, Oberdorfer was defending the Crown Zellberbach Corporation, one of the world's largest paper companies, against a Title VII employment-discrimination case involving the company's union. And Cutler's public advocacy for civil rights contrasts with his firm's private representation of the Lloyd Corporation, which won an important Supreme Court decision sharply restricting the rights of protesters to demonstrate on the "private property" of shopping centers.

Cutler's *pro bono* work includes a continuing interest in Yale Law School. He has been president of the Yale Law School Association, and in 1973 was chosen chairman of the Yale Development Board. "No individual is more important to Yale's financial future than the chairman of the Development Board," said Yale president Kingman Brewster, Jr., in announcing the appointment. "Lloyd Cutler will provide the leadership that is needed in the critical years ahead." To fulfill this task, and teach a law-school seminar, Cutler spent six months in Yale from late 1973 to early 1974 on a firm sabbatical.

Alumni *pro bono*ism, however, can have professional as well as personal rewards. Cutler's close ties to and employment of former schoolmate Donald Turner stem in part from their common Yale roots. Cutler has also utilized Eugene Rostow—former Cutler class-mate, ex-dean at Yale, and now a Yale law professor—as a some-times consultant in, for example, the FCC's KRON proceeding and the Kefauver drug hearings. Rostow's presence and position com-mand inevitable attention, a tactic Senator Estes Kefauver fully per-ceived: "You are listed in the press as testifying as Eugene Rostow. I take it you are not speaking as dean or for the Yale Law School or for any institution." Replied Rostow:

> Oh, no. I believe, though, Senator, whenever we appear, as one of my colleagues once remarked, it inevitably does involve the Yale name, and I am a firm believer in the principle of a very strict obligation on the part of any professor . . . that when he appears on a public occasion of this kind to recall that his primary obligation is that of a professor always, not an advocate.

After invoking the Yale name by dismissing it, Rostow went on to admit that he was not an expert in the drug industry, nor in patent law, nor in the act whose amendment was at issue. "Having declared his basic ignorance of all matters at hand," James Ridgeway has written, "he thereupon launched into a lengthy attack on the bill, quoting liberally from [business professor] Jesse Markam's press re-leases, which the dean had been shown by way of background material."

In June 1967 President Lyndon Johnson created the President's Com-mittee on Urban Housing to find ways to stimulate the production of low- and moderate-income housing. As committee chairman he chose Edgar Kaiser, head of Kaiser Industries and Kaiser Aluminum; Kaiser in turn chose Cutler, his own lawyer, as the committee's special counsel.

The idea of a Comsat-like corporation to fulfill a designated public need for more housing predated Cutler's work for the Kaiser committee. But it was Cutler particularly who pushed for this approach, one he was well familiar with as Comsat's counsel. It did not sit well with the working staff of the Kaiser committee, as one former lawyer there recalled in an interview:

> The whole Committee was imbued with the idea of Comsat as a great model from the start, and Cutler pushed the National Housing Partnership Corporation at the same time. . . . Cutler wrote us a memo on his Comsat idea and we tore it to pieces. He came along with nice little clichés which had no relation to reality; for example, he wanted to centralize control of decision-making in the business investors, all very wealthy people, getting large tax benefits, deciding where housing was to be built. . . . The fact that the scheme was dramatic attracted Cutler, but to the staff it seemed misleading.

But the staff lost and Cutler won. With Congress deliberating a Housing Act in late 1967, the Kaiser committee quickly issued an interim report and began lobbying for its concept of a Comsat-like housing partnership spurred by "special federal tax benefits"—an approach designed principally by Cutler and Oberdorfer. The Department of Housing and Urban Development assumed the task of drafting these ideas into legislative proposals, and then subassigned the job to Cutler and Marshall Hornblower of WC&P. Cutler then obtained a favorable tax ruling from the IRS on accelerated depreciation write-offs for the individual partners of the partnership. To secure political approval for their proposals, Cutler sat down with the staff from the Bureau of the Budget and the White House. This entire successful effort took only two weeks.

Then on to Capitol Hill, where Kaiser, Cutler, and Wally Phair, Kaiser's regular lobbyist, intensively pushed for their package. The offspring of their labors was the passage of the National Commission for Housing Partnership (NCHP) as Title IX of the 1968 Housing Act. The housing partnership puts up as much as 25 per cent cash equity in projects sponsored by partnership corporations, which take substantial paper losses due to accelerated depreciation, used to offset income. "NCHP's appeal to investors is more tax shelter than actual profit," commented *Business Week*. A NCHP brochure is candid about this tax shelter: "The most substantial return of the venture will be the tax savings generated." Kaiser and Cutler reply that these write-offs and subsidies are a legitimate way to induce industry into slum housing, an approach also taken by Senator Robert Kennedy's earlier housing bill. Among others who disagree is Paul Nelson, staff director of the House Banking and Currency Committee and as such a recipient of Cutler's lobbying for NCHP: "The housing partnership was only a gimmick, a subsidy for big corporations, another tax write-off, something they could put in their public-relations brochure to the effect, 'Look how we are helping the poor people.' "

By the time the President's Committee on Urban Housing produced its handsome report, *A Decent Home*, in December 1968, it had already succeeded in securing its organizational goal. The National Housing Partnership (NHP) was in business, with Edgar Kaiser as the chairman of the incorporators and Wilmer, Cutler & Pickering as outside counsel.

There are two ways to view the *pro bono* work of Cutler and his firm here. NHP's present general counsel, Sidney Freidberg, insists that WC&P actually made a contribution in kind of $158,385, since it has billed the NHP $343,211 from 1968 to 1971, although the firm's normal billable charge would have been $501,596. (Cutler's work for the antecedent Kaiser committee was uncompensated.) "We believe the contribution is appropriate under all the circumstances," wrote the firm in a letter to NHP, "and consistent with our firm policy of devoting substantial portions of our time to uncompensated or partially compensated work for public or social causes." On the other hand, it is hard to ignore the conflict of interest inherent in converting *pro bono publico* work into a *pro bono privato* client. WC&P's fee reduction means that instead of receiving a standard fifty-one dollars an hour for its work, it got about thirty-five dollars an hour, less than usual but still a comfortable net profit. Also, beginning January, 1, 1971, NHP began paying the law firm its standard billing rates. One former NHP lawyer, when asked if Cutler expected to end up as the partnership's lawyer, replied, "Of course; he used his Comsat background to good advantage here." So Wilmer, Cutler & Pickering made a profit and created a client because of Cutler's *pro bono* assignment, which he got because of another client, Kaiser, on whose board of directors Cutler sits.

Cutler's involvement with civil violence began with Martin Luther King's murder in April 1968, when Washington and other cities erupted with riot and arson. Hundreds of arrestees were shoehorned into jails lacking the facilities to hold and process them. Into the breach of this civic emergency swarmed scores of Washington lawyers to represent those detained without charges. "It became a matter of prestige for the big law firms to make a good turnout," observed Steve Goodman, one of the young lawyers involved. At some time during April and May, fully 90 per cent of the lawyers in Wilmer, Cutler & Pickering represented persons arrested during the riots; and during these two months, about 15 per cent of the firm's man-hours were devoted to this effort.

At the peak of confusion—when there were 150 prisoners and 150 names on arrest forms, with few matching—Cutler strode into the cellblock by the courthouse. He spotted Steve Goodman, whom he had never met previously, asked his name, and said firmly, "Young man, come with me." Goodman complied and was introduced by Cutler to United States marshal Luke Moore: "Mr. Moore, I want you to cooperate with Mr. Goodman, who will make sure that for every person there are papers, and for every paper, a body." Then the marshal and Goodman set about their task, with Goodman later noting in some awe that "Cutler was the commander"—like Patton at Al-Guettar, retrieving order from chaos.

Cutler himself worked most of the night trying to undo the bottleneck between the cellblock and the courts. Although he did not personally represent any of the defendants at the bail hearings, he worked with the judges facilitating the flow of prisoners and helped establish a record-keeping system in the cellblock to keep track of all the prisoners. But prisoners weren't the only problem. At one point fifty lawyers protested the way judges were suspending the Bail Reform Act and setting bail uniformly high, thereby preventing release. Bar leaders and Cutler denounced the head of the protest, lawyer Philip Hirschkop, for aggravating an already complicated situation. (It was not Cutler's first disagreement with Hirschkop; when Hirschkop in 1963 helped establish the Law Students' Civil Rights Research Committee, with the help of the National Lawyers' Guild, Cutler personally warned him to stay clear of the radical guild.)

For his work during the crisis, the attorney general, the mayor, and the chief judges of the local courts appointed Cutler chairman of the Committee on the Administration of Justice Under Emergency Conditions, a group created to study the response of the criminal-justice system during the rioting.

Largely as a result of his work on the Kaiser committee and the Emergency Justice Project, Cutler plunged into his most significant public-enterprise work to date: the executive directorship in 1968 of the National Commission on the Causes and Prevention of Violence. Why Cutler? President Johnson wanted a bipartisan commission, and Republican Milton Eisenhower was the chairman; he also wanted, said an LBJ aide, a Democrat he could control if it became necessary. And presumably it was not a liability that Cutler had been co-chairman of the District of Columbia Lawyers Committee for Johnson and Humphrey in 1964.

The commission began while Robert Kennedy lay dying in California. It was an inauspicious inception. Many considered it a dead-end commission, just another blue-ribbon panel to submerge issues, restate the obvious, and pacify a troubled nation. President Johnson opted so obviously for a balance of conservatives versus liberals that, according to The New York Times, "it was difficult to see how it could agree to any daring innovations." Aware of these liabilities as well as the prestige of a Presidential appointment, Cutler accepted the post—but with some apparent reluctance. When he called long-time friend Thomas Barr, of Cravath, Swaine & Moore, to be his deputy director, Cutler said, "Tom, I want to know if you are as crazy as I am."

Cutler's organizational abilities and his network of contacts—professional and personal—were fully tested. He had to organize two hundred people working on seven task-force reports and the commission's own study; he had to negotiate between the commission's crime hawks and doves, radicals and conservatives. Cutler eventually read all the reports emerging from the commission—"reading more in a month on an area than most scholars do in a year," according to Joseph Sahid, head of one of the special investigative reports. Thus Cutler helped structure the commission and oversaw its product, while the day-to-day work of the commission was handled by people such as James Campbell, a former WC&P lawyer who became the commission's general counsel.

There were, of course, problems in such a major undertaking. Many were editorial. At one point the Johnson White House balked at printing the controversial Walker Report on the 1968 Chicago Democratic Convention violence. Cutler got Attorney General Ramsey Clark to read the report to ensure that nothing in it would prejudice an existing grand jury looking into the matter. A few names were deleted, the violence commissioners pressed the White House, and the report came out in late 1968. It "put the commission on the map," Campbell recalls. At another point Eisenhower refused to publish the "Skolnik Report"—*The Politics of Protest* by Jerome Skolnik —because he thought it too radical. Cutler didn't particularly like this task-force study, but neither did he like censorship. Consensual editing eliminated many of the problems, and then Cutler approved a scheme to allay Eisenhower's uneasiness: a blurb was printed on the front of every task-force report saying, "A Staff Report, Not a Report of the Commission." Avoiding both Scylla and Charybdis, the report was published to both Eisenhower's and Skolnik's satisfaction.

Then there was the problem of nudity. A report dealing with the 1968 counterinaugural included a picture of a nude male Yippie addressing a group of listeners. "I felt that this was an undeniable part of the phenomenon we were dealing with," said report author Joe Sahid, "and it would be dishonest to omit it." He added that Cutler was upset that some innocent girl might see a male nude in a government publication. (Yet he did permit the use of the word "fuck" in the same report, although the Government Printing Office later deleted it on its own authority.) After four hours of debate on the issue, Sahid agreed to a literal cover-up: a spectator's head was printed in over the speaker's genitalia.

There was also a potential conflict of interest. Cutler represented

CBS, yet the commission expected to conduct a study of violence in the media. To resolve this dilemma, the White House pointedly announced that Cutler had CBS as a client; also, Cutler wrote a letter to the commission files disqualifying himself from further involvement in the area. (One small oversight: Cutler's daughter Deborah held an unpaid position with the media panel.) But as added insurance, the White House assigned Michael Pertschuk, general counsel of the Senate Commerce Committee, as a consultant to the media panel to ensure no conflict *actually* arose. Drew Pearson, however, charged that Cutler did exploit his double role: "He euchred or maneuvered the commission so that it went into a very superficial study of TV violence, at first. Subsequently Hale Boggs [the late House Majority leader] kicked to high heaven and now they are going into it more thoroughly." Another public official who thought Cutler had soft-pedaled the issue of media violence was President Lyndon Johnson, according to one of his aides. Cutler countered that he simply played no role in the commission's media work.

Owing in large measure to Cutler, the commission transformed from a mere amalgam of big names into a prolific policy group, concluding, among other things, that our national priorities must be re-ordered from a military to a domestic emphasis. Tom Barr saw Cutler as "the guiding genius on the commission . . . giving huge amounts of his time and using up a lot of his credit and favors for the commission."

His performance on the commission has made Cutler something of a public authority on violence. In November 1969, while the Nixon administration was refusing antiwar protestors a permit to march down Pennsylvania Avenue, Cutler sent the White House copies of the violence commission's final report—which argued that a similar permit refusal in Chicago had cocked the trigger of violence. Both he and Eisenhower went to the White House to argue personally for a permit, and it was ultimately granted. Cutler's expertise in violence in America was more frequently sought out as prisons, cities, and colleges exploded at the turn of the decade.

Here he spoke with a crisp passion far removed from the measured resonance of his courtroom legalese. "I think we are going to make

Belfast look like nothing in another decade," he told *The New York Times*. "A few more Atticas and I am afraid that terrorism is really going to take off."

"They may represent some creeps," one Washington lawyer bluntly said of Covington & Burling, "and maybe someday all the major firms will be called in to account for themselves. But Covington is the biggest goddam benevolent public-minded institution in the city." Monroe Freedman, now Dean of Hofstra Law School and formerly a prominent public-interest and ACLU lawyer in Washington, called C&B's public-service contributions "absolutely extraordinary." "If the ACLU needs somebody, we know for sure that Covington & Burling is available. We never go to anyone else as a matter of course." In fact, for the firm's *pro bono* work, the local ACLU chapter made it a co-recipient of its 1969 Oliver Wendell Holmes award for civil-liberties service. This selection, however, led a group of law students to picket the ACLU awards ceremony, the protesters complaining that Covington "qualifies for the tokenism award."

C&B has a *pro bono* committee deciding on what nonpaying or reduced-fee cases to accept. It is comprised of ten lawyers, led by firm partners William Allen and David Isbell (who in his spare time is also an ACLU official). According to an intrafirm memorandum, the committee "considers and inquires into fields and activities in which the firm can most effectively provide public services." This they do by checking for any conflicts of interest ("when a client's toes get stepped on," said a firm associate) and by rounding up associates to do requested work. Allen and Isbell represent that wing of the firm encouraging public-service work. But other Covington powers—such as Joel Barlow, Ernest Jennes, Harry Shniderman, and Tommy Austern—still seem to assume that their lawyers should only pore over Moore's *Federal Practice* seventy hours a week for Widget, Incorporated, that *pro bono* work is something of a detour from the firm's real mission of corporate law. Jennes and Shniderman so overload associates working with them that they can only with great difficulty handle *pro bono* cases. And Barlow, for example, exploded three times at one young associate for various noncorporate client work (approved by other partners) when Barlow thought the paying client required priority.

These pockets of discouragement notwithstanding, the firm fields a variety of *pro bono* work, including law reform and court-assigned cases, politics and Planned Parenthood. The type of contribution includes both the *individual* and the *institutional*, i.e., those cases reflecting solo enterprise such as Peter Hutt on alcoholism, and those involving more of a Covington group effort.

Covington's most significant institutional *pro bono* contribution has been its connection to the Neighborhood Legal Services Program (NLSP). Twice a year two C&B associates leave their carpeted luxury at 888 Sixteenth Street for a six-month stint at the bleak ghetto offices of NLSP. There they handle the usual flow of a poverty-law office, issues ranging from divorce to housing to welfare, methods spanning negotiating to telephoning to litigating.

The program began in 1969, nurtured by C&B lawyers Howard Westwood and Peter Nickles, who also happened to be NLSP chairmen in 1967–1968 and 1970–1971 respectively. This was not Covington's first fling at poverty law. From 1957 through 1964 the firm occasionally donated lawyers to the Legal Aid Bureau for a three-month visit. But three months proved hardly more than a visit, and the program satisfied no one. In 1964 Covington switched from manpower to moneypower, donating money instead of lawyers. This arrangement largely pleased the firm elders, who preferred a fixed, certain contribution to the time-consuming and disrupting contribution of lawyers. "If Tommy [Austern] wanted someone to work on a client's problem," recalled former C&B associate Gerald Levenberg, "and they were over at Legal Aid, ouch." But others were not pleased, agreeing with ex-firm member Zona Hostetler that "the notion of donating money but not time is sterile."

By 1969 the firm abandoned its contribution of money for a contribution of lawyers. Yet there was no great stampede to fill the available slots. "These guys are great on talking and short on following through," snorted Howard Westwood. The reasons for associates' diffidence were not hard to find. The *pro bono* segment of Covington had promoted and implemented the idea, but it had never been formally ratified by the entire partnership. This supposedly preserved the firm's neutrality, its tradition of not appearing to coerce anyone to do charitable work. It also created anxiety that those partners disenchanted with the NLSP program might transfer that hostility to the participating associates, thereby endangering later chances to make partnership. Also some firm lawyers feared that the legal-aid work would fail to stretch their intellectual muscles, which would become flabby over routine matrimonial cases. One considered the NLSP prospect depressing, since what a poverty client typically needed was either money or a psychiatrist. Some claimed to worry about creating a revolution of rising expectations that neither the lawyers nor even society could fulfill.

Despite such perceived obstacles, the program has continued to the present—with participating C&B lawyers largely enthusiastic. At first they felt like overtrained experts, stars of appellate-court advocacy now devoting themselves to cases requiring trial-court training. Much of the time was spent hectically putting out fires, which disabled the lawyers from spending the time necessary to get command of their subject matter. But they came to consider the work more emotionally satisfying than their C&B regimen. Chuck Herz did domestic-relations work "and thrived on it," said an NLSP lawyer; after his six months Herz wrote a divorce manual for poverty lawyers. Robert Saylor focused on housing during his NLSP tenure. "The realness of the problems hits you much harder and faster," he said. "You live with the problems twenty-four hours a day. If there is to be an eviction the next day, you keep imagining the child with asthma and thinking if only you could find one more defense that would do the trick." (Like most C&B lawyers in the program, Saylor continued to handle some NLSP work upon his return to the firm.)

The C&B-NLSP connection has gotten mixed reviews by those in a position to evaluate it. Most staff NLSP lawyers have appreciated the dedication and contribution made. But merging uptown corporate law with downtown ghetto law created strains. In the early days, Covington releasees continued to do occasional Covington work at NLSP, causing some resentment. John O'Brien, managing attorney at NLSP's Capitol Hill office, was "upset at the insensitivity of Covington" when in 1972 it recalled Michael Henke to do client work only three weeks after his arrival at NLSP. Some, such as former NLSP attorney Florence Roisman, thought the six-month term too brief, since it took at least six months to learn the ropes. "The attorney gets more out of the experience than NLSP," she said, adding that the exchange was "a selling point to get good associates into the firm." But others thought the six-month tour both an adequate period of time and a good technique to expose many young corporate lawyers to the other side of law—where a client problem meant not a depressed price-earnings ratio but a depressed stomach.

Covington & Burling's *pro bono publico* work is not limited to a few individual thrusts or to the NLSP role. Teams of lawyers sometimes become engaged in major public-policy issues, invariably involving C&B's good name. Among others, consider three cases:

• *The Culebra that Roared*—Culebra. A tiny, 7000-acre Caribbean island within the Commonwealth of Puerto Rico. Its 726 residents eke out their economic existence from cattle-herding and fishing on two-thirds of their island, since the U.S. Navy for decades has been using the other one-third as a bombing target for its Atlantic fleet. Early in 1970 the navy began increasing its bombardment of the island trying, not always with success, to keep its explosives off the inhabited parts of the island.

Mayor Ramon Feliciano of Culebra was referred by a friend to Covington & Burling precisely because it was *not* associated with liberal causes. It would therefore have a credibility that, say, the ACLU lacked (this group facing the dilemma of representing virtue too often to have sufficient clout). Covington's *pro bono* committee accepted the mayor's request for free representation in May 1970 and assigned the case to one of the firm's young comers, former White House fellow Richard Copaken. Realizing that this case called for political rather than legal or judicial action—a law suit started by other lawyers in Puerto Rico had been unsuccessful—Copaken first met with Joseph Grimes, top civilian assistant to Secretary of the Navy John Chafee, in an effort to persuade the navy to change its mind. But Copaken found the navy intransigent. National security, it seemed, required the navy to bomb Culebra. So with the aid of Tom

C. Jones, a Spanish-speaking C&B associate, Copaken set out to create the political climate in which the navy would be forced to change its position.

Well aware that their Covington connection gave them a special and respected access—one Senate-staffer they saw thought the Covington imprimatur "has an impact all its own"—Copaken and Jones booked interviews with White House, congressional, and Pentagon officials to present their case. The press was wooed, successfully, by a combination of navy blunders, good investigative work by Copaken and Jones, and skillful appeal to the human-interest side of the story. The Covington duo was even able to conscript a major military voice to their side, the *Armed Forces Journal,* which became incensed at the navy's mendacity.

On Capitol Hill, they first turned to the House Armed Services Real Estate Subcommittee with detailed testimony about the island and the ill effects of the navy's presence there. Copaken and Jones then wrote each senator requesting that he co-sponsor or support amendments to various military-spending bills prohibiting the expenditure of navy money to bomb Culebra. Other public figures were not immune from the C&B minijuggernaut. Letters went out to dozens of prominent citizens who were thought to have some influence in Washington, including Billy Graham and the Pope.

This whirlwind of activity changed Culebra from an obscure "no place" to a national *cause célèbre.* By late 1970, the Covington pair had gotten an amendment to the 1971 Military Construction Authorization Bill which required the secretary of defense to report on the alternatives to bombing Culebra. Even this prospect prodded the navy into opening negotiations to settle the dispute. The discussions culminated in an agreement on January 11, 1971, signed by Governor Luis Alberto Ferre of Puerto Rico, Mayor Feliciano of Culebra, and Secretary of the Navy Chafee, by which the navy promised to cease most of its target practice and to seek alternative sites to Culebra for operations in the Atlantic Fleet Weapons Range. Pursuant to the agreement, Secretary of Defense Melvin Laird agreed a few months later to stop the use of live shells on Culebra after January 1972 and to abandon the island completely by June 1975.

This did not end the controversy. For after reaffirming in November 1972 his agreement to leave Culebra by 1975, Secretary of Defense Laird flip-flopped in December 1972 and announced that the navy would *not* relinquish Culebra as an air-gunnery target range until *1985,* not 1975. But in May 1973, "in a rare victory for human needs over military convenience," Eliot Richardson, then secretary of defense, reversed Laird and finally ordered the navy to move its target operations by July 1975 from inhabited Culebra to two uninhabited small islands off the coast of Puerto Rico.

• *Troubled Bridge Over Waters.* In 1966, after ten years of bickering and politicking, the District of Columbia approved plans for four major freeways, including a Three Sisters Bridge to span the Potomac between Washington and Arlington, Virginia. The four roads were to cost $182 million and displace, from the poorer sections of the city, eight hundred families and over one hundred businesses. And the Three Sisters Bridge would consume at least thirty acres of parkland as well as destroy the river view from the historic Georgetown district.

These plans understandably upset many District of Columbia residents. An ad hoc coalition of citizen groups decided to challenge the plan's legality, and for help they looked to Covington. Gerhard Gesell agreed to commit the firm if the civic groups promised to raise some of the expected costs of the suit, which they did. Gesell then assigned partner Robert Owen and associate Gerald Norton to the case, and very quickly the paper began flying. The first suit was filed on behalf of thirty individuals and organizations in November 1966, beginning years of legal maneuverings of Dickensian complexity.

In February 1968 the United States Court of Appeals issued an injunction preventing further work on the highways until the government complied with requirements for planning and constructing highways, such as holding public hearings. But the city, the highway lobby, and the highwaymen's friend on Capitol Hill, Congressman William Natcher (Democrat, Kentucky), chairman of the House Appropriations Subcommittee for the District of Columbia, were far from prepared to concede defeat. Instead, they successfully attached a provision to the 1968 Federal-Aid Highway Act ordering the city to build highways and bridge "notwithstanding any other provision of law, or any court decision or administrative action to the contrary," although any construction still had to be carried out in accordance with all applicable provisions of the United States Code.

Unwilling to see their 1968 victory reversed, the Covington litigation team again wheeled into action. On October 3, 1969, on behalf of fifteen individual and organizational plaintiffs, Owen and Norton filed suit against DOT secretary John Volpe, Secretary of the Interior Walter Hickel, and officials of the District of Columbia government to stop further work on the Three Sisters Bridge, alleging multiple violations of the federal-highway laws. In January 1970 the district court upheld the government. Work on the bridge continued.

Plaintiffs appealed, and once again were saved by the court of appeals. Writing for the majority of the court, Judge J. Skelly Wright spoke of the need to protect the "voiceless minority," those voteless District of Columbia residents whose interests could be saved only by compliance with the rigorous hearing requirement of federal law. The court sent the case back to the district court for a hearing on whether those required procedures had in fact been followed.

Meanwhile, pending the new hearing, work on the bridge continued. Bridge pilings began to emerge from the muddy Potomac.

The trial itself, held in June 1970, was an extravaganza. It lasted almost three weeks and produced a fifteen-hundred-page transcript and several hundred more pages of exhibits and documents. After the trial, Owen and Norton spent their July Fourth weekend drafting a 127-page proposed "findings of fact" and "conclusions of law" to aid the judge in making his decision. Following an inconclusive district court decision, the court of appeals again and for the last time held for the plaintiffs in almost every respect—who by now felt like yo-yos on a judicial string. Essentially, Judge David Bazelon's decision on October 12, 1971, said that the DOT had thoroughly failed to comply with federal regulations in giving the go-ahead to the Three Sisters Bridge. The bridge was now dead.

Norton and Owen did not merely sit back and savor victory. Instead they filed a motion with the court for "reasonable" attorneys' fees, since they had acted as successful "private attorneys general." Judge John Sirica, however, denied their request. C&B eventually received about $10,000 from the antifreeway coalition, although normal billing for the four thousand hours spent would have netted $200,000. Some in the firm thought this case consumed an excessive amount of resources. "We've probably put more in that one case than [into] all our other *pro bono* work together," said partner Jack Schafer. "I don't expect we're going to get into any more cases like that again."

• *Office of Economic Opportunity.* In 1973 Covington & Burling joined in a rescue operation to save the much-threatened OEO legal-services program from a Nixonian execution. The threat appeared in the shape of Howard J. Phillips, a thick-set thirty-two-year-old founding member of the conservative Young Americans for Freedom, who was appointed acting director of the OEO on January 30, 1973. His assignment, underwritten by Richard Nixon's electoral landslide, was to dismantle the OEO.

He wasted little time. First, Phillips fired the acting director of the Legal Services Program and replaced him with J. Lawrence McCarty, a conservative foe of liberal Republican senator Edward Brooke in Massachusetts. Then he put the whole program on a month-to-month basis—the implication being that lawyers who deviated from administration policy would be cut off. The result was that some programs had to borrow money in order to continue operating, and others were forced to close down. Funding for back-up centers, which provide legal services projects with special expertise and technical assistance, also was curtailed, and in some instances ended. On February 10, 1973, American Bar Association officials reported that the Nixon administration had quietly gutted the ABA's legal-services advisory committee, designed to insulate neighborhood legal-services attorneys from political pressure. Phillips's attempted blitzkrieg was gaining momentum daily.

The National Legal Aid and Defender Association (NLADA), an umbrella organization for poverty-law programs, approached C&B to represent them, in part because senior partner Howard Westwood sits on NLADA's executive committee and had personally filed its incorporation papers back in the early 1950s. C&B agreed to help.

Westwood's strategy was simple: work alone and negotiate. He was somewhat slow out of the starting block, waiting some two weeks after taking on the NLADA before he acted. But on February 26 Westwood corresponded with Phillips. He patiently explained how Phillips's ukases clearly violated congressional requirements, hinted that a lawsuit might ensue if the matter were not resolved, and concluded, "Surely you will agree that a program so fully endorsed by the President, so firmly provided for by Congress, so uniquely reflecting a thoroughly American ideal should not be Humpty-Dumptied." Two days later negotiations began. Aware of Westwood's leverage as a potential courtroom adversary, Phillips compromised on a number of issues. Most significant, he resumed the normal funding of legal-services projects and agreed to give priority to grant applications of offices in financial trouble.

There was some controversy over Westwood's methods. As legal-services offices began closing—Phillips's admitted strategy was to present opponents with *faits accomplis*—public-interest lawyers felt frustrated at C&B's delays and accommodations. Some thought that negotiations with Phillips simply legitimized him when OEO supporters should have been trying to get rid of him. Westwood's arrangement with Phillips, in addition, was not legally binding. And by seeking compromise on specific issues via persuasion rather than litigation, Westwood ignored some broader issues of the Legal Services Program and the general OEO dismantlement. For example, three separate lawsuits were eventually filed on behalf of several programs and back-up centers; they saved $9 million in funds appropriated by congress but unspent by the OEO, funds that were about to revert to the Treasury Department. Another lawsuit directly challenged the legality of Phillips as acting director and the legality of all his orders. On June 11, 1973, in fact, a court ordered Phillips to cease his activities, since, among other illegalities, he had never been confirmed by the Senate. Covington refused to coordinate its efforts with such direct challenges.

NLADA's Pat Maxwell thinks Covington "accomplished quicker and produced faster than anybody else"; he favored separating the legal-services issues from the general OEO issues. But Carl Bisgaier, director of the Camden Legal Services Program, disagrees. "That's not the way we handle things in Camden," he said of Covington's reluctance to go for everything, "but maybe the way they do it in Washington." He thought an early, frontal challenge to Phillips would have alerted poverty lawyers to attacks to come, and·could have dissuaded Phillips from his attempted pillaging of other OEO programs. Alan Morrison, director of the Public Citizens' Litigation Group which filed the case removing Phillips from office, concurs. He expressed disappointment that C&B focused on the legal-services program rather than on "removing that cancer from the OEO." "These big law firms lack institutional guts," observed Morrison, who used to be in one. "But perhaps it's too much to expect more from lawyers who are in the business of business."

One almost gutsy law firm was Arnold & Porter, some of whose young associates became impatient as Westwood slowly formulated his response. They were eager to file suit. When Westwood got wind of this, he called Paul Porter and told him in so many words to lay off his case. Comity and deference being as important among Washington law firms as in foreign relations, Arnold & Porter abandoned its plans.

Nearly all District of Columbia firms of over twenty-five lawyers today do some *pro bono* work. Their motives vary from a sense of professional responsibility, to the psychological and political need to legitimize what some consider "*pro malo*" work, to an understanding of good recruiting—or some combination of all three.*

The type of program can vary as well. Firms may merely permit lawyers to assume *pro bono* cases individually and ad hoc. Some, like Covington & Burling, prefer released-time work with worthy outside groups. Others structure *pro bono* work into the firm itself. There is the five-lawyer Community Services Department at Hogan & Hartson, for example, the equal of other firm departments in terms of salary, status, and talent. Such a formal program insulates nonfee

---

* Hogan & Hartson acknowledged in an intraoffice memorandum that its *pro bono* program "may have a favorable impact on recruitment"; Edward Burling, Jr., thinks that his firm's public-service record help offset its "giant" image; and why else did Wilmer, Cutler & Pickering trot out a twenty-two-page statement to law schools detailing their *pro bono* docket? (About publicizing their corporate docket, they were more circumspect.)

work from the vagaries of law-graduate interest, an interest apparently in decline. One Hogan & Hartson lawyer thinks that although *pro bono* work generally has leveled off as law students no longer pressure for it, his firm has been unaffected.

A formal program can also insulate *pro bono* work from the invariable pressures exerted by corporate-law practice. For "law firms are businesses," not eleemosynary organizations; young lawyers on public-service cases can understandably wonder how firm partners judge their enterprise. As the *Harvard Law Review* observes:

> The work assignment mechanism—typically a partner asking an associate if he has time to take on a particular paying project—may put an associate engaged in outside work in the position of turning down a work request from a senior member because he is committed to work on a nonpaying project. . . . In these circumstances, associates, fearing the loss of good will as well as invaluable experience, are often unwilling to engage in *pro bono* work despite the stated permission.

Thus, it is generally understood that firm advancement is not hurried along by a substantial amount of nonfee cases. You are usually not cultivating a relationship with a partner, you are not necessarily developing the skills of a good corporate lawyer, and you are not promoting the interests of those who are kind enough to pay the firm payroll.

It is difficult to quantify the extent of any firm's *pro bono* investment. Lloyd Cutler's sporadic though substantial contributions or an occasional associate on a zoning case is not easily converted into a percentage of firm time. Covington's *pro bono* committee claims to have accurate data on the number of attorneys and cases engaged, but it refuses to release the information. As one measure, Arnold & Porter recently said that its *pro bono* component had probably cost the firm $200,000 annually in lost fees. Yet assuming a not unreasonable $8 million in annual billable fees (88 A&P lawyers times 35 hours a week times $50 an hour times 50 weeks), this *pro bono* "donation" is less than 3 per cent of firm gross. Alone, the Covington NLSP program consumes less than 2 per cent of firm resources. In all, it is unlikely that any Washington firm, at a given point in time, is contributing more than 5 to 10 per cent of its effort to *pro bono* work. And it appears that most of that contribution comes from young associates, not the $150,000-a-year partner who can afford it best.

A former attorney with Kirkland, Ellis & Rowe in Washington candidly elaborated some of the inhibitions working against greater *pro bono* commitments. Because Kirkland was a business-oriented, profit-oriented firm, he said, any formal commitment to a *pro bono* program would be a terrible psychological wrench for its members. Once a firm becomes conscious of itself as a social entity with social responsibility, it loses its extraordinary flexibility, or at the very least its ability to operate without a guilty conscience. What begins as an amorphous bunch of guys out to make a buck ends up as an organization of professionals who must be responsive and responsible to society as a whole.

These organizational needs and restrictions can not only limit the extent of a firm's *pro bono* commitment but the kind of cases it takes on. Rarely do they involve controversial economic issues of a kind that by definition may discomfort an important firm client. "To a point, the big firms can give and give, money, volunteer time, élan, and so on," said former Covington associate John Murphy, Jr., "but when the attack finally comes home, involving qualitatively and quantitatively the distribution of the National Goody, the firms will have to draw the line on participation." Argues the *Harvard Law Review*: "The fundamental source of opposition to a formal public service commitment by the law firm may be a fear that such work will jeopardize the firm's standing and reputation with paying clients."

Lloyd Cutler represents the people on the important issue of campaign reform. But he did not testify on the Tunney bill to reform and open up the Antitrust Division's consent-decree process. In all their years before the Federal Communications Commission and the Federal Trade Commission, has Ernest Jennes or Harry Shniderman ever suggested ways to improve agency procedure to make it more efficient and available to the consumers it serves? At a law school seminar, WC&P's Louis Oberdorfer was asked if he thought a corporate-law firm had an inherent conflict of interest when it represented consumer causes. "We're not Covington & Burling; we have some room on our shelf," he said, adding that "we don't represent any cigarette clients, and we could [challenge] the tobacco industry."

But they haven't, nor is it psychologically likely that those who labor for corporations by day will contest them at night. Consequently, *pro bono* work is usually restricted to poverty or civil-rights areas. Here the large firms have few clients and little worry that they will hurt themselves by helping the public.

To guarantee a safe docket of *pro bono* cases, firms may stretch the concept of "conflicts of interests." Lawyers traditionally do not argue two sides of a case because their advocacy would be, or at least appear to be, compromised. But conflicts are found in some handy and illogical places where public-interest clients are involved. "Threats are seen; conflicts are imagined or manufactured," wrote Ray Marks in his American Bar Foundation study. "The public interest client who poses the least risk to the firm's economic stability and the least threat to the interest of the regular clients can be accepted."

For a few examples: NLSP once asked Covington & Burling to defend some truck drivers fired in a labor dispute with the department store Woodward and Lothrop. C&B declined, not because it represents Woodward—it doesn't—but, the firm told NLSP, it *could* in the future. Richard Copaken once explored the idea of running counter-commercials for his client (if the navy advertised "Join the Navy and See the World," he would air one saying "Join the Navy and Bomb the People of Culebra"), but he was decidedly discouraged by superiors; the firm represented a network and such a move could "embarrass" it. A legal-services program asked C&B to help compel the federal government to make public employment data (percentage of nonwhites, women) of federal contractors. The firm's *pro bono* committee said no because it might adversely affect some clients— which the legal-services lawyer involved thought was hard to understand unless their client was doing something illegal. An Arnold & Porter associate once sought permission to work with local law students in a case opening up the Federal Trade Commission to public-interest intervenors; he was turned down. Arnold & Porter admitted it had no conflict of interest in the case, but any precedent could hurt many A&P clients who later found themselves at the FTC. "Remember this when you are considering where to practice law," the embittered associate told the disappointed students.

None of this really surprises critics of the large law firms. The director of the Harvard Center for Law and Education, Marion Wright Edelman, doubts that corporate lawyers possess the background or sensitivity essential for this type of work:

> They just don't understand what's at stake. These people—who are my best friends—are on civil rights boards all over the state, and when you really get into them on what the relief ought to be, or what the federal government ought to do, they all have very narrow views of the government role in private industry. . . . We don't have the industry mentality. If you have been representing private firms all your life and your big thing is to win to save their money and get your fee, you have a very different perspective than the client in Louisiana who has been screwed out of a promotion.

Others disparage the idea of occasional *pro bono* work because it does not enable a lawyer to build up the expertise necessary to have a major impact in an area. Exxon and Alcoa have full-time, not part-time, representatives looking out for their interests, it is argued; why should consumer and poverty causes be any different?

It seems clear enough that corporate law and *pro bono* law have some of the aspects of a square peg in a round hole, that many firms approach *pro bono* work with all the enthusiasm one usually brings to calling in-laws. Still, there are too many correctable injustices and too many law-firm resources to dismiss these lawyers' *pro bono* efforts, however short of their potential they may fall. For better or worse, mostly better, many law firms have made a commitment to devote some part of their manpower to defending the powerless. By this they are fulfilling the ethical obligations of the Code of Professional Responsibility, which says that "every lawyer, regardless of professional prominence or professional workload, should find time in serving the disadvantaged." Those who refuse to undertake *pro bono* work are failing their ethical obligations. "There are lawyers and there are tradesmen," Ray Marks has written. "The lawyers are carrying a burden for the tradesmen, they are retaining for the nonresponders a semblance of dignity that those nonresponders cannot truly claim until they have paid for it."

Although it is necessary that private lawyers make this contribution, it is not sufficient. More important than what corporate lawyers do in their spare time for public-service clients is what they do most of the time for their corporate clientele. *Pro bono* work can be commendable, to be sure, but should not deflect from a more generic analysis of the ethics of Washington powerlaw.

The Ethics of Powerlaw: "According to As They Are Paid"

There was a society of men among us, bred up from their youth in the art of proving, by words multiplied for the purpose, that white is black and black is white, according [to] as they are paid.
—*Jonathan Swift, on lawyers, in* Gulliver's Travels

There may be a pleasant pouch upon your client. His wallet may look fat. Suppose now that his case does not at first blush seem appealing, then what to do? Courage my friend, there is that admirable ethic of the profession which makes it clear that the lawyer is neither judge nor jury; that the lawyer has neither duty nor right to usurp the constitutional function of the judicial tribunal. —*Karl Llewellyn*

In 1924 John W. Davis, renowned Wall Street lawyer and Democratic Presidential nominee, was urged by advisors to put some distance between himself and his rich (and hence publicly unpopular) clients. But more lawyer than politician, Davis rejected this suggestion with characteristic eloquence: "Since the law is a profession and not a trade," he wrote, "I conceive it to be the duty of the priest or surgeon to serve those who call on him. . . . Any lawyer who surrenders this independence or shades this duty by trimming his professional course to fit the gusts of popular opinion in my judgment not only dishonors himself but disparages and degrades a great profession. What is life worth, after all, if one has no philosophy of [one's] own to live by." To admirers, Davis's soaring response remains the classic explanation of the lawyer's role. But others wonder exactly what philosophy it was that required Davis to devote his professional life to the House of Morgan.

A half century later the role of the lawyer remains ambiguous. What are the limits of legal advocacy? When, if ever, should a lawyer tell a client that a proposed argument or tactic is unjust? Is this judgment his to make? When, and by what standards, should a lawyer refuse to represent a particular client? Can the law-for-hire ethic provide just law?

These questions do not particularly trouble many lawyers, who simply assume that a lawyer is an advocate doing everything possible for his client to prevail, period. It hardly requires explanation that attorneys should zealously promote their clients' interests. But less appreciated is the fact that lawyers and law firms have public obligations as trustees of justice. They constitute a "profession," which by self-definition is a "higher calling" involving more than merely making money. (The word "profession" comes from the Middle English word to "profess," which originally meant taking a religious vow.) There is considerable language in court decisions, ABA formal opinions, the Canons of Ethics, and scholarly writings to the effect that lawyers take vows as officers of the court not to abuse the legal process for client benefit.* Paradoxically, the vigorous representation of a client is seen as a subordinate obligation to the process itself, for a lawyer furthers justice by advocating one position in an adversary context.

---

* In a much quoted 1917 decision, a federal district court judge wrote: "Counsel must remember that they, too, are officers of the courts, administrators of justice, oath-bound servants of society; that their first duty is not to their clients, as many suppose, but is to the administration of justice."

In 1958, a report by the ABA and the Association of American Law Schools said: "The lawyer's highest loyalty is at the same time the most intangible. It is a loyalty that runs, not to persons, but to procedures and institutions . . . those fundamental processes of government and self-government upon which the successful functioning of our society depends."

The ABA's committee on professional ethics, in Formal Opinion Number 146, asserted: "A lawyer is an officer of the court. His obligation to the public is no less significant than his obligation to his client." And EC 7-10 of the ABA Code, promulgated in 1969, reads: "The duty of a lawyer to represent his client with zeal does not militate against his concurrent obligation to treat with consideration all persons involved in the legal process and to avoid the infliction of needless harm."

Because lawyers are licensed by the state and granted a monopoly of access to the judicial system, Justice Brandeis came to regard lawyers as a kind of public utility. Former ABA president Robert Meserve said that "law is a public profession. Those who practice it have unavoidable public responsibilities." And Harvard law professor Paul Freund believes that "a lawyer owes complete loyalty to his client . . . but it is a loyalty within the bounds of honor and fidelity to the presuppositions of the system itself."

Consequently, although most lawyers assume themselves to be in "private practice," they are, in fact, members of a public profession. This view has its parallels. Whereas once businesses were small ventures locally run and owned, today's national and multinational corporations are more like economic states than "Ma and Pa" groceries; there is growing recognition of the *de facto* public status of an Exxon or a GM. Electric utilities were once simply privately owned, yet today are either publicly owned or publicly regulated. Private universities, long enclaves of learning insulated from societal turbulence, are coming to realize their responsibilities to the communities they affect. "So too perhaps should firms of lawyers," argues New York University law professor Norman Dorsen, since they are "engaged in a practice that is national in scope, services the country's largest industries, generates millions of dollars in fees, and touches on the public interest at countless points."

This public status entails a scale of obligations. In legal proceedings lawyers cannot lie, knowingly allow clients to commit perjury, knowingly make a factually insupportable argument, promote a client cause based on favors or friendship, or file a complaint or motion merely to harass or delay. Rule 11 of the Federal Rules of Civil Procedure requires a lawyer to vouch that an argument is made in good faith and not frivolously. Going further, the *Code of Professional Responsibility* says that "when an action in the best interest of his client seems to him to be unjust, he may ask his client for permission to forgo such action." ABA Formal Opinion Number 155 prohibits a lawyer from aiding or tolerating the "commission of an unlawful act, even if received in confidence. . . . He should, if unable to get the client to cease the conduct, make such disclosures as may be necessary to protect those against whom the conduct is threatening or working illegal harm." Thus, a lawyer can restrain, refuse, or even disclose a client's activities if sufficiently harmful.

The *Code* imposes more affirmative obligations yet on its adherents. It states that "a lawyer should assist in improving the legal system," and that "in assisting his client to reach a proper decision, it is often desirable for a lawyer to point out those factors which may lead to a decision that is usually just as well as legally permissible." Federal judge Charles Wyzanski has elaborated this obligation. "The modern lawyer almost invariably advises his client upon not only what is permissible, but also what is desirable," he wrote. "And it is in the public interest that the lawyer should regard himself as more than a predictor of legal consequences. His social duty to society as well as to his client involves many relevant social, economic and philosophical considerations." Because the governance of so much conduct occurs by private contract and counseling, not formal courtroom resolution, this exhortation is significant. Just as some economists are coming to realize that corporations have motivations and obligations other than merely profit maximization, lawyers should realize that they ill serve their client and society merely by engaging in legal shortcuts, end runs, and loophole hunting.

But the American Bar Association's Canons of Ethics are not very clear about how a lawyer in particular situations is supposed to resolve conflicts between fidelity to client interest and to public interest. One prominent example of this conundrum involved James St. Clair, who as Richard Nixon's lawyer often had to walk the tightrope between advocacy and obstruction. Once in 1974, when he failed to turn over subpoenaed documents, district judge Gerhard Gesell threatened to hold his well-known client in contempt of court. "You agreed to it [the subpoena], and you were vetoed, and it's wrong," Gesell chastised St. Clair in court. "You know it's wrong. We all know it's wrong. I hope you will lend your best efforts as a distinguished member of the bar to reverse this obvious affront to the process of justice." St. Clair later complied. But most lawyers, usually engaged in far less publicized cases, usually lack guidance on how to balance client and court needs. One commentator was skeptical of how they strike the balance:

> Duty to client reads in terms of taking advantage of each techni-
> cality the law may show, however senseless. It reads in terms of
> distortion of evidence and argument to the utter bounds of the
> permissible. Duty to court reads in terms of trying issues of fact
> to reach the probable truth. Duty to self resolved the conflict, as
> canons of ethics did not. The resolution was in favor of the client.

These obligations to the court and general public make many
corporate lawyers uneasy. By training, lawyers are poorly equipped to
make personal or political judgments about the injustice of a client's
position. Law schools and the legal profession stress rigorous problem-
solving within a defined issue rather than more normative analyses
about the effect of competing social policies. So a law-school class
may spend days mulling over the concept of "easement" in property
law, but spend no time assaying the social deficiencies of the probate
system, a problem perceived as not technical. "You dedicate yourself
to a concept of craftsmanship; craftsmanship becomes all," recalls
activist lawyer John Flynn of his four years with a large law firm.
"You do what law school tells you that you are supposed to do, and
don't worry about what it is you are doing. You learn to do it very
well."

And by tradition, lawyers assume that almost anything goes in
legal combat—as the judge or jury decides the winner. There is a
strict compartmentalization between personal belief and professional
advocacy. Lawyers view themselves as did Harry Caul in Francis
Coppola's *The Conversation*. Harry bugged people for a fee. He consistently maintained that he was a mere technician hired to do a job
but not to get involved in what happened after he delivered the
goods—until the day he realized an assignment might lead to
the deaths of two innocent people. Harry, like many lawyers, lacked a
sense of consequence.

And like Harry, lawyers, too, often seek to employ technique without accountability. This spares them the responsibility of having to
dump certain clients, thereby losing accounts. But technique, after all,
can be used by anyone, as technicians such as Albert Speer and Jeb
Magruder, among others, have proved so well. If corporate lawyers
want the respect of a public profession that holds itself up to higher
standards of ethics than do the rest of us, they must season rigor with

judgment. This should be especially true for Washington lawyers, whose corporate clientele have such vast impact on social policy and the general public. The larger the stakes, the larger the responsibility.

Which is not always self-evident in the behavior of Washington lawyers. It is a matter of personal choice, not professional compulsion, that Tommy Austern intimidates FDA staff, engages in ex parte contacts to influence agency decisions, uses the "work product" standard as a cover for running the Tobacco Institute's computer, and refuses to acknowledge that smoking can be hazardous. No ethical obligation required Lloyd Cutler to meet privately with Senator Kefauver's opponents, to bring the representative of a powerful constituent to his meeting with Congressman Van Deerlin, to acquiesce in client schemes that would deprive South American peasants of low-cost drugs or foist hazardous drugs on foreign consumers, or to oppose, systematically, nearly every automobile-safety improvement on behalf of Detroit.

There are many more examples. James McKay, rather than quitting the Plumbing Fixtures Manufacturers Association account or reporting its criminal conduct, at best merely swallowed hard and closed his eyes. Stanley Temko directed a delaying action that permitted the continued marketing of a drug known to be dangerous by his client and presumably by himself. Jack Schafer continues to represent ITT despite its apparent irresistible impulse to fix public policy unethically or illegally. Ernest Jennes engages in ex parte lobbying seeking to influence pending cable-TV cases. In all these situations, intelligent lawyers—choosing their clients and their techniques, often in a unique position to influence corporate policy for the better—should be held accountable for the results of their advocacy.

And if they don't like what they are asked to do, they can quit. As did Robert Wald, who dropped P. Lorillard when its position on cigarette hazards became untenable; as did the Hartford, Connecticut, law firm of Day, Berry & Howard, which apparently dropped ITT's account after the Fazzano episode was disclosed. Continental Baking, Fazzano, Dita Beard et al., Chile, war claims: with this roll call, it would not shock even the Washington legal establishment if Covington dropped ITT as a client.

An Arnold & Porter lawyer tossed out the challenge in an interview: "They like their money so much they just look the other way. But ask them: how can they be fig leaves, flunkies, for such a corrupt firm?"

The overwhelming majority of Washington lawyers interviewed for this book rejected any such criticism of their representation of business clients. Some assumed implicitly that their *pro bono* work exonerated any questionable private counseling. Few seemed to have given the problem serious thought. One Covington & Burling associate explained that he didn't have to worry about ethical issues because he's "the low man on the totem pole . . . [who] works for a great bunch of guys who really know their stuff." A firm partner reasoned, "If my wife keeps buying shoes and I tell her not to, I don't divorce her, do I?"

Beyond this homey wisdom, most interviewees repeated certain arguments, and even certain phrasing, until they became a predictable litany. Their points were essentially four:

• *It is up to the adversary system, not the lawyer, to uncover the truth.* This is largely true where the adversary system exists. But what of where it doesn't?

The adversary process is more the exception than the rule in Washington. At the agencies, as seen in earlier chapters, corporate lawyers "descend like locusts," whereas opposing consumer lawyers make only an occasional appearance. Public-interest lawyers have established themselves as an important legal presence in Washington and have won some significant victories. But it is important to realize that they number 190 on a gross budget of $13 million annually—versus 11,500 private attorneys earning some $307 million annually. Nor do government lawyers unduly worry Washington counsel, who in interviews repeatedly sneered at the quality and quantity of agency attorneys. Agency practice, then, witnesses a one-sided tilt toward a corporate sector possessing the interest and resources to mount overwhelming campaigns—a point understood by Covington & Burling lawyer John Douglas. "Our nation must assure legal representation for consumers before the federal agencies—representation which they do not now have," he wrote. "Without their own lawyers, the consumers' interests are not assured adequate attention. . . . Even where agency members and staff personnel have the best of intentions, the scales are tipped against the public. Those scales now favor the regulated industries."

In Congress, the absence of any formal adversary system is obvious. Thousands of corporate lobbyists, often lawyers, patrol Capitol Hill corridors to watch out for hostile legislation. Randomly someone from a union or citizens' organization may oppose business on a particular bill; essentially, this is like prescribing aspirin for cancer, since such groups simply lack the resources to look at more than a small fraction of the fifteen thousand bills introduced each session of Congress. Members of Congress themselves can barely keep up with the deluge of work and requests cascading over their slender staffs. "If you aren't independently wealthy," complained ex-congressman Allard Lowenstein,

> you can't have a staff that is capable of putting things together much beyond what you can come up with from the sources available to everyone—the executive departments, the lobbies, the staffs of congressional committees, the Library of Congress. That's one reason why the lobbies are so influential. They have people who are able to spend all their time collecting data on why pollution is good for River X. What Congressman can match that?

This situation leads to the breakdown of the pluralist model of competing "factions"—the political analogue of the adversary process. Political scientist Henry Kariel attributes this breakdown to a system biased against unorganized groups or those in the process of formation. Consumers are hard to organize because of what economists call "the free-rider effect": achievements such as fair labeling or stronger bumpers are "public goods" which any single consumer can receive even if he or she does not work to secure them. Also, although employment is of overriding concern to a union employee, or profits to a manager, a consumer issue is only one of the many concerns confronting citizens. Unlike labor or management, consequently, consumers have not forged themselves into a powerful political group. Nor have poor people, who lack the resources and time to lobby effectively. "Precisely because our institutions are formally open to participation by all elements in a society," explains author-lawyer Simon Lazarus of this phenomenon, "they are vulnerable to domination by the most powerful elements in society."

• *Who can say what the "public interest" really is?* There is some merit in this question. Few were satisfied with Justice Potter Stewart's now famous statement that though he couldn't define pornography, he knew it when he saw it. There is no talmudic definition of what the public interest is in every situation; and since personal subjectivity makes lawyers, who deal in the concreteness of precedent, uncomfortable, they ridicule the notion that this talisman can be used to evaluate client conduct.

But that line-drawing is difficult does not mean that no line can ever be drawn. Otherwise, scrambling into the safety hatch of "who can say," lawyers would cease to function as independent professionals.

It is not unusual that a general term has varying meanings in varying circumstances. Courts of equity have historically applied general notions of fairness; the Constitution insists on "due process of law"; the Federal Trade Commission enforces the law against "unfair" trade practices; and even the *Code of Professional Responsibility* suggests what lawyers should do when clients engage in "unjust" acts—a phrase surely as general as "the public interest" but one, in the ABA's eyes, capable of guiding ethical conduct.

To be sure, instances come to mind in which the public interest is unclear: fair trial versus free press, for example. Other times, however, the public-interest position is not balanced evenly between competing viewpoints. It is against the public interest for a lawyer intentionally to delay a proceeding or to file frivolous motions in order to exhaust the resources of an adversary; it is against the public interest to market a product with a negative cost-benefit ratio—i.e., when the harm inflicted, however indirect or difficult to trace, exceeds any benefits to users or profits to manufacturers. Equal access to the law, free speech, economic efficiency, diversity of purchasing choices, avoidance of monopoly profits, and optimal purchasing information, for example, are also in the public interest. No doubt various antisocial policies

are often wrapped in the shawl of the public interest to gain acceptance ("Covington could plausibly argue why it was all right to kill
every third person," joked a former firm member), but when it is
argued that the oil-depletion allowance is essential to a healthy oil
industry, or that GM sharply competes with other auto firms over
price, safety, and pollution controls, few people are fooled—and certainly not their lawyers.

• *It is guilt by association (what Edward Bennett Williams calls
"guilt by client") to tar a lawyer with the views of his client.* Thus,
when the ACLU defends Nazis or Communists from unconstitutional
infringements, it is wrong to perceive the lawyer as endorsing his
clients' policies; rather, he is upholding constitutional safeguards due
any citizen.

Yet this contrasts with a corporate lawyer who on a continuing
basis advises his client not merely on constitutional safeguards but
also on policy matters. As Lloyd Cutler has written, the Washington
lawyer "is not limited, as in the courts, to defending what has already
occurred. He has the opportunity of advising his client what ought to
be done—how best to accommodate its practical problems to the
emerging demands of the public interest." What if the client ignores
its lawyer's counsel, or what if the lawyer advises not what ought to
be done but what the client can get away with? It seems illogical to
criticize, say, a corporate polluter but not the Washington lawyer
whose perennial strategies may *permit* the pollution. After years of
representing only corporations, "advocacy of one interest necessarily
entails the neglect of or opposition to other interests," Congressman
Abner Mikva has argued, "and [a lawyer] cannot escape the social,
political, and economic consequences of his choice."*

Psychologists note that it is difficult for people to act one way and

---

* Charles Rhyne—Washington lawyer, once the classmate of Richard Nixon and
more recently Rose Mary Woods's attorney—deplores the tendency to identify lawyer
and client. Yet adorning his office wall is a Herblock cartoon depicting the Supreme
Court's *Baker* v. *Carr* decision establishing one man, one vote—a case Rhyne won.
One doubts whether Rhyne would similarly publicize his corporate clientele or the
city of Richmond when it moved to block a black majority by annexing a suburb.
"But lawyers cannot have it both ways," writes critic David Riley. "Either they are
to be associated with the merits of their client's case, or they are not. Rhyne is not
the only lawyer who appears not to mind the association when it is favorable."

believe another. Ultimately, either action conforms to belief or belief to action. After years of representing a client's position, it is not unexpected that a lawyer begins to agree with, if not act like, his business retainers. This lawyer-business association has been long observed—and lamented. In 1910 Woodrow Wilson said that "lawyers have been sucked into the maelstrom of the new business section of the country." But it was Supreme Court justice Harlan Stone who in 1934 put the pin to the lawyers' business balloon:

> The rise of big business has produced an inevitable specialization of the Bar. . . . At its best the changed system has brought to the command of the business world loyalty and a superb proficiency and technical skill. At its worst it has made the learned profession of an earlier day the obsequious servant of business, and tainted it with the morals and manners of the market place in its most anti-social manifestations.

More recently, corporate lawyers themselves have often invited the public to associate them with their corporate clients. Sitting on boards of directors or taking a financial interest in their client obviously cements their association with that business. Former Yale Law School dean Eugene Rostow was surprised years ago when prominent private lawyers sitting on a government antitrust advisory committee requested anonymity when they offered their views. "They were in fact so identified with views of the law they advanced in private that they would have been embarrassed, or even compromised, in their relations with clients and prospective clients by espousing a contrary view in public as members of the Committee," said Rostow. He added, "In many instances, we have become so identified with our clients, so much a part of their daily lives, that we have lost a part of our professional freedom and our professional standing, both in our own minds and in public opinion." Also deploring this growing tendency is William Cary, former SEC chairman and professor of corporate law at Columbia Law School, who said: "Lawyers in this country seem to be relied on to carry out 'the deal.' They are no longer simply issuing an opinion as would a barrister acting independently in England. They are involved in all the business aspects. In fact, lawyers have gone so far that the next case before the courts may hold them liable as underwriters and most certainly as aiders and abettors."

Lawyers continue to argue that they should not be judged by their corporate clients, even though they may perennially earn the incomes of business from business. But from Hoyt Moore's bribing of a federal judge for Bethlehem Steel (he avoided conviction because the statute of limitations had run out; the bar never moved against him) to the directorships held by lawyers in client firms (a director becomes legally responsible for certain business activity), it seems reasonable to associate a corporate lawyer with a client he continually advises in nonadversarial forums.

• *As Tommy Austern said to a hostile law student, "Would you represent Sirhan Sirhan?"* This is a refrain repeated into catechism by interviewees, a fortress to which Washington lawyers retreat when outsiders attempt to attack their work. This analogy between corporate representation and the criminal defense of unpopular clients (rapists, murderers, Communists, and homosexuals were most commonly mentioned) collapses, however, under the weight of apparent distinctions.

First, it seems odd to compare Sirhan Sirhan with, for example, General Motors. The former is alone, impecunious, without political entrée, and capable of being victimized unless stoutly defended. General Motors has more assets than most countries and cannot be similarly outclassed or victimized by a government it can influence in numerous ways. The former risks all in a criminal proceeding, but the latter can lose five cases in a row and still exist if not prosper. A single lawyer can be the *sine qua non* to an indigent defendant; a single lawyer is usually inconsequential to a GM, which suffocates problems with teams of in-house and outside counsel. Nor is it very likely that a GM will be as unpopular with the public as were, for example, Sacco and Vanzetti, Smith Act defendants, or blacks in the South—who had trouble finding any lawyers or any justice. The lawyer's oath recommended by the American Bar Association says, "I will never reject, from any consideration personal to myself, the cause of the defenseless or oppressed"—which does not seem to include *Fortune*'s "500." Thus, a GM deserves a lawyer—but there should be no anxiety that if a certain attorney refuses to defend the auto firm it may go lawyerless.

Second, a lawyer performs a more critical role in a criminal case, where a person might lose his liberty and be incarcerated, than in a civil proceeding, where property may shift hands between two well-off adversaries. Covington & Burling's clients more often find themselves in noncriminal forums. True, a civil case could conceivably damage a person as much as a criminal proceeding; e.g., the IRS has collected back taxes equal to his net worth, or the welfare office has cut her and her three children off. But such personal loss is rarely the case in business law proceedings. And a criminal trial is usually more serious, and is accordingly treated by the law more seriously. Unlike civil proceedings, a defendant is entitled by law to a lawyer in all felony cases and for some misdemeanor charges; and unlike civil proceedings, a criminal jury must conclude something "beyond a reasonable doubt" for the state to act.

In fact, human rights occupy a "preferred position" over property rights in our constitutional system. Supreme Court decisions make clear that free speech and due process of law are constitutionally more important than property rights, which can be rearranged by a state's "police power." To simplify, although a reputed democracy with a First Amendment must tolerate a speaker of verbal pollution, it need not constitutionally tolerate a producer of industrial pollution.

Third, there is a significant difference between a lawyer who just once represents an individual accused of a *past* violation and a lawyer who on retainer represents a corporation that *repeatedly* and continuously is in legal trouble. It is one thing to defend Upjohn, which continually sells a dangerous drug, or to represent Continental Baking, which seems to violate the antitrust laws with the regularity of the vernal equinox. If a court assigned a lawyer the former case, it would be unethical to turn it down; but it is not unethical to drop a recidivist client, especially in a retainer-relationship in which the attorney on an ongoing basis is supposed to counsel his client against illegality.

Finally, it is unpersuasive when Washington lawyers compare themselves with courtroom advocates to justify their lobbying activities. When Ralph Nader criticized law-firm lobbying for "cutting down consumer programs in their incipiency or undermining them if they mature," the late Thurman Arnold dissented. He spoke of the "necessity of having representatives on both sides of a case" and thought that Nader was effectively saying "that we should get rid of skilled advocates because they confuse the court." Both sides? The court? Congress is not a court with a pristine adversary process but a place of politics. To defend oneself in court, an individual almost always needs a licensed lawyer; but every citizen has the license to try to influence legislation, and in Congress a lawyer is more a luxury than a constitutional requirement of justice. It is not unusual for a Washington lawyer to defend an unpopular client in court, but heads would no doubt turn if Lloyd Cutler lobbied for the Black Panthers in Congress. Why? Because the lawyer has more latitude in choosing whom he represents in the legislative forum than in a courtroom—and consequently is more responsible for the results. Louis Brandeis captured the distinction in an analysis as often quoted as it is still relevant:

> Many bills pass in our legislatures which would not have become law if the public interest had been fairly represented; and many good bills are defeated which if supported by able lawyers would have been enacted. Lawyers have, as a rule, failed to consider this distinction between practice in the court involving only private interests and practice before the legislature or city council where public interests are involved. Some men of high professional standing have even endeavored to justify their course in advocating professionally legislation which in their character as citizens they would have voted against.

This analysis points toward the conclusion that Washington lawyers need not represent every client in every way, but can say no to client proposals or tactics. Ironically, although most Washington lawyers reject this conclusion in interviews, they at times adopt it in their practice. For law firms, including Covington & Burling and Wilmer, Cutler & Pickering, *do* occasionally refuse to represent certain business clients. Of course they have long turned away prospective clients because of inability to pay, conflict of interest, and lack of expertise—or merely as a matter of taste. But these firms, despite incantations that "everyone is entitled to a lawyer," at times make subjective and political judgments about the limits of their advocacy.

Wilmer, Cutler & Pickering refused to defend a potential gun client and refused to represent a firm opposing federal attempts to take its pesticide off the market. In an interview Cutler pointedly noted that "we don't represent any cigarette companies, you know. We would have a lot of trouble taking on cigarette clients." (One C&B lawyer harshly called this "liberal bullshit," given, he said, Cutler's other, equally unappealing clients.) In a circular sent to law students in 1969, Wilmer, Cutler & Pickering wrote, "We decline to represent clients whose objectives or tactics we find unacceptable, or who ask us to present a position on any basis other than its merits." This implies that they consider the clients they do represent as acceptable—a judgment others can then praise or criticize based on their own sense of "unacceptability."

For its part, Covington & Burling dropped the Polish Supply Mission when President Truman criticized Communist Poland in the late 1940s. In the early 1950s the firm refused to provide legal support for a move to strip scientist Robert Oppenheimer of his security classification, because it seemed to be "a witch-hunt." It represented the National Rifle Association, *but* stipulated that it would do no lobbying for that group. The firm promoted the interests of billboard people at the Commerce Department, which prompted partner Ernest Jennes—who had once warned an associate that he took a dim view of anyone refusing to work on a case—to announce that he could never defend billboards because he found them so personally distasteful. (Since Jennes represents broadcasters, his distaste simply proves the adage that beauty is in the eyes . . .)

When *Playboy* sought legal assistance from C&B, it was turned down largely out of deference to a puritanical John Lord O'Brian; when a Washington slumlord sought C&B representation at congressional hearings, he was refused, said a former law-firm member, because Covington did not want its name linked with a real-estate scandal; when a combative General Electric told Gerhard Gesell not to settle the private claims brought against the company after the electrical conspiracy convictions, Gesell parted company with GE.

Such refusals, however, appear to be infrequent. Usually, said a former C&B associate, "the firm hates to turn down any business; they'll take on anyone who can pay."

A recent SEC complaint has suddenly focused the question of lawyer accountability. It is hardly unusual for the SEC to prosecute business for violations of the securities laws. But when in February 1972 it moved against the Wall Street law firm of White & Case (the sixth largest in the country), its partner Marion Jay Epley, and the Chicago law firm of Lord, Bissell & Brook, corporate lawyers everywhere shuddered. Involved was a merger between the Interstate National Corporation and the law firms' client, the National Student Marketing Corporation (NSM). The SEC charged that the lawyers' "opinion letter" (required in a merger) deceived shareholders and investors because the lawyers were aware that an unaudited report of their client had not been properly prepared. Instead of satisfying NSM's desire to consummate this merger, the SEC said that the lawyer-defendants should have insisted that the audit be made accurate, "and failing that, to cease representing their respective clients and, under the circumstances, notify the plaintiff Commission concerning the misleading nature of the nine-month financial statements."

White & Case's recruiters groaned. Business counsel howled that the case jeopardized the attorney-client confidence by turning the lawyer into a policeman surveying client actions. To an extent, the commission *did* want the lawyers to be "officers" of the securities process, as they are officers of the court. For the investment process depends on accountants and lawyers accurately telling the investment community about the financial condition of corporations tempted at times to cut corners. "What's apparently bothering the SEC," commented the *Wall Street Journal,* "is a growing feeling that too many securities lawyers have lost sight of everything but their obligation to be an advocate. As one SEC official put it recently, 'the securities bar is getting to be like the tax bar; it's specializing in finding loopholes in the law.' " SEC chairman Ray Garrett put it even more bluntly in 1974. "A really successful fraud can scarcely be accomplished in our complex financial worlds without the help of accountants and lawyers." Instead of furthering fraud, Garrett wanted to remind lawyers to further corporate responsibility.

A 1973 court of appeals decision underscores this reasoning. The court said a lawyer could be liable for a stock fraud not only if he had "actual knowledge of the improper scheme plus an intent to further that scheme" but also if he was simply negligent in acquiescing to an illegal act. Securities safeguards "depend in large measure on the members of the bar who serve in an advisory capacity to those engaged in securities transactions," emphasized Judge Irving Kaufman. "The public trust demands more of its legal advisors than 'customary' activities which prove to be careless."

These SEC-related actions, and the tightening ethics of a community sensitized to a degree by Watergate, are helping arouse Washington lawyers to the public obligation inherent in the law. Most still talk like John Davis, who conveniently assumed an ideal system of equal justice, but some are acting more like Louis Brandeis, who understood how unideal was the lawyer's world. As a corporate lawyer, Brandeis practiced what he preached. He would lecture clients not merely on what was right for them but also on what was the right thing to do. To a union he argued for scientific management and to management he promoted the value of collective bargaining and the Sherman Act; as counsel to shippers before the ICC, Brandeis even committed the heresy of agreeing that a rate increase was justified.

In the years since Brandeis, modern technology if anything has made his ethical standards even more compelling. Modern products, from nuclear plants to flammable pajamas, can inflict damage far more severe than could their antecedents of fifty years ago. If, as a Covington & Burling partner acknowledged, a lawyer should report to the authorities a client who promised to murder someone tomorrow, what does a lawyer do with a pharmaceutical client whose dangerous drug can also "murder" or pain thousands of people tomorrow, albeit invisibly and at a distance from the client?

The ultimate issue, then, is not classic, money-under-the-table corruption by lawyers. As one walks through the handsome and elegant offices of a Washington law firm, there is hardly the odor of corruption. Instead, many of the best graduates of the best law schools represent the largest corporations in the country—corporations that are not your fly-by-night operations. But, as C. S. Lewis suggested in *The Screwtape Letters,* the greatest offenses can be "conceived or ordered—moved, seconded, carried and minuted—in clean, carpeted, warmed and well-lighted offices, by quiet men with white collars and cut fingernails and smooth-shaven cheeks who do not need to raise their voices."

What can be done about a one-sided process in which giant companies hire Washington law firms to rationalize all client misbehavior regardless of the public cost? Since we are dealing with nongovernmental institutions on matters often involving subjective judgments, there is no simple remedial law, no undisclosed panaceas to resolve this dilemma entirely. Still, the present way is not the only way.

Some radical critics would apply an antitrust analogy to the legal profession. Several Chicago state legislators, for example, recently urged a strict size limit on law firms—the theory being that smaller firms would be less likely to exhaust, delay, or inundate weaker opponents into submission. Or perhaps, no law firm could represent a business client with over, say, $100 million in assets for more than seven years. To be sure, there would be lost expertise and burdensome start-up costs every seven years for the new law firm, but it might be less likely that lawyers would find themselves indentured to dominant clients, so integrated with them that the lawyers would no longer even be aware that they had lost their professional independence. These ideas are worth exploring, but until their effects are more sharply framed, not yet worth implementing. Three more practicable approaches could reform the way Washington lawyers work.

• To a serious extent, the governmental and legal system themselves tolerate if not encourage lawyer chicanery ("I have news for Dean Burch," a lawyer has already been quoted as saying, "I'm going to try a case . . . and take advantage of every rule that's there"). *The rules governing legal advocacy can be revised to make lawyers more responsive to the process and more open in their dealings.* For example, to reduce the tactical delaying of corporate lawyers, administrative-law judges and courtroom judges should insist that strict deadlines for submissions be met and that obvious dilatory action will be referred to bar associations for sanction. Bar grievance committees, which serve a quasi-public function of overseeing a profession licensed by the state, should contain not merely in-bred brothers-at-the-bar but also some public, nonlawyer members as well; perhaps then the practices of corporate lawyers may begin to come under the kind of scrutiny reserved for ambulance-chasers and those who convert client funds.

Greater disclosure about the activity of lawyers could discourage secret influencing and better educate the public about the lawyer's role and function. The 1946 Lobbying Registration Act is, by consensus, more loophole than law; it should be amended so that whenever a lawyer-lobbyist contacts a member of Congress or his/her staff on behalf of a client (except for mere requests for information), that lawyer should register as a lobbyist and provide information about purpose, expenses, and fees. The same should be true of the regulatory and executive agencies. Meetings should be logged between Washington lawyers and their official counterparts. And regulatory agencies should require their regulatees, who by definition are in the "public" sector of the economy, to list all their legal fees (as the CAB now does). These measures emphasize the fact that information is a predicate of reform and underscore the Brandeisian wisdom that "sunlight is said to be the best of disinfectants."

• *Since part of the problem is that wealthier Americans nearly monopolize legal talent, lawyers must be encouraged to represent the now unrepresented.* This involves expanding legal services for the poor, encouraging the establishment of prepaid legal-service programs for the middle class, creating a Consumer Protection Agency to advocate consumer interests in Washington agencies, permitting foundation-supported public-interest advocates to lobby by changing the tax code, allowing plaintiffs' lawyers who bring successful lawsuits against the government to collect their legal fees from the government, and providing more funds to dues-supported citizens' groups. The responsibility for these advances is shared by the government, which can pass needed laws, by the bar, which should rewrite an "ethical" code that now frustrates access to lawyers, and by the public itself, on whom dues-supported groups depend. To the extent that the adversary system of justice truly works, Washington lawyers will be less able to prevail by default.

• Whenever and if ever any of the above changes occur, Washington lawyers will continue to have a public obligation to oversee client conduct. For they can no longer shield themselves behind the excuse of a malfunctioning adversary process—malfunctioning precisely because these lawyers represent one sector of society while they loftily urge that all are entitled to a lawyer. Sirhan Sirhan is not Upjohn and the courthouse is not the Congress or the Federal Power Commission. The making of this distinction should lead to a new lawyers' ethic: *when a Washington counsel, on a continuing retainer for past and future legal liability, represents a corporation in a civil or legislative proceeding, he (or she) should make a judgment about the likely impact on the public, and if the client desires tactics based on political influence or seeks a demonstrable though avoidable public harm, he should quit the account.*

This ethic would encourage a lawyer to make his own moral judgment about whether and how to represent clients based on a sliding scale of considerations: for example, is the proceeding civil or criminal, nonadversarial or actually adversarial, abusive of judicial procedure or not, concerned with an alleged past or continuing violation? After weighing factors like these, an attorney may choose to represent such firms, and to accept responsibility for the continuing results; but he is also free to refuse to do so, and to decide what to do with his one professional life. For there is nothing in the Code of Professional Responsibility that says a lawyer *must* represent the House of Morgan or GM. Even the Canons of Ethics say, "He has the right to decline employment," and "If a client persists in . . . wrongdoing, the lawyer should terminate their relation."

A lawyer can also simply conclude that certain business defenses can harm society more than any conceptual contribution made to the adversary process. Or he can decide initially that corporate law firms in general, whatever their legal wizardry and genteel advocacy, are institutions with negative social balance sheets.

This new ethic is no Rosetta stone instructing all lawyers what to do in all situations. Like any ethical judgment, it is subjective and personal, not universal, though the lawyer may wish others to follow his example. It is an ethic that throws the lawyer ultimately back on his own subjective preferences, his own view of "the public interest."

This is surely not new. What is the adversary process itself but a social judgment that legal combat is in the public interest because it leads to justice—a conclusion the author shares but one which, for example, China and Herbert Marcuse do not. Nor is it a neutral principle that lawyers will represent those who can pay and not represent those who cannot. This means-test effectively excludes a large class of Americans from access to legal services; it is very much a value choice. So is the new ethic of conscientious refusal. As the concept of a good German has changed, so will the concept of a good lawyer. Lawyers chafe at the accusation that they are merely hired guns following orders, but it is not surprising that some now agree with Washington lawyer Joseph Califano when he says, "I think we are going to have to start making moral judgments on our clients."

It is obviously academic to fear that all lawyers, following this guide, will rush out to conclude simultaneously that, say, an IBM doesn't deserve representation. The military draft would have collapsed if all draftees had declared themselves conscientious objectors, but military officials knew that statistically this could not happen. Any single lawyer conscientiously refusing an IBM would be secure in the knowledge that the computer giant would not go unrepresented.

Why then bother to refuse?, some might plausibly ask. The reasons are both ethical and practical. Ethically, it can be immoral to become an executioner, even though society can always find someone to lop off heads. "Someone else will do it anyway" is a standard that obliterates individual choice and can rationalize any evil. And practically, GM retains a Lloyd Cutler, and the Tobacco Institute a Covington & Burling, presumably because they can do things other lawyers cannot. To the extent that lawyers refused to expend their skills on *pro malo* advocacy, certain clients would have to use lawyers of lesser ability to make their case—a case which might not then prevail. This situation could send a message to the business sector that the best lawyers would not be merely message-takers and spear-carriers. Ideally, this spreading feedback could, to some extent, deter and reform corporate misbehavior.

Probably few individual lawyers, at least initially, will refuse corporate-client requests. Most lawyers politically agree with their clients.

Others—laboring in a capitalist economy where money buys talent—
may find their ethical qualms soothed by large legal fees. (Chicago
lawyer Donald Reuben, a powerful partner at Kirkland, Ellis, told an
audience that "as Mr. Kirkland used to say, a good lawyer is like a
good prostitute. If the price is right, you warm up to your client.")
Yet, cynics should not ignore the motivational power of not only
doing well, but doing good. Many recent law graduates claim to embrace this goal—and they are not without a model to aspire to. In
Robert Bolt's *A Man for All Seasons,* the young and ambitious
Richard Rich asked Sir Thomas More to help him become a public
official. More turned him down. Since you may not be able to resist
the corruptions of public life, counseled the wise lawyer and judge,
become instead a teacher. "And if I was," a crestfallen Rich protested,
"who would know it?" Answered More: "You. Your pupils. Your
friends. God. Not a bad public, that."

Notes

===

Chapter 1
Earthshakers, Lawmakers, Message-Takers: A Tour

page

3 Berle on law firms: A. Berle, Jr., *Encyclopedia of the Social Sciences* 341 (vol. 9, 1948).

4 Lundberg judgment on lawyers: F. Lundberg, "The Law Factories," *Harper's,* July 1939, p. 180.

4 Swaine challenge to colleagues: Swaine, "Impact of Big Business on the Profession," 35 *American Bar Association Journal* 89 (1949); see generally R. Swaine, *The Cravath Firm,* 2 vols. (1949).

5 Creation of regulatory agencies: For a background on agency development, see *Final Report of the Attorney General's Committee,* Sen. Docket No. 8, 77th Cong., 1st Sess. 7 (1941).

6 Smigel quotation on law-firm anonymity: E. Smigel, *The Wall Street Lawyers* 19 (1969 edition).

7 Metropolitan D. C. lawyers: *Washington Post,* January 17, 1974, p. E1.

7 Lawyers in government, education, business: S. Keller, *Beyond the Ruling Class* 325 (1963); Stevenson, "Making President Instead of Partner," *Juris Doctor,* March 1973, p. 10.

8 Smathers' exuberance on lush fees: J. Goulden, *The Superlawyers* 339 (1972).

8 Nine billion dollars gross legal product: Internal Revenue Service, *Business Income Tax Returns: 1971* 13, 25 (1973).

8 Zeros on the ends of problems and fees: *Washington Post,* December 26, 1973, pp. A1, A6.

8 Quotation on Richard Nixon's legal fees: L. Chester, G. Hodgson, B. Page, *An American Melodrama* (1969).

9 Annual incomes of senior partners: *Washington Post,* December 26, 1973, pp. A1, A6.

10 Comparison of Washington and Wall Street law firms: Two books on New York City law firms are E. Smigel, *The Wall Street Lawyer* (1969) and P. Hoffman, *Lions in the Street* (1973). It has been written that New York City firms have been somewhat liberalizing, at least as compared with what they were before. See Smigel, "The Wall Street Lawyer Revisited," *New York,* August 18, 1969, p. 36.

12 Freund on lawyer's obligation: P. Freund, "The Legal Profession," in R. Lynn (ed.), *The Professions in America* (1965).

12 Sommer on lawyers as auditors: *SEC News Digest,* January 25, 1974, p. 1; see generally Califano, "The Washington Lawyer: When to Say No," in R. Nader and M. Green (eds.), *Verdicts on Lawyers* (1975).

13 Lorenz lists benefits of important clients: "The New Public Interest Lawyers," 79 *Yale Law Journal* 1069, 1075, note 11 (1970).

Chapter 2
The Covington Culture: "Only a Bunch of Lawyers"

page

17 Sapienza wonders about interest in C&B: J. Goulden, *The Superlawyers* 27 (1972).

20 Portrait of Covington in 1918: Aside from interviews, much of the material in this historical section comes from D. Acheson, *Morning and Noon* (1965); D. Acheson, *Fragments of My Fleece* (1971); and Westwood, "Something of C&B's History," a talk delivered at Covington & Burling's annual dinner, November 19, 1973 [hereinafter Westwood].

20 C&B foreign clients: These statistics and names were compiled from two decades of filings at the Justice Department under the Foreign Agents Registration Act.

21 On George Rublee: See Rublee, "The Original Plan and Early History of the Federal Trade Commission," 11 *Academy of Polytechnical Science Proceedings* 666 (1926).

22 Burling view of New Deal: Quoted in the *Washington Post*, February 1, 1960, p. B1.

22 Westwood at creation of CAB: For elaboration on Westwood's role in this legislation, see Chapter 9, "Planes and Trains."

23 C&B thrives between 1945 and 1948: Westwood, p. 9.

23 O'Brian regrets hiring Hoover: *New York Times*, April 11, 1973, p. 50.

24 Firm billings 1953–1959: Westwood, p. 15.

25 Burling's "Shut up" note: This episode is described in D. Acheson, *Morning and Noon* 133–142 (1965).

26 Acheson as undersecretary of state: For a discussion of Acheson's ties to Covington & Burling during his years as undersecretary of state, see *Nomination of Dean G. Acheson*, hearings before the Senate Foreign Relations Committee, 81st Cong., 1st Sess. (January 13, 1949).

26 Schlesinger on Acheson: *New York Times*, October 13, 1970, p. 50.

26 Acheson "dies a little": *New York Times*, October 13, 1970, p. 50.

26 Acheson and Temple of Preah Vihear: *International Court Justice Reports*, 1962, p. 15; see also Thornberry, "The Temple of Preah Vihear," 26 *The Modern Law Review* 448 (1963).

27 Acheson defends colonial regimes: Acheson did not understate his case: "It will surprise some of my fellow citizens, to be told that the United States is engaged in an international conspiracy, instigated by Britain, and blessed by the United Nations, to overthrow the government of a country [Rhodesia] that has done us no harm and threatens no one. This is bare-faced aggression, unprovoked and unjustified by a single legal or moral principle." See D. Acheson, *Fragments of My Fleece* 158 (1971) (based on 1968 address before the Section of International and Comparative Law of the American Bar Association); see also Acheson, *Grapes from Thorns* 171 et seq. (1972); and *Washington Post*, December 11, 1966, p. E6.

32 Westwood reference to the management committee: Westwood, p. 12.

32 Earnings of average partner: Weil, *The Census of Law Firms* 10 (1972).

33 Female associates: Women compose only 2.7 per cent of the legal profession, although 16 per cent of the 1975 law-school graduating class are women, "Portia Faces Life: The Trials of Law School," *Ms.*, April 1974, p. 74.

34 "Oink, oink" article: Goulden, "The Washington Legal Establishment," *Washingtonian*, October 1973, p. 90.

34 Chevy Chase Club discrimination: *Washington Post*, September 14, 1968, p. B2.

34 Burning Tree Club discrimination: *Washington Post*, September 24, 1968, p. B2.

35 Bonsal on admitting women: *Washington Post*, April 12, 1972, p. C1.

40 Cappelli on Peanut Butter Case: Letter from Richard Cappelli to Marshall Beil, September 17, 1970.
42 Smigel's Wall Street success profile: E. Smigel, *The Wall Street Lawyer* 37 (1971).

Chapter 3
The Paradox of Being Cutler

page
47 Cutler promotes permanent special prosecutor: Cutler, "A Permanent Prosecutor," *New York Times*, October 25, 1973, p. 47.
47 Cutler quotation on political corruption: Statement before Committee for Public Justice, conference on "The Politics of Justice," February 9, 1974, Washington, D.C.
48 Spater describes shakedown: *Washington Post*, July 7, 1973, p. 1.
48 *Post* on Cutler's disclosure role: *Washington Post*, July 7, 1973, p. 1.
53 Evans & Novak on Johnson and Cutler: Evans & Novak, "LBJ's Non-Appointments," *Washington Post*, April 20, 1965, p. A17.
53 AP story on Cutler to Commerce: *Washington Post*, April 13, 1965, p. A2.
57 *Fortune* on Cutler: Zalaznick, "The Small World of Big Washington Law Firms, *Fortune*, September 1969, p. 120.
57 *Washingtonian* ranks Cutler: "Lobbying: The Fifth Branch of Government," *Washingtonian*, November 1972, pp. 60, 68.
58 Cutler replies to Barnett: Letter from Lloyd Cutler to Stephen Barnett, February 9, 1970.
59 N.Y. lawyer on lawyers on boards: Gartner, "Are Outside Directors Taking Outside Chances?" *Juris Doctor*, March 1973, p. 56; see also W. Hudson, *Outside Counsel: Inside Director* (1973).
60 *Business Week* decries conflicts of interest: "Conflict of Interest: The Moral Climate Changes," *Business Week*, April 14, 1973, p. 56.
60 Condemnation of Gilpatric: *TFX Contract Investigation*, hearings before the Permanent Subcommittee on Investigations of the Senate Government Operations Committee, 91st Cong., 2d Sess. (March, April 1970).
60 Charlton and FTC memorandum: *Washington Post*, September 28, 1974, p. A4.
60 Reference to Manny Cohen's phone calls: Zalaznick, "The Small World of Big Washington Lawyers," *Fortune*, September 1969, p. 120.
62 Friedenberg at Justice in America conference: Smith, "Law and Order 1970," *Nation*, June 29, 1970, p. 781.
63 Cutler letter defending Moynihan: *New York Times*, March 20, 1970, p. 46.

Chapter 4
Sentries of Monopoly

page
67 Horsky on the antitrust bar: C. Horsky, *The Washington Lawyer* 127 (1952).
67 McLaren on the antitrust bar: Speech of Richard McLaren before the Antitrust Section of the American Bar Association, March 27, 1969, p. 1.
68 Kauper view that clients dictate to counsel: Address by Thomas Kauper, "The Antitrust Bogeyman," before the New York State Bar Association, January 24, 1973, p. 20.
68 Firm advises clients to merge quickly: Smith, "What Antitrust Means under Mr. Bicks," *Fortune*, March 1960, p. 262.
68 Quotation on "looking away": Klau, "The Wall Street Lawyers," *Fortune*, February 1958, p. 144.

68 ITT politicking: M. Green, B. Moore, B. Wasserstein, *The Closed Enterprise System* 30–47 (1972) [hereinafter Green].

69 Judge Fox accepts *nolo* plea: CCH Trade Cases, *United States* v. *American Bakeries* 72, 521 (1968).

69 Arnold speaks of bogging down antitrust cases: *Wall Street Journal*, May 22, 1959, p. 1.

69 Duration of merger and monopoly cases: Green, pp. 136–141.

69 Delaying as a "specifically designated tactic": Speech of James Halverson before the Association of General Counsel, Washington, D.C., October 8, 1973, pp. 22–31.

70 Turner criticizes ABA Antitrust Section: Speech of Donald Turner before the Antitrust Section of the American Bar Association, Miami, Florida, August 10, 1965, p. 5; also speech of Turner before Cleveland Bar Association, Cleveland, Ohio, March 7, 1969, pp. 14–15.

70 Paul on public obligations of private lawyers: Paul, "The Responsibilities of the Tax Advisor," 63 *Harvard Law Review* 337 (1950).

71 Competition according to Lippmann: Quoted in Kramer, "Criminal Prosecutions for Violations of the Sherman Act: In Search of a Policy," 48 *Georgetown Law Journal* 530, 536 (1960).

71 Estimates of monopoly control over manufacturing: W. Shepherd, *Market Power and Economic Welfare* 106 (1970); R. Barber, *The American Corporation* (1969). The 1969 Cabinet Committee on Price Stability reported that the average four-firm concentration ratio was 42 per cent (*Studies by the Staff of the Cabinet Committee on Price Stability* 58, Government Printing Office, 1969). Using more refined economic data, Shepherd has put the figure as high as 60 per cent (*Market Power*, p. 106).

71 Concentration and higher consumer prices: Scanlan, "FTC and Phase II: The McGovern Papers," 5 *Antitrust Law and Economic Review* 19, 33 (Spring 1972).

71 Concentration frustrates inflation checks: J. Blair, *Economic Concentration* (1972).

71 Firm presidents acknowledge price-fixing: Green, p. 472.

71 Average corporate antitrust fines: Claubault and Burton, *Sherman Act Indictments* 40 (supp. 1967).

73 Supreme Court ruling on Von's Grocery case: 384 U.S. 270 (1966).

75 Delaware District Court ruling on cellophane monopoly: 118 F. Supp. 41 (1953).

75 Gesell's Supreme Court argument: U.S. Supreme Court, Oral Arguments; Case No. 5, October Term, 1955, *U.S.* v. *E. I. du Pont de Nemours.*

76 Supreme Court cellophane ruling: 351 U.S. 377 (1957).

76 Gesell has "horse sense": *Washington Post*, March 23, 1943, p. B5.

77 Government loses du Pont–GM merger case in district court: 126 Supp. 235 (1953).

78 Cox on Raskob memo: U.S. Supreme Court, Oral Arguments, Case No. 3, October Term, 1956, *U.S.* v. *E. I. du Pont de Nemours.*

78 Cox advocates deciding on the facts: U.S. Supreme Court, Oral Arguments, Case No. 55, October Term, 1960, *U.S.* v. *E. I. du Pont de Nemours.*

78 Supreme Court du Pont–GM ruling of 1957: 353 U.S. 586 (1957).

79 Brennan decision for divestiture: 366 U.S. 316 (1961).

79 Clifford explains du Pont switch: Goulden, *The Superlawyers* 102 (1972).

80 Cox bored with hobbyists: *Washington Post*, March 23, 1943, p. B5.

81 Herling describes electrical conspiracy: J. Herling, *The Great Price Conspiracy* 84, 157–165, 167–168, 196–198, 316 (1962).

84 *Fortune* article on plumbing conspiracy: Demaree, "Judgment Comes for the Plumbing Manufacturers," *Fortune*, December 1969, p. 96.

85 Kramer claims McKay knew: See *Transcript of Proceedings, Philadelphia*

Housing Authority v. *American Radiator & Standard Fountain Corp., Deposition of William Kramer,* pp. 1589–1593, Civ. Action No. 41773, 1970.

87 Lawyers as tax violators: *Washington Post,* October 22, 1972, p. G8.

89 Fazzano advocates merger to Cotter: *Hartford Courant,* November 8, 1970, p. 1. Transcript of *Nader* v. *Cotter,* arguments before Hon. Walter Sidor, Superior Court, Hartford County, No. 166205, January 4, 1972, at 61–99 (testimony of Joe Fazzano, represented by John Schafer).

90 Rohatyn argues for Hartford merger: A. Sampson, *The Sovereign State of ITT* 249 (1973) [hereinafter Sampson].

90 ITT antitrust activities in general: Sampson.

91 ITT and Chile: *The International Telephone and Telegraph Company and Chile, 1970–71,* Report to the Senate Foreign Relations Committee by the Subcommittee on Multinational Corporations, June 21, 1973, p. 5. See generally *Multinational Corporations and United States Foreign Policy,* hearings before the Senate Subcommittee on Multinational Corporations, 93rd Cong., 1st Sess. (March, April 1973).

93 1967 award to ITT for war losses: Foreign Claims Settlement Commission, Final Decision No. W–21523, May 17, 1967.

94 Behn secures favored status for German plants: Sampson, pp. 21–47.

96 Priorities and tradition at the FTC: See generally E. Cox, R. Fellmeth, J. Schultz, *The Nader Report on the Federal Trade Commission* (1969); *Report of the ABA Commission to Study the Federal Trade Commission* (1969); Green, pp. 321–437.

96 Campbell Soup loses marbles case: 449 F. 2d 1142 (1967).

96 Colgate-Palmolive loses sandpaper case: *FTC* v. *Colgate-Palmolive Co.,* 380 U.S. 374 (1964), *reversing* 326 F. 2d 517 (1963).

97 Jones admits "flipflops": *Wall Street Journal,* February 5, 1969, p. 8.

98 Elman criticizes ex parte basis of Broadway-Hale decision: *Broadway Hale,* CCH Trade Cases, ¶18, 692, pp. 21, 067.

100 Court of appeals overturns Geritol decision: As reported in *Antitrust and Trade Regulation Reporter,* May 21, 1974, pp. A1, D1.

Chapter 5
The Drug World

page
102 Welch receives $287,000: M. Mintz, *The Therapeutic Nightmare* 133–134 (1965).

102 Combination antibiotics called "shotgun therapy" by AMA: M. Mintz, *The Therapeutic Nightmare* 133–134 (1965).

102 Drug advertising more than R&D: National Science Foundation, *Research and Development in Industry* 76 (1970).

102 Conflict of interest between supplier and physician: *Competitive Problems in the Drug Industry,* Summary and Analysis, Senate Small Business Committee (November 2, 1972).

103 One-fifth of efficiency claims found supportable: *Washington Post,* February 2, 1971, p. A2.

103 Hospitals and adverse reactions: Hurwitz, "Admissions to Hospitals Due to Drugs," 1 *British Medical Journal* 529 (1969); Seidl et al., "Studies on the Epidemiology of Adverse Drug Reactions III: Reactions in Patients on a General Medical Service," 119 *Bulletin of Johns Hopkins Hospital* 299 (1966); unpublished data supplied by Dr. Milton Silverman and Dr. Philip Lee, University of California at San Francisco.

103 Annual adverse reactions: Cluff, "Problems in the Use of Drugs," *Proceedings of the Conference on Continuing Education for Physicians in the Use of Drugs* 9 (National Academy of Sciences, 1969); Melmon, "Preventable Drug

Reactions—Causes and Cures," 284 *New England Medical Journal* 1361 (1971).

103 Drug industry the most profitable: *Washington Post*, September 18, 1973, p. D8. Drug and medicine companies realized an average 19.4 per cent return on stockholders' investment in 1971; this total, however, understates the return for pharmaceutical manufacturing since the firms involved include many nondrug subsidiaries, whose lower returns deflate the overall average.

103 Similarity between generics and brand-name antibiotics: Simmons, *FDA Consumer*, March 1973, p. 9.

103 Price comparisons of specific name brands and generics: Statement by Senator Gaylord Nelson, June 11, 1973.

103 Orinase price comparison, Canada vs. U.S.: Statement of Senator Gaylord Nelson, June 30, 1973.

103 U.S. government buys brand names: See generally Till, "Drug Procurement: High on Profits," in M. Green (ed.), *The Monopoly Makers* 257 (1973).

104 Cutler on exorbitant drug pricing: *Competitive Problems in the Drug Industry*, Summary and Analysis, Senate Small Business Committee (November 2, 1973), p. 23.

104 Goddard describes drug lawyers: "The Drug Establishment," *Esquire*, March 1969, p. 117.

105 Harris quotation on drug legislation: R. Harris, *The Real Voice* 143 (1964) [hereinafter Harris].

105 Industry will "fight to the death": Harris, p. 144.

105 Cutler understood to speak for Dirksen: See D. Pearson, J. Anderson, *The Case Against Congress* 334 (Pocket Books ed., 1969); Harris, p. 164; Viorst, *Nation*, August 11, 1962, p. 45. In a report filed with the secretary of the Senate, Senator Dirksen reported contributions of $5450 from nine drug companies in 1962, an off-year election.

106 *Times* editorial on drug-reform bill: *New York Times*, June 15, 1962, p. 26.

106 Thalidomide increases support for stronger measure: "Conservative Congress responding to industry opposition had practically emasculated the Kefauver bill by the time the thalidomide story broke." Lessing, "Laws Alone Can't Make Drugs Safe," *Fortune*, March 1963, p. 148.

107 S1552 passed by Senate: The final bill provided that (a) before a new drug would be approved, it would have to be shown by "substantial evidence" that the drug will have its claimed effect, with the burden of proof being on the manufacturer; (b) false advertising could require that the drug be removed from the market; (c) the secretary of HEW can suspend sales of a drug immediately if it is shown to be an "imminent hazard," and a previously cleared drug must be withdrawn "after opportunity for a hearing" if the re-evaluation shows safety in danger; (d) provision was made for inspection of drug-producing plants.

107 Cutler summarizes the industry's position: *Drug Industry Act of 1962*, House Interstate and Foreign Commerce Committee, 87th Cong., 1st Sess. 249 (1962) [hereinafter DIA].

108 Cutler on "language changes": DIA, p. 251.

108 Lobbyist quotation on normal amendment strategy: Harris, p. 223.

108 Cutler and Foley buttonhole committee members: *Washington Post*, September 23, 1962, p. A1.

108 Dingell outraged: Harris, p. 224.

109 Press-corps member explains applause: Harris, p. 223.

109 PMA "war chest" against the drug bill: Harris, p. 270.

109 Drug prices still exorbitant: See Till, p. 257.

110 *Abbott Laboratories* v. *Gardner:* 387 U.S. 136 (1967).

110 Justice Clark criticizes pharmaceutical firms: 387 U.S. 136, 201 (1967).

111 *PMA* v. *Finch:* 307 F. Supp. 858 (1970).

111 Judge Latchum upholds FDA the second time around: *PMA* v. *Richardson,* 318 F. Supp. 301 (1970).

112 Cutler-Court exchange during Panalba case: Transcript of pretrial hearing, pp. 47–48.

113 Kennedy Administration looks to pharmaceutical companies: *Washington Post,* July 28, 1963, p. E3.

113 Johnson quotation on Cutler's conditions for PMA deal: H. Johnson, *The Bay of Pigs* 322–327 (1964) [hereinafter Johnson]; see generally D. Pearson, J. Anderson, *The Case Against Congress* 332 (Pocket Book ed., 1969); M. Mintz, *By Prescription Only* 369–370 (1967) [hereinafter Mintz]; Kraft, "The Washington Lawyers," *Harper's,* April 1964, p. 104.

113 Tax benefit exceeding product cost: Johnson, p. 326.

114 Merck and Pfizer profit from contributions: V. Navasky, *Kennedy Justice* 337 (1971) [hereinafter Navasky].

114 Navasky on contributors being under FTC or antitrust investigation: Navasky, 337. In all, $17 million of goods were raised, which at retail values met Castro's demand of $53 million worth of supplies.

114 Cost of McKesson generics in Colombia: *Washington Post,* July 28, 1963, p. E3.

114 Dilemma of President Comargo: Quoted in 109 *Congressional Record* 16950 (1963).

115 McKesson generic sales threatening: "In fact, one major firm is now quietly marketing drugs here [in the United States] at prices similar to those charged in Colombia, but the fear of retaliation by the drug industry has prevented the firm from publicizing it." See 109 *Cong. Rec.* 16950 (1963).

115 McKesson suppliers retaliate: *Washington Post,* July 28, 1963, p. E3.

115 Nolen alarmed: 109 *Cong. Rec.* 16950 (1963).

115 Cutler, AFIDRO, *et al.* meet: The memorandum taken at the meeting was entitled *Highlights of Discussion on Colombian Situation* (a copy is in possession of the writer).

116 *Post* sees imperialism: *Washington Post,* August 1, 1963, p. A16. The charge of Yankee imperialism is not gratuitous. The exorbitant price of drugs has caused a continuing hostility on the part of many South American countries. For example, after a coup d' état in Ecuador in 1963, the first thing the new government did was expose the inflated mark-up between the United States price and the landing price, and the portal-to-peasant price.

116 Senator Neuberger denounces conspiracy: 109 *Cong. Rec.* 16950 (1963).

116 PMA and Cutler rebuttal: 109 *Cong. Rec.* 4746 (1963).

116 Rejoinder by Walter Wein: 109 *Cong. Rec.* 4747 (1963).

118 Nelson, Cootner, Cutler testimony quoted: *Hearings on Competitive Problems in the Drug Industry,* 86th Cong., 2d Sess. 1624.

119 Chloromycetin deaths: *Washington Post,* Nov. 7, 1967, p. A18.

119 *Lancet* ads differ: *Washington Post,* Nov. 30, 1967, p. A2.

121 Warner-Lambert's Hensley and imperialism issue: *Washington Post,* May 3, 1972, p. 3; Sesser, "Special Dispensation," *New Republic,* March 6, 1971, p. 16.

122 Orinase bottle warning: The following was included on the Orinase label: "The safety and the usefulness of Orinase (tolbutamide) during pregnancy have not been established at this time, either from the standpoint of the mother or fetus. In animal studies, tolbutamide has been shown to have fetricidal and teratogenic effects at dosages of 1000 to 2500 mgs. per kg. of body weight per day."

123 Culpability under FDC Act: See *United States* v. *Dotterweich,* 320 U.S. 277 (1943).

124 Quotation on delay as injustice: Berlin, Roisman, Kessler, "Public Interest Law," 38 *George Washington Law Review* 675, 676 (1970).

125 Bromley on protraction: Bromley, "Judicial Control of Antitrust Cases," 23 F.R.D. 417 (1959).

126 Panalba frequently prescribed: Petitioner's Brief in *Upjohn* v. *Finch, et al.,* Civil Action No. 163 (D.C. W. Mich. 1968).

126 Panalba subscription statistics: See Mintz, "Public Swallows FDA's Mistakes," *Washington Post,* November 23, 1969, p. B1.

126 Panalba less effective in combination form: For example, one Upjohn study by Dr. E. L. Foltz noted: "The results show that novobiocin in combination with tetracycline produces lower blood serum levels for both novobiocin and tetracycline than the levels obtained by the use of either above. . . . there was mutual interference in the absorption of novobiocin and tetraclycline when these two agents were given in combination."

126 Novobiocin dropped by Merck: *Transcript of Hearing on Drug Safety,* Committee on Government Operations, Subcommittee on Intergovernmental Relations, May 13, 1969, p. 84 [hereinafter Fountain Hearings].

127 Adverse Panalba cases: Affidavit of Dr. William M. Kirby, *Upjohn* v. *Finch, et al.,* Civ. Action No. 163 (D.C.D. Mich. 1969).

129 Judge Kent restrains FDA: 303 F. Supp. 241 (D. Mich. 1969).

129 Kent and foundation connection with Upjohn: *Washington Evening Star,* August 15, 1969, p. 1.

130 Kent opinion overruled: 422 F.2d 944 (1969).

130 Hewitt on Panalba theft from public: Fountain Hearings, May 15, 1969, p. 223. In addition, Panalba sells at three times the price of "brand name" tetracycline and ten times as much as "generic name" tetracycline. This discrepancy and inflated price for Panalba is lower than it used to be, following the successful civil antitrust suit against three drug companies, a case in which Upjohn was a co-conspirator but not a defendant. The company was forced to contribute $6,240,000 to a $120,000,000 refund chest for the drugs involved, one of which was Panalba. See, for example, *Cong. Rec.,* February 10, 1966, S 2886–2912 (statement of Senator Russell Long).

131 Mintz on Panalba: "FDA and Panalba: A Conflict of Commercial, Therapeutic Goals?", *Science,* August 29, 1969, p. 875.

Chapter 6
Thought for Food: On Peanut Butter and Other Treats

page
132 The dangers of additives: See generally M. F. Jacobson, *Eater's Digest: The Consumer's Fact Book of Food Additives* (1972); Epstein, "Control of Chemical Pollutants," 228 *Nature* 816 (1970).

132 Additives and hyperactivity: *Washington Post,* October 29, 1973, p. A1.

132 Americans as "nutritional illiterates": See especially forthcoming Nader Report on the Food Industry, by Beverly C. Moore, Jr.

132 Sugar, fat, salt diet can cause heart disease: This position has been endorsed by the American Heart Association, the Council on Foods and Nutrition of the American Medical Association, the American Health Foundation, the National Heart and Lung Institute's Task Force on Arteriosclerosis.

132 Possible benefits of optimum nutrition: Joint Task Group of the U.S. Department of Agriculture and the State Universities and Land Grant Colleges, "Benefits from Human Nutritional Research," Rep't No. 2, An Evaluation of Research in the United States on Human Nutrition 4–10 (1971).

133 Annual food-industry overcharges: Printed in Scanlan, "FTC and Phase II: The McGovern Papers," *Antitrust Law & Eco. Rev.* 19 (Spring 1972).

133 Advertising aids monopoly overcharges: See generally Scitovsky, "Ignorance as a Source of Oligopoly Power," 40 *American Economic Review Papers and Proceedings* 48 (1950).

133 General Foods advertising budget and government research: Testimony of Ralph Nader and Beverly C. Moore, Jr., before the Subcommittee of Monopolies and Commercial Law of the House Judiciary Committee, 93rd Cong., 2d Sess. (July 17, 1973).

133 FDA enforces laws on food "definitions and standards of identity": Section 401 of Food, Drug and Cosmetic Act of 1938.

134 Austern cross-examines FDA witness: *Nut Products: Definitions and Standards of Identity—Peanut Butter*, Dkt. No. FDC-76, p. 696 [hereinafter Transcript].

135 Austern says, "Coke got theirs . . .": See J. Turner, *The Chemical Feast* 51–57 (1970).

135 Austern protests November 1 hearing date: Pre-hearing Transcript, p. 13.

136 Austern on lay people: Austern, "The Formulation of Mandatory Food Standards," 2 *Food, Drug, Cosmetic Law Quarterly* 532, 576 (1947).

137 Mechling explains not testifying: Transcript, p. 7038.

137 Austern reacts to Mechling's imputation: Transcript, p. 2205.

138 Austern slowly questions FDA official: Transcript, p. 2214.

138 Cappelli refers to lengthy transcript: Letter of Richard Cappelli to Marshall Beil, September 17, 1970.

138 Foley comments on lost consumer-attitude survey: Transcript, pp. 2148–2150.

139 Austern warns against arrogance: Austern, "Exploring Expertise: Some Pragmatic Aspects of Practicing Law," speech delivered at Harvard Law School, November 18, 1968, p. 32.

139 Final standard without 3 per cent limit: 33 *Fed. Register* 10506 (July 1968).

140 FDA's two new sections on hearing rules: 31 *Fed. Register* 3003, 3008 (February 1966).

140 Udall charge on access to Nixon and Mitchell: *A Report on the Circumstances Surrounding the Proposed Sale of U.S. Postal Service Bonds*, Postal Service Subcommittee on the Post Office and Civil Service, 92d Cong., 1st Sess. (September 27, 1971).

141 Austern lampoons nutritional labeling: Austern, "Legally Required Voluntary Labeling," 27 *Food-Drug-Cosmetic Law Journal* 312, 314 (1972).

141 Court upholds "using influence": *Troutman v. Southern Railway Company*, 441 F. 2d 586 (1971).

142 Racial discrimination at American Can: See generally U.S. Commission on Civil Rights, "Bellamy Alabama: Company Town Revisited," Fall 1969, p. 12.

144 Austern wants individual references deleted: Vitamin Hearings, pp. 7665, 7670 (*Revising the Regulations for Foods for Special Dietary Uses*, 21 C.F.R. Parts 80, 125, Dkt. No. FDC-78).

145 Criticism of food and drug bar quoted: J. Goulden, *The Superlawyers* 194 (1972).

146 Austern exhorts National Canners clients: R. Lamb, *American Chamber of Horrors* 195 (1936).

146 Austern urges FDA to secrecy: Austern, "Drug Regulation and the Public Health," 19 *Food, Drug, Cosmetic L.Q.* 259 (1964).

146 Austern says standards are political: Austern, "The Formulation of Mandatory Food Standards," 2 *Food, Drug, Cosmetic L.Q.* 534–535 (1947).

Chapter 7
The Law of Smoke

page
148 Cigarette-related deaths per year: FTC Hearings on Proposed Cigarette Advertising Rule, July 1, 1969, p. 105 [hereinafter FTC Hearings]; S. Wagner, *Cigarette Country* 204 (1971) [hereinafter Wagner].

148 Death rates for smokers and nonsmokers: C. M. Fletcher and D. Horn, *Smoking and Health* (1970). National Clearinghouse for Smoking and Health, *Unless You Decide to Quit, Your Problem's Going to Be Staying Alive,* DHEW Publication No. (HSM) 73-8705 (revised December 1972).

148 Life expectancies of smokers and nonsmokers: U.S. Department of Health, Education, and Welfare, *Chart Book on Smoking, Tobacco & Health* 12 (based on study by Dr. E. C. Hammond) (1972).

148 Carbon-monoxide study: U.S. Public Health Service, *The Health Consequences of Smoking. A Report of the Surgeon General: 1971,* DHEW Publication No. (HSM) 71-7513 (1971); see also R A. McFarland, "The effects of exposure to small quantities of carbon monoxide on vision," *Annals of the New York Academy of Sciences,* October 5, 1970, pp. 301–312.

148 Eye irritation for nonsmokers: F. Speer, "Tobacco and the Nonsmoker: A Study of Subjective Symptoms," *Archives of Environmental Health,* March 1968, pp. 443–446.

148 Children of smokers: National Tuberculosis and Respiratory Disease Association, *10 Million Women Have Quit Smoking* (leaflet).

148 Natal deaths and smoking: C. M. Fletcher and D. Horn, *Smoking and Health* (1970); see generally T. Whiteside, *Selling Death* (1971).

148 Austern not convinced: Austern, "Exploring Expertise: Some Pragmatic Aspects of Practicing Law," lecture at the Harvard Law School, November 18, 1968 (in a response to a student question asking why he represented the Tobacco Institute).

148 Childs on Tobacco Institute: Childs, "Tobacco Institute Fighting to Prevent Check on Ad Flow," *Washington Post,* July 25, 1969, p. A29.

149 Austern argument that FTC lacks authority: A court of appeals decision in 1973, overturning a district court decision, decided that the FTC did have such substantive rule-making authority. *Nat'l Petroleum Refiners Ass'n* v. *FTC* 340 F. Supp. 1343, *rev'd* 6–27–73, No. 72–144 (D.C. Cir. 1973).

149 Commissioners become irritated: Wagner, p. 140.

149 Davis on the unconstitutional argument: K. C. Davis, *Administrative Law and Government* 55 (1960).

149 Fritschler's view of industry opposition: A. L. Fritschler, *Smoking and Politics* 81 (1969).

150 Drew comment on labeling bill: "The Quiet Victory of the Cigarette Lobby: How It Found the Best Filter Yet—Congress," *Atlantic Monthly,* September 1965, p. 76.

151 FCC rejects rehearing petition: 32 *Federal Register* 179, p. 13713 (1967).

152 Covington arguments against Banzhaf's appeal: Brief for Interviewing Party, National Association of Broadcasting, *Banzhaf* v. *FCC* (4, No. 21285) (D.C. Cir. 1967).

152 *Midwest Television* v. *FCC:* 364 F. 2d 674 (1966).

153 Commerce Committee on witnesses' financial ties: Wagner, pp. 157–158.

153 Cullman 1969 testimony: Hearings before the Committee on Interstate and Foreign Commerce, House of Representatives, Cigarette Labeling and Advertising, 91st Cong., 1st Sess. (1969).

153 FTC report on *True* magazine incident: *1967 FTC Report on Smoking to Congress,* June 30, 1968, p. 30.

154 Antismoking ads hurt more than commercials help: *New York Times,* August 16, 1970, p. 63.

154 Wasilowski angered: Schneier, "The Politics of Tobacco," *Nation,* September 22, 1969, p. 277.

154 FTC refers to Public Health Service report: 1967 Report of the Public Health Service, *Health Consequences of Smoking,* p. 3.

154 Stewart on cigarette advertising: Hearings before the Committee on Interstate

and Foreign Commerce, House of Representatives, *Cigarette Labeling and Advertising,* 91st Cong., 1st Sess. 9 (1969).

155 *New York Times* notes industry concession: *New York Times,* July 1, 1969, p. 40; see also editorial, "Anybody . . . Knows It's a Hazard," *New York Times,* July 4, 1969, p. 20.

155 Austern letter denounces article: Letter from Thomas Austern to James Reston, executive editor of *The New York Times,* July 7, 1969.

157 Wald explains his ethic: Zalaznick, "The Small World of Big Washington Lawyers," *Fortune,* September 1969, pp. 120–125.

158 Quotation on institute's problem with Hill & Knowlton: *Wall Street Journal,* March 17, 1969, p. 1.

159 Corcoran on "head start": "They Build Bridges to Washington," *Business Week,* April 23, 1966, p. 87.

159 G&W for retaining Washington counsel: "Why the Corporate Lobbyist Is Necessary," *Business Week,* March 18, 1972, p. 64.

161 Drew Pearson accuses C&B: Pearson, "Thirty-five Years on the Merry-Go-Round," *Nation,* July 7, 1969, p. 11.

Chapter 8
Car Counsel

page
163 1973 auto deaths: Moskin, "Life and Death in Your Automobile," *World,* March 13, 1973, p. 14. Annual auto deaths have increased from 20,000 in 1925, to 40,000 in 1956, to 55,000 in 1968, to a record 56,700 in 1972. National Safety Council, *Accident Facts* 40 (1973).

163 1971 cost of auto accidents: *Societal Costs of Motor Vehicle Accidents,* app. B, p. 1 (1972).

163 GM engineer's safe car: McLean, "A Sensible Safety Vehicle," *World,* March 13, 1973, p. 36.

163 Cutler quotation on industry safety progress: *Traffic Safety Act of 1966,* Senate Commerce Committee, 89th Cong., 2d Sess. 2, as written by Lloyd Cutler according to Senate Commerce Committee general counsel, Michael Pertschuk.

164 Non-monetary prices of cars: See generally J. Jerome, *The Death of the Automobile* (1972); D. Randall and A. Glickman, *The Great American Auto Repair Robbery* (1972).

164 Overcharge due to concentration: See Scanlan, "FTC and Phase II: The McGovern Papers," 5 *Antitrust Law & Eco. Rev.* 33 (Spring 1972).

164 Barr blames drivers: *New York Times,* January 28, 1965, p. 14.

165 Drew Pearson on Cutler hiring: *Washington Post,* May 5, 1966, p. F16.

167 VESC tire guideline: Drew, "The Politics of Auto Safety," *Atlantic Monthly,* October 1966, p. 99 [hereinafter Drew article].

167 AMA laughed out of hearing room: Unpublished dissertation by Paul Sitton, Harvard Graduate School (1970).

168 Drew on a Cutler amendment: Drew article, pp. 100–101.

168 Criminal penalties supported by Hartke: 112 *Cong. Rec.* 13603 (1966).

169 Mansfield schedules floor vote: See C. McCarry, *Citizen Nader* 86 (1972).

169 Cutler additions to final committee report: "The American automobile industry has been for many years one of the most dynamic factors in the entire economy. . . . The industry's growth and productivity have been outstanding. And American cars—whatever their shortcomings—are among the world's safest.

"Moreover, the hearings produced evidence that the automotive industry has made commendable progress in many aspects of automobile safety. With respect to such critical components as its brakes, and suspension systems, the automobile of 1966 demonstrates marked improvement over its predecessors." *Report, Traffic Safety Act of 1966*, Senate Commerce Committee, 89th Cong., 2d Sess. 2.

The following Cutler write-up, obtained from the Archives File on the law's legislative history, was *not* inserted: "The Committee expects that the Secretary will act responsibly and in such a way as to achieve a substantial improvement in the safety character of vehicles without impairing the efficient operation of the automobile industry and its ability to deliver safe and economical transportation to the American public at the lowest possible prices."

169 Cutler's boxing-match analogy: Remarks of Lloyd Cutler, February 16, 1967, before the Federal Bar Association Briefing Session on Safety Standards.

170 Large companies that lobby: "Why the Corporate Lobbyist Is Necessary," *Business Week*, March 18, 1972, p. 64.

170 FDA chief complains of lobby pressure: *New York Times*, December 31, 1968, p. 1.

170 AT&T–Justice private meeting: For a description of this incident, see the hearings chaired by Emanuel Celler, *Consent Decree Program of the Department of Justice*, House Antitrust and Monopoly Subcommittee, H.R. Rep. (H. Res. 27), 86th Cong., 1st Sess. (1959).

170 Former congressmen as lobbyists: *Congressional Quarterly's Guide to the Congress of the United States* 301a–303a (1971).

170 Committee aide describes lawyer-lobbyist tactics: *Washington Post*, December 14, 1969, p. 1.

171 Auto air pollution in California: *Third Annual Report*, Council on Environmental Quality (citing EPA data), p. 6 (August 1972); *The Automobile and Air Pollution: Part I, Report of the Panel on Electrically Powered Vehicles*, U.S. Department of Commerce, p. 11.

173 "The Great Detroit Smog Caper": 113 *Cong. Rec.* (1967), October 26.

175 Turner explains view on criminal charges: Letter of Donald Turner to Ralph Nader, October 8, 1969, p. 2.

176 Willens argument on cross-licensing: *Washington Post*, August 6, 1969, p. B15.

176 Cutler called the best lobbyist: Fowlkes, "GM Gets Little Mileage from Compact, Low-Powered Lobby," *National Journal*, November 14, 1970, pp. 2498, 2502.

177 Nineteen Congressmen complain: Letter from Congressman John Blatnik et al. to Attorney General John Mitchell, September 2, 1969.

177 McLaren announces consent decree: For a discussion of what the decree included and did not include, see M. Green, *The Closed Enterprise System* 260–262 (1972).

177 Rankin expresses frustration: *Washington Post*, October 29, 1969, p. A2.

178 Von Hoffman quoted on upheld decree: Von Hoffman, "Smog Trial," *Washington Post*, October 31, 1969, p. B1.

178 Students picket Cutler: See generally Riley, "Influence, Picket Signs and the Public Good: A Debate on the Lawyer's Role," *Potomac Magazine* [in the *Washington Post*], March 15, 1970, p. 18.

179 Cutler's hands tremble: "Law Students Trade Charges with Leading Lawyer in Capital," *New York Times*, October 10, 1969, p. 30.

180 Public-interest lawsuit on truck wheels: *Washington Post*, September 16, 1970, p. A3.

182 Plaintiffs denied right to collect damages in smog cases: *In Re Multidistrict Vehicle Air Pollution*, CCH Trade Cases, No. 74, 540 (June 18, 1973).

182 Judge Real refuses retrofitting order: Memorandum, Opinion and Order, *In Re Multidistrict Vehicle Air Pollution* (D.C. Calif., November 21, 1973) (J. Real); see also *Washington Post*, November 27, 1973, p. A2.

183 Air Force harness tests: "Comments on Ford Motor Company's Ad on Airbags," June 21, 1971, NHTSA # 69-7, notice 9, item 59.

184 Court decision upholds NHTSA's authority to require installation: *Chrysler et al.*
     v. *Department of Transportation*, 472 F. 2d 659 (6th Cir., 1972).
185 Air bags and "real world" crashes: Kielty, "How 'Real World' Crashes Are
     Increasing Air Bag Acceptances," *Traffic Safety*, April 1973, p. 18.
185 Department of Transportation study: *Washington Post*, August 28, 1974, p. A4.

Chapter 9
Planes and Trains

page
186 International travel percentages: *CAB Handbook of Airline* 523–530 (1969).
186 CAB study of interline tickets: Ross and Passell, "The CAB Pilots the Planes,"
     New York Times Magazine, August 12, 1973, p. 9 [hereinafter Ross and
     Passell].
187 Estimates of air-fare price reductions: Jordan, "Producer Protection, Prior Mar-
     ket Structure and the Effects of Government Regulation," 20 *Journal of Law
     and Economics* 151, 161 (April 1972); Pillai, "The CAB as Travel Regulator"
     in M. Green (ed.), *The Monopoly Makers* (1973); see studies of Theodore
     Keeler cited in Ross and Passell; see generally Levine, "Is Regulation Neces-
     sary?" 74 *Yale L. J.* 416 (1965).
187 Americans who have never flown: Pillai, "Consumer Protection in Aviation Rate
     Deregulation," 38 *Journal of Air Law and Commerce* 219 (1972).
187 American aviation in mid-thirties: For a detailed look at the legislative struggle
     culminating in the 1938 law, see Westwood and Bennett, "A Footnote to the
     Legislative History of the Civil Aeronautics Act of 1938 and Afterward," 42
     Notre Dame Lawyer 309 (1967) [hereinafter Westwood].
188 Gorrell statement on Westwood: *Regulation of Transportation of Passengers
     and Property by Aircraft*, hearings before Senate Commerce Committee, 75th
     Cong., 1st Sess. 428 (1937).
188 Westwood view of aviation regulation: Westwood, p. 320.
188 Opposition to federal aviation agency: Westwood, p. 322.
188 Gorrell quotation on competition and monopoly: *Civil Aeronautics Act of 1938*,
     House Committee on Interstate and Foreign Commerce, 75th Cong., 1st Sess.
     67 (1937).
188 Kolko thesis on regulation: See G. Kolko, *Railroads and Regulations, 1877–
     1916* (1966) and Kolko, *The Triumph of Conservation* (1963).
189 Legislation attributed to Gorrell and Westwood: See *Monopoly Hearings in
     Regulated Industries: Airlines*, hearings before the Antitrust and Monopoly
     Subcommittee of the House Judiciary Committee, 84th Cong., 2d Sess. (1956).
189 American Legion on policy making: Quoted in R. Harris, *The Real Voice* 90
     (1964).
190 Federation of American Scientists' criticism: See *Federation of American Sci-
     entists Newsletter*, April 1973, p. 7; testimony of Jeremy J. Stone, director,
     Federation of American Scientists, before the Minerals, Materials, Fuels and
     Mining Subcommittee on Interior and Insular Affairs, U.S. Senate, June 19,
     1973, p. 7.
192 CAB approves interchange plan: 12 *CAB* 518 (1951) (Lee dissenting).
193 Opposing counsel on consolidation move: "Answer of Continental Airlines to
     American's Motion for Consolidation of the Dallas to the West Case with
     Southern Transcontinental," May 8, 1958, pp. 1, 4; CAB Dkt. No. 7984.
193 Dallas protests case consolidation: "Answer of the City of Dallas to American's
     Motion . . . ," May 12, 1958, p. 4; CAB Dkt. No. 7984.
194 Cost of awards to American Airlines: Letter from J. William Doolittle, Jr.,
     attorney at Covington & Burling, June 22, 1961; CAB Dkt. No. 7984.
195 Westwood brief on Kerkorian's high rollers: For the details of this entire con-
     test, see CAB Dkt. No. 20786.

196 CAB dismisses Western's request for declaratory ruling: CAB Order 69–4–17.
197 1968 route proceedings for SAA: CAB Dkt. No. 20054.
198 1973 route request approved: CAB Order 73–10–2.
199 Laylin on Covington representing SAA: J. Goulden, *The Superlawyers* 58–59 (1972).
200 Spater predicts profits from merger: *Aviation Week*, March 29, 1971, p. 27.
201 Private meeting with CAB members quoted: Hearing transcript, p. 325 (June 1971), CAB Dkt. No. 22916 [hereinafter Transcript].
202 Metcalf muses on the private meeting: *Advisory Committees*, hearings before the Subcommittee on Intergovernmental Relations of the Committee on Government Operations, 92d Cong., 1st Sess. 51 (1971).
202 *Airline Management* characterization of Flanigan: *Airline Management*, August 1971. See also "Flanigan's Shenanigans," *Time*, March 20, 1972, p. 14.
203 Henzey on DOT's authority: *Airline Management*, September 1971.
203 *Aviation Daily* on DOT's authority: *Aviation Daily*, July 16, 1971, p. 83.
203 Spater on Stans: Testimony of George Spater before the Senate Watergate Committee, November 15, 1973.
204 Connally close to Woodward: *Washington Evening Star*, August 12, 1971.
204 Antitrust Division opposes merger at meeting: *Aviation Week*, September 6, 1971, p. 22.
204 Spater denies meeting with Baker: Transcript, pp. 269–270 and 689–690.
204 Spater denies lobbying Justice and DOT: Transcript, pp. 328–329.
205 Spater recalls no other meetings: Transcript, p. 329.
205 Spater remembers Connally meeting: Transcript, pp. 430–431.
205 Hydeman criticism of ex parte contacts: Transcript, p. 220.
205 Legal and lobbying fees: *Time*, "Diverging on Merging," September 13, 1971, p. 80.
205 CAB ruling on merger: CAB Order 72–7–92.
205 Seattle Chamber of Commerce: *Aviation Daily*, July 2, 1971, p. 13.
206 Spater "overplayed his hand": *Newsweek*, "Requiem for a Merger," September 13, 1971, p. 92.
206 Robertson answers no: *Washington Post*, June 12, 1971, p. D7.
206 Cutler answers Robertson: *Washington Post*, June 12, 1971, p. D7.
206 Aug questions propriety: *Washington Evening Star*, August 12, 1971.
206 The EJA case: For detailed versions of the Executive Jet Aviation Story, see *Case Study of a Penn Central Subsidiary: Executive Jet Aviation*, Staff Report of the Committee on Banking and Currency, House of Representatives, 91st Cong., 2d Sess. (1970) [hereinafter Case Study]; J. Doughen and P. Binzen, *The Wreck of the Penn Central* (1971) [hereinafter Doughen and Binzen].
207 Lassiter's expenses: *Newsweek*, "Penn Central: Pandora's Box," November 9, 1970, p. 76.
207 Memo in EJA's files: Case Study.
207 Cox informs Penn Central of illegality: Doughen and Binzen, p. 183.
208 Wilson letter to Sundlun: Doughen and Binzen, p. 183.
208 Cox again warns Penn Central of illegality: Doughen and Binzen, p. 184.
208 Cox's knowledge documented: Doughen and Binzen.
209 Penn Central and EJA fined: CAB Order 6a–10–67.
210 Cutler appearance before House Banking Committee: The Banking Reform Act of 1971, Hearings before the House Committee on Banking and Currency, 92d Cong., 1st Sess. 796–821 (May 3, 1971).
210 Cutler remark on conflict of interest: Aug, "Rail Agency's Law Firm Has Ties to Pennsy Case," *Washington Star News*, August 13, 1974, p. A12.
211 The *Star* on Pollak: *Washington Evening Star*, February 1, 1967, p. 1.
212 On Penn Central merger generally: See M. Green et al., *The Closed Enterprise System* 42–44 (1971).
212 *Time* praises Saunders: *Time*, January 26, 1968, p. 71A.

213 Bankruptcy proceedings called a lawyer's dream: *New York Times,* January 22, 1973, p. 1 [hereinafter Shenker].

213 Guthrie federal loan blocked: *Los Angeles Times,* February 10, 1970; see also Goulden, pp. 246–255.

215 Quotation on spending $10,000 for a $2000 case: Shenker.

215 Vandestar baffled: Shenker.

215 Countryman views procedure as a mistake: Shenker.

215 Blanchette against reduced fees: Shenker.

Chapter 10
The Media Lawyers

page

217 Adult TV watching: "The TV Networks Shrug Off New Competition," *Business Week,* March 27, 1971, p. 90; N. Johnson, *How to Talk Back to Your Television Set* 11 (1970).

218 Percentage of stations receiving network programing: L. Brown, *Television* 16 (1971).

218 Newspaper ownership of stations: Hearings before the Antitrust and Monopoly Subcommittee of the Senate Judiciary Committee, *The Failing Newspaper Act,* 90th Cong., 2d Sess., part 7, p. 2410 (1968).

218 Chain ownership: See generally Johnson, "The Media Barons and the Public Interest," *Atlantic Monthly,* June 1968, p. 43; Moore, "The FCC: Competition and Communications," in *The Monopoly Makers* 35 (M. Green, ed., 1973) [hereinafter Moore]; Bishop, "The Rush to Chain Ownership," *Columbia Journalism Review,* November/December 1972, p. 10; FCC *Annual Report* 152–164 (1970).

218 Network profits: *New York Times,* August 22, 1973, p. 1.

218 The Middle America market: Moore, pp. 51–52.

218 TV censorship: Johnson, "The Silent Screen," *TV Guide,* July 5, 1969, p. 6.

218 FCC resistance to cable TV: See generally Johnson and Dystel, "A Day in the Life: The Federal Communications Commission," 82 *Yale L. J.* 1595 (1973); Moore, pp. 62–70; report of the Sloan Commission on Cable Communications, *On the Cable* (1971); hearings before the Subcommittee on Communications and Power of the House Interstate and Foreign Commerce Committee, *Cable Antenna Television* (CATV), 92d Cong., 1st Sess. (July 22, 1971).

219 Multiplicity can become uniformity: Bishop, "The Rush to Chain Ownership," *Columbia Journalism Review,* November/December 1972, p. 10.

220 Comsat bill passes: See generally J. Goulden, *Monopoly,* 104–143 (1968).

220 Cutler selected to write by-laws: See generally *Hearings on Communications Satellite Incorporators Before the Senate Commerce Committee,* 88th Cong., 1st Sess. (1963).

220 Cutler proud of articles of incorporation: *Washington Post,* Feb. 2, 1963, p. C9.

222 Supreme Court turns down Cutler and Cox: 395 U.S. 367, 375 (1969).

223 Minow on the FCC: Quoted in Drew, "Is the FCC Dead?" *Atlantic,* July 1967, p. 29.

223 Cutler testifies on lack of non-network sponsors: In the Matter of Amendment of Part 73, before the FCC, hearings held in July 1969 [hereinafter FCC Hearings].

224 Cutler response to Johnson: FCC Hearings, p. 9932.

225 Supreme Court rules against joint newspaper ventures: *Citizen's Publishing Co. v. United States,* 349 U.S. 131 (1969).

225 Lobbying for the Newspaper Preservation Act: Lea, "Lobbying Overwhelms Opponents of Newspaper Preservation Act," *National Journal,* July 7, 1970, p. 1606 [hereinafter Lea].

225 *Chronicle* treatment of Cohelan protested: Lea, p. 1606.

226 Hruska protests omission of retroactivity: *Newspaper Preservation Act,* report of the Senate Judiciary Committee, 91st Cong., 1st Sess. (November 18, 1969).

226 FCC allows KRON to retain license: *In Re Applications of Chronicle Broadcasting Co.,* 40 FCC 2d 755 (1973).

227 Staggers' committee references: *Subpoenaed Material Re Certain TV News Documentary Programs,* Special Subcommittee on Investigations of the House Interstate and Foreign Commerce Committee, 92d Cong., 1st Sess. (1971).

229 WC&P spokesman protests lobbying label: All quotations in this paragraph are from *The New York Times,* July 18, 1971, section 4, p. 3.

230 On the tactics of inundation and obstruction: See generally R. Marks, *The Lawyer, The Public and Professional Responsibility* 254–255 (1972).

232 Clagett et al. oppose 50-50 proposal: FCC Hearings, p. 9903.

232 Moore quotation on access: FCC Hearings, p. 9802.

232 Clagett on the price of network time: Brief for CBS affiliates in proceeding, FCC Hearings, p. 6.

232 Clagett not familiar with details: FCC Hearings, p. 10015.

233 Court of appeals upholds commission: *Mansfield Television, Inc.* v. *FCC,* 442 F. 2d 470 (1971).

233 One-to-a-market rule: 33 *Federal Register* 5315, 12 F.C.C. 2d 912 (1968).

233 One-to-a-market not to affect existing ownership: The briefs of both the Department of Justice and Earl Moore urged divestiture of such interlocking ownerships as the only effective way to reduce the monopolization of the airwaves.

234 Licenses for WHDH and WLBT not renewed: In WHDH, a group of community residents and academic professionals challenged the existing license in 1967, and the FCC granted the license to the challengers. 16 F.C.C. 2d 15 (1969). In WLBT, a license challenge was brought by community leaders and the United Church of Christ; after the FCC turned them down, an appeals court decision held in their favor on the grounds that the former licensee had radically discriminated in hiring and air practices. 38 U.S.L.W. 2002 (D.C. Cir., June 20, 1969).

234 Proposal to reduce challenger filing time: In the Matter of Amendment of Section 1.580 of the Rules, FCC 69–253, Dkt. No. 18995, March 20, 1969.

235 Jennes for filing time reduction: Brief of CBS affiliates, In the Matter of Amendment of Section 1.580 of the Rules, FCC 69–253, Dkt. No. 18995, March 20, 1969, p. 23.

235 Johnson dissent to 60-day filing time: 16 R.R. 2d 1512 (1969) (emphasis in original).

237 FCC's "Second Report and Order": See "FCC Final CATV Decision," *Television Digest,* 1966, p. 3.

237 Harris letter on AMST visit: Letter to Ben F. Waple, secretary of the FCC, from Jack Harris, president of AMST, May 30, 1967, p. 4.

238 FCC on responsibility of parties to restricted meetings: 10 R.R. 3d 641 (1967).

238 Jennes's two San Diego cases: *United States* v. *Southwest Cable,* 390 U.S. 157 (1968); *In the Matter of Midwest Television,* 13 F.C.C. 2d 478 (1968).

Chapter 11
Pro Bono Publico?

page
243 Fortas in *Gideon* v. *United States:* See Lewis, *Gideon's Trumpet* (1964).

245 Lawyers' committee like Abraham Lincoln Brigade: R. Marks et al., *The Lawyer, The Public and Professional Responsibility* 128 (1972).

245 Lawyers' committee 1969 projects: Lawyers Committee for Civil Rights Under Law, *Annual Report*, 1968–1969, p. 11.
245 *Alexander* v. *Holmes County Bd. of Education:* 396 U.S. 19 (1969).
245 Lloyd Corporation decision: *Lloyd Corporation* v. *Tanner,* 407 U.S. 551 (1972), modifying *Amalgamated Food Employees Union* v. *Logan Valley Plaza,* 391 U.S. 308 (1967).
246 Rostow commentary before Kefauver: J. Ridgeway, *The Closed Corporation* 94 (1968).
246 Ridgeway on Rostow's testimony: J. Ridgeway, *The Closed Corporation* 97 (1968).
247 Comsat-like corporation for housing: See, for example, *New York Times,* November 27, 1966, p. 1.
247 Partnership to have special tax benefits: Wilmer, Cutler & Pickering Memorandum, "Methods of Stimulating Private Investment and Management Participation in Urban Housing Projects," August 11, 1967.
248 NCHP's appeal as tax shelter: "Housing Wins Big Partners," *Business Week,* February 14, 1970, p. 83.
248 Kaiser & Cutler argue that write-offs legitimate: See statement of Edgar Kaiser, House Ways and Means Committee, March 31, 1969.
249 WC&P's efforts during riots: Response of Wilmer, Cutler & Pickering to Harvard Law School questionnaire, November 1969, located at Harvard Law School Placement Office.
249 Cutler establishes cellblock record-keeping: For a general description of the situation, see B. Gilbert, *Ten Blocks from the White House* 127 (1968).
250 Cutler appointed head of riot justice committee: See *Justice in Time of Crisis* (W. Dobrovir, ed., 1969).
250 *Times* on violence committee: *New York Times,* December 14, 1969, section 4, p. 2.
252 Pearson on Cutler and TV-violence study: Pearson, "Thirty-five Years on the Merry-Go-Round," *Nation,* July 7, 1969, p. 11.
252 Commission calls for domestic priority: "The Eisenhower Commission has done a brilliant job in setting out what is wrong and what can be done to correct wrongs. Its recommendations are a clear call for responsible national action on urgent domestic problems." *New York Times,* December 14, 1969, section 4, p. 12.
253 Cutler sees U.S. becoming Belfast: *New York Times,* September 21, 1971, p. 1.
253 ACLU picketers complain: *Washington Post,* December 2, 1969, p. B2.
258 Richardson reversal of Laird "a rare victory": *Washington Post,* March 25, 1973, p. 1.
258 February 1968 court of appeals injunction: *D.C. Federation of Civic Associations* v. *Airis,* 129 App. D.C. 125, 391 F. 2d 478 (1968).
259 January 1970 district court decision upholding government: *D.C. Federation of Civic Associations* v. *Volpe,* 308 F. Supp. 423 (1970).
259 Final court of appeals ruling: 459 F. 2d 1031 (1972).
261 Lawsuits save unspent OEO funds: Arnold & Porter brought one suit for the Michigan and Colorado Migrant Legal Aid Programs, Roza Unida (Ohio), New England Neighborhood Legal Services and NLADA Technical Assistance Program. Wilmer, Cutler & Pickering brought the other two on behalf of D.C. Migrant Legal Action Program, a back-up center, and Community Legal Services, Inc., of Mississippi, respectively.
261 Phillips ordered to cease activities: *Williams* v. *Phillips,* 360 F. Supp 1363 (D. D. C. 1973); motion for stay denied, 482 F. 2d 669 (D.C. Cir. 1973).
263 *Harvard Law Review* quotation *pro bono:* Note, "Structuring the Public Service Efforts of Private Law Firms," 84 *Harvard L. Rev.* 410 (1970).
264 *Harvard Law Review* on law firms' fear of jeopardizing reputation: 84 *Harvard L. Rev.* 414 (1970).

265 Marks on the public-interest client: R. Marks et al., *The Lawyer, The Public and Professional Responsibility* 128 (1972).

265 Copaken discouraged from countercommercials: J. Goulden, *The Superlawyers* 363 (1972).

265 Arnold & Porter refuses FTC *pro bono* case: The courts interpret conflicts far more strictly than these lawyers. "It is doubtful if the Canons of Ethics are intended to disqualify an attorney who did not *actually* come into contact with materials substantially related to the controversy at hand when he was acting as an attorney for a former client now adverse to that position." *United States* v. *Standard Oil Corp.*, 136 F. Supp 345, 364 (Kaufman, J) (S.D. NY 1955).

266 Edelman on corporate lawyers: "The New Public Interest Lawyers," 79 *Yale L. J.* 1064, 1108, n. 66 (1970).

266 Marks on lawyers and tradesmen: Marks et al., *The Lawyer, The Public and Professional Responsibility* 128 (1972).

Chapter 12
The Ethics of Powerlaw: "According to As They Are Paid"

page
268 On Davis's career and philosophy: See W. Harbaugh, *Lawyers' Lawyer: The Life of John W. Davis* (1973).

269 Attorneys should zealously promote clients' interests: ABA Opinion 280 (1949): "The lawyer . . . is not an umpire, but an advocate. He is under no duty to refrain from making every argument in support of any legal point because he is not convinced of its inherent soundness. . . . His personal belief in the soundness of his cause, or of the authorities supporting it, is irrelevant."

269 Vow not to abuse legal process: *In Re Kelly*, 243 F. 696 (1917).

269 ABA on the lawyer's highest responsibility: "Professional Responsibility: Report of the Joint Conference," 44 *ABA J.* 1159 (1959).

270 Meserve on law and public responsibility: Speech of Robert Meserve before the Bar Association of the District of Columbia, July 9, 1973, p. 4; see also Griswold, "The Legal Profession," in H. J. Berman (ed.), *Talks on American Law* 250 (1971).

270 Freund says system comes before client: Freund, "The Legal Profession," in K. Lynn (ed.) *The Professions in America* 35, 40 (1963).

270 Dorsen on law firms: Dorsen, "The Role of Lawyers in America's Ghetto Society," 49 *Texas Law Review* 50, 56 (1970).

270 What lawyers can't do in proceedings: See American Bar Association, *Code of Professional Responsibility* (1969); see also V. Countryman and T. Finman, *The Lawyer in Modern Society* (1966).

270 Permission to forgo unjust action: American Bar Association, *Code of Professional Responsibility*, EC 7–9. See also "Professional Responsibility: Report of the Joint Conference," 44 *ABA J.* 1159, 1161 (1958) that counseling in a lawyer's office "often deters his client from a course of conduct technically permissible under existing law, though inconsistent with its underlying spirit and purpose."

271 *Code's* affirmative obligations: American Bar Association, *Code of Professional Responsibility*, Canon 8 and EC 7–8.

271 Wyzanski on counsel obligation: Quoted in B. Levy, *Corporation Lawyer: Saint or Sinner* 105 (1961).

272 Quote on duty to client and court: Llewellyn, "The Bar Specializes—With What Results?" 167 *Annals of the American Society of Political Science* 177 (1933).

272 Flynn on law schools and craftsmanship: "The New Public Interest Lawyers," 79 *Yale L. J.* 1096, 1138 (1970).

274 Annual budget of Washington public-interest lawyers: These statistics compiled during a survey done by author of fifty Washington public-interest law groups; survey available upon request.

274 Agency corporate tilt: There is much literature on this point. See, for example, L. Kohlmeier, *The Regulators* (1970); J. Turner, *The Chemical Feast* (1970); D. Zwick, *Water Wasteland* (1972); M. Mintz and J. Cohen, *America Inc.* (1972); M. Green (ed.), *The Monopoly Makers* (1973); S. Lazarus, *The Genteel Populists* (1974).

274 Douglas argues for consumer representation: *Los Angeles Times*, opinion section, August 31, 1969, p. 1.

275 Kariel notes bias against unorganized groups: H. Kariel, *The Decline of American Pluralism* (1961); see also Wright, "Professor Bickel, the Scholarly Tradition, and the Supreme Court," 84 *Harvard L. Rev.* 769, 789 (1971).

276 Lazarus that open institutions are vulnerable: S. Lazarus, *The Genteel Populists* 27 (1974).

277 "Guilt by association" argument: See E. B. Williams, *One Man's Freedom* 19 (1962); see also Williams, *New York Times*, March 22, 1974, p. 39.

277 Cutler on advising what ought to be done: Cutler, Book Review, 83 *Harvard L. Rev.* 1746, 1751 (1970).

277 Mikva argues that advocacy means choice: Mikva, "Interest Representation in Congress: The Social Responsibilities of the Washington Lawyer," 38 *Geo. Wash. L. Rev.* 651, 663 (1970).

277 Riley on Rhyne: Riley, "The Challenge of the New Lawyers: Public Interest and Private Clients," 38 *Geo. Wash. L. Rev.* 547, 583 (1970).

278 Wilson reference to lawyers: 35 *ABA Report* 419 (1910). See also Dos Passos, quoted in J. W. Hurst *The Growth of American Law* 342 (1950).

278 Justice Stone on the lawyer-business connection: Stone, "The Public Influence of the Bar," 48 *Harv. L. Rev.* 1, 6–7 (1934).

278 Rostow on lawyers identifying with clients: Rostow, "The Lawyer and His Client," 48 *ABA J.* 146 (1962).

278 Cary discusses lawyers and "the deal": Cary, "Professional Responsibility in the Practice of Corporate Law—The Ethics of Bar Associations," 29 *The Record* 443, 445 (May/June, 1974).

280 The "preferred position" of human rights: *Murdock* v. *Pennsylvania*, 319 U.S. 105, 115 (1943); *West Virginia Board of Education* v. *Barnette*, 319 U.S. 624, 639 (1943); *Thomas* v. *Collins*, 323 U.S. 516, 528 (n. 12) (1945); *contra*, *Kovacs* v. *Cooper*, 336 U.S. 77 (Frankfurter, J. concurring) (1949).

280 Arnold dissent to Nader criticism: Hearings before the Subcommittee on Executive Reorganization on S.860 and S.2045, Senate Government Operations Subcommittee, 91st Cong., 1st Sess. 430 (March, April, July, 1969).

281 Brandeis distinguishes court from legislative practice: Brandeis, "The Opportunity in the Law," 39 *American Law Review* 555, 558 (1905).

282 C&B drops clients: For an interesting court case depicting a situation where C&B declined to make a questionable defense on behalf of an aggressive client, see *United States* v. *Jacobs*, 298 F. 2d (1961).

283 SEC and NSM case: *SEC* v. *Nat'l Student Marketing Corp.*, Civil Action No. 225–72, D.C. Dist. Ct., filed February 2, 1972, p. 35.

283 *Wall Street Journal* quotes SEC official: *Wall St. J.*, February 15, 1972, p. 1.

283 Garrett on lawyers and financial fraud: *SEC News Digest*, May 31, 1974.

284 Kaufman ruling in stock fraud case: *SEC* v. *Spectrum, Ltd.*, CCH Sec. Reg. No. 94, 300 (December 4, 1973).

284 Examples of Brandeis advising on what is right: Freund, "The Legal Profession," in K. Lynn (ed.), *The Professions in America; J. W. Hurst, The Growth of American Law* 342, 344 (1950).

286 Responsibility for access to legal talent: These subjects are dealt with at length in a subsequent work, *Verdicts on Lawyers* (R. Nader and M. Green, eds.) (1975).

287 Lawyer's right to decline employment: *American Bar Association Code of Professional Responsibility,* DR–110(c), EC 7–8, EC 7–9.

288 Lawyers as hired guns: See "Mr. Nader's Legal Profession," 56 *ABA J.* 146 (1970); contra Nader, "Law Schools and Law Firms," *New Republic,* October 11, 1969, p. 21; "Lawyers as Hired Guns," *Harvard Law Record,* November 14, 1969, p. 8.

289 Goal of recent law graduates: There is evidence that law graduates enter law firms with the same frequency as those of earlier generations (Green, "Goodbye to Pro Bono," *New York,* February 21, 1972, p. 29), although they may do with more demanding standards for client conduct and *pro bono* work. The following chart is based on telephone interviews in June 1974 with the placement offices of the six schools listed.

Where Law Graduates Go Upon Graduation*

	Boston University			Columbia			Harvard			New York University			Pennsylvania			Yale		
	'69	'71	'73	'69	'71	'73	'69	'71	'73	'69	'71	'73	'69	'71	'73	'69	'71	'73
Law firms	34	40	42	55	66	59	49	55	67	41	47	49	39	42	47	38	39	53
Industry	11	6	7	4	0	3	3	3	2	12	5	8	8	6	5	2	3	3
Clerkship**	7	9	13	25	20	10	12	18	13	12	11	13	29	20	17	22	27	21
Public Service***	19	10	13	0	5	4	6	7	4	4	10	14	0	10	6	15	11	5
Others****	29	35	25	16	9	24	30	17	14	31	27	6	24	22	25	23	20	18

* Based on those students reporting their jobs to the school's placement offices, which is usually between 80 per cent and 90 per cent of all students.
** An estimated 75 per cent to 90 per cent of all judicial clerks enter law firms following their clerkships.
*** Includes legal aid, public interest law firms, VISTA (now called ACTION), Peace Corps, NAACP, ACLU.
**** Includes teaching, graduate study, government, and military service.

Index

About the Author

Mark J. Green is a twenty-nine-year-old lawyer and writer whose books include *The Closed Enterprise System,* the best-selling *Who Runs Congress?, Corporate Power in America, The Monopoly Makers, With Justice for Some,* and *Verdicts on Lawyers* (forthcoming). His articles have appeared in such publications as the *New York Review of Books,* the *New Republic,* the *Yale Law Journal, The New York Times Book Review,* the *Washington Post,* and the *Nation.* He was editor-in-chief of the *Harvard Civil Rights–Civil Liberties Law Review* (1969–1970) and director of communications for Ramsey Clark's senatorial campaign in New York (1974), and is currently the director of Ralph Nader's Corporate Accountability Research Group, a public-interest law firm in Washington, D.C.